BEING Ram

INSIGHTS INTO RAMAYANA

Protection

YOGI ADITYANATH

Honorable Chief Minister, Uttar Pradesh

Guidance

MR. JAIVEER SINGH

Honorable Minister,
Culture and Tourism Department, Uttar Pradesh

Direction

MR. MUKESH KUMAR MESHRAM

Principal Secretary, Culture and Tourism Department,
Uttar Pradesh, President-Institute

MR. SHISHIR

Director, Directorate of Culture, Uttar Pradesh
Vice President-Institute

Executive Editor

DR. LAVKUSH DWIVEDI

BEING Ram
INSIGHTS INTO RAMAYANA

A COMMENTARY ON GOSWAMI TULSIDAS'S SHRIRAMCHARITMANAS

Kartikey K. Poddar

VANI PRAKASHAN GROUP | AYODHYA RESEARCH INSTITUTE

First Edition : 2023

VANI PRAKASHAN GROUP

4695, 21-A, Daryaganj, New Delhi 110 002
Phone: +91 11 23273167, 23275710
India

Branches

Ashok Rajpath, Patna 800 004, Bihar
Coffee House Campus, Mahatma Gandhi Marg, Allahabad 211 001, Uttar Pradesh
Mahatma Gandhi International Hindi University, Wardha 442 001, Maharashtra
36/A, Shakespeare Sarani, Rani Birla Girls College, Kolkata 700 017, West Bengal

sales@vaniprakashan.in

vaniprakashan@gmail.com

In Association with

ESTD.-1986

Ayodhya Shodh Sansthan
presents

Being Ram : Insights into Ramayana
by Kartikey K. Poddar

ISBN : 978-93-5775-929-8
Religion/Culture

Price : ₹ 2000

Printed and bound in India at R.K. Offset, Shahdara, Delhi-110 032

Vani Prakashan's signature motif is created by Artist Maqbool Fida Husain

DEDICATION

I dedicate this book to my Mother, Father and Gurudev as I have inspired and gained this vision by them

...by Kartikey K. Poddar

Shri Ram: Sharanam Samastjagatan...

References to Ramkatha are found in the Indian literary history that is more than two and a half thousand years old. In every century, Ramkatha was written in its own way. Apart from India, there are many countries in the world where Ramayana is read, heard and recited in some form or the other. Mughal rulers like Emperor Akbar, Jahangir and Shahjahan also got Valmiki Ramayana translated into Urdu. Famous German scholar Father Kamil Bulke came to India from Belgium in 1935, who first undertook authentic research and survey and wrote a book on Ramkatha, which proved to be a guide and a milestone for many scholars to come. According to the research of Father Kamil Bulke, more than four hundred Ramkathas exist all over the world.

It is a well-known opinion that the first book on the life of Lord Shri Ram is Ramayana written by Maharishi Valmiki. Ram's name is also found at one or two places in the Vedas, for example in the Rigveda.

According to historical evidence, the first mention of Ramkatha is found in 'Dasaratha Jataka' which was written about 400 years before Christ. The tradition of literary writing on Ramkatha started from Dasharatha Jataka and Valmiki Ramayana. Goswami Tulsidas ji's Ramcharitmanas and many other writers after him worked on Ramkatha. There is a need to compile all such texts and keep their brief description at one place. Not only this, the diversity and uniqueness of Ramkatha attracts and influences all of us in many ways. From this point of view, it is necessary to collect the available literature on Ramkatha in one place.

The work of compiling all such Ramkatha literature and bringing it to light has been started by Dr. Rajesh Srivastava, working in the Charitable Works Department of Madhya Pradesh Government, who is a leading scholar of Global Ramayana. The introduction of more than a hundred Ramayana texts in this book on 'Ramayana Darshanam' by Dr. Srivastava will be an innovative experience for the readers. The learned author has prepared this compilation with utmost hard work, which is being presented by the institute before you, attentive readers and curious people. Your suggestions and ideas will make this book more effective, hence they will also be awaited.

— Dr. Lavkush Dwivedi

Director,

Ayodhya Research Institute,

Introduction

One problem that human beings are facing since time immemorial is **'Dukha'** (Unhappiness), so much so that we have accepted sadness, dissatisfaction, anxiety, and frustration as an inevitable part of life. Over the period of human evolution, the physical aspect has been evolving and transforming, but the way nature has been programming the human mind, remains the same. Times have changed, the physicality has changed, but the way our mind deals with the world, has not changed. However, with the passage of time, number of the ignorant minds have increased substantially, creating problems both at individual and collective levels. History is full of instances of crime, hatred, suppression, and violence committed by humans under the influence of desires and fears. Millions have died because of the mind's insanity, and the struggle is not yet over. Even though the ignorant world has accepted 'Dukha' as a part of life, but that doesn't mean that untrue will become real, and insanity can be accepted as 'customary.'

No matter how much asset one accumulates or how much planning one does for a safe and secure future, one cannot free oneself and others from the multifaceted impacts of 'Dukha.' We all are living a dejected life. Humans are quick to blame others, destiny, circumstances, and just everything except themselves. *The reality is that the cause of all 'Dukha' is not the situation but the way we 'Deal' with the situation.*

Most of us don't even know how to conduct life correctly. The reason is our mismanaged mind. One part of the mind that is 'I' is working obsessively to empower the other part of the mind that is 'Mine.' The fundamental problem is that both 'I' and 'Mine' are misbelieved as true, whereas the 'Self,' which is the actual reality, is neglected in unawareness. This infectious, lethal, and chaotic state of mind is what I call as Dysfunction of mind.

As a disease gives unwanted pain and suffering to the body, similarly, dysfunction of mind is compulsively and continuously giving a turbulent and unsettled condition. When just a small headache is intolerable for us, imagine how much we are suffering unknowingly, living every moment with this dysfunction. The problem is of grave concern. It's not only affecting the part of 'You'; rather, the problem is 'You.' As beings suffer from varied ailments, available medical treatments are also diverse in nature. But interestingly, the cause and effect of mind dysfunction are more or less the same in all beings, and so is its treatment. If not sooner than later, the symptoms of body illnesses are traceable. But unfortunately the mind dysfunction, in most cases, *never* gets diagnosed.

A whole lifetime of 70-80 years gets wasted without us realizing the real cause of 'Dukha,' the incessant and compulsive pain and suffering. Just one in thousands acknowledge it, and one in those puts up an effort to correct this dysfunction. Although human psychology has advanced a lot, still this dysfunction of mind is something that cannot be permanently cured by counseling, therapies, or medicines. Had it been so, every being of the world would have been happy by now. A simple pill cures a headache within a few minutes. But there is no such pill that can cure the dysfunction. Sedatives and psychedelic drugs give some relief for a while, but as soon as their effect is over, 'Dukha' comes back again.

One can never get a permanent solution to get rid of the effects of dysfunction by doses of medications, intoxications, adrenaline rushes, comforts and luxuries or ego gratification. The solution lies in first acknowledging that there is a problem and then restructuring the mind to original settings. We must understand that it is us who have spoilt the God-programmed settings, and, therefore, nobody else is to be blamed than us. One universal and greatest manual of procedures that joyfully cures the dysfunction and restructure the mind is none other than the holy 'Ramayana.' It is that one single bouquet that has flowers of inspiration, truth, righteousness, pleasure, courage, determination, love, and, of course, grace. The sole objective of Ramayana is to establish 'Ram-Rajya,' in every being which ensures the permanent cure of dysfunction of mind, and absolute freedom from 'Dukha.'

'Ram-Rajya' is essentially a state of self-consciousness that is entirely free from worldly fears and desires. A place where there is no insecurity and dissatisfaction. 'Ram-Rajya' truly signifies the uninterrupted flow of divine intelligence and bliss, which is the essential nature of all beings beyond the realm of mind, body, and physicality. Ramayana is an eternal universal consciousness that leads every being to perfection. This manual doesn't just showcase step by step pointers but a very absorbing tale of relationship, friendship, revenge, love, and most importantly, the victory of good over evil. It carries the objective of Supreme Lord Rama and a pledge that whosoever will have full faith in Ramayana will attain that level of success, strength, and peace, which he has never witnessed before.

As neither the humongous celestial bodies of other galaxies nor the minute cells in the grains of rice can be seen with naked eyes but requires sophisticated instruments. Similarly, the essence of Ramayana cannot be recognized and appreciated without the sophisticated attributes of discipline, commitment, perception, and intellect. The present era is very much impatient. It wants quick and instant solutions. Since birth, we believe that the only purpose of life is to accumulate power and pleasures, and the only relationship we know and value is 'give and take '. However, there are also hidden gems, the enlightened souls, saints, and sages who, without any expectation of returns, have committed their lives in the devotion of Lord Ram. They are the real heroes of humanity who are learning, contemplating, and retelling the spiritual- scientific principles of Ramayan for the greater good of humanity.

The life, miracles, and wisdom of Lord Ram, 'the human Avatar of Supreme Consciousness,' are the very essence of Ramayana. It gives purity, satisfaction, relaxation and realization, which every human being yearns for. The in- depth, insightful, and thought-provoking meanings of Ramayana have been first internalized and then presented by many learned ones over a period of many centuries. The greatest one among them is Saint Goswami Tulsidas, the creator of 'Shri Ram Charit Manas.' Based on his teachings and ideas of Shri Ram Kinkar, I have put my humble effort to simplify the insightful concepts that Ramayana upholds. I hope it will appeal to the logical minds of the present era and will attract them towards the greatness of Lord Rama. May the Grace of Lord Rama always remain with all beings, and may the divinity of Ramayana enlightens every soul with **'Sukha,' the ultimate bliss.**

Why am I writing on Ramayana?

It is my deepest desire to see RamaNam in thought, speech and action of not just follower of 'Sanatan Dharma' but of all faiths. So far Lord Rama's name has been exploited for all selfish interests except for welfare and well being of mankind. Reader will find new perspectives of Ramayana not discussed in the present era at all. Most importantly I assure the reader that whosoever studies Ramayana, will become eligible for the Grace of Lord Rama. And whosoever attains His Grace lives a fruitful and rewarding life free from pain and suffering.

Finally consider Ramayana text like an open source code. There can be new interpretations and insights that you may discover. There is no end of Ramayan. The more you delve into it the newer knowledge will reveal to you. Minds of present era appreciates scientific, logical and questioning approach. For the first time readers will get answers to the many 'Why's and 'How's of Ramayana.

Ram-Rajya

Where every man is like Rama,
And every woman is like Sita.
Every brother is like Laxmana,
And mother like Kaushalya.
Where the city is like Ayodhaya,
And every family is like Raghukula,

Where loyalty, courage and strength like Hanumana,
And where there is no fear of Kaala.
Where renunciation is like Bharata,
Where penance is like Urmila,
Where kids are like Luva and Kusha,
And where there is no obsession for Maya.

Reverence of parents is like Shravana,
Devotion is like Shabri mata,
Where every home worships Lord's Paduka, And where there is no place for Bhed Bhava.
Where teacher is like Vashishta,
Where mentor is like Vishwamitra,
Where friends are like Sugreeva,
And associates like Vibhishana.

Where the pure waters of Saryu flow,
Where the flowers like in Pushpa Vatika grow,
Where the trees are Kalpatru,
And where earth is Kamdhenu

Where father is like Dasratha,
And relatives are like family of Janaka.

Where martyrdom is like Jatayu,
Where youth is like Angada,
Where there are challenges like Lanka,
And victory, like that of Vanar Sena.

Where one only seeks Lord's grace,
And love is filled in every space.
Ram Rajya is not a place but is Lord's kingdom,
Attained by the one who lives life with Devotion.

Contents

AYODHAYAKAND

ARANYAKAND

KISHKINDAKAND

SUNDERKAND

LANKAKAND

UTTRAKAND

BALAKAND

Chapter 1

Rise of Ravan : The Evil Desire

The ten-headed Ravana prayed at Brahma's feet,
Other than monkeys and men, me, none can beat.

RAVAN'S STORY

Once an Asura named Ravana did extraordinary penance or 'Tapasya' to please God Brahma. Brahma got pleased from him and offered him to ask a boon. To establish his dictatorship over the world, Ravana asked for eternal immortality. But Brahma refused to grant this wish as it was against the principles of nature and told him to ask something else. Ravana was a shrewd diplomat, so he cleverly modified his wish and asked for a boon that none other than humans and monkeys could kill him. He intentionally chose these two exceptions because he used to consider both of them too weak and inferior to be a threat to the Asura clan. Brahma granted him this request.

Empowered by the blessings of Brahma, Ravana became a superpower. He conquered the three worlds and started torturing beings in all possible ways he could. He, along with his cavalry of Asura, even defeated the Devta, who were considered all-powerful. But once he confronted Bali, the monkey king of Kishkindha, and lost to him in fierce combat. For a highly intuitive ruler like Ravana, it did not take long to understand that it was an indication that monkeys were in no way inferior to him. Guided by his innate diplomatic instinct, Ravana wisely made a compromise with Bali and refrained from troubling Kishkinda after that.

After his defeat against Bali, Ravana could have realized that his immortality could be challenged, and it was high time that he should mend his evil ways. But his ever- growing mind-ego and pride prevented him from doing so. He continued with his sinister maneuvers and did not even hesitate to abduct Mother Sita believing that a mere mortal like Lord Ram could do nothing to him. However, he finally received his due chastisement when he got killed by Lord Ram for his unrighteousness.

Egoic sense of superiority made Ravan commit the biggesst mistake of his life. He underestimated monkeys and humans and was overconfident of his power, which ultimately led to his downfall. The reality which ego fails to understand is that no power is supreme in this world. Everything has a beginning and an end, and nothing is beyond vulnerability. It is essential for beings to realize this trick of ego before it spoils life.

Meaning of freedom from evil is to realize that it is never a good proposition to control, harass, or manipulate others. Whenever the mind sends thoughts of superiority, which happens quite frequently, remind yourself, the outcome of Ravana.

KUMBHAKARNA'S STORY

"This wretch will gulp the world and still crave,
I give him one day, after spending many in dark cave."

Ravan's brother Kumbhakarna was also undertaking a severe penance to get bestowed by a boon from Brahma. The sheer size, ferocity, and endless hunger of Kumbhakarna made Brahma apprehensive of his intentions if he is granted a boon. He was worried that such a blessing would encourage him to consume the entire world to gratify his insatiable hunger and bring atrocities to the world with his violent acts. Devta sensed this dilemma of Brahma. They played a trick by manipulating Kumbhakarna's tongue for a few moments, which made him mispronounce his wish for 'indrasan' – a state of supreme power, glory, wealth, pleasure, and glamour – as 'nidrasan' – a state of eternal slumber. Brahma was more than happy to grant him that.

Kumbhakarna realized the error he had committed. He pleaded for clemency from Brahma and requested him to give him some solace from this state of eternal sleep. Brahma became merciful and allowed him one day of awakened state after every six months of sleep.

When reflected upon the story of Kumbhakarna, it can be realized that he is a personified representation of the unending desires of human beings, which can grow to take a humongous form if not checked and controlled on time. Desires of a man is an outcome of his ego, which makes the man believe that the more of everything is better - one must opt for more power, more pleasure, more wealth, more honor, and so on to be happy. That is why everybody craves for 'indrasan'.

However, this is nothing but a delusion that has been befooling human beings since time immemorial as Indra, the actual possessor of 'indrasan desires for 'Brahmasan'. So when even Indra is not satisfied with his present state, where is the end? Where is the satisfaction? The prolonged slumber of Kumbhakarna indicates that obsessive desires needs to be quieted. If the being fails in doing so then at one stage it will transform in a punishment.

Blessing of sleep prevented Kumbhakarna from doing wrongful things induced by the fickleness of mind and somewhat purified him. Therefore when Ravan asked him as a brother to fight Lord Ram, Kumbhakarna replied that he would only fight because of brother-dharma. He straightforwardly said to Ravan that by abducting Mother Sita, he had committed the ugliest crime. He counseled Ravan to return Mother and Surrender to Lord Ram. The ever merciful Lord will forgive him and so Lanka will be saved. But Ravan paid no heed and forced him to fight.

It was owing to his abstinence from evil thoughts and deeds, his goodness was acknowledged by Shri Ram and Lord liberated him from 'Asura yoni', a miserable state of existence, to the highest state of eternal bliss.

Being cannot eliminate desires or the Kumbhakarna as the 'intent of elimination' itself is also a desire. It is, however, possible to Surrender all desires in the lotus feet of Lord Ram. Then elimination of desires and purification becomes Lord's responsibility. Gyan or knowledge that comes with Surrender (Samarparna) enables the being to realize the true purpose of life.

Ravan lifted Kailasa to show his might,
None in this world can face me in a fight.

As Ravana became dominant with the boon from Lord Brahma, he relinquished the spiritual penance and started his journey of malevolent conquest. First of his acts of domination was forcefully marrying a pious lady named Mandodari in the Asura fraternity. She was the possessor of heavenly persona. Such was her divinity that Lord Hanuman mistook her for Mother Sita when he first visited Lanka in search of her. Mandodari was compelled to marry Ravana because of his overbearing influence over her father. After marrying one of the most beautiful women, Ravana's next malicious venture was to capture the grand fort of Lanka from his stepbrother Kuber. He defeated Kuber without much effort and established the capital of his empire centering the fort.

These feats did not satiate Ravana's desire for power and possession. He followed the already defeated Kuber to the Himalayas with a huge army to snatch away his magical aircraft 'Pushpak Viman'. There also he achieved success. While returning, the entourage reached Mount Kailasa, the abode of Lord Shiva. There Ravana performed a contemptuous act by uplifting the Mount Kailasa in his masculine arms as a demonstration of his strength and pride. His action impressed everyone, and he was applauded for his power and courage. The admiration from different corners for his marvelous accomplishment boosted Ravana's ego further. It made him believe that he is invincible and insurmountable and at par with Lord Shiva, if not less.

Ego wants to demonstrate qualities and achievements thereby proving self as superior to others. Ego does not leave the smallest of opportunities to boast in terms of power, beauty, wealth, intelligence, talent or respect. Doing so, it believes that it will attract more attention and it is a fact that others' attention is a booster for ego.

Urge to show off takes away humility from character and makes one believe that he is the doer of all the successes. Mind is filled with thoughts like 'I did this, and I did that,' and as a result, it starts expecting credits for everything. If appreciation is not as expected, mind shoots thoughts of dissatisfaction, frustration and in extreme cases, insanity and violence.

When Ravana was attempting to lift Mount Kailasa, the omnipresent and eternal God Shiva was watching with great amusement. He was already enthralled by the devotion of Ravana and wanted to make His devotee happy. In fact, he lightened the weight of the mountain intentionally so that it became easy for Ravana to complete the task. But proud Ravana failed to see the 'Grace' of Lord Shiva and believed that it was he who made the impossible possible. Though later, at the Swayamvar of Janaknandini, Ravana could not move the Bow of God Shiva even by an inch, let alone lifting. This proved that he was not that powerful as he thought himself to be. But Ravana did not accept that and continued believing foolishly that he had unparalleled strength.

Ego deludes us from believing and acknowledging Grace. Being becomes eligible for Grace only after complete Surrender of self to the Supreme. Surrender (Samarparna) is to realize that not even a pin can move without Grace and whatever one achieves is because of Grace. Realization of Grace is death of mind-ego. Therefore to obstruct being's acceptance for Grace, mind gives irrelevant thoughts that are based on 'I' ness' that is 'I am the doer - I am the achiever - I am the best' and so on. These were the same egoistic thoughts of Ravana, which didn't let him accept Lord Ram as Supreme in human avatar.

Ultimately, he earned an unfortunate death and misery for his family.

Vibhishan, the second brother of Ravana, was a devotee of Supreme Ram. He was no match to Ravana in terms of strength and knowledge. But he was a great devotee who always tried correcting Ravan and yet the foolish Asura ousted him from Lanka. Vibhishan then completely Surrendered to the lotus feet of Lord Ram. In return, Lord bestowed the throne of Lanka to Vibhishan, and he continued to rule over the region peacefully for the rest of his life.

These two brothers but opposing believers, Vibhishan and Ravana, represent Surrender (Samarparna) and Ego. respectively. Ravana acted in a most unbecoming manner and committed blunders for which he had to pay a hefty price. Vibhishan, on the other hand, believed in Grace and Surrendered unequivocally to the Supreme and led a happy and peaceful life.

To prevent oneself from getting digressed by ego, one needs to follow the path of Surrender (Samarparna). Grace is the cause and effect of every action. The purpose of the birth of a human being is just to make efforts or 'purushartha' to become 'eligible' for Grace. Ramayan explains the implications of both ego and Surrender (Samarparna) in simple story form. Ultimately choice is with beings, to be trapped in ego like Ravana or to attain the greatest treasure which is Grace of Lord Ram.

■■

Chapter 2

Ravana Defeated Devta : Non-Absoluteness in Righteousness

"Devta defame me behind my back and are my enemy, They flee away when called for a confrontation with me."

There are ample instances in human history that showcase that apparently stronger people blame their weaker counterparts of conspiring against them. They threaten the weaker opponent of dire consequences if they do not Surrender before their might. Some choose to bow before the strong despite knowing very well that their claims are untrue. This is a method using which so-called strong entities spread their control over the not so strong entities and ensure continuity of their predominance. This happens at all levels, be it nations, politics, business or institutions.

Defeat of Devta

Ravana followed the same tact to dominate those whom he thought to be weaker or equally powerful as he was. He took an overview of his situation to find that he had befriended all the demons and entered into a friendly contract with the monkeys of Kishkinda. Humans were inconsequential to him. The only source of threat for him was the Devta or demigods who hailed from 'Swarglok'. He therefore, decided that to establish his supreme command over the world, the Devta clan must be defeated.

His first step towards his goal was to convince his massive army of demons about the perceived threat from the Devta. Ravana told them that the demigods are colluding clandestinely to ensure downfall of Asura clan but were afraid of face to face confrontation. Ravana also knew that demons were pleasure-seekers who enjoyed moral or immoral acts of lust without any hindrances. They used humans arbitrarily to satiate their bodily desires, and Devta obstructed to this.

Ravana successfully used this cue to manipulate the minds of his fellow demons and made them believe that they were victims of various cunning maneuvers of the Devta and must fight against them to fulfill their desires without any hindrances.

To further strengthen his arguments, Ravana concocted a Manushya-Devta (Man-God) nexus and showed to his followers that it was the Yagya or oblation from the humans that empowered the Devta who in turn provide the human society the security and satisfaction. It was a give and take relationship. Thus, to overpower the demigods, their source of power must be destroyed ab initio so that they become weak and incompetent to fight or escape. Then they would be forced to Surrender before Ravana, who in turn would pardon or punish them.

Ravana's first target was to defeat Indra, the chief of demigods to devastate the morale of the rest of the Devta clan to fight against him. He sent his mighty yet deceptive warrior son Meghnad to accomplish the feat, which he did successfully. Then, he ordered his army of demons to spoil the Yagya or offerings of the humans and he led another army to attack the Swarglok. Devta were petrified by the sheer power and valor of Ravana. Most of them chose to elope to a safer zone in the caves of Meru Mountain while some preferred admission of defeat before Ravana.

Ego Trap of Us Vs Them

The story so far talks about the triumph of evil over truth and virtue. It was the same evil ego motives of the demons that bonded them together and made them work towards the achievement of the corrupt ideas. Their ego compelled them to make a distinction between 'Us' and 'Them' with 'Us' indicating the demons and 'Them' the Devta and all other opponents. It ignited a sense of hatred for the entities belonging to the group 'Them' in Asuras minds and encouraged them to disturb the order or 'Dharma' and set up a new one where only the demons would rule.

However, sinfulness is not limited to any clan or group of entities. In the tales of Ramayan, as there are astute characters like Manthra and imprudent characters like Kekayi among the humans, there are also devout characters like Vibhishan, Mandodari, and Trijita in the Asura clan. No group can, therefore, be generalized as totally evil or totally good.

Those who are strongly identified with ego crave for control and power without caring about right and wrong.

The ego forces them to create false enemies and encourage them to perform immoral acts so that they have complete control. Control is again an ego-created illusionary idea which in reality holds no ground. Unless there are hatred and conflicts, they will never be able to rule and control to the satisfaction of their ego. This phenomenon is evident even today. Influential leaders manipulates collective people ego and so create the 'Us vs. Them' scenarios in the context of caste, language, religion, nationality, skin color, and just anything so as to create drama and hatred in order to ensure their own control.

Influential Evil

The ego indeed has the competence to bring together those with similar ideology and inspires them to work collectively in pursuance of their heinous objectives. However, the question that creeps into the minds of readers is how the evil Ravana could rout the righteous Devta? Not just during the era of Ramayan, even today we witness the over-dominance of negativity over positivity; falsehood over truth; and evil over goodness. The moot point is why evil is so domineering? Where lays its strength over virtue?

The answer lies in the fact that to overpower the evil, 'absoluteness of righteousness' in thoughts and action is a must. There cannot be any loose ends. Those who will stand for Dharma or righteousness must be beings of pure mind, body, and soul. Although the Devta were mostly righteous, they too were not above the nefarious influence of ego and arrogance. Indra, the King of the Devta, was himself a proud person who flaunted his power and used his position to fulfill his personal desires. He indulged in unrighteous deeds like illegitimately engaging himself with Lady Ahalya in the guise of her husband and deceiving her to commit a mistake. Other demigods too had their fair share of misdeeds which could be termed as misuse of divine power for pleasure purposes. The unrighteousness of demigods weakened their power of goodness.

Consequently, since they were not free of sins, Devta could not uphold the dharma and fight for its protection against the Asura. Ravana, on the other hand, stayed true to his purpose and practised this 'policy of completeness' conscientiously. His strong determination, which, although was for evil motives, paved his path to success.

Be Cautious

Undetermined Dharma comes with a risk of deprecation while adharma associates no chance of being dismissed from its path. One small mistake can make the spiritual aspirants fall from righteousness, and hence, it becomes imperative to be very careful in life. While the already fallen one, who is ignorant of the truth, has no morality to lose. When there is a conflict between the dharma and adharma, adharma seems to have a competitive advantage over dharma because of this incompleteness in the practitioner of dharma. Those standing on behalf of dharma draw their power from their noble deeds, and any digression from this path makes them weaker. Contrarily, those treading the path of adharma gain strength from their misdeeds. That is why Asura became more controlling than the Devta.

Power of Righteousness (Dharma)

In real life, practising dharma may seem to be complicated or sometimes impossible due to the negative conditioning of our minds and external influence. On the other hand, wrong doings come naturally with mind-created justifications - 'If everybody is doing so, I can also do so'. Therefore, it may appear that leading a life like Maryada Purushottam Ram is a trying mission. To prove to the ordinary human beings that it is very much possible to conduct life along the path of dharma, God Ram took human avatar. He demonstrated that no matter what, if one decides to lead a life of dignity and honor, nothing in the universe can stop him. Lord Ram is the symbol of 'completeness in righteousness'.

Lord Ram encountered all the challenges of his life rightfully and righteously, which elevated him from an ordinary to a Supreme figure. He also showed that treading the path of dharma calls for sacrifices and tough decisions against and above one's own will and interests. It takes a lot of courage and emotional robustness to pass through the journey of dharma. What was right at that time is valid today as well. Those who will walk the path of righteousness will face hard challenges and uncalled sacrifices to reach the Supreme state of Maryada Purushottam. But along with this, also do remember the promise of Lord Ram – "Those who uphold Dharma, to them I become the protector and promoter."

Chapter 3

Corruption of Manushya Society : The Vulnerable Mind

Demons did everything in their power to destroy morality,
Virtue, goodness, and righteousness deteriorated in human society.

After conquering Devta, Ravan wanted to consolidate his control over them. He realized that to keep Devta subjugated, their source of power must be tampered. It was the Yagya and practice of dharma by humans or Manushya that used to empower the demigods. Ravan cleverly strategized to degenerate dharma so that humans refrain from worshipping Devta and thereby curtail the flow of power to Devta to fight him back. Ravan never wanted to destroy humans as they were resources which could be used for menial work and satisfaction of the carnal needs of Asura.

Manipulation to Rule

Ravan's first step towards that goal was to send members of his Asura clan to Manushya societies. These demons entered the community in disguise of humans and got engaged in different walks of life, such as priests, saints, yogis, reformers, preachers, and nationalists. In those days, human society functioned following the principles of Veda, which preached dharma or righteousness as the way of life. These demons were sent with the aim to ruin the fiber of the society and denigrate dharma. As priests and yogis, they started criticizing the Veda as impractical and obsolete. They intentionally misinterpreted the preaching of the Veda, terming them as dogmatic and restricting. Using their power, they exhibited magical tricks and influenced humans to believe in them instead of the enlightened Saints.

They tried to shift the focus of humans from astuteness and austerity to luxury and lasciviousness by the blatant display of wealth and power and mocking the traditions and values as orthodox. They emphasized that thc principles of Dharma are the chains inhibiting individual freedom and enjoyment. Proclaiming spiritual life as dull and boring, these Asura drove Manushya towards indulgence. They further numbed the spiritual seekers by asking for proof of the existence of God and made people believe that there was no God.

The outcome was unsurprisingly evident. Humans changed their mindset and strayed from the path of Dharma. Upasana, Bhakti, and Tapasya that represent worship and devotion were considered superstitious practices. Mocking and disregarding those who followed the path of Dharma became a common practice. Schools of spiritual practices were cornered and marginalized. People began believing that chanting the name of God was a mere waste of time. The ecstatic state attained by consuming narcotic drugs and bliss state of Samadhi that is attained by Yog Sadhana were considered one and the same. They were also convinced that control over thirst and hunger through penance was wasteful trouble for the body and detachment from worldliness or Vairagya was nothing but escaping from one's responsibilities.

The overpowering impact of the Asura on humans led practitioners of Dharma or Sages to move away from society and hide in forests. People were so engrossed with the satisfaction of their bodily desires that they didn't even utter a mantra or God's name for once.

Once Ravan achieved his much-desired objective, he became very active in eliminating any form of Yagya anywhere. If he would ever get the news that a Yagya was being performed somewhere, he would rush to that place with his army and destroy that. Ravan was so paranoid that he would not even leave the responsibility on his commanders. He was afraid that these generals might be sluggish in the discharge of their duties, and he would not achieve what he desired. Those who practised Dharma were severely punished and thrown out of society.

Deterioration by Attraction

Ravan's relentless evil endeavors bore fruits. Human society became corrupt, and vices like hatred and jealousy spread like wildfire. People started having negative feelings about each other. Ravan rewarded injustice, exploitation, and plundering. All human virtues like compassion were made to appear weak and tools of manipulation. It was promoted that nobody on this earth does anything to another person without any self-interest. People were acknowledged as charming and intelligent if they could play clever on wealth or get into illicit affairs with other women.

There is no doubt that Ravan made a consorted effort to pollute humans or Manushya and took them out of the path of Dharma, but humans were no less responsible for their deterioration. They allowed demons like Ravan and his faction to manipulate them and distract them from the path of righteousness. It was their choice to embrace negativity and imprudence. If Ravan were the only root of all problems, then Supreme Ram would have killed him from heaven instantly and solved the problem forever. But that was not the solution. Humans were involved in the process of transforming society towards unrighteousness and immorality. That is why Lord Ram decided to play an 'Avatar leela' of a lifetime like a mortal human being to purify the disillusioned human race and restore Dharma.

Lord Ram set an example before the misguided human beings on how to walk the path of righteousness even in the most challenging times of one's life. He also showed that Dharma could be practised without studying Veda. All one needs to do is hold on to three pillars of Dharma: tolerance, acceptance, and sacrifice. Absoluteness of humanity is dharma. Every human being is capable of practicing it irrespective of the conditions of their lives. Dharma can be practiced at reasonable times as well as in times of hardship. It is through Dharma that one can achieve fulfillment in life. What was relevant in those days stays pertinent even today. The message remains the same. Follow and practise the life of Lord Ram and attain perfection.

■■

Chapter 4

Proclamation of Narayana : Divine Intervention

"I will take avatar as a human being and restore order, In Raghukul I shall be born as Ram, the evil up-rooter."

The Request

Denunciation of dharma in human society created mayhem in the world. There was rampant plunder of nature and its resources. The misdeeds of the miscreants of Asura burdened Mother Earth who realized that it was Ravana who was the root of all evils. He was destroying nature slowly but surely like a cancerous growth in the body. Perturbed with the developments, but unable to find any solution, she visited Devta and sages who were hiding in the Meru Mountain. They together went to Lord Brahma to pray for security against Ravana.

Brahma gave them a patient hearing, although, at heart of hearts, he smiled with the thought that everyone remembers God only during the tough times. With great sympathy, he explained to them that Ravana had performed hard penance to earn his blessings and also was a devout follower of Lord Shiva. Since two of the trinity had sanctified Ravana, they couldn't do anything that contradicted their previous behavior. That is, they could not punish Ravana for his unruliness. However, Brahma guided the disappointed petitioners that they could approach the Supreme entity of the trinity that is Narayan, who is the preserver of the universe and always stands by the side of His devotees.

Easily approachable

Fathoming the internal dilemma of the requesters about the place and the way to find Narayan who was inaccessible even to the Devta, Lord Brahma explained that Narayan is Supreme and omnipresent. He need not be looked for in places. His seekers can recourse to him from wherever they are. As he is the creator of past, present, and future, there is no particular time rather anytime is a good time to seek Him. Being the Supreme Knower, he understands every beat and vibration of the universe and hence, knows mind, heart, and deeds of all His beings. He need not be said anything as he already knows everything.

Lord Brahma further clears the doubts of the petitioners by saying that one should not hesitate to approach the Supreme Narayan as He is merciful, kind and compassionate towards all. One must not hold any guilt, thinking that since I have committed sins in the past, I am not eligible to come under his aegis. Shri Narayan can forgive the gravest of criminals with His love. It is He who puts one through pleasurable and painful circumstances for one's benefits. None can understand his mathematics. Thus, there is no need to worry about the future. Just be in the divinity of the present moment. Brahma then explained to them the easiest way to approach the Supreme.

> *'Evil wants control over others, materialistic wants worldly pleasures, Wise wants peace for all, but a devotee only wants Love of the Lord.'*

Lord Narayan is connected with all the creatures of the universe with the bond of love. He is the owner of the world, and hence, no one can offer him anything material. Charity, temples, fasting, scriptures, worships, oblation, and pilgrimage are mere tools to purify oneself of all the worldly meanness. To get united with Him, one must have sincere love, attachment, affinity, and devotion or Bhakti, which can grow only in a pure heart.

No Complacency

Hearing the soulful plea of the group, Shri Narayan could not resist and replied from Baikunth Dham, the highest Heaven, saying, "Fear not O sages and Devta, for your sake I will assume the form of human and shall be born in the glorious Raghukul family, the dynasty of Ikshvaku."

Being assured by the Supreme Lord, the petitioners felt relieved, and they returned satisfied. Surprisingly, after that, the Devta began a phase of overwhelming celebration. This was because they realized that Shri Narayan would not only restore dharma on earth but also defeat Ravana and give Devta back their power and possessions, which Ravana had taken away. Despite being divine creatures, Devta were self-seeking too. Their ego could see only their benefits over others.

From time immemorial, history has witnessed the outcome of such 'self-seeking ego' where the 'haves' have refused to share their resources and bounties with 'have-nots' leading to hunger, diseases, violence, poverty and misery across a significant proportion of humanity.

Mentor's Counsel

Lord Brahma being a wise older person did not like the gestures of the Devta. He reprimanded them, saying, "Don't rejoice like selfish fools. All of you, too, must go to the earth and assist the Supreme Avatar." Upon awakened by Lord Brahma, Devta immediately took millions of avatars as the mighty and knowledgeable monkeys, apes, and bears and got spread in the forests of Kishkinda. There they patiently awaited the arrival of the Greatest Hero Lord Ram for years.

Lord Brahma counseled them with his wise words that although the divine protection or Grace is there with them, however, that did not mean that they should become complacent with the assurance that Lord Ram would take care of everything. Instead, they should start working doubly hard or become '*purusharthi*' to express gratitude while awaiting the changes to take place. Selfless action is the most exceptional service to the Supreme.

If Grace is the energy, then '*purushartha*' is the medium. Without the medium, energy will still be present, but without energy, the medium is of no use. People must neither be inactive nor be overtly self-conscious on their doership. In Ramyan, Lord Ram has bestowed Grace on this devotees wherever he has gone. With this Grace Hanuman, Sugreeva, Vibhishan, Ahalaya, Shabri, Jatayu, Vanar Sena and others could put their *purushartha* in different purposes to serve Prabhu Ram and put an end to all their suffering.

■■

Chapter 5

Yagya of Dasaratha : Give and Take is Imperative

'The King of Ayodhya was sad, for he had no son,
He performed the Mahayagya for Lord's intervention.'

Dasratha's pain

The noble king of Ayodhya, Dasratha was unhappy because despite having three wives, he did not have an heir to the throne to take his legacy forward. None of the queens could give him a son. Worried and depressed, he visited the Royal Sage Vashisht and sought a solution from him. Vashisht suggested that performing a Yagya for son by offering oblations to the Supreme would yield results. The Yagya was successful and pleased by the efforts of the king, Agni Devta appeared with a divine potion and asked Dasratha to distribute the same among his queens.

Kaushalya is Knowledge

King Dasratha divided the divine potion into sixteen parts and gave the first eight parts to his first queen, Kaushalaya. If Dasaratha could be compared with dharma, Kaushalaya could be associated with Gyana or Knowledge. She was a wise lady. By offering the largest part of the divine potion to Kaushalaya, the king indicated that knowledge must be given the highest priority in a person's life as dharma is incomplete without knowledge. The consecrated union of the two brings righteousness and balance in one's life.

Kaikeyi is Action

The king then gave four parts to his second queen, Kaikeyi, who symbolized purushartha or action. This act of the king symbolized that action comes after dharma and wisdom. Activities that are supported by dharma and wisdom lead to outcomes that are not only beneficial for the doer but also for society at large. If action is devoid of dharma, it is bound to be a failure as was seen in case of Ravan who despite being a great achiever of many feats met with disappointment because he was not on the path of dharma and lacked sensitivity towards others. Action-oriented beings are usually very ego-centric and must be given due importance else they can create problems and spoil peace and harmony.

Sumitra is Emotions

After that Dasratha divided the remaining portion into two parts and gave one part each to Kaushalaya and Kaikeyi with a request to deliver it to the third and youngest queen Sumitra. Instead of presenting the potion directly to Sumitra, the king followed a hierarchical structure to indicate that grace must flow from senior. The Supreme Lord had given it to Agni Devta who passed it onto Dasaratha and who, in turn, gave it to Kaushalaya and Kekayi and asked them to offer it to Sumitra. This process of bestowing grace involved the inclusiveness of all participants.

Sumitra is a symbol of 'Bhava' or feelings for Supreme. 'Bhava' is free from ego and indifferent to ups and downs of life. It hardly mattered to Sumitra whether the king himself offered her the potion or it came through the two elder queens. Those who are filled with 'Bhava' are totally pure at heart. Even if one is in dharma, knowledge, and action but lacks Bhava, then is as good as deadwood. 'Bhava' is the essence of life. Sumitra passed on her unique quality to two of her sons Laxman and Shatrugan who became an epitome of commitment and service for elder brothers Bharat and Lord Ram.

Everything is planned

After consuming the divine potion, the three queens conceived and gave birth to four sons with Sumitra having a twin. The whole incident was a prelude to the arrival of the Avatar of Supreme Narayan on the earth. The Supreme Lord had made up his mind that he would take a human Avatar as an offspring of King Dasratha. He choreographed the divine intervention so effortlessly and with so much precision that it was beyond the cognitive understanding of mortal beings. Only enlightened sages like Vashisht who possessed the celestial eyes could see that providence in earthly incidents.

Dasratha was a principled man with utmost devotion or Bhakti for the Supreme. He envisioned Him as his son in his previous life. In Shri Bhagavad

Gita, Lord states that He manifests in whatever form the devotee wishes. It could be a father, friend, enemy, son, friend, servant or master. That is why the Supreme blessed Dasaratha with the honor of being the father of His human avatar, Lord Ram.

Problem of Attachment

Everything about Dasratha was excellent, leaving one flaw that was 'attachment' or 'moh' which eventually led to the disturbance in his family. When King Dasratha announced Lord Ram as the successor of the throne of Ayodhya, action-driven queen Kekayi became self-obsessed under the destructive influence of Manthra a 'Kusangati' or evil company. She rejected dharma and began seeking her narrow self-interest by exploiting 'attachment' or 'moh' of the king towards her. She asked for the exile of Shri Ram and the throne of Ayodhya for her son Bharat. She was oblivious of the consequences of her foolish deeds and thought that it was for the benefit of her and Bharat. Dasratha had no choice but to grant her the wish. As a result, Shri Ram had to set out for fourteen years of exile. Dejected King Dasratha died with much agony. After his soul departed the mortal body, the ever merciful Narayan gave him salvation. Queen Kekayi regretted her act till the end of her life and everybody else, including her son Bharat, discarded her and she led a life in remorse. What boils down from these events of the epic is that one must keep on making efforts to achieve the desired goals but at the same time must ensure that the means and the end are in accordance to Dharma, totally free from flaws. Else the outcome is painful.

The concept of Yagya is based on reciprocation and is applicable for all, at all times. Without the exchange of tangible and intangible oblations, this world cannot function. Moreover, a give and take relation brings a sense of oneness among all. Although King Dasratha organized the Yagya for his purposes, he invited his friends, family members, saints, and acquaintances to take part in it. This symbolized another thing that any initiative cannot be successful by the efforts of an individual only. It is a team effort that leads to success.

Importance of Give and Take

In today's world, beings are obsessed more on taking and less on giving, and this is the cause of unrest. By focusing more on giving, the balance will be restored. As Swami Vivekananda has said, 'ask not what I have got, contemplate what I have given.'

Supreme incarnated in Raghukul and blessed the king and queens for their unwavering devotion and good deeds. The king of hearts, Lord Ram, brought glory to the dynasty with his significant actions that uplifted the righteousness and destroyed the evil. Following the footsteps of Lord Ram, which is an admixture of Dharma, Gyan, Purushartha, and Bhava, people can reinstate balance in the world and make life an unforgettable precedent.

■■

Chapter 6

Advent of Lord Ram : The Supreme Godhead

Arrival

Time has come, lights are on, let's celebrate the auspicious day, For now, we will witness eternity's greatest epic and play.

Today we will celebrate the personification of beauty and purity,

Because today Lord Ram has manifested as King Dasratha's family.

The sun, the sky, the breeze and the water are pleasant, Beings are elated, and the seekers danced that instant.

Gods from Heaven are emptying the flowers from the barrel, The joy of Ma Kaushalaya and Raghukul is unexplainable.

Immediately the priests and preachers were called,

Let the ceremonies began, and every other work be stalled.

Sounds of music and blessings have filled the palace, People have finally found the much-awaited solace.

Streets are decorated with colourful jewels and flags, The saints are giving away hundreds of years of virtues, Without any discrimination and tags.

The ladies of the city in beautiful attires are hymning songs for the prince,

The lanes are soaked with fragrances of perfumes ever since.

Each man and woman is dancing in ecstasy, Dismissing their class, stature, and decency.

Uncountable material, elephants, horses, cows, and gems, Are distributed by the King with generosity,

To prostrate before the Lord, the supernatural energies, All have reached the palace with alacrity.

There is celebration everywhere around, But the Asura are unhappy and drowned.

Just a drop from the sea of bliss makes Shiva and Brahma Supreme deity,

Today that sea of bliss is flowing in ten directions of Ayodhya city.

Every household of the abode is glowing with ecstasy, Clusters of men and women are lost in frenzy.

Queens Kekayi and Sumitra also have given birth to beautiful sons,

Even Ma Saraswati cannot describe the euphoria of millions.

The night came to see Lord Ram, impatiently in brusque,

But seeing the Sun Devta got scared and sheepishly stayed like dusk.

The sparkling gems on the ceiling are like celestial stars, The white pinnacles of the palace are like lunar czars.

Chanting of mantras is like the chirping of excited birds, Beautiful kids were running back and forth in herds.

Seeing the spectacle, the Sun forgot his course, Month passed by, but He stood still with his horse.

No mortal could know how the month passed by,

When Sun didn't move, then how could the night come by?

God Shiva and Brahma arrived at the celebration, together, But because of their human form, no mortal could remember.

Ecstatic in the joy, those two were roaming in the lanes like crazy creatures,

These sacred traits of Gods were only understood by Ram Nam chanters.

Everybody was coming, going, celebrating, enjoying and blessing, The king was showering wealth with open arms without asking.

Naming Ceremony

Then King Dasratha asked the great Sage Vashisht to name the royal princes,

Ram is the treasure of peace and purity, in front of whom the power of evil eclipses.

Bharat will look after the wellbeing of the world, And in front of Shatrughan, no enemy can stand.

Laxman is the one, who is the abode of noble characteristics,

Henceforth, the land of Awadh was sparkling with the charisma of the princes.

Since beginning Laxman became Brother Ram's, loyalist ardent, Bharat and Shatrugan were like friends and attendant.

Though the mothers fondly gaze at the beauty of the two lovely pairs,

But it is magnificent Ram who is the ocean of bliss in all the heirs.

His heart illuminates like the moon and he smiles like twilight, Mothers play and fondle with him with immense love and delight.

The formless, all-pervading, creator of the universe, Paramatma, whose slave is Maya,

Out of pure love and devotion is baby playing in the arms of Mother Kaushalaya.

His form is like a deep blue lotus, possessing Kamdev's beauty a million times,

Feet are like a red lotus, on which the toenails are sparkling like pearls in primes.

A string of tiny bells is encompassing the waist,

And outstretched arms are decorated with ornaments of unique taste.

Mark of tiger claw is on the chest, and the diamond looks fascinating,

The neck is like a conch shell, and the glow of the face is captivating.

Lips are like rose curtains, unveiling beautiful little teeth,

Curly hair and fluffy cheeks are like alluring daffodils on velvet heath.

The beauty of the Lord's form is not in Veda's perception,

Supreme creator crawling on tiny hands and knees is beyond my comprehension.

In this way, the father of the universe, enchanted Ayodhya citizens, A demonstration of how devotion is paid back by Lord of Heavens.

Lordsport - Leela

For the delight of his followers, the lord is sporting as a child, Watching the baby in a rocking cradle, Mother Kaushalaya smiled.

Enthralled in her child's love, she forgot the passing of day and night,

Once she left the baby in the cradle and went to her deity's sight.

There she saw her baby playfully eating the oblation of the deity, Shocked she was and ran back to the cradle,

But found the baby sleeping, beaming with beauty.

Confused she was and again rushed back to the temple, And yet again she found the royal prince eating an apple.

Trembled with fear, her mind found no rest,

How come at the same time the baby was both on the east and the west?

'Is this an illusion or magic', Mother was scared,

Lord understood mother's dilemma and Supreme form He revealed.

What the great Lord Krishna showed to Arjuna after much deliberation,

Lord Ram showed to Ma Kaushalaya out of pure love and devotion.

There were countless universes in Supreme endless flavour,

Mother was trembling after seeing the Creator who had arrived as her toddler.

Lord comforted mother, 'but don't tell anybody about my real form',

I will never, but want you back as my baby, mother role I want to perform.

Thereafter Lord indulged in childish sports to the great delight of His follower,

With mother and father, Little Ram would play hide and seek with mirth and laughter.

In the company of His playmates, he was smeared in the dust, Then he would run to father and jump on his lap like a gust.

The one who cannot be comprehended by humans as well as Gods,

Was chased by Mother in annoyance, and witnessing it, the universe laughs.

Unfortunate are those who cannot enjoy Lord's mesmerizing leela and drama,

Only a pure devotee can feel the restlessness and playfulness of little Ram.

Growing up

Whose one breadth has more than all Vedas knowledge,

On attaining boyhood, he for education, would be sent to college.

Proficient in learning and perfect in politeness, virtues, and decorum,

Seeing the four brothers passing by in the streets, all hearts played the drum.

Ram was dearest to every child, man, woman, and elder

Every younger was taught by Him, the meanings of Vedic scripture.

He would rise early and busied self with brothers in city affairs, King Dasratha was very glad to see the work of his successors.

The eternal, all-pervading, omnipresent and mighty creator, Was doing earthly acts for the sake of His lover.

How do I elaborate on the scene of the highest paradise?

Only the one who seeks the lotus feet of Lord Ram, can advise.

Please forgive my misdeeds, O Lord Hari's incarnation, And bless me with your eternal and exquisite devotion.

One cannot free self from the web of samsara, which is intangible, If is not devoted to Lord Raghunath's feet, which are incredible.

Chapter 7

Vishvamitra Seeks : Nobody is Perfect

The great sage felt very troubled in mind,
Without the Lord's intervention, Asura will not die.

Vishvamitra's Story

Sage Vishvamitra is an exceptional character in the epic of Ramayan, who has been associated with many amazing stories. Right from King Harish Chandra to Lord Ram, he tried the kings of Raghukul dynasty numerous times just for their own benefit. He also played a crucial role in nurturing and shaping the characters of Prince Ram and Laxman. The sage himself was a great achiever who had transformed himself from an arrogant emperor to a self- realized Saint, a feat that is seldom heard in history. He was the first to speak the Gayatri Mantra and was spiritually very powerful. Wise sages and mighty kings would bow before him.

Vishvamitra, a Brahma Gyani that is the highest position of knowledge, felt helpless when he heard about the sufferings of the sages in the hands of the Asura of Ravana. These sages had approached him with a plea to rescue them. Despite his power acquired from years of hard penance, he realized that these Asura who were spoiling the Yagya of sages were no less powerful owing to their association with Ravana. Ravana was the emerging superpower. He had earned his might through unmatched spiritual knowledge and penance and was extremely courageous and determined.

Although Vishvamitra was empowered with celestial weapons from Lord Brahma, Shiva, and Vishnu as rewards for his extreme penance, he did not use them against the Asura. He always believed in non-violence as a part of his spiritual practices.

Flaws of Mind

Readers may find this apparent timidity of the mighty sage surprising and rather confusing. Questions may arise, how come such a great *rishi* feared Asura? What were his reasons? When with the power of his *tapasya* and penance he could easily destroy millions, then why did he feel helpless? What was his reservation in using celestial weapons against the Asura? Wasn't this ploy of non- violence another form of weakness and lack of courage against evil? Readers may also feel disheartened seeing the triumph of evil over dharma and the fear of the righteous of the evil. However, the answers perhaps lied somewhere else.

In the battle against the evil, what matters most is the purity of heart and an absolute righteous character. Any incompleteness in dharma is the cause of the weakness. The same applied in the case of Vishvamitra. The three Asura- Tadaka, Subahu, and Maricha who were creating trouble for the sages were symbols of anger, fear, and desire. One who is above these three 'vratti' or binding characteristics of mind could fight against them, which sage Vishvamitra was not despite his years of *tapasya* and practice of righteousness. He, being a seer or *Gyani,* was well aware of his shortcomings.

Earlier, the sage believed that everything is achievable by efforts and penance but eventually realized that it's not true. So now Vishvamitra decided to seek the help of the Lord to free himself of the 'vratti' of anger, desire, and fear, which were the last hurdles in his spiritual journey.

Surrender (Samarparna) of Vishvamitra

He very well knew that Lord has taken avatar as the Prince of Ayodhya and so he decided to approach Him for protection from Asura. Thus, instead of venturing out to fight the Asura himself, Vishvamitra decided to approach Lord Ram for help. This was his first step towards Surrender (Samarparna) and devotion for Lord. The move sends out the message that the ultimate way for liberation is Surrendering to the Supreme. As mentioned in the Gita, Lord has promised to Arjuna, "Abandon all dependencies and Surrender unto Me, I shall free you. Do not ever fear."

The so called achievers may find this logic difficult to digest as they believe that people themselves are responsible for all their deeds, successes, and failures. They are the doers. Whatever someone achieves is an outcome of his or her passion and hard work. They also hold that Surrendering to the

Lord is an excuse for complacent, lazy, and non- performer and dependence on Grace is escapism.

Vishvamitra also felt the same during the early years of his spiritual life. The principle of accomplishing feats through hard work and penance made him achiever of many triumphs but posed a barrier against his realization that one needs to Surrender to Lord and acknowledge His Grace. However, his encounter with sage Vashisht changed his perception. He began to realize that no matter how much one tries, there remain some aspects which are beyond the control of humans. It could be own characteristic limitations or circumstantial impediments, hindering people from achieving their best potential. In fact, without questioning and analyzing self, the seeker must Surrender to the Supreme and seek His solace.

The epic of Ramayan portrays both the perspectives of acknowledgment and non-acknowledgment of Grace before the readers. It is up to us to choose which path we think is most suitable for us in our journey to the fulfillment of life.

■■

Chapter 8

Story of Lady Ahalaya : Power of Penance

Lord Ram saw the statue which was uncommon,
The sage then narrated the story of Ahalaya, a heart broken.

Story so far

Threatened by the repeated attacks of the Asura on the sages and on their *Yagya*, Sage Vishvamitra approached King Dasratha and asked for his two sons Ram and Laxman for fighting those demons out of the region. With the consent of the king, both the princes followed the sage to the forest and destroyed the demons. Pleased Vishvamitra gifted Lord Ram his celestial weapons and taught him many warfare skills along with spiritual knowledge. To safeguard the *Yagya* of Sages, Lord Ram and his brother Laxman stayed at the ashram of Vishvamitra for some time. After ensuring that the forests were free of threats from demons, Vishvamitra took the brothers to Janakpur, the city of Princess Sita where God Shiva's *Dhanush Yagya* was taking place for Her *Swayamwar*. On their way to Janakpur, they came across an old, lifeless, and decayed ashram where Lord Ram noticed a strange statue of stone in female shape. He became curious and asked sage Vishvamitra about the mysterious rock. The sage narrated the tale of unfortunate Lady Ahalaya to Prince Ram and Laxman.

Ahalaya's Story

Maharishi Gautama was a great sage who lived with his lovely, committed, and pious wife, Ahalaya. The king of the demigods Indra was fascinated by the beauty of Lady Ahalaya and secretly and illegitimately longed for her. He used his magical spell to turn one midnight into a 'Brahma Muhurta' or the time of daybreak. Sage Gautama believing that the dawn has arrived woke up from his sleep and left the hut to the river to perform his usual morning rituals. Indra then entered the hut disguised as Gautama and involved himself with acts of physical intimacy with Lady Ahalaya who too was deceived by Indra's magical spells and believed that it was her husband who had come to her. Thus, she allowed him to indulge with her.

On the banks of the river, Maharishi Gautama realized that something was wrong as it was still pitch dark there. Perplexed, he returned to his hut to find that Indra was coming out of his room in his guise. Things became clear to him, and he could reason out all the mysterious incidents happening to him. Indra got caught. Raging with anger, Sage Gautama cursed him an embarrassing form. He did not even spare his innocent wife. He cursed Ahalaya a lifeless existence. Ahalaya immediately accepted the mistake and pleaded for solace from Gautama. The sage realized that he had acted harshly with his wife under rage and impulse, and hence blessed her that when Lord Ram would touch her, she would regain consciousness. He also promised that he would return at that time and accept her again. After that, discarding the ashram, the sage went to the Himalayas, and Ahalaya got transformed into a rock. Since then the ashram became deserted. No humans, not even animals or birds ever came near the cursed ashram.

After narrating Ahalaya's story, Vishvamitra told Lord Ram that since then the poor lady had been chanting 'Ram Nam' and patiently waiting for His arrival. Upon hearing the heart-wrenching story of an innocent and deceived woman, Lord Ram could not stay calm. He went ahead and touched her to free her of all the sins that she got involved in unknowingly and unintentionally. Maharishi Gautama also returned and accepted her again as his wife.

Illegitimate Desires

In the epic, the incident of illegitimate pleasure-seeking happened twice. Once Indra took advantage of the naivety of a pious lady, and on another occasion, Ravana took the sense of honour of Lady Sita, to his ride. In both instances, the perpetrators disguised themselves as sages. This is highly symbolic. But the moot point here is that Indra was the King of Devlok, the up-keeper of Dharma and Ravan was an evil Asura King with no regard for righteousness whatsoever. How come both acted similarly and committed hideous crimes? So, where lays the difference between Devta and Asura, when both are slaves of their animalistic desires?

The fundamental question is, is every being a slave to the carnal instincts?

Is it the same for Indra and Ravan or for that matter to human beings? Therefore, our scriptures and sages have always given high importance to control of desires. Some may argue that Indra was the King of demigods and far too superior to humans, so the comparison is not valid. But if a Devta could falter in the path of controlling an illegitimate bodily desire, then what power do humans hold against it?

No matter what the status of the creature is, controlling one's desires that lead them to the path of wrongdoing is entirely in one's hand. It must be understood that such illegitimate acts always cause spiritual, mental, and physical deterioration. The root of the problem is that beings do not like to accept their shortcomings. Those who are enslaved by their bodily desires think that they can somehow escape the repercussion of a wrongful act and will continue to lead a happy and peaceful life. But that does not happen. Neither Lord's Dharma nor beings' own conscience allow them to be satisfied, and they mentally run helter-skelter to find justification for their deeds using some corrupt logic. Their immoral thoughts never permit them to introspect and check their conducts. They fail to realize that irrespective of them getting caught for their unrighteous acts or not, the karmic account will balance itself. If not today, maybe tomorrow but there is no escape.

Ahalaya is Intelligence

The next significant question that arises out of this tale is why was Ahalaya punished? She was unaware of the trickery of Indra and was under the influence of his magical spell. Then what made her husband curse her?

Notwithstanding her sheer innocence, Ahalaya who represents 'Buddhi' or intelligence which failed on reasoning, on that occasion. The cause of all her suffering was her complete reluctance to apply her mind to the context of the circumstances. Maharishi Gautama was a very learned sage, not like Dhobi Bhadra of Ayodhya who discarded his wife out of baseless suspicion. He could very well see that his wife was innocent. But what infuriated the sage was the lack of logic in his wife to judge the situation and act accordingly. Sage Gautama had always led a life of celibacy, and Ahalaya was very well aware of it. So how can he indulge physically? This is the reasoning that Lady Ahalaya failed to identify.

Righteousness Vs Pleasures

The intelligence in human beings has two options like that of Ahalaya. One is

Gautama who symbolizes 'Dharma' or righteousness and second is Indra who symbolizes 'Bhoga' or pleasures. Leading a righteous life can result in two outcomes. One is the attainment of Heaven, where all the desires of mortal life get fulfilled. The second one holds no value for pleasures and is an utter state of 'Vairagya' that is indifference and dispassion towards all pleasures and pains. All enlightened people in every era have always subscribed to the state of Vairagya with the purpose of searching for knowledge and realization of truth. The idea of glories and pleasures of Heaven is to either coax or manipulate lower intelligence.

Intelligence always chooses Dharma over Bhoga, but only when it is alert and focussed. However, in reality, no matter how hard one tries, there are situations when intelligence loses focus and alertness and tends to get attracted to Bhoga. In a similar weak moment, Ahalaya or Buddhi got indulged in Bhoga and believed it to be the reward for her sincere practice of Dharma.

Therefore, alertness and righteousness is imperative but not the ultimate solution. Gautama was the symbol of alertness and righteousness, but still, he was helpless. He perceived the mistake of Ahalaya as his own mistake. After realizing his utter harshness in cursing Ahalaya, he comforted Ahalaya with the boon that she would regain consciousness when Lord Ram blesses her.

The full proof solution

Ahalaya gladly accepted Gautama's judgment, and she kept on chanting the name of Lord Ram even in her petrified form. Buddhi can be purified only by devotion or Bhakti, which also eliminates the attraction for Bhoga forever. It is exactly what happened with Ahalaya as she got her intelligence purified treading the path of Bhakti. She pleased Lord Ram with her intense Bhakti and became purified with His blessings. Ahalaya or Buddhi was then in union with the Supreme and she attained enlightenment, which is the highest reward for a human being to be free from all worldly sufferings.

In the state of enlightenment, even the most luring Bhoga that is Indra fails to gull Mother Ahalaya, the purified Buddhi. Moreover, that is also the reason why Sage Gautama accepted her wholeheartedly. To be with Ahalaya was now no less than a reward for Gautama.

Thus, no matter what the past is, and no matter what right or wrong one has committed in one's lives, everyone is eligible for devotion or Bhakti at any stage of life. Lord has assured that whenever someone calls Him with a pure heart, He will respond and make them free from all the sins and suffering.

We can, therefore, either embrace Bhakti and get liberation like Ahalaya or continue indulging in Bhoga and face its bitter consequences. Ultimately the choice lies with us.

■■

Chapter 9

Blossoming of The Greatest Love Story

Janakpur

After liberating Ahalaya,

The sage with the two Princess reached Janakpur shortly, King Janaka was pleased with their arrival,

And welcomed them hurriedly.

Seeing Lord Ram and Laxman, King's heart was overwhelmed, 'Who are these two ornaments of divinity?

I have lost control of my eyes,

Seeing the most fascinating form of Infinity.'

Sage replied, 'All beings love them,

Sons of Dasaratha, they are Ayodhya's pride, They slayed the demons, freed Ahalaya and Established Dharma at our ashram side.'

'O sage, their beauty is beyond descriptions,

My good Karma of past life has finally been obliged,' The King then escorted them to the royal guest palace,

For the first time, King Janaka, in his life, was hypnotized.

Vishvamitra speaks, 'You are the upholder of morals O Ram, And you are the epitome of reverence,

Why don't you feast the eyes of Janakpur citizens,

And let them relish, the human form of impermanence?'

Clad in royal garments with graceful bow and arrow in hands, The two Princes graced the city,

Like fire, the news spread, and all citizens hastened to see them, As if paupers were rushing to grab a priceless property.

A million eyes got satisfied, seeing the master of the universe, Walking past their homes,

Young pretty damsels blushed from the sides of their doors, As the Lord of million Cupids casually roams.

The two lads, fair and dark were of tender age And the embodiment of grace,

The fondness of damsels is pure and sacred –

'We didn't know the Princes are of beauty scarce'.

Union of Ram and Sita is brought about by providence, There is nothing in this eternity that can change it, This is the groom our Princess Janaki deserves,

And it is Heaven's order, so none can challenge it.'

And yet, there will always remain doubting and unsure beings, Unable to feel divinity because of sheer ignorance,

But then just one chant of RamNam can destroy, Any quantum of idiocy and arrogance.

Like benighted beings of Kaliyuga,

Few ladies of Janakpur seemed uncertain about Ram's competence, 'Shiva's Dhanush is mighty like Mount Kailasa,

While this lad is of subtle and delicate appearance.'

Just then a wise lady intervenes-

'The one, whose touch has liberated Ahalaya from the darkness of years,

The Creator who has fashioned Janaki with beauty and skills Has zeroed on Ram to be her groom, irrelevant are your fears.'

The two brothers spreading supreme joy reached Dhanush Yagya arena,

Which was magnificent and grand, Decorated lavishly with gold and silk,

The whole coliseum was a wonder of Bharat land.

Innocent children were joyfully playing with Prince Ram, And showed Him around,

He distributed them presents and escaped playfully,

To return to the sage upon hearing the evening conch sound.

Lord who bats an eyelid to any terror,

Today like an obedient ward is bothered at being late, And so, hurries to reach his guardian Vishvamitra,

This is the joy of devotion, lovingly served on every devotee's plate.

The two brothers saluted the sage apologetically And entered with his permission,

Vishvamitra smiled affectionately

Then they all retired to rooms for relaxation.

The Lord whose lotus feet are sought by millions By Yoga, Jap, Tap, Seva and Bhajan,

Was getting immense satisfaction in massaging feet For the comfort of Vishvamitra, His guardian.

Pushp Vatika

Both the princes woke up early in the morning, And went to the royal garden to collect flowers, With the consent of gardeners,

They began plucking from the most beautiful floral clusters.

Meanwhile, Sita with her companions arrived in the garden temple

To pray to Ma Bhawani, the Goddess of Energy,

While she was engrossed in Dhyan, someone announced The presence of the charming princes with alacrity.

All of them rushed to see the two glaring stars of righteousness and divinity,

But it was Sita who was most anxious to see her soulmate of eternity.

The tinkling of bells and ornaments of ladies, Gently attracted Prince Ram's attention,

Lord turned around and saw the symbol of purity, In the same direction.

His magnetizing eyes became motionless,

As if the eyelids had forgotten their function,

His heart was filled with admiration for her beauty But he couldn't utter a single word of adoration.

He felt as if Creator has put in all His creative competence In this divine manifestation, for the world to see,

She emanated charm, like a flame of light in the house of beauty, It seemed she enlightened the world, obliviously,

There are no comparisons I can think of, To match her blissful dignity,

Even the greatest of thinkers lack the imagination To paint words for Her Excellency.

Gazing at Shree Ram,

Sita's heart rejoiced as if it has found long-lost treasure, The Ganges of love that was flowing between them, Turned her blind to objects minor.

Then beholding the image of Lord in her eyes, She swiftly closed her eyes' shutter,

Knowing Sita being overpowered with love, Even a word, her companions couldn't utter.

Sita then returned to Temple,

Adoring Goddess' feet, with folded hands she prayed,

'Glory to you O mother of the universe,

The keeper of righteousness, evil from you, is afraid.

There is no beginning and end of You

And You are responsible for birth and destruction, You adore your Shiva as God,

Whose infinite grace is the being's only consolation.

You have always cared for my heart,

Now please listen to my humble request, I plead,' Mother replied, 'Don't worry my child,

The suitor whom you desire will be yours, indeed.'

Thanking, again and again, Ma Bhawani, Overwhelmed Sita returned to her royal abode, Lord Ram also returned to Sage Vishvamitra, And innocently narrated him the day's episode.

'Ram you are the cause and effect,

May your desire be accomplished,' blessed the great sage, Brothers were glad to hear his approval,

Eager, the two lions are now for tomorrow's stage.

■■

Chapter 10

Joy of Janaka : Just Knowledge is not Enough

Unexplainable is Lord's attraction, Logic doesn't work with emotion.

The Enlightened Janaka

King Janaka had an unexplainable unique experience on seeing Lord Ram. Goswami Tulsidas described the overwhelmed state of the king in great detail. Janaka was speechless, almost hypnotized, and lost his power of reasoning. He confessed this state of his before Vishvamitra. This event is very significant in terms of spirituality. King Janaka was an exceptionally wise and knowledgeable person. He was titled 'Raj rishi' and 'Videhraj' as an honour for his Gyana (Knowledge) and Atman Sakshatkar (Enlightenment). Rarely any king in the history of Sanatana Dharma has had the credential to attain such position. It was the sages who could reach the highest plateau of knowledge.

Form Vs Formless

Janaka being an enlightened individual, very well knew that beings are not body or mind; instead, they are the manifestation of the supreme consciousness. Consciousness is 'Nirguna' that is, it has no attributes and 'Nirakar' that is, it has no form. Janaka firmly believed in this universal truth. Despite that, he was swayed by the human Avatar of Lord Ram, who is the physical manifestation of Supreme. This is rather an unusual reaction for a Gyani (Knowledgeable) like Janaka. How can someone who believes in formless, get attracted to physicality, matter or form?

The underlying reason is that the form, aura, attraction, energy, and essence of Lord Ram are infinitely charismatic. Avatar Ram shattered the beliefs of a non-believer of forms. Janaka couldn't reason out why he got immensely attracted to the Lord. Praising and loving a Form of the Supreme is the unique quality of Bhakta or devotee like Hanuman and not of Gyani or self-realized ones like Janaka. In the Gita, Lord has declared that to Him, Bhakti is superior to Gyana as He does not long for knowledge but love only.

Sprouting of Devotion

King Janaka, for the first time in his life, felt the divine joy of Bhakti. Those who emphasize logic and reasoning can know the Universal Truth, but only those who unconditionally love Him can enjoy the pleasure that the Truth ensues. That very moment of glancing at Lord Ram shook the belief system of Janaka for which he was widely revered.

This tale may provoke immense joy in the minds of a lover of Lord Ram, but it has the potential to develop an insight for the inquisitive seeker (Jigyasu) that logic, reasoning, and questioning will give knowledge but not the ultimate satisfaction. Treading the path of knowledge without devotion gives intellectual superiority, which generates a sense of pride and entraps the seeker in ego, the most significant impediment to reach the final destination.

Attraction of Forms

The reputation of the two princes had spread across Janakpur even before they reached there. The citizens of Janakpur were immensely curious to see the brave boys who had slayed Tadaka and liberated Ahalaya. They too, like their king, were overwhelmed after seeing Ram and Laxman. They formed a connection with Lord Ram instantly and secretly wished that it is He who must win the bow challenge and marry their Princess Sita so that they would have the privilege of seeing Him again and again. Citizens were not enlightened like their King Janaka. They just relished the beauty of Prince Ram without indulging in 'How' and 'Why.'

The attraction in divinity is such that it makes people forget themselves, let alone their desires and welfare. Their sole wish remains to be in the company of their Lord. This is 'Prema Bhakti' or love-devotion where the being forms a relationship with the Supreme.

Love is tough for self-obsessed ignorant people to apprehend. That is why there is so much criticism, condemnation, and violence in the pretext of 'My' beliefs and 'Your ' beliefs in world's history. A devotee doesn't contest others' beliefs rather acknowledges all beliefs and faiths as one, as all of them lead to the Lord. Devotee remains indifferent towards the material and about desirable or undesirable situations. He only cares to be with the Lord. Many believe that Lord Ram took human Avatar to destroy Ravan, but the truth is He had come for the joy of His devotees. Wherever Lord Ram went, there the beings experienced the ultimate bliss and ecstasy which was missing in their lives.

Purity in Love

I have enough of loss, enough of gain;
I have my Love, what more can I obtain?

Both Sita and Ram fell in love with each other at the very first sight. Tulsidas narrated the gleeful moments of their encounter vividly. Siya-Ram connected immediately and realized that they are made for each other. There was absolute clarity in emotions without a trace of sensory desire. Siya-Ram followed the code of conduct and didn't interact then, though they were mesmerized by each other. They just hoped of becoming one and waited for the opportune moment to unveil its outcome.

Now the question is – like other love-struck beings, why didn't they try to express their feelings to each other? Answer is simply because They had taken Avatar to set instances for the world to believe in Surrender (Samarparna) of Supreme for fulfillments of desire. They knew that whatever He feels right for them would actually happen, irrespective of what the worldly forces want. Words are required to express when clarity and surety are missing.

Expectations is the problem

Surrendered devotees don't need to use smartness and cleverness to make things happen. They just stay aware of the present moment and to whatever situation life puts them in. They have gained the power of acceptance. For them every happening is the will of the Lord. Surrender (Samarparna) gave purity and gracefulness to the love of Siya-Ram and insight to others. Elements of desirability, impatience, anxiety, control, insecurity, and expectation in relationships signify that connection is still not complete. Instead, it appears more like a mutual agreement to fulfil the emotional and physical needs of each other. Such a relationship goes on well as long as there are conscious efforts to satisfy one another. But for how long can one play roles. So when the real nature of one surfaces, the expectations of the other are not fulfilled and then, problems start cropping up. In the relationship between Lord Ram and Mother Sita, there is only giving and never asking. There is also a sense of gracefully accepting the situations that life puts them in.

Cleverness doesn't works

Many may argue that the Maryada and Dharma practised by Siya-Ram are very difficult, and almost impossible to implement in present times. In reply, it can be said that before passing our judgements have we ever cared to try? People tend to succumb easily to what is happening around them. That is why we may not witness real relations around us. However, that doesn't mean they don't exist. There still exist meek noble ones who follow the footsteps of Siya-Ram and lead an honourable life.

Sita after seeing Ram returned to the temple of Goddess Bhawani and prayed for Prince Ram to be her husband. Ma Bhawani blessed her and granted the wish. Again, most people say that such incidents between the devotee and God only take place in fictitious mythological stories. Generally wishes of people hardly get heard or granted by Supreme. Therefore, they very conveniently conclude that praying doesn't work. But perhaps what we are overlooking here is the purity, honesty, and Surrender (Samarparna) in Sita's worship to Ma Bhawani.

Everyone is bestowed with a certain degree of intelligence to contemplate their thoughts and actions. While dealing with worldly affairs, they always maintain a clever approach of 'If not this, then that.' They cannot let go of this craftiness even when interacting with God. The element of conditionality in the prayer dilutes its effect. One needs to Surrender unconditionally to the Lord inside out.

To feel His grace, beings need to first purify themselves and keep shrewdness and conditionality out of their lives. Reading about characters of pure souls is an effective way to purify oneself, and that is exactly the reason why Shri Ram Charit Manas is considered the greatest epic. It is the saga of the divine grace of Surya Vanshi King Ram and Janaknandini Sita that epitomises purity and is a treasure trove of eternal learning and wisdom.

■■

Chapter 11

Verdict of Laxman : Unwavering Faith

You are the Sun, you are the Light,
Remove the darkness and set things right.

Laxman's assurance

In the comforts of Janakpur, the two brothers woke up early in the morning. It was still dark outside. Ram could not sleep the whole night. He was love-struck for the first time and spent the entire night staring at night sky engrossed in thoughts of Sita. He, not in his usual spirits, lamented to Laxman that soon the Moon would fade away.

Realizing the sentiments of his brother, Laxman replied that the bow of Lord Shiva is like the darkness of the night and the contenders are like dim-lit stars in the night sky. They can merely flicker but cannot remove the darkness. Therefore, they will never win the challenge. They will show off and boast of their strength but are no comparison to Him. It is Lord Ram who must become the Sun to end the long darkness of night and spread light all over for the pleasure of his devotees. When the sun shines, the stars vanish. Laxman foretells that Lord Ram will break the Bow of Shiva effortlessly and win the challenge. He and only he will get the hand of Princess Sita.

World of Sycophants

The statement of Prince Laxman is very significant not just for the devotees of Lord Ram but also for the understanding of the human psyche. Like the clever egoist contenders of bow-challenge, in present times too, there is a segment in society which despite not being extraordinary, pretend to be one. They boast about and show-off their not so unique qualities and possess admirable stamina to talk about themselves at every possible opportunity.

Lost in their self-obsessed thoughts, they do not even hesitate to undermine others. Their sole objective is to influence people to acknowledge their superiority over them and create a gang of sycophants, who mesmerized by their illusionary strength, will follow them to fulfil their ulterior purpose which is 'Yog & Shem,' that is to achieve what they don't have and to protect what they have.

Laxman referred to those kings with a false sense of self- aggrandizement, who have assembled for the bow challenge with an expectation to win it and marry Princess Sita. By declaring their ineffectuality, Laxman removes the last iota of doubt of those who are unsure of Lord Ram's victory. People with lesser intelligence, weaker-will, wrongful and unrighteous conduct get attracted to the boastful fake leaders very easily. These benighted followers form the class of **sycophants**. Unsurprisingly, this kind of people constitutes the majority portion of the human population on earth. Sycophants usually suffer from low self-esteem and hence, desire to find recognition, satisfaction, and solace through connection and identification with a stronger personality and powerful associations.

Sensible Seekers

Then there are seekers or the wiser ones. They are significantly lesser in number than sycophants. They, due to their good karma in the past, are bestowed with the Grace of Lord and remain uninfluenced by the ridiculousness of the phony leaders and their gang of sycophants.

Seekers are essentially those individuals who are experiencing emptiness in life. Things that generally offer satisfaction to the common beings hardly appeal to them. Therefore, they do not get impressed by the boastful portrayals of fake people or leaders. Seekers are neither entirely worldly nor wholly settled in spirituality. They live in a twilight zone. Being confused, they sometimes experience immense joy while at other times suffer from intense exasperation. They are in the middle of a process of awakening; in the middle of illusion and truth.

Ordinary worldly solutions for happiness are not something they crave for. They are like flowers of Lotus dwelling in the muddy water yet staying unscathed by the filth. The flickering dim lights of the stars in the night sky may be sufficient for ignorant-nocturnal beings but not for seekers of light. Seekers live with a hope that one day, there will be sunrise that will engulf the darkness of ignorance and eliminate petty fakers and megalomaniacs.

However, not all seekers can put their faith in the Sun under the spell of darkness. But those who can, become eligible for the grace of Sunlight. These arc the true devotees who have committed their lives in the service of the

Lord. It is they who the Lord loves the most. They find peace and happiness the moment they place their faith in the Supreme, and it was so overwhelming and gratifying for them that other than Lord, they expect nothing else from life. Only such devotees are entitled to the divine love and deserve to be pleased by the Supreme. Laxman, therefore, is requesting Lord Ram to become the Sun and give the ultimate bliss to His devotees.

Everyone encounters challenging and tough situations in life. It is the ignorant ones who try to find solutions in this fake world based only on self-capability and self- intelligence. On the other hand, a devotee Surrenders to the Supreme. The Lord accepts the difficulty of the devotee on Himself and solves the tough situations to ensure uninterrupted peace for His devotee.

Patience Pays

O Lord, Please your devotees, they have suffered a lot, Brutally attacked by ignorance, yet their faith was not lost.

Later in the morning, the two royal brothers went to Dhanush Yagya, the Bow-Challenge ceremony, with Sage Vishvamitra. News of their arrival spread like wildfire in the city. Men, women, kids, and seniors leaving their task at hand rushed to see the Lord in action. The citizens of Janakpur, the seekers, were hoping that their darkness of life would end. For some reason for which they had no explanation, they were drawn to the arena. Something inside them was utterly convinced that Lord Ram is the Sun they had been waiting for all their lives. Today, as soon as the bow would be broken, there would be Sunrise and in its light, the agony of the long night would end.

The fake ones and their sycophant followers compromise with the darkness. For them, the feeble light of flickering stars is good enough. They are hopeless and helpless and unable to put their faith in the right place. They wear masks of confidence, arrogance, cleverness, and happiness to hide their inner pain. Seekers tolerate the foolishness, the condemnation and the violence of ignorant people but never succumbed to them.

The seekers and the devotees of Janakpur had patiently waited for a very long time. The day of Lord Ram's arrival to the Dhanush Yagya was the day of their salvation. Sun rose then, and the Sun has risen even today. In Sunlight, the emptiness of life will end. But the question is, shall we continue to burn in the fire of ignorance throughout our lives or for once should we put our faith in Lord Ram and attain peace and perfection?

■■

Chapter 12

Countless Portrayals of Lord : One Truth, Many Perceptions

Each one perceived Lord differently,
As per their perceptive, individually.

Prince Ram and Laxman, accompanied by Sage Vishvamitra, entered the arena where the Bow challenge was supposed to be conducted. Thousands present there were enthralled to see Lord Ram. They were helplessly captivated by His majesty. To them, He was the incarnation of the Supreme consciousness. The seeker, ignorant, and sinner perceived the Lord differently, according to their intentions.

Many Reflections

Great warrior kings saw the reflection of the God of War, Kartikey, in Lord Ram. For them, he stood as a symbol of courage, valour, honour, and supreme master of warfare. The wicked kings quivered with fear as if their worst nightmare had come alive as they saw God Narsimha in Him.

The Asura who had joined the challenge disguised as Kings, witnessed the imagery of the God of Death, Yama, in the Lord. They realized that no matter how clever they are in befooling others with their fake demeanours, they cannot escape the Eyes of Death. The wise sages were bewildered after seeing the divine aura of the young man and couldn't flip their eyelids in astonishment. They were as thrilled as the Gopis of Braj used to be after seeing the most attractive and divine personality in the whole universe, our very own, Lord Krishna.

The young ladies blushed like red roses as they observed the shadow of the God of Beauty, Kamadeva, in Him. The enlightened ones saw Vishwaroop in Lord Ram. They witnessed infinite heads, hands, and feet; there was no beginning and no end. They watched that creation and destruction were transpiring simultaneously in Him.

The relatives of King Janaka saw Lord Ram like a family member. Even before anything was finalized, they accepted Him as husband of Sita and related with Him as their brother or son in law. The Queens saw Lord Ram as their dear child, and found motherly love and affection flowing in their hearts.

The Yogis witnessed the 'Element' of Supreme having attributes of peacefulness, purity, evenness, innateness, and naturalness. The Devotees saw their 'Ishta' or 'Personal God or Goddess' in Lord Ram. They were overwhelmed by the very glimpse of Lord Ram, and their minds were filled with the ultimate joy that they had longed for all their lifetime.

Princess Sita felt natural love and gladness seeing the Lord. Her feelings could neither be described in words nor imagined in thoughts by the mortals. One can explain earthly things only. We can relate to the love between a man and a lady because we can see and experience it. Nobody is aware of the eternal and omnipresent bond of Lord Ram and Mother Sita and therefore, cannot explain. What we have read in scriptures is that theirs was a Love of Union and Oneness, an association of consciousness and nature through which the universe is created.

The Lord is infinite, and so are His forms. Everyone defines Him within their boundaries of intellectual abilities. If birds had a developed intellect, they would have perceived God as a bird. Thus, human beings perceive God as human. Who is wrong and who is right?

Perceptions

Once a bird was chirping,
To someone, she was
singing, To others, she was
laughing, To one she was
chanting,
For another one, she was crying,
Each one judged the bird's chirping, as per own
perception, But what she actually meant was out of their
comprehension.
Goswami Tulsidas had a deep understanding of the human
mind. He was well aware that different people tend to

perceive the same object or occurrence differently. No one knows the reality in absoluteness. Therefore, while describing the reactions of the diverse group of people after seeing Lord Ram, he wrote that each spectator viewed Lord Ram as per their perception. This has a very significant meaning in general as well.

People with their limited intellect are incapable of knowing the complete truth. Hence, perceptions among people differ. Problem arises when people start believing that it is their perception of a thing or event that is the ultimate truth and turn adamant by labelling others as false. Intellectual constraints and lack of tolerance towards the viewpoints of others lead to conflicts and disputes. No matter how much people try to understand the perspectives of each other, there will always remain a gap.

Everything is One

The point here is that, it is fine to have limited intellectual abilities and also to disagree with other viewpoints. What is not right is to be obstinate with a point of view and rejecting the opinions of others. The truth is that every particle and every action is part of one universal energy. This is not a spiritual belief but a proven quantum physics observation.

Spiritualists believe that universal energy is the Supreme Intelligence, who is managing the whole system. Thus, when the sceneries are one, onlookers are one, eyes are one, minds are one, the consciousness of beings is one, then where is the difference? Why there is a disparity in perspectives? This is because the Lord has bestowed human beings with the independent power of reasoning and therefore, being is free to take their own decision. No belief is imposed by the Lord.

To be able to accept and tolerate contradictions wisely, one must believe in the truth of Oneness. With disbelief or ignorance for Oneness, one cannot practise tolerance. Lord Ram sees all and knows all. He merely manifests himself in different forms for the satisfaction of people with limited intellects and narrow minds. He makes things easier for His seekers by allowing them to perceive Him as per their minds. That is why for an ignorant, Lord Ram is an ordinary human being, whereas, for a wicked and evil, He is terror and death.

So far, using intellect, we have read about perceptions and presumed to have understood it as well. But the question remains whether we have actually accepted it. This we have to leave to the time to tell. Till then, we can be sure of one thing that, for now, peace and harmony among human beings is a far cry. Proofs of conflicts and commotions are galore for ages.

One must understand that sheer dependence on intellect is not enough for developing higher insight, let alone enlightenment. More importantly, what is needed is the understanding to Surrender intellect to the Supreme and accept Him as the controller. The realization that truth is not what can be logically explained; instead the truth is what can be felt with the heart, mind, and soul; something that is beyond the comprehension of intellect; something that surpasses all reasoning and logic is what needed to bring about the change. It is only the ultimate faith in the grace of Lord Ram that can help, and nothing else.

■■

Chapter 13

Realization of the Challengers : Wisdom gives Peace

Thoughts of feast cannot satiate hunger,
Mind-ego is humanity's biggest manipulator.

King Janaka came forward to greet the Sage and the two Princes warmly and seated them at the pavilion reserved for most important guests. The contenders at the arena gradually regained reasoning after being spellbound by the divine form of Lord Ram. All of them accepted defeat at heart after knowing that Lord Ram is going to contest for the Bow Challenge. The flickering stars recognized the Royal Sun. There was no doubt in their minds that He was going to come out victorious. Most of them started putting forward lame excuses to escape the challenge. "Now, there is no point in participating here, the bride would choose the most handsome man, that is Prince Ram," they discussed among themselves.

Foolish Greed

However, the Asura disguised as wicked egoistic kings laughed out loud, mocking others. They began making tall claims that they could have broken the bow instantly the moment they had entered the arena. But then, that would have spoilt the ceremony which they did not want and hence, were following the procedure. Moreover, in that case, there would have been chaos and conflict, which would have made deciding the winner difficult. They also chose to attempt last to give a fair opportunity to everybody and prevent losers from foul cry. The Asura emphasized that until the bow was broken, the winner could not be decided and thus, who would be the fortunate person to marry Princess Sita remained uncertain. They further boasted that they could even conquer 'Kaal,' that is death itself for Lady Sita, so someone with a stature of Ram did not seem undefeatable.

Warning of Wisdom

The contenders, who had attained wisdom seeing Lord Ram, heard the ludicrous claims of the wicked contenders and smiled. They informed that these two princes were sons of King Dasratha and they were strong enough to defeat not only the misunderstandings of mind but also the illusion or Maya that had engulfed the world. These kings even warned the Asura that foolish ones trying to act smart create unnecessary hindrances on the path of a divine event often get killed in the process. Therefore, useless boasting would not achieve anything, and the stupid braggers would not win.

They further added that Sita is the mother, and Ram is the father of the universe. They represent the epitome of beauty and divinity that beings have never seen before. Everybody must seize this opportunity to feast their eyes with this Heavenly Pair because such an occasion might not happen again in their lifetime. They further counselled that those who would ridicule the competence of Prince Ram and run after the mirage, would pay through their lives and gain nothing. "We have spoken the truth, now each one is free to make their assessment. We know that today, we have been rewarded with the fruit of our birth," the wise concluded.

Ignorance compelled egoistic Kings to desire that which was beyond their means that is Princess Sita. In present times too, ignorance and unrealistic approach give less delight but more pain to the beings. Irrational desires and expectations only lead to frustration and embarrassment, thereby making beings restless and violent. Greed when remains unchecked bring sheer loss and sadness. But the urge to acquire is so intense in beings that even after knowing the implications, they are unable to apply sense.

Invaluable Wisdom

Generally beings mistakenly believe that wisdom is something that is acquired from outside and that it is not for everybody, but just for spiritual practitioners. This misconception deteriorates their condition further because then there is no motivation to correct self. Moreover, the misconduct of some pretentious spiritualist practitioners in the present times have further spoiled the value for religion and spirituality in general perception.

Lord has stated the universal truth in Gita that every human being is born with wisdom in absoluteness, which is higher than the sagacity of all the Vedanta scriptures put together. Wisdom is an innate characteristic of the soul or 'atman'. But when the soul comes across the physical matter, it gets disillusioned and starts identifying itself with the body forgetting its real identity. This leads to loss of wisdom, and the beings ('Jiva' that is atman attached with shareer) are then entrapped in greed-driven thoughts.

Wisdom frees the being from this trap and changes the approach of the being, and henceforth his desires become utility-driven rather than attraction-driven. But we should also know that anyone or all spiritual practices are just a minuscule contributor to this process of wisdom- realization. Broadly, it is the Grace of the Lord that brings the overall change in the mind-set of beings. In the arena of Bow Challenge, it was because of the Grace of the Lord, that the veil of ignorance was removed and divine vision was bestowed upon the sensible Kings.

Wisdom allows the realization of endless traits of mind-ego like unreasonable wants, fake pleasures, superiority, gain and loss, and so on. As beings attain wisdom, they start understanding that what so far they have considered as essential is, in reality, not so. Through the eyes of wisdom, they understand how the mind-ego manipulated and compelled them to act foolishly by making them believe that such actions were necessary for survival, growth or security.

Fear of Loss of Pleasure

The mind-ego of the wicked kings made them helplessly laughable by desiring Princess Sita. Unfortunately, they were intensely infatuated to the magnificent beauty of Princess Sita only. Doesn't the same happen to us as well? Just like them, we also basis our likes and dislikes on outer appearance. Acknowledgment of real qualities comes quite late or never. A beautiful thing desired by many automatically attracts a higher value. Just a few ones know the actual reasons for desirability and most of the ones simply chase, seeing the mass interest.

By acquiring a valuable something, we derive a sense of superiority and pleasure. But sooner rather than later, the sense of superiority and pleasure associated with the beautiful thing fades away. The pleasure from a valuable thing excites initially, but soon we become habituated to it. Then another beautiful thing shows up, which again attracts us. We again compete and struggle to acquire it to feel superior again. Beings are only interested in those things in which many others are interested. As soon as the mass interest shifts to another thing, being too loses attraction in the previous thing.

Beings fear to visualize a life devoid of pleasures. Hence, they continue to struggle to acquire new and beautiful things to ensure the uninterrupted flow of happiness. This is an ongoing cycle that runs until the end of life. It keeps beings occupied with running and chasing. This is how ignorant beings waste their precious lives. The wise kings saw beyond the outer appearance of Lord Ram and Princess Sita. They instantly realized that Supreme Mother Sita is not something to be acquired but to be Surrendered to.

Significance of Lord's Darshan

Now the question is how mere sight of Lord Ram could generate divine realization? Explanation is that the energy and vibes of a 'pure entity' ceases the obsessive-compulsive thoughts and give clarity in mind. In present times too, we gain insights and clarity of mind in the company of a pure and holy person (Sage) or thing (Idol) or place (Temple). But this happens with those who have purified self to a certain level.

Once the beings attain insight, the helpless urge to acquire pleasures diminishes. Then rises the moments of Wisdom (Gyan) and Devotion (Bhakti) that truly give ultimate satisfaction. But soon the worldly attractions again take over, and the peace is lost. And the being again returns to the same old running and chasing business. This is because of the past conditioning of the mind of many years. Practice of awareness is needed to extend the period of wisdom and diminish the influence of mind-ego.

The wise kings after witnessing Supreme Ram and Sita felt great joy and satisfaction. We may not have the privilege of witnessing Lord Ram like them, but we do have the power of faith with us. When we start giving value to faith, the mind-ego loses strength automatically and wisdom dawns. Ultimately, the question remains what is the purpose of our life - pleasure or perfection?

■■

Chapter 14

The Bond of Love : Grace is Everything

With an anxious heart Her eyes looked for Lord Ram in the crowd,
Seeing Him she was relieved, while the courtesan announced loud.
Whoever will break Lord Shiva's mighty bow today, Will be wedded to the Princess without any delay.

Princess Sita, who is essentially the embodiment of charm and excellence, was escorted in the arena by her companions. All the contenders were spellbound seeing her divine aura. They were caught in the grip of infatuation. She cast a glance at the kings present there, but her anxious heart was only looking for Prince Ram. For a moment, the eyes of Siya-Ram met. Both of them felt as if they had found a long lost treasure. Drawing Lord Ram into Her heart, she shifted the gaze out of modesty.

The Challenge

The courtesan then narrated the story of Supreme Shiva's Bow. The mighty bow was presented by Lord Parshuram to King Janaka as a reward for his Gyan and Dharma. It took thousands of men to lift and position the bow. But one day Janaka was surprised to find that little Sita could lift it effortlessly. Lord Parshuram also observed the incident and realizing the divinity of Sita, he told Janaka that only the one who could tie the string of this bow would be eligible to be her husband. He would be no ordinary person but her companion of eternity. When Princess Sita reached the right age, Janaka organized the Swayamwar with the bow- challenge to find that eternal partner for Sita who would be equal to her stature.

The story was already written by the providence. The outcome was pre-determined. Nothing could change the unification of Siya-Ram. Lord Ram and Mother Sita are incarnations of Supreme Narayan and Laxmi, who dwell together beyond the dimension of form, space and time. But their 'Avatar-Leela' or earthly play was necessary as they wanted to teach Dharma to the beings through Ramayan.

Every journey of life is already written by providence even before it begins. Every life has an objective to fulfil. Nothing happens without a purpose. Following the directions of Supreme Intelligence, beings can not only meet their life- goal with perfection but also set an example for others.

Doership is an Illusion

However, in our world, things rarely happen the way they should. The reason is our incapability to read the divine plan. Supreme Intelligence has chalked the path of life but has, at the same time, given us the freedom to decide. Beings using this freedom, take decisions which are not aligned with the divine plan and therefore become subjects of earthly experiences of pain, suffering, and frustration. Ignorance surfaces when beings do not contemplate on reality. Ignorance emanates from the belief that all lives are supposed to follow the same predictable pattern. Comparing one's life with that of the other, beings ignore the words of wisdom. When Supreme Lord Ram and Mother Sita, the Avatars of divine Supreme did not interfere with the plan and willingly faced all challenges and hardships, how can mere mortals think that they can reshape the plan? But surprisingly people do believe that they are the sole determiners of their fates and thereby spoil the course of their lives.

Righteous Conduct

For Siya-Ram, interfering with the divine plan like ordinary human beings would have meant privately marrying and thereby avoiding the challenge, rejecting father 's order to go to exile, refusing to testify Mother Sita through Agni-Parisksha and not going to an exile again for the unjust satisfaction of citizens of Ayodhya. But never did they compromise on Dharma or Duty, irrespective of their sufferings. Self-contemplation is asking oneself, 'Am I ready to face the difficulties yet stay righteous, or shall I shy away from challenging situations just for the sake of convenience?'

For Siya-Ram, life was never about wealth, power, and pleasures, but to follow Dharma and stay righteous in the face of adverse circumstances. That is why they became legends. Not every being's life needs to be filled with grave challenges and hardships as that of Siya-Ram, but the idea here is to remain virtuous in all problematic situations regardless of magnitude and severity.

Beings neglect Dharma, either to satisfy their desires or out of fear. Compromise and cleverness can give instant satisfaction, but nobody can escape the effects of karma that lies ahead. Our sages understood this long ago, and, therefore, in Ramayan, utmost importance has been put on 'Tyaga' or sacrifice and renunciation. When rightfully practising Tyaga, no matter how much every being loses materialistically in life, he or she ultimately emerges as a winner, earning reverence from all corners. Lord has stated that unless the means and the end are not perfect, the story is not over, be it Ramayan or Mahabharata.

Shrewd Escapes

The foolish contender Kings were desperate to win. The most powerful Asura of that era, Ravan, also attended the ceremony. However, realizing that he could not lift the Shiva's Bow, he left the arena quietly to save himself from the embarrassment of defeat. The other contenders knew that they were no match even to Ravan let alone Lord Ram, yet they were obsessed with the thought of Princess Sita and meekly hoped to win the challenge. If they had some sense, they would not have acted stupidly.

Stupid Desperation

Immediately after the announcement, the foolish kings rushed to win the challenge. Each one sought the blessing of victory from his 'Ishta' or Personal God before attempting to raise the bow. But a thousand others also prayed to their 'Ishta' for his defeat. More than achieving their successes, every being takes a greater interest in ensuring others' failure. Each contender tried one by one. They arrogantly clasped the bow with steady grip and exerted all their strength but failed to move the bow an inch, let alone lift. Finally they withdrew in utter dismay. The bow was absorbing the might of the contenders, making them weak. This is what desires, and attractions do to the being's energy. Out of greed, beings lose not only their righteousness but also their abilities.

Then the contenders formed a group and collectively tried to lift the bow hoping to win the challenge. This was yet another act of sheer stupidity. In their spree to win, they forgot that even if they could raise the bow collectively, how could they decide the winner? They thought that it could be decided later, as of now the aim was to win by any means. It is another instance of how greed consumes our intelligence. However, despite consorted efforts, they could not move the bow a bit. Spectators laughed at them, and they retired embarrassed.

Although the contenders had accepted defeat, they did not leave the arena. Instead, they went back to their seats and waited. They now thought that since everybody had lost, King Janaka might change the conditions of the challenge and so they still have chances. Even after being mocked and insulted by others, the pathetic greed of foolish contenders gave them hope. Not every hope that gives motivation is correct. They lost their respect and honour, but the desperation was not yet lost.

In present times also, we see similar desperations. What we think of as our firm resolution to achieve is actually our desperate desire to acquire. Without assessing our own strength and the situation, we just jump to grab. The incidence of bow challenge reflects this stupidity of being. This is how mind-ego plays with thoughts and manipulates being. Dreams or fantasies of pleasures associated with the winning of beautiful thing shadows intelligence, compelling beings to act irrationally and eventually leads to loss, defeat, and disappointment.

Everything happens with Grace

We need to realize that whatever we achieve is because of Grace, and whatever we lose is also because of Grace. Our talents and abilities are just instruments to achieve. The extraordinary skill with which some beings achieve greatness is again a special gift of Grace given to them. Thus, there is nothing to be proud of and nothing to boast of. Foolishness and failures will keep frustrating us till we don't acknowledge Grace and stop assuming ourselves as the doer.

Now the obvious question that arises in our minds is that then what beings are supposed to do in their lives if everything is choreographed by Grace? Is there anything in beings' control?

The answer is that every being's purpose in life is to become 'Eligible' for Grace by conducting themselves correctly in every situation that life puts him in. Whatever one requires is bestowed by Lord, and this means there is no need for struggling, chasing and running. In other words, it's acceptance of gains and losses as His will.

With the blessing of Lord Ram the moment Sugreeva changed his approach, from being an ousted coward he became the King of Kishkinda. He had lost all his hope and strength in self. But he instead of doing 'ifs and buts,' just relied on the assurance of his friend Lord Ram. Question is what is it in this world that we can fully depend on? On what should we place our 'Shraddha' or absolute faith in – on ourselves or Grace of Lord Ram?

■■

Chapter 15

Laxman's Challenge : Power of Faith

If Lord permits, I will lift the globe like a ball,
And smash it like an ill-baked earthen pot.

Frustrated with their pathetic performance in the bow- challenge, the shameless contenders blamed King Janaka for intentionally disrespecting them by throwing an impossible challenge. Out of sheer disgust, they even questioned the legitimacy of the birth of the Princess. That is how people are. To divert mass attention from their defeat and to justify their failure, they can stoop down to any level and accuse others and the circumstances. They find acceptance of failure, be it a loss of valuable treasure or a small argument extremely painful because the mind-ego considers any level of loss or defeat, equivalent to death.

To save itself from dying, mind-ego shoots thoughts of fear, threat, and aggression incessantly. Being identifies with these thoughts and therefore, to deal with the perceived threat, reacts either offensively or defensively. In most events, such impulsive reactions cause more harm than doing any good. But the wise ones, who are in awareness of the functioning of mind, don't get carried away by unreal thoughts. They have trained their minds to ponder over only useful ideas. Mind no more controls them. In the state of awareness, there is only the right response and no attachment to success or failure.

Janaka's pain

Infuriated King Janaka retorted and silenced those menacing voices. He reminded the defeated contenders that nobody was invited to participate in the challenge. It was their voluntary decision to join in. He further said that since none could budge the bow even by one unit of grain, nobody had the right to call himself a great hero. Janaka explained that as a father, it was his duty to ensure that his daughter gets a husband who was at par with her.

Therefore, he organized the mighty Bow challenge. He had hoped that he would perhaps find the right match for her daughter on that day. With great disappointment, he asked the failed kings to leave the arena, as he thought it was not the will of the providence that his daughter Sita must get married. The devastating outcome of the challenge and the reaction of the defeated kings made him forget that Lord Ram with Laxman and Sage Vishvamitra was also present in the arena.

Laxman's Announcement

Owing to the offending words of King Janaka, Prince Laxman got furious. For him, insult of all contender kings was also the insult of Lord Ram because He too was present in the arena. Laxman, the avatar of the Great 'Sheshnag,' cannot tolerate anything against his Lord Narayan. Laxman stood up and shouted back that nobody should dare to ridicule an assembly where his brother, the most powerful, Lord Ram was present. He openly challenged that if Lord Ram permitted him, he would lift the globe like a playing ball and smash it. He further announced that he could pick up the so-called mighty bow and carry it to four hundred 'yojan' (ancient measurement unit) before shattering it into pieces. He concluded saying that if any of his claims turned out to be false, he would never touch a weapon in his life. As he was finishing, the earth shook suddenly. Everyone in the arena trembled in fear and Janaka became concerned. Lord Ram sensed the anxiety of the beings and lovingly pacified Laxman.

The shaking of the earth after the claim of great Laxman was a signal to atheists and those who undermined devotion that what he was saying was accurate. The earth shook the belief system of ignorant beings. It was needed to awaken them from the slumber of idiocy. Whenever the old structures of false beliefs crumble down, the cynical people tremble in fear. But this fear is essential for their advancement towards truth.

Power of Faith

Laxman had first sought Lord Ram's permission before replying. This act of Laxman indicated that a devotee could make huge claims and roar like a lion, depending on Lord Ram. A devotee doesn't have baseless confidence in self, like ordinary ignorant people. A devotee is dispassionate and indifferent to the world. He doesn't care for his insults or dishonour or personal loss.

Things which are of great value to the worldly people, barely make any sense to a devotee.

His purpose of life is only to please and serve his Lord Ram. But when there is any direct or indirect attack on the honour of his Lord, a devotee roars back with great power. His purpose of life is to be of some use in the service of his Lord. He doesn't fear death and considers it as reunification with Lord. For him, it is a win-win situation. There is no power in this universe that can harm a fearless yet meek devotee. He rarely reacts, but when he does, nature corroborates him.

Observing the response, Lord Ram and Sage Vishvamitra first smiled as they expected this behaviour from Laxman. However, seeing the situation turning complicated, the Lord intervened. He didn't scold or silenced Laxman, rather pacified him very lovingly. This signalled that Laxman's role as a devotee was now over. A devotee can make any claims, now it is up to the Lord to fulfil the words of His devotee. In the Gita verse 18.66, Lord has assured His devotees, "Abandon all dependencies and Surrender to Me. I will free you from all troubles, fear not". The act of Laxman was in accordance with Bhakti-Dharma. So long as the devotee is in righteousness, he enjoys the right to love and care of Supreme.

Another significance for pacifying Laxman was to send the message that members of Raghu-Vansh or Solar Dynasty, that is Prince Ram and Laxman, were real heroes who believed more in action and less on speech. Boastful words are used by those who are doubtful of their capabilities. The one who has real mettle just performs and proves his worth. Secondly, the responsibility of the Ruling class or Kshatriya-Varna lies in upholding Dharma and safeguarding honour.

The Two Roles

Act of Laxman must be viewed more as the sentiment of a Bhakta than as a response of a Raghu-Vanshi Kshatriya. Being can earn the merit of good karma by practising Swadharma that is the worldly role according to their class and family. But the being in pure devotion attains Lord. To a devotee, one moment of Lord's love is much greater than the merits of all Punya or merits of virtuous actions accumulated in all lifetimes. Bhakti is greater than 'Varna & Vansh' that is lineage and class. The idea here is that being must practise 'Swadharma' that is playing the earthly role as per his 'Varna & Vansh' but from inside be devoted to the lotus feet of Lord Ram.

This understanding of the difference between the outer and inner roles is not possible without knowledge of truth. And only when being feels a sense of emptiness from inside, does he venture out to seek the truth that is the love of the Lord. The feeling of emptiness in the lows as well as highs of life is very agonizing. Every being wants relief from all worldly sorrows, but because of lack of true-knowledge, he never gets that. One tries to seek the solution in regular ways of society, that is by keeping busy or getting engaged in exciting activities. This may divert his mind for a while, but the vacuum doesn't go. Medication or intoxication can offer some relief, but once their effect is over, the pain again surfaces. Life, therefore, becomes a pendulum oscillating between distress and enjoyment. Although being has the solution close by, yet he doesn't have faith in it. And without faith, no treatment can work.

Fortunate are those who experience a similar state of dejection which Prince Arjuna also experienced before Lord enlightened him through the verses of Gita, which marked the beginning of the journey of truth. Unconditional acceptance of the words of scriptures and sages is the only way to come out of the state of dejection. But if we keep on criticizing scriptures as dogmatic and sages as fake, shall we ever find a permanent solution to the sufferings? We must not forget that it is because of the Grace of Lord Ram that we have reached this level of understanding. Now, whether to move ahead or return is ultimately our choice.

■■

Chapter 16

Time has Come : Doubts Block Peace

Sant, Devta and Bhakta were elated,
Fallen Dharma will soon be reinstated.

Turn of Prince Ram

Right action is not always about proving oneself or achieving something. Instead, it is about doing what is righteously needed to be done in a given situation. To know the appropriate step, mentorship of wise sages is imperative. A lot of drama had already taken place in the bow challenge arena, but Prince Ram was unmoved. Sage Vishvamitra was delighted to see that even after the provocative claims of His brother, Lord Ram didn't react. He waited patiently for the permission of the sage. Vishvamitra gently said, 'Rise Ram and do the needful.' The subtle message was that now was the auspicious time to break the bow, not for Ram's love-interest or to show off His extraordinariness or to disrespect anybody but to end the agony of the Royal Sage King Janaka and for the honour of the Princess. Also, the sage wanted the world to know about the arrival of Lord Ram through the bow-challenge, and that is why he brought the two heroic brothers to Janakpur. Vishvamitra played a notable role in Ramayan that was bestowed on him by the Supreme.

Lord Ram, with his innate grace, stood like the Sun that rises after a long night. The magical aura of Prince Ram spread in all directions. Here was one man who had the courage and confidence to attempt the bow challenge even after seeing the failure of the mightiest kings of the world. Whether he succeeds or not, we will find out later. But the message is that being must neither bother about success or failure nor think about appreciation or criticism of people when approaching a task of righteousness. Even in isolation when none else is witnessing, the one who dares to face the toughest of challenges for 'Dharma', is acknowledged and rewarded by the omnipresent Supreme.

Seeing Lord Ram rise, the enlightened sages, devotees and Devta were thrilled with contentment. They knew that the beginning of the end of Asura Ravan had begun. The 'Jigyasu' or the curious seeker of Truth quenched their age old thirst. The spiritual citizens of Janakpur got excited as they realized that the pain of their King was about to end, and Janakpur would be filled with happiness, never seen before. The hearts of wicked contender kings sank. They lost the last hope of having Princess Sita.

Unending Doubts

But there were some in the spectators who doubted Lord Ram and his abilities. One of the prominent doubters was Queen Sunena, mother of Sita. After all, this was a crucial matter regarding her daughter's life, and she too like Janaka was very disturbed with the happenings at the arena. She shared her dilemma with a companion. Sunena was more than happy to have Prince Ram as Sita's groom. But her apprehension was how a young prince of such a delicate frame notwithstanding his majestic persona would be able to lift God Shiva's Bow when the mightiest of the kings failed miserably?

Doubts about Supreme and His Grace obviously arises as nobody has seen or heard Him. Beings relies only on what their senses and mind can perceive. What they can perceive is right for them and what they cannot is false. But we don't outrightly reject the presence of God because we do witness His scriptures, sages, devotees, religions and at times, miracles also. For beings, there is indeed something beyond perception, but until the what-s, how-s, why-s and when-s are not satisfied, doubts don't go.

Sunena's companion was a wise and firm believer of Lord Ram. She replied that competence could not be judged merely by size or structure. She further explained to her that the moon is like a small dot in the night sky, but it effortlessly sways the tides of vast oceans of the planet earth. A slight shift of Moon can create humongous tidal waves that can swallow every inch of land on the planet. She also reminded that Pranav or 'Aum' is a mantra of the single letter yet contains the power to sway the Supreme Creator, the Preserver, and the Destroyer. 'Aum' is the sound of the universe. But again, the problem is that since beings don't believe in it, they don't practice it.

Unescapable Loop

Majority of people are living with endless doubts in their minds. Some don't even care to sort them, and those who do are generally not satisfied with the answers. The cause of endless doubts in beings is that there are very few real spiritual practitioners whose words have the power of truth that can satisfy being's eternal quest. Secondly, beings lack the purity and maturity required to absorb the knowledge of truth.

Unending doubts are thoughts that the mind-ego creates to keep being entangled in ignorance. This entanglement doesn't let the being experience reality. And this is exactly what mind-ego wants because it knows that being's knowledge of truth would mean the end of its existence. And naturally, nothing wants to die. Mind-ego also weakens the ability to perceive truth and hence, being finds it very difficult to trust the words of sages and scriptures. They cannot believe in anything unless they go through an experience that gives them concrete evidence.

Owing to unawareness, people react foolishly either by countering or mocking or turning violent against the knowledge of the truth. Foolish being only trusts the one who speaks what he wants to hear, shows what he wants to see and gives what he wants to have. And in this give and take policy, there is no consideration of right or wrong. Although the main culprit is mind-ego, yet beings cannot escape their responsibility.

It is because a being doesn't value 'Vivek', he gets trapped in the mind-ego. A trapped being, irrespective of relaxed external demeanour, lives and dies in dissatisfaction. Having doubts is very humane and rational but rejecting the words of wisdom is sheer foolishness. Mind-ego is not easy to overcome. Even at the zenith of enlightenment, doubts keep knocking. The solution is not to cling but let them pass. Only the faith in the Lord can give the strength to let go. Without faith, the chaos cannot be sorted and stopped from coming back.

Seek Truth rather than answers

A true friend is the one who gives you the right perspective and rescues you from this never-ending maze of doubts. For Sunena, it was her companion who firmly concluded that she must rest all her doubts because it was definite that Supreme Lord Ram would break the bow. Words dipped in the nectar of truth always work, and so Sunena was immediately relieved from all her doubts and anxiety.

It is only with the grace of the Lord that a being can free him or her from the chaos of doubts and disbelief. To Surrender without getting convinced is the leap of faith, which one has to take to cross the ocean of confusions and troubles. In Kaliyuga 'living life on my own terms' kind of attitude is commonly appreciated. But the problem is that with such an attitude the humility to value the words of wisdom gets lost. Therefore, people usually remain confused in life. Confused beings make wrong choices which then lead to frustration and depression.

'One, who believes that he knows everything actually knows nothing.'

In Ramayan, we can see that even the Supreme Avatar Ram, who is the epitome of knowledge and consciousness,

worshipped His Lord Shiva and always valued the teachings of Sage Vashisht, Vishvamitra, Bharadwaj and more. Message is that only by having full faith in the Lord and in the teachings of wise, one can lead a peaceful and satisfying life. Ultimately it's the being's choice; either he can keep on doubting or learn from the story of Lord Ram and attain peace and prosperity.

Chapter 17

The Mighty Bow Breaks : Nothing is Insurmountable

The bow symbolizes the ego that traps & shackles the being, But Lord Ram ensures His devotee's freedom & well-being.

A Girl's Heart

As Prince Ram was approaching the bow arena, Princess Sita's heart started beating faster. Siya-Ram had already formed a connection and started seeing each other as a life partner. Although Sita was pretty confident of Lord Ram's victory, yet she prayed to the Gods, especially to Lord Shiva, to lighten the weight of the bow for Prince Ram. She was perturbed with her father 's insistence on the bow- challenge. However, logically speaking, she knew that the bow-challenge was the best way to find and bond with Lord Ram. Lady Sita considered strength and decisiveness as significant as intuition and emotional connection. And this extraordinary understanding made her feminine love more magnificent and vibrant.

Here we must not forget that Mother Sita and Lord Ram are the manifestations of the same Supreme Consciousness. They took different Avatars and are playing earthly roles for a purpose. They are well aware of the supreme truth but are displaying their feelings, thoughts, body language and emotions like a mortal being. This is the way for Siya- Ram to become one and connect with mankind.

Sita was dubious as well as apprehensive just like any common human being - what if Ram was unable to win the challenge? Fear of losing emerges when there is a close connection or attachment between two individuals. Lord declares in the Gita that if one continuously contemplates an object or person, then he develops an attachment to it. And Attachment leads to a desire for the object or person. If the desire is not fulfilled, then anger emanates, and when the desire is satisfied, then the fear of losing arises.

Elucidating desire, Lord further says that beings must avoid contemplating on mundane objects. But if he does, then he at least should be careful about attachment. Even if he gets attached, then he should be cautious of the desire connected to it. And, if the being cannot control his desire, then at least he should try to avoid expectations for its fulfilment. Fulfilled desires take the being towards new dreams, while unfulfilled desires give birth to frustration and anger.

Princess Sita, in her heart, had already become one with Prince Ram, and so the fear of losing Him was bothering her. After getting carried away by her feelings for a while, she immediately regained her 'Vivek' or power of discretion. Someone who is in 'Sadhana' or spiritual practice cannot be trapped by mind-ego for long. She experienced her thoughts and emotions, not as a participant but as a witness who observes things with detachment. This is known as 'Sakshi Bhava' wherein being separates awareness of self from mind and thoughts.

Witness your Mind

To understand the 'Being witness' better, try to visualize the chaos that occurs in a long traffic jam on the road. Getting carried away means trying to drive your way through the jam. Being witness or 'Sakshi Bhava' means flying over the jam. Involvement with thoughts is the prime cause of being's unhappiness. On the other hand, detachment with thoughts helps the being realize the inner self. And the eternal nature of self is 'Sat-Chit-Anand' that is purity, truth, and bliss.

However, one must not underestimate the mind-ego as it has the tenacity to entrap the witness again and again. Being, who values 'Vivek' or power of discretion can outsmart the mind-ego, but it is something very challenging to do. But in the case of 'Bhakti' or devotion, Lord does the needful for His devotee and frees him from the entanglements of mind-ego. A 'Bhakta' or devotee cannot be entrapped and bothered by mind-ego.

In awareness, Princess Sita recollected that the Supreme fulfils a 'Satvik' wish if it is on the side of Righteousness, Faith, and Welfare. Her longing for union with Ram was in sync with the said criteria, and thus, she was very assured in her heart that her wish would be fulfilled. Here we must understand that Princess Sita's 'Satvik' wish is more of divination than a desire.

Saint Tulsidas now sums up and says that Fear of Princess Sita, Doubt of Queen Sunena, Pride of Lord Laxman, Anger of Parshuram, Distress of King

Janaka, Yearning of contender kings, Anxiety of Devta, and Ignorance of the beings, all imposed additional weight on the bow. Fear, doubt, pride, greed, distress, ignorance, anger, and anxiety are the traits of mind-ego that create hindrance for being in realizing the self. Lord Ram's Avatar role was to remove these obstacles and bless the being with ultimate bliss. And, therefore, Lord's breaking of the bow, was a symbol of defeating the mind-ego. Lord Shiva with Mother Parvati, from His abode, Mt. Kailasa, was cherishing 'His Lord Ram' in action.

The Bow Breaks

Lord Ram, before attempting the bow challenge, thought of Lord Shiva and sought His blessings. He glanced at Princess Sita And Instantly felt the state of her heart. He said to himself that it was time now to finish the task without any further delay. Harvesting the farms is of no use when the crops had dried up.Therefore, He must provide comfort to all the beings in pain before it gets too late. Lord Ram gripped the centre of the bow and in a fraction of a second, lifted, bent, and broke the bow in two pieces. At that moment, thunderous lightning flashed from the bow and encompassed the whole universe. Nobody could behold Lord's action but could just witness a glimpse of the light. They were all awestruck with the Heavenly luminescence.

The onlookers were only seeing the two broken parts of the bow lying on the floor beside the Divine stature of Prince Ram. At that very moment, the earth shivered, and everybody cheered in excitement. The union of Supreme Ram and Sita was sealed, and it was to be witnessed by the whole universe, a sight that would be cherished for ages. Furthermore, this event marked a step ahead towards the end of Adharma and the establishment of 'Ram-Rajya.'

The Bond is Sealed

Shatanand, son of Lady Ahalaya, and the royal minister of King Janaka settled the crowd and initiated the 'Jai-Mala' ceremony. For the first time, Lord Ram and Princess Sita came closer and adorned each other with the garland made of most beautiful flowers one could ever find. They were elated with the outcome and smiled, looking at each other. The whole of humanity rejoiced, and Janaka's family started the celebration. Devta, Sages, and Devotee showered flowers and prostrated themselves to the feet of Siya-Ram. Lord Shiva and Mother Parvati were getting prepared for attending the royal marriage. They wanted to bless the Supreme couple. The Asura were trembling in fear, but somehow they consoled themselves thinking that Lord Ram is ever kind and merciful, and he would perhaps pardon even the gravest and ugliest sins of His followers. So assuming they might have a chance, they comforted each other.

Finally, what was destined to happen had actually happened. Now comes the days of celebration. The

breaking of the bow and the union of Siya-Ram are the sights that always give the utmost peace and happiness to the devotees. The event of bow-challenge reaffirmed the truth that whenever and wherever people seek help from the Lord for any reason, He would arrive and free the being. There is absolutely no power in the universe that can harm a 'Bhakta' who dedicated himself to the pious feet of Siya-Ram.

■■

Chapter 18

Wrath of Parshuram : Anger doesn't Solve Anything

The one who has broken the bow is my enemy,
My cruel axe has exterminated even an unborn baby.

Parshuram's Story

Just when the celebration of the holy marriage of Lord Ram and Lady Sita had begun, an ultra-masculine figure walked inside the arena. Recognizing Lord Parshuram, the whole assembly was petrified. Everybody was wondering about the reason for his arrival. In the past, whenever and wherever Lord Parshuram had arrived, destruction had ensued. Parshuram had heard about the extraordinary incident of breaking the sacred bow. He immediately rushed to Janakpur to find out who dared to dishonour the bow of Lord Shiva. Once at the arena, he saw the broken pieces of the bow and got infuriated. He threatened to devastate the whole Janakpur if people present there did not disclose the name of the person to him who had the audacity to disparage the bow. Understanding the situation, Lord Ram stepped forward and tried to assuage Parshuram in a calm and composed manner. But Parshuram, in his blind rage, kept on threatening and abusing. This irked Lord Sheshnag Laxman, and he confronted Parshuram courageously and sagaciously.

This was probably the first time in the history of 'Sanatan Dharma' when two Avatars confronted each other; one was Lord Ram, and the other was Lord Parshuram. That is why this was a unique occurrence. Lord Parshuram was extremely devoted to Lord Shiva and perceived the breaking of the bow as an insult of his Lord. On the other hand, Laxman discerned threatening utterances of Parshuram as an abuse of Lord Ram. Lord Ram was God-Master-Father figure to Laxman. Therefore, both Parshuram and Laxman could not resist anything against their 'Ishta' Gods. Parshuram's wrath loomed as terror shivering spines of all present there. They were well aware that it was the same Parshuram who had eliminated the Kshatriyas or the Ruler-Class twenty-one times from the face of planet earth. Everybody was aware of his prowess. But that did not intimidate Laxman. He remained unfazed and derided Parshuram. Although Lord Ram was trying to pacify Laxman, this time Laxman refused to back out.

Anger Issues

Parshuram was an un-absolute or 'Apoorna' avatar of Supreme God Narayan. He was divine and pure but possessed many of the humane characteristics, prominently 'anger'. This created inconsistency in his demeanour. On the one hand, he was terrorizing people and threatening to kill Laxman, but on the other hand, he was wholeheartedly blessing Siya-Ram and King Janaka. Despite being discourteous, he expected Laxman to treat him with respect. Though an avatar, he was not free from mortal anger.

Anger is stimulated when things do not happen in the way one expects things to happen. Expectations arise when a human being considers himself as separate from others. This is 'Dvait Bhava' or Dualism. 'Advaita Bhava' or Oneness means that everything is made up of one Supreme element. There can be a difference in appearance, quality, and nature of the objects, but the element is one and the same. Let us understand this clearly through some examples. Suppose a person bites his tongue mistakenly with his teeth, does it mean that he will punish his own teeth? If, by mistake, one breaks a precious object, does it mean that his hands must be punished?

One or Seperate

Similarly, if one's own child does something wrong for which that person suffers a loss, he may scold or punish the child, but he will not allow his anger to take any drastic step against the child. It is simply because the child belongs to him. This is 'Advaita Bhava' wherein the tongue, hand, and child are believed to be part of one's own entity.

But the question is, will that person tolerate the loss if caused by any other, such as a friend, colleague, enemy, or stranger? The answer will be no, because of 'Dvait Bhava,' as the person does not consider others to be part of his own self. Saint Tulsidas edifies that all people must inculcate 'Advaita Bhava,' which means everything is one and the same. When there is no duality in perspective, then there cannot be a feeling of separation. And, when there will be no perception of separateness, then the being will see all other beings as his own. And then the repercussions of mind-ego such as anger, hatred, intolerance, and negativity will automatically shrink.

Control is the Key

For practical and social purposes, the value of anger cannot be overlooked. Supreme Lord Ram himself had shown anger against others, but only when He felt that necessary. But His angry disposition was outrightly aimed at the welfare of others and not for his own selfish purposes. Here one must have a vivid understanding of the difference between controlled and uncontrolled anger. Controlled anger is for welfare, whereas uncontrolled anger always leads to devastation. For example, controlled fire is beneficial for cooking, but the same fire when goes out of control can create havoc and destroy vast tracts of land. While the friendship of Lord Ram and Sugreeva was sealed with the sacred fire as a witness, it was the same deadly fire with which Lord Hanuman had burnt the Lanka.

Control comes with 'Vivek' or power of discretion. Laxman's anger was controlled, as Lord Ram, the Supreme personification of 'Vivek,' was beside him. Laxman's confrontations with King Janaka and Lord Parshuram ultimately proved to be beneficial for both of them. Not only did they feel obliged to Laxman for proving them wrong but also because it was for him that they could realize the truth of Supreme Ram and henceforth accomplished the purpose of their lives.

Parshuram's uncontrolled anger arising because of the breaking of the sacred bow was utterly baseless and illogical. Despite knowing the fact that Lord Shiva had given the bow to King Janaka as a gift, he unnecessarily got upset, believing that breaking of the bow was a sheer insult of his Master Lord Shiva. Once an object is gifted, the giver holds no right whatsoever on the object and its subsequent usage. King Janaka was, therefore, free to use the bow as per his choice and requirement and Parshuram should not have any concern about that. Moreover, when Supreme Lord Shiva had no objection in the Bow- Challenge ceremony, then Parshuram had no authority to interfere and take action. If Lord Shiva wanted, then He would have intervened Himself.

On the contrary, Lord Shiva was ecstatic to be a participant in the union of Siya-Ram. In fact, by unnecessarily creating a scene at the arena, Parshuram was disrespecting the sentiments and feelings of his Master, Lord Shiva. A devotee can in no way act against the will of the Supreme Lord. Also, Parshuram should have realized that once the bow had been broken, it could not be joined back, so his annoyance had no relevance. What has happened has happened, there is no point in avenging or grieving for it afterward.

Ending Hatred

Lord Parshuram's angry disposition was obligatory prior to the era of Lord Ram, wherein the Rulers had turned evil and were torturing innocent beings. Parshuram's sole purpose in life was destroying and subjugating the evil rulers, which he did for the greater good of humanity. Now, although both his role and his era were done, his hatred for the ruling class did not subside. Now was the age of Lord Ram, who was born as the noblest ruler with the foreordained purpose to destroy evil Asura and reinstate Dharma. However, Parshuram was yet to come to terms with this fact.

Impulsiveness brings Problems

The anger of Laxman proved to be immensely beneficial as it inspired Lord Ram to compete for the bow challenge, win it, and become one with Princess Sita. In replies to Parshuram's threatening statements, Laxman used witty and intelligent words. He said that without a servant, the master has to bear the burden of the load. But once the servant is there, the master must transfer the weight to him and feel comfortable. Similarly, Parshuram must transfer the responsibility of reinstating 'Dharma' in the ablest hands of Lord Ram. Laxman also reminded Parshuram with the conviction that because of his destructive anger, he had killed his innocent mother, which was unacceptable under any circumstances. Parshuram had slaughtered his mother just on his father 's command without giving a second thought. His father doubted the integrity of his wife though he had no proof or evidence against her. His father questioned his beautiful and pious wife driven by inferiority complex and insecurity. However, immediately realizing the grave mistake, his father asked him to bring back his mother to life, along with erasing the memory of the brutal act. This impulsive and injudicious act, though, remained as a black spot on Parshuram's character.

Beings, therefore, need to be very cautious of their impulsive actions. Parshuram had divine powers, so he brought back his mother to life. But mortal human beings don't have such ability, and therefore, the harm once done in impulsiveness cannot be reverted. Also, unlike this incident, ordinary people cannot erase the black spot of their inhuman or senseless acts.

Ultimately, the satirical yet beneficial words of Laxman and humility of

Lord Ram transformed Lord Parshuram's perception and guided him to the ultimate truth. Parshuram realized that only an Absolute or 'Poorna' Avatar of Supreme God could be as Heavenly as Lord Ram. For the first time in his life, he learned to value apology and forgiveness. When he understood that the new era had actually downed in the potent hands of Supreme Ram, he at once Surrendered to Lord Ram and finally found peace.

Acceptance

In Kaliyuga or the present era, peace is something which everyone is searching for, but the question remains how to attain peace? Although the soul or atman is innately connected to the Supreme, still our mind is busy in seeking the solution in the material world. Since birth, every being starts believing the material world as true. Whatever the child learns from the environment, first from parents, then family, then society and then the world, becomes his mindset for the rest of life by default. As the surrounding environment is itself confused about the truth, the same confusion is passed on to the children while they grow up. Because of such confusion, beings lose control over their minds. Driven by uncontrolled mind, as long as being endeavour to seek solutions to his problems in the material world, peace remains unreachable. It's only by valuing 'Vivek' that is the power of discretion and Surrendering to the pious feet of Lord Ram, that beings can come out from the ever-growing influence of ignorance. Lastly, but most importantly, ordinary human beings merely need to accept the connection with the Lord and leave the rest to Him to take care. The whole idea of spirituality, religion, psychology, and philosophy boils down to one question

What is your Acceptance or 'Svikriti'? Is it the material world in which you live, eat, and work, or is it the Absolute One who is unperceivable to the senses?

■■

Chapter 19

Liberation of Parshuram : End of Hatred

The moment he realized Lord's supremacy,
His heart brimmed with love and ecstasy.

Incorrect Diagnosis

In the past, Lord Parshuram executed Sahastrarjun of 'Kshatriya Varna' an evil King who was tormenting the innocent beings. His treatment with Sahastrarjun was similar to that of a surgeon who removes the malignant tumour to save the patient's life. But Parshuram didn't just stop after the surgery. He instead incorrectly diagnosed that the infection had spread to the whole body. He kept on annihilating all the Kings of 'Kshatriya Varna.' Because of his unchecked mind-ego and misconceptions, all the Kings of the ruling class seemed evil to him. His acute hatred for Kshatriya reached to such an extent that he did not even hesitate to kill their innocent unborn and new-born offsprings. He was so utterly blindfolded with hatred that he himself got transformed into one he hated the most. The vengeance of Parshuram was totally based on 'Varna' or Class and not on merit. Had he wanted, he would have killed Ravana for his evil actions, but he didn't, just because Ravana was an Asura and not a Kshatriya. The hatred and anger, therefore, disoriented Parshuram.

But this time, Lord Ram was the Supreme Avatar who was born as Kshatriya, and he was the greatest and noblest King of the world. One of the reasons behind His incarnation was to prove that a 'Varna,' community, class, or clan cannot be held responsible for the evil acts of some of its members. The same logic was applied to Asura also. Lord Ram killed only those Asura who didn't leave their evilness. He made friends with others and never harboured ill-feelings for them. Parshuram was also noble but with some flaws. He was like a peaceful river that created havoc only during flood times. At the bow challenge arena, Lord Ram built a barrier-dam to contain the fury of the river and released Parshuram from the burden of hatred he was carrying, forever.

The Treatment

The battle between Lord Ram and Ravana happened much later. Before that, Parshuram was defeated by Lord not by weapons but with the power of compassion, purity, and of course righteousness. During his encounter with Lord, Parshuram was raising his legendary axe again and again to fight, but Lord Ram repeatedly made sincere efforts to pacify him. He did not even reply in aggression for once. He knew that Parsuram's hatred for Kshatriya was merely based on a wrong belief and not on any wrong intention. Misconceptions can in no way be cleared by violence, because violence just gets entrapped in the loop of avenge and revenge, and never solves the problem. Instead, the problem can only be sorted out by effective communication and understanding. Like Parshuram, Lord Ram too always carried his mighty Bow and Arrow. But unlike him, Lord believed that weapons cannot solve a problem. Instead, weapons were always the last and the least choice for the Lord to resort to. He always tried to address every issue with patience, acceptance, and tolerance first.

In present times also the world is filled with collective dissension where communities, nations, and established religions are harbouring hatred for each other. Millions have died because of the violent, hateful intentions of a handful, and the situation is worsening further. Humanity has tried many a time to solve the issue with peace talks, but that too has not worked. Why? Because we are just like Parshuram who are carrying acute repugnance for others that spoils all negotiation efforts.

None is Lesser

Parshuram was getting very angry at Laxman's sarcastic and fearless replies. To scare Laxman, he was, again and again, raising his axe but was very surprised to see that it did not affect Laxman at all. He failed to recognize that the reason for Laxman's impudence was the same axe. Had Parshuram kept the axe aside, he would have found the real Laxman who is extremely polite and courteous. It reflects another reason why we fail to settle conflicts in our times. We want to settle the issues but only by showing our power and superiority. But the fact is today nobody likes to be imposed upon, whether they are dominant or weak. Therefore, the feeling of harmony never inculcates between the sides, and the issues remain unresolved. Neither a Parshuram nor a Laxman but only a Ram can bridge this gap and bring harmony between the adversaries.

Humility Works

Saint Tulsidas describes in his writing that in response to Parshuram's anger, Lord Ram politely replied that one who has broken the bow must be his loyalist servant. It confused Parshuram, how can a loyalist do such an unacceptable act? Lord Ram's reasoning and feelings can be understood with an example. Let's say a master asks his servant to clean the house properly and neatly. A sincere servant will not just wipe off the dirt but will also remove unused waste objects which were occupying space for long. The intention here is not to incur a loss, or cheat the master but to diligently perform the cleaning job. A wise master will understand and appreciate his servant's commitment. The old bow had become useless for Supreme Lord Shiva, and he gave it to King Janaka, who kept it as a prized possession. By breaking the bow, Lord Ram has fulfilled a loyalist servant's duty of cleaning Janaka's attachment for the Bow. Though being the undisputed and most powerful persona, who can uproot the whole earth instantaneously, Lord dealt with the situation with extreme humbleness and honour. Addressing self as 'Das' or servant reflects the humility in our Hindu culture.

It is the law of nature that a small and un-absolute entity gets automatically attracted to the large and absolute entity. The ocean doesn't send invitations, and yet the rivers rush to unite with it. Similarly, beings devote all their lives to find the cause of their attraction towards the Supreme. Lord Shiva's bow could be best embellished in the hands of Lord Ram. Parshuram was awestruck, seeing that another bow of Lord Vishnu, which he was carrying, automatically floated in the hands of Lord Ram. It was sufficient proof for Parshuram to realize that this young, beautiful, and charismatic lad is no other but Supreme Lord Himself.

Liberation of Parshuram

Parshuram Surrendered to the Lord and in front of the whole assembly requested Lord Ram to shoot an arrow on his ego from the Bow of Vishnu and release him from the burden of anger and hatred. After the realization of truth, his heart was filled with great joy, love, and devotion. With deep emotions, he praised the Lord and happily left the arena. It is amusing to note how the benevolence of Lord Ram even changed the most ruthless heart like Parshuram's. Saint Tulsidas says that by studying the life of Lord Ram and repeatedly contemplating on self, a being will attain self-realization that he had been yearning for all his life.

The being will also realize that other than Surrendering to the lotus feet of Lord Ram, there is absolutely nothing worth doing or proving in this world. Like Parshuram, we will also find peace as soon we come out of the anxiety of 'doing' and focus on just 'being' in the company of Lord Ram. And then only Lord can free us from all the burdens that we are carrying all our lives. So when Lord is taking our sole responsibility, then there is absolutely nothing to worry about.

Free yourself from load,
Keep your soul in the rest mode, Believe in His grace,
And reciprocate His embrace.

■■

Chapter 20

The Bride and Groom : Darshan gives Fulfilment

Shiva, Vishnu, Brahma, Kartikey and Indra were standing in the line,
Darshan of Bridegroom Lord Ram is more than owning a celestial goldmine.

'Darshan' of Supreme Deity is given great significance in 'Sanatan Dharma.' While Darshan literally means 'to see,' the real meaning is to 'have a vision of' something. Here having vision means to pay homage, be grateful, to acknowledge the grace, and to absorb the divine quality of deity. To have the Darshan of Lord Ram as a bridegroom riding on the beautiful horse was itself an ecstatic spectacle for which all the Gods left their abodes and lined up in Janakpur. Saint Tulsidas has enticingly elaborated on the feelings and qualities of God. His purpose is to make us realize how mere 'Darshan' of Lord Ram brings extraordinary happiness and advantages to Gods and beings alike.

Destroyer

Lord Shiva was the first in the line who had Darshan of Lord Ram with His 'third eye.' The common perception of the 'third eye of Shiva' is destruction. Here the symbolic meaning of 'destruction' is detachment or 'Vairagya,' and Lord Shiva is the highest personification of 'Vairagya.' In the real sense, the 'third eye' is to look inside, to introspect, to reflect, and to contemplate on self. Being's mortal eyes can see only the materialistic outer appearance and not the inner-self. It is only with the 'third eye' of Vairagya that one can realize the confinements of mind-ego. Here Lord Shiva conveys the message that only the one who has valued the third eye and contemplated on self, can actually have 'Darshan' of Lord Ram.

Preserver

God Vishnu was next in line with Mother Laxmi. Saint Tulsidas says that God Vishnu had Darshan of Lord Ram not just from eyes but also from heart, which signifies that eyes are just a medium. Unless the love and grace are felt from the core of the heart, one is not entitled to the Grace of Lord Ram. Mother Laxmi was well aware that Lord Ram is pleased with the one who serves His beloved. So to please the Lord, She is eager to confer on unimaginable wealth and fortune to His devotee. It, therefore, means that by seeking the grace of Lord Ram, the devotee automatically gets entitled to the blessing of Mother Laxmi.

Creator

The message from Creator Brahma is to believe in the truth of creation, and that is everything is one. Creator and Creation are one, neither separate nor different. By Darshan, beings must try to witness self in Lord and Lord in self and relish His grace.

Warrior

Lord Kartikey is the symbol of war and courage. On the path of spirituality, mind-ego creates hurdles. Many a time, the seeker, out of frustration of defeats, gives up and falls back. Here the clear message from Lord Kartikey is that beings need to tackle mind-ego with valour and firm determination. The awareness of self drives us towards the Supreme, but the mind-ego always pulls us back towards worldliness. In the path of seeking the Lord, one always has to wrestle against the false self. Winning or losing doesn't matter. Courage lies in trying. The seeker who takes up this challenge gets blessings and Darshan from Lord.

Submission

Lord Indra symbolizes worldly pleasures. Worldliness is all about leading a luxurious, flourishing, joyful, and secured life by dedicating self in accumulation of maximum objects which hold high value in others' perspective. But here, Indra conveys an important message to the being that no worldly objects can match the immense pleasure derived from Darshan of Lord Ram.

Journey to Perfection

Being's journey towards truth and Lord Ram begins with emptiness and inquisitiveness. The intensity of desire to know the truth determines the distance being will cover. Reading, understanding, and talking about Ramayan evoke the urge in the blessed ones to know the truth of Lord Ram. Our intrinsic nature is to achieve perfection. The material and mundane world is imperfect and perishing, yet we are attached to it because of our 'Karma' and Conditioning. It takes high intelligence, keen interest, and lots of courage to walk on the 'road less travelled,' like a baby who crawls towards an attractive toy leaving the comfort and security of the parent's lap. Seeking is walking consciously with full faith in Lord towards a beautiful yet unknown destination, leaving the secured comfort zone behind.

Darshan is witnessing the quintessential divine beauty of Lord Ram. An ideal beauty, on the one hand, gives blissful vision to our eyes while, on the other hand, leaves us with a sense of insufficiency. No matter how hard we try but mundane objects cannot fulfil this sense of insufficiency in us; instead, they will only give us pain and failure, sooner or later. Whereas when we devote this sense of insufficiency to the Supreme Lord, then He naturally gives us ultimate bliss, satisfaction and peace.

Whatever is pointing towards truth will eventually lead us to perfection and power, which is much more superior to what this world can ever offer. The highest reverence that can be offered to the Lord is by realizing that without His grace, life is impossible to deal with. And whence the being Surrenders his everything and asks Lord to take charge of his life, thence he is blessed. Lord incarnates in each era to destroy pride and ego. He slays the stubborn evil ruthlessly. Yet the 'Mahakaal' or Destroyer melts instantly on just one humble and earnest prayer of the being. Lord says 'I will give up everything for that one smile on the face of my child.' All beings are dear to Him, but only the meek who calls Him out helplessly from the bottom of the heart is dearest to Him.

Stop waiting for that one perfect moment, When you are done with worldly involvement, Because such moments never arrive,

And now is the time to realize,
That 'Darshan' of His manifestation,
Is the most effortless way to embrace perfection.

■■

Chapter 21

The Four Pairs : Setting Life Priorities

The four endeavours and the four states of consciousness are unified together,
The handsome grooms and beautiful brides are made for each other.

Purpose of Life

So far, many a time, we have talked about eliminating desires and liberating the self from the materialistic world as the ideal way to connect with the Lord. However, everyone, including me lies, when we claim that we have no desires and are totally free from materialism. As a matter of fact, the one who is actually free from desires never claims. As mentioned by Lord, every being is carrying forward a 'karmic account' from his previous births. Desires of the present are based on past "karma" or deeds in the account. Each birth is like a playfield, designed by Lord Himself, to neutralize the account and get liberated. The best way for neutralizing the account is by 'inaction.' Inaction means not doing anything which can bind us again, that is to live out the pleasures as well as pains with detachment and non-reaction. Without going further into details, it is well understood that it's very difficult rather impossible for the beings to practice 'inaction.' In fact, doing action and having desires are unavoidable parts of human nature.

Goals in life are a must which can be accomplished only by firm determination, perseverance and industriousness. As per the principle of 'Karma Yoga', the offering of goals, actions and results to Supreme and Surrendering to His will is the way to attain perfection. Phoney spiritual gurus, while quoting selective verses from Vedic scriptures, often misguide others and justify their own indolence. One may boast about knowledge to prove His intellectual superiority, but without applying them to life, the inestimable life-opportunity simply gets wasted. There can be no alternative or excuse for 'Purushartha' or hard work.

Lord says that only when the being realizes the ultimate joy of inner-self, he can get liberation from desires and materialism. It is like, one who swims in the ocean, does not get attracted to small ponds ever. Even the Vedanta scriptures are like small ponds in comparison to ultimate bliss and wisdom that dwell inside every being. Materialism and Bliss of Consciousness are inversely related. As the level of awareness of consciousness escalates, the attachment with materialism automatically diminishes.

But this bliss can only be realized when one puts in sincere effort or'purushartha.' Life is not just about enjoying worldly pleasures, but it's a priceless opportunity to do penance or 'Tapasya' to attain the Supreme goal. Vedic scriptures talk about four 'Purushartha' or endeavours and four 'Avastha' or states of consciousness, a clear understanding of which gives the much-needed transparency in setting the goals and attaining them.

Four Types of Actions or Purushartha

Saint Tulsidas says that at the holy matrimonial alliance of Siya-Ram, the attendees had the unique opportunity to witness the darshan of four 'Purushartha' or four endeavours in the four grooms. Prince Bharat symbolizes 'Dharma' or righteousness, Shatrughan symbolizes 'Arth' or wealth, Laxman symbolizes 'Kaam' or passion and Lord Ram symbolizes 'Moksha' or ultimate salvation. Lord states that beings must give equal importance to all the four endeavours. The endeavour of 'Arth' gives the right to accumulate wealth for self, family, and society. 'Kaam' gives the right to work for the fulfilment of desires. 'Dharma' states that actions must not be immoral, unethical, and illegitimate. 'Moksha' is about liberation from 'Maya' or the materialistic world.

Shatrughan is a silent protagonist of Ramayan who follows Bharat uncritically. It signifies that the endeavour to earn money must be totally in accordance with righteousness, without illegitimacy and pride. Laxman, on the other hand, is full of energy and enthusiasm, having only one purpose that is to serve Lord Ram. Similarly, the desires must be pursued with zeal, but for one purpose only, that is liberation. Therefore, before setting goals, one must contemplate deeply on them. The fallacious aspect of mind gives endless thoughts of desires like 'I want this or I want that.' Beings need to analyse every single thought in terms of its fruitfulness. Each desire-thought must be weighed, questioned and observed cautiously. If it is trapping us further in worldly affairs, then it is to be avoided.

Conversely, if it serves a righteous purpose, then it ought to be pursued.

Lord says that by continually evaluating thoughts with alertness, one will eventually discover the true aspect of mind and will become aware of the fact that the one and only purpose of life is freedom from worldly pursuits and realization of self. Desires cannot be eliminated by negating because the idea to eliminate desire is itself a desire.

Once the being sets his priority to attain liberation from 'Maya,' he must dedicate his life to serve this priority. Just like Laxman dedicated his life in the service of Lord Ram. All the duties, roles, situations, and responsibilities that life entrusts on the being must be dealt with, keeping in mind that the ultimate purpose of life is liberation. Actions that are performed following the ideals set by Ramayan, best serve Lord Ram and are the ways to please Him and attain 'Moksha.'

Four States of Mind

Saint Tulsidas relates the four Princess Brides with the four 'Avastha' or states of consciousness of human beings. Princess Urmila, who's married to Laxman (Kaam), symbolizes 'Jagriti' or state of waking. It signifies that beings must be wide-awake in pursuing desires. Shrutkirti who's married to Shatrughan (Arth), symbolizes 'Sushupti' that is the state of sleep. To properly understand this union, one first needs to understand and accept the principle of 'Karma Yoga' that one has the right to action but not on the fruits of action. Gains and losses are ascertained by 'Prarabdha' or 'Karmic Account.' Thus fruits are not in being's hand and are unalterable. Although being has full control on action, he has absolutely no influence on result. It, therefore, means that the being must give great importance on wealth earning activity without emphasizing on the outcome. 'Sushupti' with 'Arth' signifies that being must be indifferent to wealth just like he is indifferent to the world in sleep.

Princess Mandavi, who's married to Bharat (Dharma), symbolizes 'Svapna' that is the state of dreaming, signifying that one must stick with righteousness in such a way that even in dreams he would not go against it. Finally, Mother Sita symbolizes 'Turiya' that is the state of enlightenment, signifying that only the one who seeks Lord Ram can realize the truth of the Universe and become the 'enlightened one.' Lord Ram and Mother Sita are complementary to each other which essentially means that without Sita, Ram is not reachable and without Ram, Sita is not attainable. One must remember that all beings experience waking, sleeping, and dreaming states naturally, but there are very few who works for 'Moksha' and 'Turiya.'

Urmila and Sita always stayed together, which signifies that enlightenment can be attained only with alertness. Shrutkirti and Mandavi were very close, thereby reflecting that dreams are seen only in sleep. Sleep means pausing the mind-ego activity, which calms and relaxes the beings.

Uncontrolled mind, if not given a break will lead to insanity and even death. Therefore the value of sleep must not be underestimated. As the control over the mind improves, the need for sleep automatically diminishes. In dreams, when the eyes are not performing their actual role, there is an eye of awareness that observes and witnesses the mind activities. At that time, both the picture and seeing the picture happens simultaneously inside the mind. The state of dream indicates the presence of eye of awareness which is beyond the limitations of mortal eyes. Only by practising scrupulous observation of mind activity, being can become 'Sakshi' or witness that is the ability to consciously behold from the eyes of awareness. By being a witness, one frees self from the ups and downs of life and attains the unwavering ultimate bliss.

Surrender (Samarparna) is Freedom

For a lucid and coherent understanding of these four significant endeavours and states, one needs to have a superior level of intelligence & 'Vivek.' But what ultimately matters is the urge for knowing the truth. A meek devotee realizing self as helpless and ineligible Surrenders his everything to Lord. Such a devotee is blessed with special attention and love of the Lord. All beings are dear to Him, but the devotee is the dearest. 'Bhava' of Supreme Lord for the devotee is, 'This child, weeping in the anguish of My love, is totally dependent on Me, and has refused all the worldly pleasures that I have fixed for him. Now it is My duty and My Dharma to give My everything to Him'. Supreme Lord is obliged to reciprocate love. Lord expeditiously frees the devotee from his 'karmic account' and ensures 'Turiya,' 'Moksha,' and, most importantly, 'Bhakti' for him.

The grand wedding of Siya-Ram was an overwhelming sight for Saint Tulsidas. He had the 'Darshan' or the vision of Supreme love and bliss. Blessed is the one who in all four 'Purushartha' and four 'Avastha' fixes his mind only in Lord and nothing else. Blessed is the one, whose single endeavour fulfils the obligation of wealth, desires, righteousness, and salvation. Blessed is the one who in any four states of waking, sleeping, dreaming and self- enlightenment, sees nothing else but the lotus feet of Siya- Ram. It is because only the blessed one is eligible for the deific affinity of Siya-Ram.

■■

Chapter 22

The Pranking : Value of Humour

The groom doesn't talk at all, is He mute or arrogant? O Prince, look beside and see your conceit melt.

Why so Serious?

Vedic rules and traditions are purposefully meant to ensure system and order in both worldly and spiritual life. These traditions are the constitution of our religion which is religiously laid down in our holy scriptures. Beings are expected to conduct life following these traditions. Lord Ram is recognised as the most fervent practitioner of Vedic constitution among all. However, living in the compulsion to practise rules and disciplines all the time arouses a claustrophobic feeling of being confined in a cage. Therefore, ordinary and straightforward beings look for an opportunity to escape such an enclosure. Wise or 'Viveki' is the one who understands this aspect of human nature and enjoys the light and humorous moments to ventilate. Such moments are enjoyable for everybody. Missing out these moments brings dryness of strict rules and regulations in life, making it lifeless, dull, depressed and dead.

Saint Tulsidas was very well aware of the value of 'Ras' or nectar of enjoyment in human life, and therefore he beautifully incorporated knowledge with enchantment in Ramayan. A great tale is essentially the one where the reader experiences 'Ras' or nectar of bliss and 'Gyan' or wisdom connately. It is the aim of all epics, poetry and stories in Sanatan Dharma to make learning not only inspiring but also enjoyable. If not, for this reason, rule books would have been published. Even the greatest spiritual guide, 'Bhagavad Gita' has a background of an interesting tale like 'Mahabharata'. Only those pieces of 'spiritual art' that help radiate the nectar of joy have qualified the tests of time, thereby helping in the expansion of consciousness considerably. A very serious life always gets too boring to spend. Therefore Path of Devotion or 'Bhakti' is considered the greatest of all because unlike Gyan (Knowledge),

Karam (Action) and Dhyaan (Meditation), there is an innate amusement and joy attached to 'Bhakti' right from the beginning.

Fun Time

Lord himself planned one such incidence of joy for His devotees just after the grand holy marriage ceremony. The formal proceedings of marriage were finished. The ceremony was conducted strictly in accordance with Vedic norms by eminent and virtuous sages and priests. All the attendees were expected to participate with sincerity and seriousness. As the formal ceremony ended, the ladies of Mithila took the brides and the grooms inside Queen's palace because now is the time for celebration and that celebration essentially means singing, dancing, laughing and of course, playing pranks with open hearts. Here 'Sages', 'Rules' and 'Discipline' are not allowed to interfere. The whole atmosphere remains filled with informal and exciting interactions. Here irrespective of status, one can speak freely without any strings attached. The centre of attraction was obviously the supreme couple Siya-Ram. The thoughtful teasing of ladies made Prince Ram blush, and he couldn't even utter a word in embarrassment. That further prompted the ladies to pun. The graceful bride, Princess Sita, was shy and wasn't even lifting her eyelids but was staring downwards with a gentle and divine smile on her fair, beaming face. Her feelings towards Ram's uneasiness along with her protectiveness for him were not hidden from anybody.

One of the princess's friends made fun, saying, 'Why Prince Ram is so quiet? Is he mute?' Hearing this, Lord Ram smiled. It was amusing to note that the Supreme Lord of the universe who is sought by Vedas was participating in pranks for the pleasure of beings. The teasing continued, and another friend replied, 'He isn't mute but is proud. He doesn't consider others at par with him and so doesn't care to look or talk with them.' To which the first one placing Sita's hand on Ram smilingly said, 'If it so then O Prince Ram, just have a look here. Your self-admiration and vanity will melt off.' The sweet pun meant that Sita had a very fair complexion whereas Ram was wheatish. And so he had no reason for such self-superiority. The statement though was said in innocence, not in sarcasm.

Only the one who is either purely innocent or totally insane can mock the King of Ayodhya with such casualness. Lord Ram understood the pun and smiled blushingly, lowering his head. Princess Janaki to prove her non-participation in this wordplay removed her hand in haste. The hall was filled with sheer laughter. The only one who was grumbling inside was Prince Laxman. It's because Lord Sheshnag always takes his job of serving his master too seriously. But Lord Ram signalled him to take it easy. The ladies continued with their pleasantries, and they started laughing even more loudly than before. They were not ready to leave any opportunity to tease the grooms that day.

Humour is the Food for Life

Such light moments of joy and humour in one's life must not be undervalued. These moments are like rainfall for barren land, mother's milk for the infant and gold for the pauper. Since the day Lord Ram left Ayodhaya with Laxman and Sage Vishvamitra, this was the first occasion of merriment for them. Life is not always smooth. It keeps on throwing challenges continuously to evaluate the mettle of beings. Righteous way of life always keeps one busy, in contemplating, pondering, assessing and doing. But then life also bestows these precious cheerful moments through little windows of pleasantness to cherish to the fullest. Such revitalising moments are essential for all without any bias. The Siya-Ram 'Vivah' or Holy Marriage is the 'Ras-Leela' part of Ramayan.

There is no denying the fact that such an intriguing interaction represents pure love and a feeling of togetherness. There is no end of variety and anxiety in love. What a bag of gold means for greedy or Samadhi means for Yogi is how the playful past-times (Leela) of Lord matter to the devotee. Just like an insecure miser who is always busy in counting his cash, a devotee continuously checks and evaluates reciprocation of his love from the Lord. Until Siya-Ram got separated in exile, Lord ensured and also enjoyed light moments of joy and romance in life. Display of affection and altercations are part of all relations. Similarly, ups and downs are an integral part of life. Dharma gives the strength and courage to tackle difficult times fearlessly but, 'Ras-Leela' is what helps to heal even the most painful bruises.

■■

Chapter 23

The Divine Touch : One Needs Eyes to See

She is eyes for the blind and voice for the mute, Whatever she touches at once turns into gold.

Philosopher's Stone

Today the three queen-mothers of Ayodhaya were overwhelmed with love and jubilation because the stars of Raghukul, the four prince-brothers with their soul-mates, have returned home after the holy matrimonial alliance. The whole kingdom of Ayodhya danced in euphoria as this is the time of celebration. It was undisputedly the most glorious event in the history of 'Arya' civilisation. Wedding of a prince is, no doubt, a joyous event for the citizens, but what was the reason for their overwhelming happiness today? What was so special about it? This situation reminds us of the story of a pauper. Long ago, a pauper was sitting outside the village, thoroughly depressed with life. He was disillusioned and couldn't figure out any solution. Unmindfully sitting there, he picked up a stone and casually started playing with it. From then on, he kept the stone with him, and whenever he felt like, he used to play with it to pass his time. He was unaware that he was carrying the philosopher 's stone, a unique stone that turns any metal it touches into gold. Once accidentally, his philosopher 's stone touched an iron nail and turned it into gold. The pauper exclaimed and danced in sheer exuberance.

Just like this pauper, we also have philosopher 's stone within us, but just like him, we are also unmindful of it. Saint Tulsidas says that a spiritual seeker constantly ponders over attaining the ultimate bliss. Though all holy epics and scriptures have always stated it, yet the seeker neglects the fact that bliss is being's innate nature. We are the consciousness. It is just that we have forgotten about it.

Forgetfulness of Beings

The people of Ayodhaya were suffering from the same forgetfulness. Supreme Lord Ram was born and brought up amongst them. He was easily approachable to all of them. They also loved Him as their Noble Prince, yet they didn't have any knowledge whatsoever about His divinity. It was only after Princess Sita arrived with Him to Ayodhaya that beings could unveil the truth. Mother Sita is the eyes of wisdom that is 'Vivek', without which Supreme Ram cannot be recognized. It requires proper guidance of sages and contemplation on self to realize our true identity. Lord says that once the being is settled in truth, then nothing can stop him from flowing in the ocean of ultimate bliss.

A Yogi seeks Supreme consciousness by 'Neti-Neti' or discarding all that is untrue. Not everybody can see the difference between true and untrue. Anybody can become a seeker, but only the one with 'Vivek' can become a Yogi.

Saint Tulsidas says that mothers are the seekers, and Ram is the Supreme consciousness. As soon as Princess Sita, the 'Vivek,' arrived at Ayodhaya, mothers apprehended the truth of Ram and attained ultimate bliss.

Sita is the Eyes

Although the royal sage Vashishta had already announced Lord Ram's divinity publicly at his birth, still, the mothers were far away from knowing the bliss. Beings repeatedly see, read, and hear the spiritual lessons, but because of their undeveloped 'Vivek,' they are not able to grasp and recollect the knowledge. Therefore, beings like the royal mothers even tend to forget the knowledge given by Heavenly Sages like Vashishta. Sita, as a daughter-in-law, blessed the kingdom of Ayodhaya and bestowed the 'Vivek' that was missing in their lives. With the grace of Sita, the mothers at once realized that the one whom they believed as their mortal son was none other than the Supreme Lord Himself.

Tulsidas questions, a person may own all the luxuries and pleasures of the world, but if he is unwell, without a healthy body and mind, can he make use of them? Can he enjoy them? Similarly, beings already possess the greatest wealth of the universe, but they are not aware of it because of the ill mind. Beings don't need lectures on consciousness and bliss; all they need is a cure for the illness of mind. And the best treatment for all kinds of mind-ego disorders like attachment, desire, like-dislike, anxiety, fear, anger, and dissatisfaction is 'Bhakti' or devotion. No medicine and no psychiatric treatments can cure these disorders other than love for Supreme. Indulgence in the so-called feel-good or stress-busting activities like socializing, partying, shopping, travelling, improvisations in lifestyle, the art of breathing, and so on may give short-term pleasures and satisfaction. But the ultimate panacea that eliminates all diseases from the root is devotion or 'Bhakti' of Siya-Ram.

We have a beautiful world around us, but can a blind appreciate it? One needs eyes to see it. Saint Tulsidas mentions that Ram is the beauty that can only be seen with divine eyes that is Sita. We don't know the cause of our relentless struggling with life. We don't even understand where the problem is. We always find ourselves short of words in explaining our actual state of sorrow. It's just one lock that is stopping us from opening the doors to freedom. We spend our whole life looking for the key to that lock but fail miserably. However, that day, thankfully, the royal mothers got the key for the first time in the form of Sita, and immediately the lock of their mind-ego got removed. It was like for the first time, they were blissfully flying in the boundless sky, just like a golden eagle. For the very first time, they comprehended Supreme Ram, and for the first time, they found the words that give peace to the heart and eyes to relish the greatest beauty.

The Battle Inside

Mothers' feelings were similar to the peace and happiness of the patriotic-warrior, who, after years of battle, is finally able to free his land from the evil attackers. Lord has always guided beings to win the combat that keeps happening inside each of us. The true courageous warrior is the one who can deal with this inner-war and yet doesn't strive for victory. The other outer tussle is of no significance for that 'Mahavir' or the Great Warrior, who has defeated the mind- ego. Here one must understand that being is the warrior; courage is Mother Sita, and victory is Supreme Lord Ram.

One important thing that Tulsidas often quotes is that no matter how brilliantly, creatively, and meaningfully he tries to explain 'Bhava' or feelings, neither he nor any other spiritual thinker can express the Bhava in words in totality and in real sense. In fact, just words cannot perfectly portray Mother Sita, who is the personification of Bhava that flows in every heart. The problem with us is that we don't value Bhava and give more importance to the material world. Beings must understand that nothing is more valuable than 'Bhava,' not even the Supreme Lord. Only the one who gets rid of the hard shell of mind-ego can understand the true meaning of 'Bhakti.' Only the one who has Surrendered 'I'ness to the Lord can have the privilege to feel the flow of pure love. Pure love embedded in 'Bhakti' is the philosopher 's stone that turns whatever comes in its way into gold.

Chapter 24

Lord's Adolescent Phase : Recitation brings Progress

Lord smiled seeing Ayodhaya glittering and celebrating, This is just a pause in the story, a lot still left for learning.

Trusting Vs Knowing

One of the most important purposes of Ramayan is to eliminate 'fear ' in beings. So what exactly is this fear? Why every being throughout his life, lives in some or the other fear? Fear is a persistent apprehension of harm to self, and the absolute absence of this apprehension is fearlessness. Fear can broadly be categorized as outer fear and inner fear. Outer fear arises from external factors like criminals, animals, or enemies and poses a threat to the security and safety of physical self. The improvements in self, like

- letting go of addictions, immoral associations, venturing out of comfort zone creates a sense of loss of pleasure and uncertainty in mind. Uncertainty again gives rise to fear. Inner fear, on the other hand, is based on probabilities of the threat to self in respect of loss of honour, wealth, and comforts. The one who is insensitive, brutal, cunning, and unjust with others, though appears to be invincible,

also lives in an unabating fear as he dreads the same to happen to him. Fear of failure makes beings doubt their self abilities, and they refrain from taking up endeavours in life. These are the most common forms and causes of fear in beings. The list is endless and dealing with fears one by one is impractical. What is important for us to know is that, as the being progresses on the path of truth, his reliance on physicality and materialism diminishes, and fears automatically get reduced. Faith in Lord brings miraculous changes that nobody can fathom. Knowing how faith works scientifically doesn't help beings in any way. So it's always better to trust the word of learned enlightened Saints like Tulsidas to benefit the self.

Fear is the cause of Suffering

There is no being in the world who can claim to be completely free from fear. It is because the state of absolute fearlessness cannot be attained by acquiring power, courage, wealth, experience, or confidence. But it is only accomplished by an enlightened devotee who has taken refuge in Supreme. Lord says, as long as one identifies self with mind and body, he cannot free himself from fear. Self is a reflection of one indivisible, universal consciousness. Separateness arises when self identifies with the body as 'I' and sees another self-identified body as 'You.' Body is not eternal like consciousness. It lives and dies. Essentially whatever entity that comes to life becomes attached to life. As it is unable to detach with life, it fears death.

Self-identified-body spends all its mortal life in search of immortality. This effort never gives any result, instead brings chaos and trauma in life. It can be concluded that fear of death is the primary cause of all troubles and pains in one's life. Every problem of human life stems from the seed of fear. Although we try all the tricks up our sleeves, we just are not able to free ourselves from fear. In Sanatan Dharma, this fear is described as 'Mahabhaya.'

Another primary cause of fear is 'Dependence' which is coded in the DNA of all human beings. 'Purushartha' or endeavor for independence is again a wasteful endeavour. Solution lies only in shifting our dependence from material to consciousness, and the simplest way to bring this 'shift' into effect is 'Bhakti.' Saint Tulsidas believes that 'Bhakti' can be practised merely by studying or 'Paadth' the journey of Lord Ram from His birth to departing Ayodhya with Sage Vishwamitra and His return to Ayodhya with Princess Sita. This part of Ramayan is called as 'Balakanda.' By regular 'Paadth' of 'Balakanda,' the 'Antaha-Karana' or conscience of seeker purifies, and faith in the Lord magnifies. With the rise in faith, being's dependence on materialism will gradually decline, and the seeker will steadily and effortlessly be free from fear.

Be Assured

Saint Tulsidas shows immense confidence in the unadulterated Bhakti of Lord Ram. He invites seekers from all around the globe to get immersed in the divine nectar of the glories of Lord Ram. He advises all materialistic beings to practice 'Bhakti' without any bias. As a mother offers the temptation of gift to her child to make him study hard and reward his sincere efforts, similarly,

Saint Tulsidas assures the materialistically obsessed beings, of the fulfilment of all their desires just by studying the life of Lord Ram. In fact, the Saint is fully confident that whosoever will read, speak and think glories of Lord will unconditionally be benefitted. He has, therefore, repeatedly mentioned in Ramayan that beings who Surrender at the lotus feet of Lord Ram will find all their wishes come true, even much sooner than they anticipated.

Useless Logic

However, there are so-called rational intellectuals who always question the relevance of 'Bhakti.' Their thinking process is primarily based on logic, and whatever that doesn't quench their endless queries with logical explanations is not acceptable to them. Often I have heard them asking, how can a mere study of a book fulfil desires? Although I have scientific answers to their queries, I have seen that no quantum of explanations can satisfy the endless Hows and Whys of mind-ego trapped rational intellectuals. Believe it or leave it, the only way to happiness is by practising Bhakti. Lord in Shri Bhagavad Gita has concluded to Arjuna, that one who will Surrender to Him abandoning all dependencies, He will free him from all worldly sufferings. Other than this, being doesn't need to do anything. If one sincerely study Ramayan, he will also know the how and why of Surrender (Samarparna).

A musically enriched song has two important aspects. One is wordings, and the other is the tune. A typical listener enjoys the song when it has both the words and tune, but for an admirer of classical music, musical notes and tunes alone are sufficient to relish the melody. There is no compulsion for words. Devotion is like classical music, which appeals 'less' to the logical minds, and 'more' to the loving hearts. Saint Tulsidas concludes the 'Balakanda' saying that he has narrated the story for self-purification. Here again, the mind-ego trapped being asks, how can a story narration can be of any help? And how does self-purification help? Shouldn't one be committed to the accumulation of wealth instead of wasting time in studying Ramayan? How God, who signifies formless consciousness, can take Human Avatar? If Ram is Supreme God Himself, then why did he have to go through so many ordeals during His human incarnation? The common worldly perception is that 'Bhajan-Bhakti' is one thing, and practicality is different.

But in the real sense, these questions don't take you anywhere. No matter how good explanations are put forward, a questioning mind remains stranded from where it started. But the questioning is still considered far better than ignorance because at least there are possibilities to get to somewhere notable. At least there is a curiosity to know something valuable. Only the seeker himself can quench his thirst for answers; none other can spoon feed him. Of course, there are guidance and advice on how to find the answers. But only the genuinely inquisitive one will sincerely work hard to seek the answers. The others will either keep on questioning or won't bother themselves about knowing the truth at all.

Questions and more questions

Our minds are so conditioned by the external environment that we are unable to think beyond forms and figures. For us, each thing has to be quantifiable, measurable and comprehensible by our sense organs. Unless an entity is not scientifically proven, we do not accept it. But does that mean Supreme Lord is not there? Do our perceptions, limitations, and beliefs make any difference to the truth? What does God want from us, and why? What is the meaning of a Devotee? How is a devotee different from others? When the one who harms others is labelled as criminal and is supposed to be punished, then why Lord Ram, who has executed millions, not considered guilty?

Who is Lord Ram?

We need to understand that Lord Ram is both the supreme consciousness and physical manifestation. His body form is not an amalgamation of consciousness with 'Trigunatmak Prakriti' or 'three modes of nature' like that of mortal beings. Rather His mortal form is limitless, eternal, indestructible, formless and consciousness. Lord Ram is not born out of any karmic cycle but out of His omnipotent divine will. Mind that is programmed by the environment to function in forms and figures finds it very difficult to accept Grace. To understand it better, let's take an example of electricity wire lines that are running parallel to each other. Without the flow of current, all wires are uncharged. But when current is passed through a wire, it gets charged and becomes powerful because it is carrying electric energy. Touching a charged wire can cause death, but the same wire, when runs a life support system for critical patients, saves lives too. Similarly, Grace of the Lord is like energy which flows through the devotee. As a charged wire can pass current to other wires and charge them too; likewise, a devotee not only gets himself enlightened but also enlightens others.

The act of slaying by Lord is nothing but the grace of the Lord as He frees the unrighteous beings from the cage of mind-ego and also ends their threat to others. Lord is the Supreme consciousness, an energy that is present in every particle. All forms are made up of very subtle vibrations charged with one and the same universal energy. A devotee who is himself charged with His grace sees His grace in everything. Ignorant beings who don't know or believe in His grace cannot understand Him. The perception and limitation of ignorant beings are only because of their disbelief. The laws and principles of universal intelligence are always there, irrespective of those who believe it or not. Like whether one believes or not, the law of gravity is still there. As the two cars charged with same electricity can race with each other, similarly, one manifestation of the Lord can play with other manifestations of Lord. There is no 'I' or 'You.' There is only One that is 'Vasudeva Sarvam.' Hence the one who is slaying and the one who is being slayed is one Supreme Lord. A devotee sees the One Supreme Universal Energy & Intelligence as Lord Ram.

Conclusion

After the Grand Wedding, King Dasaratha, with sons, daughters, sages, courtiers, and citizens returned to Ayodhya from Janakpur. Ayodhya is glowing with joy and celebration. Mothers are praising the feats of their Ram and have opened their hearts to the newly wed brides. Everyone is crediting Sage Vishwamitra for the happiness of Ayodhya. As the role of Sage Vishwamitra in Ramayan is served, he now leaves but much against the will of Prince Ram. Everybody is happy. But the question remains - has the Ram-Rajya arrived? Has the Lord fulfilled His purpose of incarnation? No, not yet. There is a lot more to be learned and cherished. This is just the first halt, says Saint Tulsidas. It just brings us to the conclusion of 'Balakanda,' the childhood part of Lord Ram.

It was well past midnight, but Prince of Raghukul was still awake. He stepped out of bed and stood by the window. He looked at the city and was surprised to see that celebrations are not over yet. He smiled, seeing the beings happy. But the lessons are, however, need to be learned. Neither the

Lord's nor a devotee's life is free from ebbs and flows. But one thing is assured that fear, pain and suffering cannot touch the one who has trusted Ramayan and Surrendered himself at the lotus feet of Siya-Ram.

■■

AYODHAYAKAND

Chapter 2.1

Mirror Effect : King Dasratha's Retirement

Time has come for the Crown to be handed over,
And fulfill the purpose of life, which is to surrender.

Fourteen years had passed by since the matrimonial union of Siya-Ram, and in these fourteen years, silver clouds of meritorious deeds had poured showers of joy on Awadh. One fine day King Dasratha was sitting with all his courtiers in the royal state assembly hall. All of a sudden, the king casually checked his face in the mirror and set his Crown straight. He observed that his hair beside ears had turned grey. It seemed as if old age was whispering in his ears - "O king, it's time to make Ram your regent and thereby fulfill the prime objective of your life."

Mirror is a genuine friend of human beings. It reflects the exact and precise image of the looker without any distortion. Although nobody likes to be shown his shortcomings, and the mirror shows our clear-cut flaws, yet we don't despise it. It is because a mirror is always unbiased and trustworthy, and it's only purpose is to inspire us to look better. We value the opinion of the inanimate mirror more than alive beings as we presume that among beings, there are no real well-wishers, and every being is infected with the germs of hatred and jealousy. Well, the fact is that we only see others through the point of view of our own mind-ego. And as said earlier, mind-ego has hardly any correlation with the actual truth.

For mind-ego, a mirror is unprejudiced and a reliable friend whose only purpose is to make the external egoic appearence beautiful and be appreciated by others. Most beings live to be acknowledged by others. And acknowledgment is like oxygen for mind-ego. Everybody can see the external self in the mirror. But commendable are those who get inspiration from the mirror to contemplate on the inner self. King Dasratha was one such rare and great being who though being the most powerful entity of Raghukul Empire, still contemplated on life, and its purpose. In the history of the world, rarely do we find an influential leader or monarch believing in self-contemplation or renunciation. Mostly their mind-ego works till last breath, to sustain and expand the control.

The value of self-contemplation rises even higher when one does it publicly instead of in isolation. In those times the royal courts were occupied by sycophants who could flatter their King endlessly and shamelessly. Kings were habituated of hearing their false praises day and night and so were entrapped in an unreal self-image. Most of them were oblivious to the reality of life. Principally, a self-obsessed being never contemplates on truth as he sees himself through the eyes of others. But King Dasratha was highly 'Viveki' or wise. He didn't judge himself through the words of sycophants. In fact, on hearing the fake praises of sycophants, he became even more alert and analyzed the situation with conviction. Somebody of his stature checking himself in the mirror in public may sound weird, but it conveyed an important message to the sycophants that this King could not easily be trapped in fake flattery.

The crown on his head was out of its position, signifying that Dasaratha has entered the fourth stage of life wherein the mind and body are tired serving for the worldly obligations. Now is the time to pass over the ruling-control in the young and able hands of Prince Ram. The advent of old age also signifies that now he must quit the worldly affairs and contemplate on the higher purpose of life. The body of an elderly person may lose its strength, but his introspection, receptive and thinking ability become even sharper and more developed. Multifaceted experiences of childhood, adolescence, and adulthood present beings with those immensely realistic insights which no book or preceptor can ever teach.

Wise is the one who truly recognizes and values life insights and liberates the self from worldly traps of ambitions and insecurities. It is assumed that everybody in old age retires and hands over their accumulation to their successor with pleasure. But the truth is that even after physically handing over, beings cannot let go of the attachment and control.

Just a mere tilt in the crown was a good enough indication for Dasaratha to understand the required course of action. But, on the other hand, even after multiple occasions of the toppling of the crown on the floor, Ravan couldn't grasp the signal of 'intelligent life.' Instead, every time Ravan picked up the crown and wore it again without an iota of embarrassment. Ravan essentially symbolizes the strong influence of 'Moh' or attachment. In fact, Ravan is the finest example of how a being can be insanely attached to his crown of worldly accumulations. Lord says that no matter whatever a being intends to do in life, his primary focus must always be fixed on the end result. And the end result of Ravan or Attachment-'Moh' is nothing, but death and destruction.

King Dasratha was a great devotee of Lord Ram. In a previous life, he wished to become the father of Lord. Lord has declared that a devotee can establish any relationship with him. And He is obliged to reciprocate devotee's chosen relationship. Ravan was also His devotee, and in a previous life, he chose to be His enemy. Now, on the one hand, there is a devotee like Ravan who doesn't want to return Lord's supreme-mate Lady Sita. While on the other hand is a great devotee like Dasratha who wants to surrender everything in the lotus feet of Lord Ram and accomplish the ultimate objective of life. Blessed are those who with complete awareness and free will, surrender everything to Lord. He serves each of His beloved devotees unconditionally exactly the same way He served his father-devotee King Dasratha.

Chapter 2.2

Plotting of Devta : Unashamed Insecurity

Devta prayed that some trouble might brew in the meantime, The royal rejoicing didn't please them,
Just like moonlight is disliked by a thief in the night time.

The Announcement

King Dasratha officially announced that tomorrow Prince Ram would be crowned as the King of Ayodhaya. Hearing that pronouncement, every being of Ayodhaya was overwhelmed with joy and was anxiouslylooking forward to the ceremony. But the self-serving Devtawere not happy and hence were plottingmeans to spoil the crowning. They approached Goddess Saraswati and begged Her to help them in this plot so that they could somehow stop the ceremony.

Dasaratha divulged his desire to make Ram the King to the royal sage Vashishtha before announcing it to the public. It didn't take long for the Sage to understand the 'Bhava' or holy feelings of Dasaratha behind such desire and so he asked him to proceed without any delay. As crops get damaged if not harvested at the right time, the sage felt that it was the right time to make Ram the king and that the sacred resolution aroused in the heart of Dasaratha should be executed immediately. Otherwise, mind-ego is so powerful that it can corrupt even the heart of a devotee like Dasratha and spoil his spiritual progress. Retirement from active worldly life and crowning of Ram as the King is a step towards spiritual progress for Dasratha. The announcement was, therefore, made without further delay.

Godless Devta

Now the question arises, why were Devta against the dawn of Ram-Rajya? It is quite understandable if Ravan, a wicked Asur had desired to put hurdles in the ceremony. But the fact that righteous Devta, who are residing in Heaven, are making such a conspiracy against Lord Ram, to whom they are themselves devoted, sounds quite astonishing. It is on the request of Devta, that Lord Ram had taken avatar, to destroy Ravan. Because Ravan had become a superpower and had defeated Devta and captured Heaven.

Saint Tulsidas explains that a human being, through his accumulation of meritorious deeds, attains the status of Devta. By virtue of those deeds, he isthen allowed to reside in Heaven where there are endless pleasures, no fear of death, and, of course, the fulfilment of all desires. Heaven is considered as the highest abode which inspires human beings to do 'Punya' or meritorious deeds in their mortal life. But another crucial aspect is related to it.

Although Heaven serves asan unlimited source of pleasures, the dwelling Devtacan only enjoy them as per their individual merit. Each one of them has his shareof pleasures. And there lies the problem. It is because wherever there is inequality, it gives rise to jealousy, and just as mortal beings, Devta were no different in this case. In the beginning, to encourage righteousness, Devtas bless and support the seeker of truth, as his spiritual endeavours empower them too. But as soon as the seeker progresses further and higher towards 'Vairagya' and is seen to be conquering the cause and effect of pleasures, Devtas get concerned. They are very much attached to pleasures and don't want the seeker to change the rules.

A liberated enlightened being is given the highest positionin Heaven, and therefore, it is a potential threat for the Devta, who are currently holding the position. It is because of this concern for pleasures and to safeguard their positionthat Devta wanted to spoil the efforts of the devotee. These are the reasons why Devta wished to ruinthe final spiritual endeavour of Dasaratha, of making Lord Ram the King and renouncing worldly life.

After establishing Ram-Rajya, the final resolution of Dasaratha would have been accomplished, and he would have attained enlightenment. But Devta, instead of supporting this great feat of Dasaratha, were more concerned about their interests. The second reason for their worry was that Raavan had defeated Devta and restricted their enjoyment of pleasures and so they were desperate for the destruction of Raavan. And that was only possible when Lord Ram instead of ruling Ayodhayawould go tothe forest in exile. Hence for these two reasons, the self-seeking Devta were conspiring against the crowning of Prince Ram.

Thoughts of Ram

Now another question that crops up here is why Lord Ram, the Supreme of Universe,had let Devta successfully execute their plot? Firstly, Lord's avatar purpose was outright meant for the establishment of 'Dharma,' and for that to be the King of Ayodhaya was not a compulsion. Secondly, Raavan was, without any doubt, destined to be slayed by the Lord whether as a King or a forest dweller. Foolish are those who think that they can manipulate the Leela of the Supreme.

Dasratha was a practitioner of 'Gyana,' or Knowledge Path of seeking where the onus to attain spiritualsuccess lies more on the seeker and lesser on Lord. Had Dasaratha been on the path of 'Bhakti', of absolute surrender, then Lord would have taken full responsibility for his well being. But that was not the case,soLord allowed Devta to interfere with the sacred resolution of Dasaratha and spoil the Crowning ceremony.

Firstly pleasures and fulfillments of desires must not be the objective of spirituality. Secondly, what beings believe as their clever manipulation is actually the planning of Supreme Intelligence. We must know that nothing is in human-being's control. No Faith or Yoga or Practice or Religion can match the Path of Surrender or 'Samarparn & SharranagathiBhava' in the lotus feet of Lord Ram. Lord loves all His beings equally, but the surrendered one is dearest to Him. Had Dasaratha practised absolute surrender, he would not have faced a gloomy end. Had Devta learned to be detached from pleasures and let go of their cleverness, they wouldn't have been tormented by Ravan.

Chapter 2.3

MANTHARA : The Game Changer

News of ceremony distressed her heart,
Tonight the joy of millions shall be torn apart.

Her Story

Mother Saraswati understood the shrewdness of Devta very well, however, for the sake of the welfare of all beings, she agreed to create obstacles in the Crowning ceremony of Lord Ram. Now she had to find that one pawn, which could be used for this purpose, and she found the dimwit maid of Queen Kekayi as the most suitable for the purpose. It's interesting to note how an insignificant, deformed, low-born, and illiterate woman like Manthra did something that changed the destiny of the Ayodhaya Empire. The name 'Manthara' cannot be erased from the history of Sanatan Dharma. The shrewd conspiracy of a weak and timid being like Manthara defeated the mightiest emperor of the Land of Bharata, King Dasratha.

Manthara's heart was burning out of jealousy and hatred on hearing the news of Lord Ram's Crowning. It's not given in Ramcharitmanas but through other texts, we come to know that in the past, Lord Ram and Laxman had disciplined Manthara for her stupid acts and therefore she was looking for revenge. Her evil mind at once started plotting a way which would spoil tomorrow's ceremony. She knew she had only that one night left to execute her plan. She evaluated and found that the instrument for this evil conspiracy is Kekayi. No wonder, brilliant was that 'Manthara' mind that was able to manipulate a knowledgeable and matured Queen like Kekayi.

Now the question that arises here is why Goddess Saraswati chose Manthara? The answer lies in the manner in which a contagious disease affects beings? The germs of a contagious disease always attack the vulnerable ones first. Every being has a certain level of inbuilt immunity. In whosoever the resistance power is least, germs always target him first because of the high chances of success. Manthara was cunning yet a vulnerable target. At the time of the matrimonial alliance of Dasaratha and Kekayi, Kekayi's father had put one condition that the son born to Kekayi would become the successor of Dasaratha and the next king of Ayodhaya. Dasratha immediately agreed because firstly, he had no son till then and also because he was so fascinated with Kekayi that he didn't even think over the condition at all before accepting it.

Kekayi's father was a crafty diplomat. He sent Manthara with Kekayi to Ayodhya as he knew that Manthara being a maid will always be with his daughter overlooking the happenings in the palace. Being deformed, others will pity her and consider her harmless. However, he very well knew that though she may be physically insignificant, yet she had a very shrewd intellect and knew how to manipulate things in her favour. Accordingly, if anything goes against Kekayi's interests, Manthara would be able to handle the situation. From the perspective of Royal Diplomacy, qualities of Manthara were beneficial for Kekayi's father, and her wickedness also made her a usable character for Mother Saraswati to execute Devta's plot. Wicked one may think too highly of oneself but for intelligent ones is actually an easy target who can be manipulated. Mother Sarswati, the Goddess of intelligence in a split second easily manipulated Manthara, a wicked and complex being.

Manipulation of the Manipulator

'Sam' or cajoling, 'Dam' or corrupting, 'Dand' or punishing, and 'Bhed' or provoking one against others are the four aspects of political diplomacy. Manthara was the symbol of 'Bhed Buddhi' that is having expertise in provoking others to fulfil self-interest. Although to a wicked being, it appears that provocative skills bring immediate victory, but at the base of every action, there is one universal principle, which is 'Dharma' or righteousness. Any action against 'Dharma' may appear very rewarding at first, but will ultimately bring destruction and punishment to the 'Bhed Buddhi.' The same happened with Manthara. To see and listen to the wicked is already the beginning of wickedness - Confucius.

It is easier to deal with real suffering than imaginary suffering, which cannot be wiped out quickly by any means. Manthra built unreal castles of fear in the mind-ego of Kekayi. She made Kekayi believe in an imaginary future of her suffering if Prince Ram is crowned as the King. The power of unreal fear is such that even a mother like Kekayi, who lived all her life for her loving son

Ram, suddenly felt threatened by Him in just a span of a few minutes. For the first time, the 'Manthara' mindset of 'My' son Bharat and 'Kaushalya's' son Ram penetrated Kekayi's mind. Fools are those who consider Ram and Bharat as separate and different when, in reality, they both are One in thought, speech, and action.

Kaikeyi's Boon or Curse

Human-beings must be very cautious while choosing the source of taking advice because one single mistake can make life crumble down. Kekayi's only mistake was that she listened to evil Manthara and believed her words. A boon, if incorrectly applied, can turn into a curse, but 'sincere acceptance' has the power to transform a curse into a blessing. Kekayi asked for two boons from Dasaratha, which perfectly suited her and Bharat's interests. But since the inspiration of the boons was selfishness, jealousy, and impure interests, the same blessings turned into a dreadful curse for both Kekayi and Manthra.

On the other hand, when Ram left Ayodhaya, He was just Prince Ram, but when He returned to Ayodhya after fourteen years of exile, He became 'Maryada Purushottam Bhagwan' Ram. Lord accepted the exile orders with utmost sincerity which was acknowledged by the whole world. This is the power of 'Dharma'. This is also the perfect instance of how an ordinary person becomes extraordinary. It is not real hardships, but the 'Fear' of difficulties that bothers beings the most. Like Kaikeyi, beings spend their entire life dealing with imaginary insecurity and fear. Our biggest enemy is our own fear and nothing else. It's only at the dusk of life that human beings realize there is nothing worth chasing and escaping. Great are those who realize this truth early in their life that nothing is of much significance other than surrendering in the lotus feet of Supreme Ram.

Chapter 2.4

MANTHARA : THE STUPID

Not only did she created suffering for others,
But also painted her destruction in dark colours.

Balanced Equanimity

It is very humane to feel troubled in adverse situations. But when there is no threat or harm to self, yet the mind-ego feels agonized just because the other one is prospering, indicates 'Asuri' or demonic quality. Staying unmoved and level-headed in a highly favourable or extremely adverse situation signifies saintly quality. Neither the news of the Crowning ceremony overwhelmed Lord Ram with joy nor the news of exile from Ayodhaya could bother Him at all. Many believe that such a great attribute is only possible for a divine entity rather than mortal beings because, from a practical perspective, nobody can remain unperturbed when confronted with a loss.

Saint Tulsidas points out with conviction that more the being progresses in the path of spirituality, more the lines of separation between 'Me' and 'You' minimizes, and ultimately 'Bhava' or the feeling of Oneness emerges. From a worldly perspective, a devotee, yogi or seeker may interact with others as regular beings, but his inner 'Bhava' is always in Oneness with all. The soul and body of every mortal being are made up of one and the same Supreme Element. The sense of separateness from others is a characteristic attribute of mind-ego. The mind of every being has been conditioned to believe self as separate, which is the fundamental cause of tormenting fear in a being's life. Spiritual progress is unconditioning of mind. Although Lord Ram annihilated Asura, His 'Bhava' for all beings, irrespective of Devta, Asura, or Manushya was One and the same, that is affection.

The 'Manthara' inside Beings

The mind-ego of Manthra was polluted to such an extent that she could not accept the glory of Prince Ram. So far, such hateful thoughts were contained inside her, and as such, they were harmless. But the day she brought her evil thoughts to action, she herself paved the way for her destruction. An unchecked mind-ego feels distressed and cannot tolerate the well being of others. The core thought which gives rise to jealousy and hatred is *'If I am not happy, how can you be happy.'* And therefore, mind-ego always resolves to ruin others happiness so that the other also becomes miserable like itself.

The same thing is also happening to us. We tend to become unhappy seeing other's success. Our pain lessens as soon we come to know about other's loss. In every unchecked mind-ego, a Manthara resides whose only purpose is to unnecessarily manipulate thoughts with delusional fears. One must get rid of this inner Manthara before it gets too late and further spoils life bringing irrecoverable destruction. One can lessen its influence by being aware of the Manthara's tricks, but to uproot Manthara entirely, the only way is 'Bhakti.'

Whether Ram or Bharat becomes the King, Manthara knew that neither her status as the Queen's maid would change, nor would she get the throne of Ayodhaya. And yet she conspired against beloved Prince Ram. Her foolish hatred delayed the advent of 'Ram-Rajya' and brought unnecessary pain and agony for the innocent people of Ayodhaya. To execute her plot, she unscrupulously capitalized on Kekayi's egoic sense of separateness. The whole of Ayodhaya was a testimony to the fact that Kekayi had loved Ram more than Mother Kaushalya. But still, she could not get rid of the egoic affliction that Ram was not born from her womb. Therefore, she became an easy target for manipulation for Manthara.

Success or Stupidity

'Manthara' means a slow and steady mover. She never got excited and always took every step with calculative patience. Kekayi blasted her when she first spoke ill for Ram but eventually yielded to her persistence. The strength of negativity must not be underestimated. Many people, including King Dasratha tried to persuade Kekayi to change her stand but failed. This shows how strongly influential the evil Manthara was.

Ultimately the question remains whether the exile of Lord Ram is considered as Manthra's success or her stupidity? Because whenever one plots to do harm to others, he or she must contemplate deeply on the implications. A woodcutter may possess a sharp axe with which he can effortlessly cut the branches. But if he uses the same axe to cut the branch which is supporting him, then he would obviously be labelled as a fool. Manthara was no doubt very sharp, but she used the same sharpness unwisely against herself. We must know that this is the consequence of all wicked ones who only know how to play skillfully but don't have a far-sighted vision. And therefore, Manthara or a wicked woman was tagged as 'Mandmati' or dimwit by Saint Tulsidas.

Chapter 2.4

Friends Congratulate Prince Ram : Meaning of Friendship

Great power involves great responsibility,
Lord honoured His friends with great humility.

Old - New Equation

The announcement of the crowning ceremony of Prince Ram brought enchantment in Ayodhaya, but the overwhelming joy in the hearts of His childhood friends was inexplicable. As soon as they heard about the crowning announcement, they all hurried to the palace to congratulate their age-old friend, who would become their king, the next day. But they witnessed an unexpected change in His behavior. No, it wasn't ego, vanity, or superiority, but tonight they found in him immense reverence for them with natural affinity.

Usually, as one attains great power and position, a transformation in behavior occurs. Mind-ego necessitates a change in the equation of relationships to upkeep the glory of the newly attained superior status. Therefore, ego suddenly draws a line between self and old associates with whom there has been a comfortable and informal relationship of equality so far. The ego seems to convey the message that the way things went earlier between them now needs to be changed. And they are expected not to cross the line demarcated by mind-ego.

It is but natural that the old associate's feel surprised witnessing this unexpected transformation in their old friend, especially when they have grown up, studied, played, and spent the most memorable phases of their lives together. But then, they willingly accept the newly drawn line. But if one of them agrees with this new relationship equation without any surprise or hesitation, then there must be a secret motive behind it. The mind-ego of a so-called ordinary being always wants to be associated with the mind-ego of a so-called important-being for only one purpose, which is to become bigger and safer.

Quality of Selflessness

However, Prince Rama is definitely not the one who allows the mind-ego to trap Him in the new identity of a King. Instead, He sets an example for others on how to deal with the new power equation in an unexpected but most appropriate manner. As such, His friends were amazed at the immense modesty of their very own Ram. Today the relationship status has definitely changed. But the superior position was attained by not Rama but the friends. Lord says that the 'Niswarth Bhava' or selflessness of His friends has put them in a higher place than His. He felt that acceptance of the throne has made Him smaller in front of his friends. Ram tells them very humbly that tonight, by congratulating Him with their hearts open without any trace of bitterness or jealousy, they have attained a higher position. Hence, today He gave them high respect. Selflessness is always given a higher order in 'Sanatan Dharma' than power and position. Lord knows that change in the relationship equation pains the lesser privileged one the most. But in His friends, there was no trace of pain and no manipulation of mind-ego, rather a glow of Renunciation of ego.

The ones who are considered as friends by the Lord Himself cannot be ordinary mortal beings. They are the devotees who have won over the traps of mind-ego. Since childhood, His friends have always shared their possessions with the Lord, but today the Lord says that He has become very selfish by not sharing the throne, which he received as a gift based on his birthright and not on the merits. Today He feels embarrassed and inferior for his selfish act and, therefore, wants to honor His large-hearted friends with extreme affinity.

Meaning of Friendship

The impact of Lord's heart pouring submission was such that His friends, while returning from the palace, had their eyes moistened. Listening to the soul-stirring words of the Lord, they couldn't stop praising the heartfelt affinity, love, and humility of their dear friend, Ram. Their only wish was, if they are born again, they must spend their lives serving their heartiest pal Lord Ram.

The act of newly attained power by one usually infuses a sense of bitterness to lesser privileged others towards him. In contrast, one's humility in rising grandeur evokes a divine 'Bhava' or feeling of love in others towards him. Ram-Rajya essentially means where love and respect must come from inside without any compulsions or obligations whatsoever. Loyalty cannot be inherited. It is to be earned. By contemplating on Lord Ram's mannerisms that gave Him massive followership, one will automatically absorb and demystify the divine qualities. One will easily attain the highest position in all the worlds by just surrendering in the lotus feet of Lord Ram.

Now, how does one achieve greatness? Is it merely by the material success that comes with selfish endeavors, or is it by attainment of others' love and loyalty that comes with selfless actions? What is the use of spirituality, religion, or devotion if the self-seeking sense of superiority still remains there? What is the essence of real leadership? Is it just earning followership by selling hatred and capitalizing on fears, or is it by setting examples of endearment and equality?

True Relationship

Relationships are a lifelong journey that cannot be the same throughout. No matter who is rising and who is falling, only thoughtful behavior ensures longevity in a relationship. Lord's highly matured way of handling relationships may be contrary to the present norms of our society, but critically ask yourself when did our society, with its thousands of years' history, last acted maturely? When did collectively as a society, we have contemplated managing relationships wisely? The excitement of worldly success and frustrations of failures overshadow the light of 'Vivek' or intelligence.

However, 'Viveki' or wise ones, who practice righteousness and awareness, who know how to value both outer and inner relationships. The most important relationship is not outside but is the one which the being has with his own 'Self.' Self is not a physical identity but is a reflection of the Supreme. Realization of Supreme, that is valuing the relationship with self, ensures peace, prosperity, and highly rewarding life. Just like Prince Ram's friends went to congratulate Him without any hesitation and ill-feeling, beings too must approach Him wholeheartedly. In return, Supreme Lord Ram places them at a higher position than Himself.

Chapter 2.6

Curse of Kaikeyi: Insecurities are Loud

What did I think of and what just happened,
Because of one woman, everything got ruined.

A Bolt from the Blue

That night Kaikeyi, the second queen of King Dasaratha and mother of Prince Bharata, was burning with anger and jealousy. The evil fire of Manthara had encapsulated her. King Dasratha was concerned when he got the news that she had entered the 'Kop-Bhawan', the private chamber. He nervously entered the chamber and inquired about the matter from her. Then an unexpected and shocking thing happened, which totally destroyed the spirit of Dasaratha. Kaikeyi, asked for her two boons, which was given by the King to her, a long time ago. First, she demanded that instead of Ram, the next morning her own son Bharata must be crowned as the next King of Ayodhya Empire. Hearing such an uncustomary request, Dasratha got very disappointed, but he agreed to it. But the second demand of Kaikeyi shattered him into pieces. It was because she asked that Prince Ram should be sent to forest exile for fourteen years to live a life of an ascetic.

Story of Kaikeyi

Now the question is why Dasaratha agreed to such selfish demands of Kaikeyi despite his utter disappointment? Ever since the two met, King Dasratha was not just smitten by Queen Kaikeyi's alluring beauty, but also by her larger than life qualities. Queen Kaushalya was a woman of reserve and serious nature, while Queen Sumitra was the symbol of selfless service. Thus it was only Kaikeyi, with whom Dasaratha could relish the games of romance and physical intimacy. She was bright, extroverted, sharp, beautiful, and had a great persona that was appreciated by all. Not just that, she was also a courageous and skilled warrior who participated in wars with the King. In the past, in a war against Asura, she once saved Dasratha's life by aligning the wheels of their royal cart with her fingers, thereby not letting the cart to disassemble until they reached a safe zone. Dasratha admired her for this brave and intelligent feat and rewarded her with two boons, which she could ask any time in their conjugal life. Being a sensible and wise person, Kaikeyi didn't accept the boons that time as she considered her act as nothing extraordinary but a wife's duty towards her husband.

At the time of marriage, it was decided between Kaikeyi's father and Dasratha that in future, her son, and no other queens' sons, will be the first successor to the throne of Ayodhaya. She was indeed large-hearted then as she didn't mind giving up this right. Later on, seeing the great qualities of affectionate Ram, she herself urged Dasaratha and insisted on making Ram the King. Kaikeyi always thought in terms of larger interest and for the welfare of the empire. Her nobility and acumen were appreciated not only by Ayodhaya but also by other empires. Her aura overshadowed the modest and humble personalities of Queen Kaushalya and Sumitra, and yet there were no traces of ill-feeling between the three queens.

Dasratha felt fortunate to have a towering persona like Kaikeyi as his wife. However, no matter how a mighty structure may look beautiful from the exterior, only a strong internal foundation can ensure its longevity. Similarly, appearance can be impressive, but what is more important is the 'Bhava' or the intention of the being. Behind every beautiful outer aura, the trap of mind-ego remains hidden. It makes the foundation of life so vulnerable that even in a small quake, the whole massive structure collapses. The same happened with Kaikeyi.

Her Conditional Love

'Rajo Guna' or the mode of passion was dominant in Kaikeyi. She was hungry for name and fame. She always had an intense craving for respect and appreciation. There was a good reason why she was so affectionate towards Prince Ram. When Manthara first tried to paint a negative picture of Lord, Kaikeyi defended Ram, saying that out of all mothers, He respects and loves her the most. She even tested the authenticity of Rama's feelings many a time before and found His endearment for her, unaltered. Rama's true sentiments had successfully passed all tests.

Kaikeyi failed to realize that love is not an object of the test, and that true feelings are never conditional to show off. The 'Bhava' or heartfelt feelings are always pure and pious. Kaikeyi doubted the affinity of Ram and wanted to check if it is consistent and not fake. A mother, doubting a son's affection, is apprehended as a shallow thinker. Insecurity is a lethal trap of mind-ego which wants to check and ensure others' loyalty again and again. A positive response makes it feel satisfied, important, and superior.

Before serving a meal, it is always sensible to be careful about the choices and tastes of the guests. There was always a hunger of respect, acknowledgment, and superiority in Kaikeyi's heart, and therefore, the 'Creator of Universe' Lord Ram served her what she wanted. The simple-hearted Kaushalaya and Sumitra were not attention seekers like her, and so Lord didn't try to practise the same with them. Lord loved all His three mothers equally and ensured servings that suited the tastes of each one of them.

Egoistical Agreement

Love is not dependent on speech and expression. It is silent and makes one peaceful, not loud. It's the trap of mind-ego that doesn't let beings appreciate true feelings. Beings are foolishly attracted to expressive and loud gestures. Beings display fake intimacy just to please the other one. Why is other people's sense of satisfaction so vital for us? Mind-ego likes to form newer and stronger partnerships. It loves to be appreciated, always. Unreal but loud expressions of affection are an unspoken agreement between the two parties. Since 'I' have given 'You' a sense of self-importance, so 'You' must also ensure the same for 'Me.' This will make both of 'Us' feel important and special in others' eyes. Self-importance serves as oxygen for the mind-ego, which makes it feel alive and expanding. The only objective of the mind-ego is to see acceptance for itself in everyone.

Love is Fearless

Manthara misled Kaikeyi showing her an imaginary horrific future where if Rama becomes the King, she will fall from her important and superior position. Manthara didn't stop here and further explained that being the mother of the King, the highest position will go to Queen Kaushalaya, who then will treat Kaikeyi like a maidservant, and she will have no option but to obey her orders as a subordinate. Dasratha and Lord Rama will not intervene in Kaushalaya's affairs, and Kaikeyi will forever rot in this hell-like palace. Mind-ego can be very creative in designing a negative situation. Manthara played a trick, but if Kaikeyi had the least sense, she could have questioned, did anything happen in so many years which hints towards an adverse situation like this? Did Kaushalaya, Dasratha, or Prince Ram ever make her feel lesser? The influence of insecurity is such that it totally overshadows the 'Vivek' or intelligence and compels beings to take a drastic step, which only ruins lives.

'Tolerate their misunderstanding' - Lao Tzu.

Lord Rama did not just tolerate the injustice, but he continued loving His mother, Kaikeyi, the way he used to, even after knowing the cause of her insecurity towards Him. The message He gave to mankind was that the power of love and tolerance is much superior to insecurity, hatred, and jealousy. There will be tests and trials in life, but ultimately 'Love' will emerge victorious. By taking refuge in the lotus feet of Lord Rama, one will always find the strength to tolerate all worldly chaos and be able to tread on the testing path of Love.

CHAPTER 2.7

Curse of Kaikeyi : Who is the Real Culprit?

Crowning of Ram will bring glory to His mother, not you,
Make your son the King, and your dreams will come true.

Lust for Power

Lord Ram always held mother Kaikeyi in high regard more than anybody else. He admired her day and night like a true-hearted son, yet her hunger for respect and importance was not satisfied. Not just Prince Ram, but she desired that everybody should acknowledge that 'Ram is Kaikeyi's son.' In the History of Ayodhaya, she wanted to be mentioned as the mother of King Ram. But she also knew that practically it was not possible in this lifetime. Now the question is, why was she so desperate to be known as Ram's mother? Why couldn't she relish motherhood of the greatest symbol of Dharma, Prince Bharata?

The only reason was her Rajoguna (the intense urge for name and fame) because of which she neglected the pure and divine affection of Ram and Bharata. The distinct qualities of Bharata were not known to the people of Ayodhaya until the announcement of the crowning of Prince Ram as King. Bharata was not as popular a figure as Ram, and therefore Kaikeyi's mind-ego was attracted to the towering achievements of Lord Ram, whose glory had already spread in all directions. Ram had single-handedly destroyed Tadka, Marichi, and Subahu and gave protection to the Sages in the forest. He even broke the mighty bow of Shiva, which thousands of contenders together couldn't even lift. As the whole world acknowledged the heroism of Ram, the ever-growing hunger of Kaikeyi's ambitious mind-ego could be satisfied only by becoming a mother of such an eminent personality. Neither Dasratha nor anybody else could realize the underlying thoughts of Kaikeyi, and thus they became utterly shocked by the sudden change in her.

Threat to Her Ambitions

Meanwhile, Kaikeyi was sure that as Ram loved her the most, so when he would become the King, she would be recognized as the mother of the King and honored not only in Ayodhaya but in the whole Land of Bharata. But that night, Manthra tricked her mind by convincing her that it will be Kaushalaya who would be recognized as Ram's mother and not her. This one thought made her insecure towards her position and aspirations at once. By maneuvering the boons of Dasratha to make Bharata the King, and send Ram to exile, she just wanted to safeguard her interests. She thought that since Bharata is her real son, she would now definitely get the desired recognition as King's mother.

It was not about 'My' son or 'Her' son, it was just about 'I, Me & Myself.' Mind-ego can stoop to any level for its self-vested interest. Not only Ram and Bharat, but she played with the future of the entire Ayodhaya Empire for her selfish purposes. That night Kaikeyi's insecurity and hunger for recognition overshadowed the purest relation of child-mother. She was so stubborn that no reasoning or advice could change her stance.

Here one must try to understand why the attributes of recognition, self-importance, and Rajoguna were so dominant in Kaikeyi? The nature of a being in the present is the result of the causes and effects of past Karma. Now one may ask, was Manthra responsible for Kaikeyi's wrongful deed? The answer is, "No." Manthra was just a spark that fuelled the flame of Kaikyei's ambitions, which was already lit. Was Kaikeyi the reason for Lord Ram and Sita's suffering? No, beings are just a medium. Everything is programmed by universal intelligence. Can the wrongful deeds be justified based on this reasoning? Of course, not. Right or wrong ideas may sprout in a being's mind anytime, like a thought, but the execution of that idea is in his hands that is, the final choice always remains with the being. Is Kaikeyi a villain? No, not exactly. It is because when Lord Himself never held any grudges for her, who are we, the mortal beings, to put the villain tag on her. We must not forget that Mother Kaikeyi spent the rest of her life in self-abasement and penance after realizing her mistake. She was accepted not just by Lord, but also by everybody from Raghukula.

Chapter 2.8

Ram, the Target : Tolerance is not a Sign of Weakness

It is the first time I am seeing such a thing happening in the palace,
Let me hurriedly bring Ram here, for only His presence ensures solace.

As we thoroughly go through Ramayana, we come to know about three types of beings. First, the one who, because of the fear of obstacles, doesn't even take any initiative. Sugriva was among them who, instead of confronting Bali for abducting his wife, ran away from Kishkinda and took shelter in a safe zone. Second, who do initiate work, but when they face any obstacles, deviate from the path they set to follow. Vanar Sena was like them, who enthusiastically shouldered the task of searching for Mother Sita. But when they couldn't find her, they gave up and thought of ending their lives.

Third, are the great ones, who, no matter what the situation is, do not stop until they have achieved the goal. They are the perfect ones who always do the right job, at the right time. Lord Hanumana faced many obstacles and challenges, but he acted as needed at that time and didn't return without getting the news of Mother Sita. Then beyond all these types, there is one and only 'Maryada Purushottam Raja' Ram,who taught the world how to conduct life in the most unexpected and extremely adverse situations.

King Dasratha's heart sank, seeing the adamance of Kaikeyi. The thought that tormented him the most was that because of his boons, innocent Ram is being punished for no fault of his. He fell on the floor numb and lost the sense of his surroundings. Kaikeyi called the minister Sumantra and asked him to bring Ram immediately. She ignored Sumantra's concern for the King and asked him to follow the order. Seeing the situation, Sumantra got very concerned and hurriedly rushed to bring Prince Ram.

Obedience is an Act of Faith

Now the question is why Kaikeyi insisted on calling Ram and didn't reveal anything to Sumantra or anybody else? Kaikeyi was very sure that in the whole of Ayodhaya, one person who would never disobey her even when the orders were against him, is her son, Ram. Even Manthara knew this fact, and that is why while corrupting Kaikeyi's mind, she didn't target Ram. Instead, she portrayed Kaushalya as a villainess. She knew that it's easy to trick mind-ego and create insecurity in the mind of Kaikeyi by picking Kaushalya. Kaushalaya and Kaikeyi were co-wives, which means they were at par in position. However, as Kaushalaya was older in age, she had the upper hand. Commonly, beings display large-heartedness towards juniors and respect towards seniors. It's only with equals that a feeling of competition, comparison, and insecurity prevail.

Manthara shrewdly plotted the scene where both the schemer as well as conspirer is Kaushalaya. Ram is just a puppet in her mother's hand. Kaikeyi always believed that Ram is pure, vulnerable, and innocent and, therefore, he will never disobey her. And if Dasaratha refuses to accept her demands, he would be blamed for being a liar and also considered a black spot on Raghukul. So he, too, will honor his promise. When both Ram and Dasratha would accept her demands, there would be no option left with Kaushalya but to accept Kaikeyi's demand without any protest. In this way, by making Bharata the King, Kaikeyi would attain the highest position and put an end to Kaushalaya's threat forever.

Just like Prince Sidhartha of Lumbini, Lord Ram was also kept away from any sorrow, pain, or tragedies. Father Dasratha had given special instruction to the teachers and mentors not to expose Ram to anything which could pain his heart. It was, therefore, the first occasion that Ram would witness such dreadful circumstances.

The most historical moment ever of not just Ramyana but in the history of the world was that moment when Lord Ram accepted Kaikeyi's orders. Generally, in the lifetime of a being, there occur only one or two extreme events, which alter the entire course of life. Mostly these are the daily petty matters or insignificant criticism or misbehavior or manipulations, which keep on bothering us. Often we feel life is unfair to us. So whenever an intense grudge surfaces in your heart towards the unfair treatment of life, just remind yourself the way Lord Ram accepted the harshest judgment ever passed by a mother to a son. And take refuge in the lotus feet of Lord Ram to get the strength to tolerate. Remember, tolerance is the most courageous human quality, which is rarely found. It's only one in millions who attain the position of 'Mahaveera'.

Chapter 2.9

Exemplary Acceptance of Ram : Finding Bliss

No person, place or time can influence happiness,
For the one who trusts the Supreme consciousness.

Expect the Unexpected

Prince Ram got very concerned when he saw the troubled state of his father Dasratha. He at once inquired from mother Kaikeyi about what went wrong, to which Kaikeyi replied in single breadth, "Your father is unable to bestow the two boons he has promised me. On the one hand, there is 'Dharma' or righteousness, while on the other hand, there is 'Moha' or attachment for a dutiful son." Anxiously she spoke, "Ram only you can pacify your father, and only you, by accepting the conditions, can solve the crisis and give peace to your father."

Normally, human-beings get very worried when they are confronted with any unexpected adverse situations in life. But if the being tries to view who is the creator of the situation and search for an answer to 'why' of the situation, then he would possibly smile and shine just like Lord Ram did, when he heard his mother's curses for him. Kaikeyi may have lost trust in the virtues of her son, but Ram's forever feeling of faith, love, and devotion for his mother's endearment never ever swayed, even by a bit. The mother who feeds sweet sugar to her child does not hesitate to give bitter medicine if it's necessary for her child's health and wellbeing. The child, who sees a mother's affection only in sweetness and not in bitterness, cannot be a deserving child. After hearing his mother's conditions, Lord Ram felt elated.

People Doesn't Matter

Whatever situations, whether good or bad, beings experience in life, revolves around three external factors - PERSON, PLACE & TIME. Whatever be the experience, whether joyful or sorrowful, if it is dependent on external factors, it can never be real and stable. And therefore, Prince Ram, for his state of eternal bliss, never depended on any person, place or time. Had it been so, you could well imagine what his state of mind would be, on hearing the order of exile to the forest on the very day of his crowning ceremony.

Had his state of bliss been based on Kaikeyi and her endearment, then after seeing a wicked transformation in her, he would have been utterly devastated. That night, the venom of hatred and revenge had completely spread in the mind-ego of Kaikeyi, and the only thing she intended was to weaken Kaushalya by making Ram suffer. But Lord Ram knew that no person, be it his own mother, can spoil the 'Ananda' or true bliss that forever remains inside every being. He always believed and trusted the 'Sat-Chit-Anand' or 'Truth-Consciousness-Bliss' attributes of Self.

Place Doesn't Matter

Now, if Ram's joy was solely dependent on the place, that is the Kingdom of Ayodhaya, then don't you think the harsh orders of leaving Ayodhaya and dwelling in the forest for fourteen long years would have shaken the core of his existence? But he believed that life is an ongoing journey, and the city of Ayodhaya is just a temporary halt. And that is why without wasting a single moment, he very effortlessly left Ayodhaya and excitedly ventured on the 'road less travelled.'

Time Doesn't Matter

Again, if Ram had believed that his good time had ended and bad time set forth, then the moment he heard about the curse would have been extremely harrowing for him. But the 'Supreme Blissful' Ram neither lived in Past nor in Future. He very well knew that the Past only gives 'remorse' while the Future only gives rise to 'worries.' The truth, beingness, and bliss are always in the present moment and nowhere else. He never averted or delayed anything because he knew that anything could be influenced, but nothing can affect the 'Power of Now.'

Lord Ram has declared that whoever reads, follows, and sees Him and believes in his 'Darshana' will attain the permanent state of bliss which no person, place, or time can dare to influence. He wants to bless all beings with that potent strength, with which they don't have to expect anything from the world, not even from the Supreme Lord Himself. Lord Ram doesn't say that *'I am Supreme, ask from me.'* Instead, He wants the being to realize that whatever is Supreme, is already there inside, in the 'Self' and that beings don't need to ask for anything from anybody or anywhere.

But we all know where the problem lies. The influence of mind-ego, worldliness and Maya' is so immensely powerful that even after trying hard and practising righteousness consistently, we still get bothered. In fact, all our efforts or 'Purushartha' has limitations. But what is beyond all worldly boundaries, and 'Maya' is 'Surrender' or 'Samparna Bhava.' We need to unconditionally Surrender all our attachments relating to person, place, and time in the lotus feet of Lord Ram and attain the never-ending Bliss or 'Anand,' which is our eternal truth.

Chapter 2.10

Inspiring Words of Ram : Power of Words

Just as a seasoned traveler leaves no tracks,
A good speech lacks fault-finding & threats.

Hearing the unexpected conditions of Queen Kekayi, Prince Ram replies, "Fortunate is that son who follows the instructions of his parents. Look, mother, he is one in a million who can give happiness to parents. I am really blessed as now I will also be able to meet the great sages and saints who dwell in the forest. On top of that, I have my father's and your permission."

Let us set aside the real identity of Lord Ram that he is Supreme God and consider him as an ordinary mortal, and then see that his qualities as a human being are remarkable and learnable. The popularity he amassed among people of not just in Ayodhaya but also everywhere else was not because of his divinity but his mannerism. Goswami Tulsidas says that even enemies like Ravana praised him. His behavior and especially his speech and selection of words would melt the heart of the rocks.

Man's Beauty is in his Tongue

Incorrect speech with inappropriate words is the one biggest factor that creates confusion among beings. Commonly an unfavourable situation evokes undesirable emotions in beings, which have a tremendous impact on their speech. For example, hearing the curse of Kaikeyi, an ordinary person would have replied with hatred, authority, and anger. The tongue has very little tolerance towards distasteful food and also with unkind experiences. Tongue forgets that it itself has to bear with distasteful food. But it is someone else who has to bear tongue's offensive speech. As a being is careful about the choice of food he eats, he must also be very cautious with his speech. But only the one, who blooms like a lotus in muddy water, can be careful with both words and speech and still maintain composure in overwhelming times.

In archery, putting an arrow on the bow and hitting the desired target with absolute accuracy and right velocity requires a good amount of skill and practise. Similarly, delivering a good speech is also a skill. It requires intellect, control, balance and farsightedness. Vedic scriptures say that one cannot expect a decent and reliable speech from four kinds of beings, and they are diseased, retarded, possessed, and intoxicated. One who is not infected with any of them and yet speaks thoughtlessly actually has little control over his mind. Be it archery or speech, one thing that is imperative in achieving excellence in any department of life is 'Alertness.' No matter what the situation, experience, or emotion is, one who doesn't lose alertness of mind manages life splendidly.

In front of Kaikeyi, the Sun of Raghukul, Ram was standing with the familiar radiating face and a beaming smile, which she had always witnessed on him since his childhood. Her speech was so intimidating that every being of Ayodhaya was intensely hurt, so much so that King Dasratha lost his life. Surprisingly, one who was the main target and who ought to be the most hurt from her deadly attack was standing with the same bliss and unfazed stature as always. The poison of her words was utterly defeated by the extraordinary calmness of Lord Ram.

On the stage, a good orator makes thousands of spectators spellbound just with his speech. But many a time, in day to day life, hearing the same orator appears like someone has stripped the beautiful ornaments of an ugly being and revealed his real appearance. One can stage fake speech to please others, but not for long. Still, fakeness has become the ornament of every being because it is an instrument of mind-ego to influence others.

Priority Matters

Keep aside the fact that Lord Ram is Almighty for a moment and learn from his composed reply in the most agonizing situation one can ever experience. Try to understand the point that no matter what the circumstances are, one must not lose control of mind, and only then delivering a delightful speech becomes possible. Ultimately the question that one must keep on asking himself is, 'What is the priority of my life'? If it is name, fame, and wealth, then he becomes pretty vulnerable to attacks like that of Kaikeyi.

But if it's fulfilment of the purpose of life, then nothing can disturb the innate peace because every being contains in 'Self' all the fixings required to achieve perfection. Just an awareness of the fact that devoting and surrendering life in the lotus feet of Lord Ram is the only purpose of life gives tremendous power to the being. The being can then triumph over the deadliest threats, attacks, and challenges of the world effortlessly.

Chapter 2.11

Lord Ram visits Mother Kaushalya : Power of Bhakti

Situation and reaction - it takes two to tango,
Fear and attraction are the cause of all mumbo-jumbo.

Nobody can deny the fact that the primary cause of Prince Ram's exile is both Manthra and Kaikeyi. Still, to some extent, mother Kaushalaya too didn't play wisely. All this while she was very excited about Ram's crowning and her becoming the mother of the King of Ayodhaya. In this enthusiasm, she completely ignored or better to say took for granted Kaikeyi's expectations. Although Queen Kaushalaya had pure feelings with no ill intention for anybody, however, being the eldest and seniormost after Dasratha, she needed to be extra careful and sensitive. Since the very beginning, she was well aware of the ambitious and egotistical nature of Kekayi. Had she given little importance to her expectations and dealt with responsibility and understanding, Manthra would have never succeeded in poisoning Kaikeyi's mind.

To err is human, but to be perfect is Ram.

That night Queen Kaushalaya was sitting alone in her palace, eagerly looking forward to the next day's crowning ceremony of her loving son Ram. Soon Prince Ram came to meet her with a smiling and radiating face as always and touched her feet. She blessed and embraced him for many moments. Lord gently spoke - "Father has given me the kingdom of the forest, which in all aspects is very beneficial for me. Please give me your blessings with a happy heart, so that my journey ahead gets filled with joy and success."

Kaushalaya's motherly embrace was filled with the joy and comfort for Ram, yet the temptation of her embrace could not divert Lord Ram from 'Dharma' or the path of righteousness. Not even for a moment did he think of rejecting the exile orders given by his stepmother and stay back for his real mother.

Fear and Attraction

Almost all human-beings are governed by two factors, fear and attraction. These two forces drive them towards 'Adharma' or unrighteousness. Often we see that whoever is indulged in clever and wrongful pursuits achieve success, such as Ravana, who created Lanka of gold and ruled the world. Seeing such offenders flourish in their lives, others also get tempted to follow the same path of unrighteousness or 'Adharma.' To restrain this unlawful thought, Vedanta states about the Law of Karma, which clearly says - the cause and effect of all deeds do not begin or end with birth and death of the being's physical body. Instead, the account is carried forward to the next birth with the subtle body or consciousness of the being. And nobody can escape the consequences of his right and wrong actions or 'Paap & Punya.' Therefore it can be concluded that every being must be very cautious with his conduct in order to have a trouble-free tomorrow. Although the purpose of the Law of Karma is to contain the unrighteous instincts of human-beings, unfortunately it hadn't seen much success in doing so.

Study of Ramayana inculcates the 'Satoguna Vritti' or the pure instinct, which leads to 'Bhakti.' Unlike the Karma theory, Bhakti effortlessly and joyfully replaces the contradicting thoughts of fear and attraction with the evergreen virtues of wisdom and love, thereby leading to righteous actions. All the principal characters of Ramyana were able to rise above their fears and attractions with the incarnation of Lord Ram in their lives.

Pran jaye par Vachan na Jayi.

Kaushalaya was kind of an opportunity for Prince Ram to declare Kaikeyi's orders as null and void. Had Ram had the slightest of attraction for the throne of Ayodhaya, he could have easily said, "I am not interested in accepting the throne, but for a son, mother's position is superior to father. Therefore for the satisfaction of my real Mother Kaushalaya, I got to accept the throne." Every being of Ayodhaya would have happily agreed to Ram's verdict, and nobody, not even Kaikeyi, would have dared to say anything against him. But we must not forget that here we are talking about none other than 'Maryada Purushottam' Ram, who cannot be influenced by any sort of worldly attachment. And therefore, he didn't let Kaushalaya's affection and aspiration divert him from his firm determination and word of honour.

This was only the first incident with many more to follow wherein Lord Ram sets an example to make the beings realize that *'Your commitment is more important than your life.'* We must learn from Lord Ram that righteousness is superior to even a mother's love. And therefore, no matter what happens in life, the devotee of Lord Ram must not compromise on values. Devotee must also try and establish in himself the vision of Ram-Rajya, which is not only his ultimate destination but also his quintessential destiny.

Chapter 2.12

Ifs and Buts put to an End

Lord never took decisions emotionally,
Instead, He looked after the larger interests logically.

The Promise

Like all previous times, this time, too, Lord Ram was firm in following the forest exile orders diligently, though it was against the wishes of everybody. Many 'Ifs' & 'Buts' were raised, but Lord clarified each one of them with both logic and righteousness. It is only through understanding His perspective meticulously that the seeker can get priceless insights on dealing with challenging life situations.

The first objection was that, if King Dasaratha was obliged to fulfil Queen Kaikeyi's promise, then he was also obliged to fulfil the promise of crowning Ram as the King of Ayodhaya. By ordering Ram to go to forest exile, he was honouring one promise but, at the same time, breaking another promise. Dasratha himself said to Ram that he has all the right not to accept the forest exile order. More than Kaikayi's curses, Dasratha felt guilty for breaking his promise to Ram.

But Prince Ram clarified this dilemma and safeguarded his father's honour. By giving the Ayodhaya Kingdom to Bharata, he has fulfilled his promise he made to Kekayi. And by giving me the throne of the forest, he also kept his promise, which he gave to Ram. Ram further clarified that the forest region is larger than the city region of Ayodhaya Kingdom. So considering both in terms of area and responsibility, Dasratha has given more to Ram than Bharata. In this way, according to Ram, his father, Dasaratha, has successfully accomplished both the obligations.

No Time to Waste

Before the announcement of crowning, Bharat left with Shatrughan to meet

Bharat's ailing maternal grandfather 'King Kaikay.' The other objection was why Ram was in so much haste to execute the orders the very next morning. Ram could wait until Bharata returns, and make his final decision then. To this, Lord replied, "Both me and Bharata are given separate kingdoms, and since I am the elder one, I must be first crowned as the king. Secondly, today is also the auspicious time or 'Mahurat' for my crowning. Therefore I must not wait till the arrival of Bharat, and I must immediately take up the responsibility that father has entrusted me with."

Actually, the underlying fact is that Ram very well knew that under no circumstances, his dear brother Bharata would allow him to leave Ayodhaya. Bharata was devoted to Lord Ram to the extent that he would have even ended his own life rather than letting him leave Ayodhaya. But Ram also knew that his forest exile is 'Vidhi ka Vidhan' or 'Will of Supreme.' Secondly, there is also a much greater life purpose, which he needs to fulfil. So just to avoid the hurdle of Bharata's pure love, he decided to leave Ayodhya before Bharata returns.

Here Lord wants to give us a message that nothing is more important than the purpose of life. Whenever 'Maya' observes that one is going to accomplish his life goal, Maya puts hurdles of fear, temptation, and attachment in his path. That's the most significant role of Maya. She creates conditions that give fear (Kaikeyi's curse), temptation (Kaushalaya's embrace), and 'Bandhan' or boundation (Bharata's attachment). The point is that no matter what the hurdles are, one must always look for ethical solutions and religiously stick to his path.

Forest Throne

Everyone knows about great rulers and fascinating kingdoms, but it's the first time in history that we hear about something as unusual as the throne of the 'forest.' It appears as if the Lord is tricking us again by giving the logic of the forest throne. But Lord had a very sound and in-depth reason behind saying that, which only a visionary and highly intelligent or 'Viveki' King can think of. According to Lord, by ignoring the forest region of the kingdom, the rulers have committed a grave mistake. Empire doesn't mean the cities and capital only. A ruler's duty and accountability do not end only by working towards the development of cities. History is filled with incidents where, by neglecting the forest region, the Kings had given the scope and opportunity to enemies to invade and attack their kingdoms.

King Dasratha believed that his kingdom is safe and secure and that he has been a successful ruler. Yet, Vishvamitra had to walk hundreds of miles himself to inform him about the brutality of Asura in the forest region. Khar and Dushan, the evil cousins of Ravana, had already established their cantonment with an army of fourteen thousand demons in the Dandakaranya forest, which was inside the borders of Ayodhaya Empire. Thousands of innocent beings and sages of the forest had already lost their lives. Despite that, Dasratha was ruling peacefully in the comfort of his palace. The royalty was, therefore, only satisfied with the fact that Ayodhaya city was safe, peaceful, and prospering while conveniently believing that everything was alright in their empire.

Lord Ram, therefore, didn't want to let go of this opportunity of forest exile. He knew that the throne of Ayodhaya city was just an obligation where his skills, competence, and power are of little use. Therefore he gave himself a paramount purpose to execute his divine capabilities. In fact, he himself wanted to go for forest exile to provide protection to his people and also to set an example for other kingdoms.

Objectives of Forest Exile

Lord Ram was also well aware of the fact that to free the world from Ravana's evil grip, the holy war was imperative. But the question was, what would be the way of war? Whether it will be fought from Ayodhaya city or from its forest region? He contemplated that Dasratha's situation was not only vulnerable, but he also was not at all fit for a battle against the mighty Ravana. Secondly, because of his fatherly attachment, he would have never let his son Ram fight the deadly war. So, in that case, His job of eradicating evil would be left incomplete. Understandably, Lord felt that to get engrossed in the apparent and available pleasures of Ayodhaya city is sheer foolishness. He knew that to achieve greatness, one requires to leave the comfort zone and venture on a challenging path.

Finally, forest exile was like a blessing for Him because great sages, yogis, and devotees dwell in the forest region. Ram strongly believed that by regularly having their 'Darshan' and gaining knowledge from them, one acquires immensely beneficial spiritual strength, which leads to wellbeing and perfection. So he discarded all fancy princely costumes and wore the modest attire of an ascetic. But he didn't forget to take his weapons because he was going there as the protector of the forest. Moreover, as per 'Kshatriya' customs, a warrior must always remain prepared.

Here we must understand that Lord Ram took human avatar for a purpose, and that purpose could only be fulfilled by leaving Ayodhaya. Manthra, Keikayi, and others are just instruments of 'Leela' or divine play. Their role is just to act in sync with the Lord's purpose. In our lives, we tend to get worried at once when we see an unfavourable situation. Also, we always find faults and blame others for our troubles. But most of the time, we fail to understand the cause of the situation and the possibilities that lie ahead. Point is to realize that every person and situation that affects us is actually acting in sync with our life's purpose. It is our non-acceptance and misinterpretation of the situation that leads us to unhappiness.

The bottom line is that like Lord Ram, every situation, whether favourable or unfavourable, ought to be embraced wholeheartedly and acted upon with full courage and enthusiasm to achieve higher goals and the purpose of our life. Consistent contemplation and unconditional Bhakti of Ram will eventually give rise to the forgotten spiritual powers in Self and take the human-being to the greatness for which he actually takes birth.

Chapter 2.13

Sumitra enlightens Laxman : Meaning of Sacrifice

Both you and I are very fortunate and blessed,
For you have devoted your life to Ram and progressed.

Laxman's obstinacy

Lord Ram tried His best, but he finally had to accept defeat in front of Laxman's incorrigible obstinacy to accompany Him to the forest exile. Ram knew well that once Laxman decides something, then nothing can change his decision. But before leaving for the forest, Ram asked Laxman to take the permission and blessing of Mother Sumitra. It may appear to us that since Sumitra is the real mother of Laxman, Ram asked him to do so. But there are always deep and insightful reasons behind every action of Ram, and things are not as simple and straightforward as we perceive them to be.

Sumitra, who also symbolizes 'Upasana' or Devotion, instead of feeling depressed like ordinary beings, got really content in sending her son for the forest exile to serve his 'Ishta Ram.' Although both her sons Ram-Laxman were going on a fourteen years exile, yet very unlikely for a mother, she didn't come out to bid them adieu. It is because she had absolute faith in her God and, therefore, left everything on Him. She just stayed inside being engrossed and surrendered in her 'Upasana.' Undoubtedly, such a notable instance of faith is rare to find in the history of Sanatan Dharma.

Essence of 'Tyaga'- Renunciation

Today Laxman, the symbol of 'Tyaga,' was sacrificing name, fame, power, wealth, luxuries, comforts, security, and relationships and leaving with Ram for forest exile of fourteen years. It was no surprise because he never wanted anything else from life except the 'Seva' or service of his loved 'Bhaiya,' Ram. However, what is the real essence of Ultimate Renunciation or 'SarvaTyaga'? Many seekers in the excitement of spiritual ambitions renounce their homes but soon give up as they cannot live without family and material belongings. Question to them is, why is there a need to leave home for the spiritual quest? Aren't they merely interested in getting other's attention and applause? Deep inside, aren't they actually expecting respect for renouncing worldliness? Like all worldly ambitions, there are spiritual ambitions too, wherein undeserving ones in the desire of becoming like Adi Shankracharya or Gautama Buddha or Great Mahavira pretends to have discarded materialism to attain the honour or 'Aadar' reserved for 'Sarva-Tyaga' or Ultimate Renunciation.

However, in spirituality, renunciation does not necessarily require leaving one's home or to display an act of sacrifice to the world. Neither by wearing ascetic robes and emptying pockets, one becomes 'Mahatma' (Great One) nor immolating self wilfully, does one become 'Sati' (Epitome of Self-Sacrifice). In fact, living in the agony of separation from Supreme yet fulfilling all worldly responsibilities without complaining and still always being hopeful of reunification is the greatest Spiritual Practise. This is what Mother Sumitra symbolizes.

Sacrifice of Sumitra

True 'Tyaga' means renunciation of not just family, home, and wealth but also of the desire for recognition. Only one in a million can practice it in absoluteness. Lord Ram knew that Mother Sumitra is the embodiment of absolute devotion and therefore sent Laxman to her as He wanted him to learn the real meaning of renunciation from his mother. Ram wanted to make sure that egoistical thought of self-greatness for sacrificing the worldly possessions does not arise in Laxman's mind. Not just that, He also wanted Laxman to understand and realize that Mother Sumitra's sacrifice is far greater and significant than his.

As soon as Laxman passed on the shocking news of the fourteen years of forest exile of Lord Ram to Sumitra, she couldn't control her feelings and burst into tears at once, though it didn't take her long to clearly understand the rationale. 'The 'Rajoguni Vritti' or 'Self-Centered thought' had played through Kaikeyi,' she thought to herself. Seeing tears in mother's eyes, Laxman got concerned thinking that now mother will possibly stop him from accompanying Lord Ram to the forest exile.

But after hearing Mother Sumitra's thoughtful reply, Laxman was both surprised and embarrassed. He immediately realized that Mother's renunciation is far greater than his renunciation. He also understood the fact that after seeing the ego of 'Tyaga' in him, Lord had purposely sent him to Sumitra for purification. A devotee's mother sacrifices that which is dearest to her, even more than her own life, and that too without expecting anything in return. A devotee like Laxman may get the deserving honour and recognition, but often the sacrifice of the mother goes unnoticed. It is only the mother who bears all the pain of departure of her son and nobody else. Others may empathize but can never feel what the mother endures.

Greatest Dharma

Vedanta says that a son must always obey his mother and father, no matter what. The thought is no doubt noble but is somewhat confusing for a logical mind to understand. From a spiritual perspective, being takes many births, and in every birth, his mother and father are not the same. So under this condition, parents of which birth should be considered as true? And what if there is a difference of opinion between mother and father? By the said condition, what is the 'Dharma' or duty of the son? To whom should he respect more or give more importance, father or mother? Mother Sumitra, the greatest source of wisdom, clarifies this dilemma. She enlightens Laxman that the true mother and father of each and every being are none other than Mother Sita and Maryada Purshottam Ram. Whenever the being contemplates deeply, he will figure out that the relationships of the human body begin and end with this lifetime, but the relationship of the being with the Supreme is beyond the purview of a lifetime or 'Kala' and, therefore, eternal. Hence, every being must only consider the divine connection with the Supreme as real and final and that every worldly relationship is just an extension of being's innate connection with the Supreme.

Discarding anything you possess is a sacrifice or 'Tyaga,' but is there anything in the world that the being can say he possesses? Because whatever he possesses has been bestowed to him by Supreme. And when he doesn't own anything, then what actually is he sacrificing? Sumitra has an answer to this. She says to Laxman that if by any chance, by leaving Ayodhaya for Lord Ram, Laxman considers himself as a great noble one or 'Mahatma,' then it is just a delusion. The Creator and the owner of the universe are one and only Supreme. So only He can claim sacrifice or 'Tyaga.' Lord Ram is the rightful

Ruler of Ayodhaya, which he is sacrificing. Therefore, only Lord ought to be recognized and honoured as 'SarvaTyagi' or Ultimate Renunciator and nobody else.

Ram is the Supreme who had taken human Avatar for the upliftment and greater good of humankind. He didn't even need to arrive on 'PrithviLok' for fulfilling that purpose because He could have accomplished it by just a blink of His eyes. Had Ram not wanted, then the very thought of cursing him for the forest exile would have never aroused in the mind of Kaikeyi. We must know that the cause and source of every inspiration, thought, and idea in our mind is Supreme Ram - ***'Urr Prerak Raghuvansh Vibhushan'***

But then the question arises, what is the purpose of forest exile? Mother Sumitra concludes that the reason for taking Laxman along in the forest exile is to allow him to serve his Lord Ram or do 'Prabhu Seva.' Ram is sacrificing His everything just for brother's sake as Laxman always wanted that only he and nobody else must serve Ram. With these inspiring words, Mother Sumitra wants to instill gratefulness in Laxman. Just for his well-being, Lord has happily accepted the suffering of exile. This is how a devotee must connect himself with his Lord's Leela or story.

Mother Sumitra very well knew that the mind-ego is very clever and immediately shoots thoughts of superiority whenever beings act for others sake. But in reality, beings must be grateful to others for allowing them to serve. Mind-ego doesn't want the being to realize this fact, so it always creates unnecessary thoughts of recognition and respect for his own 'so-called' selfless acts. Therefore the right words at the right time are very much needed to evoke 'Vivek' or intelligence in the seeker so that he always sees and understands the real picture in a higher perspective and be grateful. Ultimately Mother Sumitra is proud of her son Laxman for understanding his purpose of life, which is to wholeheartedly surrender in the Lotus feet of Lord Ram.

Chapter 2.14

Sumitra's Ram : Devotee obliges God

Just like the Day is where the Sun is,
Likewise, Ayodhaya is where the Lord is.

Mother Sumitra aptly rejects any notion that reflects Laxman is bearing any pain or hardship for Lord Ram by accompanying Him to the forest exile. She firmly believed that Ayodhaya is wherever Ram is. Real Ayodhaya is not a geographical entity, rather it is a living consciousness that always follows Ram. Wherever and whenever the name-'Ram' is thought of or uttered, divine Ayodhaya establishes there itself. Ram is the 'Sun' or the cause, and Ayodhaya is the 'Day' or the effect.

Essence of Bhakti

Hearing Sumitra's heartfelt and inspiring words, Laxman was overwhelmed with emotions. He expressed his gratefulness, saying today mother had given him a new insight on 'Tyaga,' sacrifice, and renunciation. He realized that a devotee is just a servant of the Lord, whose only purpose is to serve and be surrendered to Him. A servant has no choice, desire, hope, and wants of his own, and he is totally committed to giving comfort and pleasure to his Master Lord. But the materialistic beings who are under the misleading influence of mind-ego traps that are hatred, jealousy, anger, greed, and cleverness can neither understand the meaning of 'Bhakti' nor can they serve Ram wholeheartedly. Their life is just like a puppet that dances on the whims and fancies of their destructive mind-ego.

Sometimes lust rules, sometimes anger burns,
Sometimes greed manipulates, and sometimes fear resonates.

Whatever the servant or 'Bhakta' possesses is only for one purpose, that is, to serve others for the pleasure of his Lord. Mother Sumitra, in loud and apparent terms, declares that only by giving birth to a 'devotee-child,' a mother accomplishes her purpose of life. If there is a lack of devotion in her child, then it could have been better for that mother to be infertile. Only that tree is useful whose fruits give nutrition and health to others. But if a tree bears poisonous fruit, then by being infertile and fruitless, the tree is actually serving the society better. Its infertility will save many beings from the poison. Devotion is divinity, which uplifts whereas mind-ego is an illness that always degenerates.

Real Mother

Sumitra strongly believes that the focal point of all worldly relations like friend, father, mother, or brother is Supreme. However, it appears to Laxman that there is a contradiction in her statement. On the one hand, Sumitra says that Sita is Laxman's real mother, while on the other hand, she speaks for herself that she is the most fortunate mother to have a son like Laxman. Sumitra explains that in the forest, if Laxman remembers Sumitra as his mother, then he will get distracted from the service of Siya-Ram. But in Ayodhaya, if Sumitra remembers Laxman as her son, then it will bring her closer to Siya-Ram. And hence Laxman must only consider Sita and not Sumitra as his mother, but she will continue to consider him as her son. Here we are witnessing an exceptional occurrence wherein a mother is asking her son not to consider her as his mother anymore.

Indebted Ram

Now the question arises here is, why didn't Lord Ram visit Mother Sumitra himself and inform her about Laxman going with him? Ram has always loved and respected Sumitra as much as Kaushalaya and Kaikeyi, so doesn't he have a moral responsibility towards Sumitra, especially when he is taking her real son Laxman along with him to the forest exile? The answer lies in the fact that Ram sees himself as a borrower or debtor and Sumitra as a lender or creditor. Already Sumitra has given utmost care and love to Ram since his childhood, and now she is offering Laxman, her own son, for His service. Ram feels very indebted to Sumitra, and just like a borrower avoids facing the lender, similarly, He doesn't want to face Mother Sumitra. Ram feels that throughout His life, the mother has only given and never asked for anything. And instead of repaying her or doing something for her, He is again taking away her most precious possession, Laxman.

But the next question is if Ram couldn't face Sumitra, then at least she could have come outside and seen Ram? After all, Ram was also her dear son, who was going on fourteen years of forest exile. This is one of the very few instances when the Supreme God of the universe kneels down in front of the greatness of an enlightened being. Ram knew that Sumitra didn't come outside to see Him because she didn't want Him to feel lesser. Moreover, in the presence of mother Sumitra, Ram would have hesitated in taking along her own Laxman. She didn't want to make Ram feel bad or guilty in any way, and so great Sumitra avoided bidding adieu her sons.

Saint Tulsidas says that when a devotee like Sumitra with a pure and honest heart serves, then even the Lord gets puzzled. The reason is that the Lord is so concerned and humble that He finds it very challenging to decide what to bestow in return to the devotee for her selfless service. Ram forever remained indebted to Mother Sumitra and took utmost care of Laxman as He could not afford to take away anything more from her. Such an instance of divine relation between Lord and Devotee is scarce.

Generally, intelligent and worldly beings without an iota of hesitation, ask, and expect the Supreme to fulfil their desires. Long queues at the temples are filled with mostly two kinds of beings, one of the two types is who wants happiness, and the other who wants to get rid of the pain. By chanting, fasting, offering, or worshipping once in a while, they want to prove themselves as pious and expect the fulfilment of their desires. And here we have a devotee like Mother Sumitra, who has always practiced righteousness, bore all sufferings patiently, but has never asked or expected anything, instead offered her everything to the Lord. Like her, whoever selflessly surrenders, offers, and serves Lord Ram becomes greater than Himself in the eyes of the Lord. In return, the Lord ensures the well-being and happiness of that devotee. Saint Tulsidas says that by learning from the selflessness of Mother Sumitra, seekers will realize that the only purpose of life is to surrender in the lotus feet of Lord Ram.

Chapter 2.15

Transformation of Nishadraj : End of Untouchability

This encounter marked the end of an age-old evil social system,
And, announced the advent of Ram-Rajya to end the mayhem.

Ram leaves Ayodhaya

Following Mother Kaikeyi's order, Lord Ram with Sita and Laxmana left Ayodhaya the very next morning for the forest exile of fourteen years. It left the whole of Ayodhaya in utter dejection as they saw their beloved prince leaving them in such a manner. The citizens of Ayodhaya, out of pure love for Ram, followed Him to the forest. Lord slipped away at an odd hour of the night to make people return to the city. The three of them then reached the borders of Ayodhaya Empire and entered the forest region from where the territory of a scheduled tribe, 'Nishaad', starts. Their king Nishaadraj was an old alliance of Lord Ram.

On hearing the news of Lord Ram's arrival, King of Nishaad, along with his companions, rushed to the spot. With pleasantries and gifts, they respectfully greeted and welcomed Lord Ram, Sita, and Laxman. Following the customary social rituals, Nishaads prostrated to show his deep respect for the Lord. As the Nishaad tribe was considered 'untouchable' and was not allowed to come closer to upper caste ones, Nishaads saluted maintaining a distance from the Lord. After that, what happened was beyond the imagination of people present there. Lord hugged Nishadraj like a dear old friend and made him sit next to Him. At that very moment, the prohibitions of old evil customs shattered, and the advent of Ram-Rajya was declared.

The meeting of Lord and Nishaad was the beginning of the implementation of Ram-Rajya. It was much needed for replacement and rejection of the prevalent flaws of the ancient social system. Instead of Ayodhaya, the throne of the forest excited Ram more because He felt that this was an excellent opportunity for Him to bring his vision of Ram-Rajya to reality. More than the urban centres, bringing changes in other regions of the empire was vital for him.

Practise of Untouchability

The Practise of Untouchability was essentially based on Vedanta principles of a social system or 'Varna Vyavastha.' It is a universal truth that Vedanta is the utterance of God. However, did God ever want this unrighteous and evil practice of Untouchability to be implemented in human society? Is God partial towards Higher Caste and biased against Lower Caste? Did God want to establish a system where one segment of beings would be ill-treated by others on the basis of birth?

Lord Ram had taken human avatar just to make the society understand the practical meaning of Vedantic principles. Whenever beings need clarification and correct understanding of the Vedantic tenets, they must thoroughly study and observe the life and conduct of Lord Ram. So what exactly was Ram's perspective on 'Varna Vyavastha' or caste system? What was his stance on the social taboo of Untouchability? The answer lies in the meeting of Lord Ram and Nishaad. The insights into this meeting are, in fact, more relevant in present times than before.

Followers of the 'Sanatan Dharma' firmly believed in the concept of Rebirth. They believe the soul is eternal and that the body changes in each birth. Some of them believe that whoever does good deeds in past life is born in the upper caste in the present life, while those who have done evil deeds in past lives are born in lower caste in the present life. It thus signifies that the lower caste ones are primarily sinners and so they must not come in contact with the so believed pious upper caste. It was also believed that the lower castes ones deserve this suffering. The privileged ones used to see themselves as the face of noble doers, and they took pride while justifying their rejection of untouchables.

Vasudeva Sarvam

Vedantic laws are there to make beings contemplate and thoughtful, and not to be used to exploit others. Now the question for the believers of Untouchability is that if the Supreme has written Vedanta, then why can't you leave the application on Him as well? Did Lord give you the authority to decide the cause and effect of the Karma of other beings? Does any being remember his acts of past lives? If you can justify Untouchability on the grounds of Vedanta, then you should also consider another principle of Vedanta, that is, 'Vasudeva Sarvam,' that is, the Supreme Lord is in every being. If One Supreme is the identity of every being, then how can one consider himself as superior and others as untouchable?

The more the upper caste was cruel and insensitive towards the untouchable, the more it considered itself to be religious and true practitioners of Vedanta. The concept of cause and effect related to rebirth is scientific, but instead of bringing any good results, it has resulted in greater disharmony. In every era, wise souls have always tried to solve the untouchability issue. On the surface, results have been quite positive. However, inside the polluted hearts of society, the feeling of hatred and division still existed. In present times too, a division based on religion and race is still very dominant.

Hatred, Fear and Desire

However, there was an exception, and that exception was Lord Ram, who, with the essence of 'Love,' had been able to succeed in eliminating this evil. In those times, society stayed away from untouchables as they didn't want the germs of sinful Karma to infect them. Therefore the 'Untouchables' were pushed far away from urban centres and forced to live on minimal resources. Besides, rulers in those times used 'fear' and 'greed' as instruments to exercise their power and control over abandoned people. By power, the rulers would instil fear, while by giving resources, they would satisfy greed.

On the contrary, the divine vision of Ram-Rajya was a society that would be both fearless and desire-less and meant to be governed with only one universal principle, which is 'Love '. In their meeting, Ram extended the same love to the abandoned Nishaad tribe. Lord's heartfelt affection not just ended the untouchability complex from the root, but also aroused the blessed feeling of surrender-ship in Nishaad naturally. For the first time ever, Nishaad experienced unconditional and unbiased love.

True Relationship

Lord lovingly addressed Nishadraj as 'Sakha' or friend, and this word at once washed away all the frustrations and pains in all of them, instilled by society. From a worldly perspective, this marked the end of the division based on the caste system. While from the spiritual aspect, Nishaad was reminded of the eternal and genuine connection that exists between God and Being. Relationships in human society are not stable because they are mostly governed by 'utility' rather than by 'actuality.' Till the other one is of some use, there is a display of love. And, with the end of the 'use,' the pretentious love also evaporates. Love is an absolute and essential need of every being. So to be loved, being wants to become useful for others. And therefore, being's whole life is spent in the endeavour of gaining a superior position in class, religion, caste, money, and power to attract the attention of more and more people.

But the relation between Lord and the being is unconditional and causeless and therefore is real, joyful, and eternal. As soon as the being realizes this divine relation, his insistence, and dependence on worldly society are eliminated. He no longer feels the urge to indulge in worldly affairs to build connections and forever lives in ultimate peace and bliss of Self. It is 'Vairagya' or indifference, which is the innate quality of a devotee. Nishaadraj was untouchable, downtrodden, repulsive and dim-witted for society. But for Lord Ram, he was an enlightened seeker of truth. Knowing your relationship with the Lord is the highest knowledge. To recognize the Grace of the Lord and surrender to Him is the indication of enlightenment.

The Transformation

Everybody welcomes and greets a King with reverence, but the one like Nishaad who surrenders even to an exiled one, has only love and humanity in him. Saint Tulsidas says that this is the outcome of 'Darshan' or realization of Lord Ram by Nishaad. He further states that whoever realizes Him, actually realizes Self. And this means beings understand that their innate nature is nothing other than truth, consciousness, and bliss.

After meeting with Lord Ram, Nishaad became both fearless and desireless in life. Later, when Bharata arrived in search of Ram, with his whole army, Nishaad had mistaken him as an enemy of Lord. However they didn't fear fighting with Prince Bharata's army of thousands of soldiers, though they were just a handful of companion warriors with him. Also later, Nishaad didn't accept the tons of gold that Bharata offered him as a token of friendship. He was, therefore, free from desires too. Nishaad had realized that fear and desire are meant for the mind-ego, not for Self. Also, he had understood that love, peace, and bliss are the real essence of life.

In the materialistic society, the gravity of feelings is quantified by the value of the gift one gives to others. But Supreme Lord Ram doesn't care about objects. All He needs and craves for is unconditional 'Love' of His devotee. Nishaad offered Lord whatever material property he had, which Ram didn't accept. But Lord was more than pleased to accept the 'property of love' offered by Nishaad. Point is that when surrender-ship is honest and love is innocent without an iota of cleverness, the Creator of the universe himself becomes both a friend and a servant to a mortal being.

Chapter 2.16

Baffling but Adorable 'Kewat' : Love is the Soul's Treasure

I won't take you across unless you let me wash your feet,
For whatever you touch, becomes a lady and breaks free.

Cheerless Times

When Lord Ram with Laxman and Sita left Ayodhaya, King Dasratha sent his minister Sumantra with them to look after and also to convince them to return. After spending a night with the Nishaad tribe, all of them with the King of Nishaad tribe resumed their journey to the forest and reached on the banks of the holy river Ganges. There Ram asked Minister Sumantra to return as he had come quite far with them. Lord asked Sumantra to tell the King that Ram is determined to complete the forest exile. Both Sumantra and Ram were very close to each other. Having completely failed in his efforts to convince Prince Ram to return, Sumantra, with a heavy heart and tears in eyes, bid them farewell. Lord too, felt very depressed with his departure. The incidents of the past few days had made Ram dispirited and emotionally drained.

The journeyers were waiting on the riverbank when King Nishaad called a boatman 'Kewat' to take all of them across. Kewat's encounter with Lord is a significant episode so much so that Lord made sure that he again meets Kewat while returning from Lanka in air-vehicle 'Pushpak Viman.' Kewat, a miserable, rural, innocent, unsophisticated yet wonderful being, did something in that short meeting that made him quite an adorable personality for Lord Ram and His devotees.

Weird Request

As Kewat with his boat came closer, Lord politely asked him to take them across the river. But surprisingly, he refused at once. His rude and abrupt refusal stunned everybody. On being inquired of the reason behind his refusal, he replied that if Lord Ram wants to enter his boat, then Lord must first let Kewat wash His feet. Kewat continued that he had heard that any lifeless object, when touched by the dust of the Lord's feet, becomes a beautiful woman. He was actually referring to the Ahalaya incident wherein a dead statue converted into a woman as soon as Ram touched it. Therefore Kewat wanted to wash off the dust of the Lord's feet himself. He can't afford his boat to become a woman, as this was the only source of livelihood for his family.

Laxman and Sita were shocked at this misbehavior, but after a long time, this bizarre yet whimsical demand of Kewat brought a smile on Lord's face. Laxman angrily scolded Kewat, how dare he make such mischief with the Prince of Ayodhaya. To which Kewat stringently insisted on his condition that if Prince Laxman wants, he can shoot him at once with his arrow, but Kewat won't let Lord Ram step in his boat unless He allows him to wash His feet. It didn't take Lord Ram long to understand the underlying feelings of Kewat. He, therefore, stopped Laxman and accepted Kewat's demand smilingly.

Kewat had sensed the heaviness in the journeyers and hence, tried to lighten the atmosphere with his weirdness. Also, being a devotee of the Lord, he didn't want to lose any opportunity to serve Him. Had he directly requested Lord, then out of his hesitation and humility, the Lord would not have allowed him to wash His feet. Therefore he made up this 'boat transforming to lady' story to somehow touch the lotus feet of Lord Ram. It was a rare opportunity for Kewat, and he couldn't afford to miss it at any cost. Now Laxman, Sita, and Nishaad also understood the feelings or 'Bhava' of Kewat and were pleased with his humorous and innocent request.

Pure Devotion

That day, nothing was more vibrant on this earth than Kewat and his wife, who together had the rarest privilege to wash Lord's feet. Needless to say, their joy knew no bounds. After taking them across the river, Kewat prostrated to Lord, who felt very indebted as Kewat had not only lightened the mood but also refused to take the boat fare. Lord was wondering what He should give him in return. It was just then that Mother Sita slipped out a precious ring from her finger and offered it to Kewat. "Supreme Ram always wants to give something to His devotee, and 'Yogmaya Laxmi' Mother Sita fulfils His resolution. What more can the being ever ask for?"

But seeing the offering, Kewat, instead of being happy, got disheartened and embarrassed. He felt that probably because of his salutation, Lord thought of offering him something as a token of his boat service. A servant who expects from his Lord Master can never serve him wholeheartedly. "What will future generations think of me, when they will come to know that Mother Sita had to take off her ornament because of me? I am no less than Kaikeyi," he thought to himself. Kewat with joined hands bowed and said-

Flaws, pain, and poverty had ended,
Luck has changed, and I am enlightened,
I am waiting here for your return,
After fourteen years, bestow me what I deserve.

All his life, Kewat complained to God Brahma that He had written only suffering in his destiny. He worked hard each day, yet struggled to make ends meet. That day Brahma replied, 'What can I do, beings receive only on the basis of their past Karma. I cannot intervene in the cause and effect of Karma. But today Supreme Lord Ram is coming to you who is beyond the laws and principles of the Universe. He bestows beings not only considering Karma but also 'Bhava' and devotion. So ask from the Lord.'

Greatest Spiritual Practise

But surprisingly, the day when Kewat actually had the unique chance of getting the treasure of his life, the difficult 'vritti' of desire just evaporated from his mind. Saint Tulsidas insightfully suggests that beings need not ask for anything from this world, for it has nothing to give. Asking is the typical nature of mind-ego, whereas offering is the innate nature of true Self. Being must only offer unconditional love and service to Lord Ram and patiently wait for His response. Beings must also understand that the painful occurrences in life are the Lord-sent lessons that need to be learned. In fact, sufferings are nothing but squaring off past bad karma. 'Acceptance' of unfavourable situations without any anger, complains, or resistance is the highest level of 'sadhana' or spiritual practice.

Saint Tulsidas says that human-being pray all their life to the Lord to end their suffering and fulfil their desires. But when the Lord arrives to grant, all desires automatically get vanished from the root. It was exactly what happened with Kewat. As a great devotee, Kewat had the once in a lifetime opportunity that day to ask for anything from the Lord, but he couldn't, and the Lord gave him the greatest gift of His 'friendship.' Moreover, Tulsidas asserts that like Kewat, whoever doesn't bother for treasures, but devotes and surrenders himself wholeheartedly, attains the Creator of all treasures, who is Supreme Lord Ram.

Chapter 2.17

The Prayagraj : When the 'Sought' becomes the 'Seeker'

O Sage, please guide Me, which path must I take,
O Ram, your every step is for beings' welfare sake.

Guidance of Sage Bharadwaj

After crossing the sacred river Ganga on Kewat's boat, the angelic journeyers along with Nishaad reached Sage Bharadwaj Ashram situated at 'Triveni Sangam,' the holy confluence of Ganga, Jamuna, and Saraswati, at Prayagraj. Ram prayed to Sage Bharadwaj to guide him on the right path he must follow. The sage laughed up his sleeve and replied that whichever path Lord Ram takes, automatically becomes the correct one. This short conversation between the Lord and the Sage is very significant and insightful.

Commonly human-being first sets his target and then enquires about the path that leads to it. But from a spiritual perspective, every seeker's aim or destination is one and the same, that is, Supreme God. Therefore Lord doesn't find it necessary to talk about the target, and he simply asks about the path. This inquiry seems unusual because Ram knows that He, Himself is the target of every seeker. It is indeed strange to note why that day the One, who is sought by all, has Himself become a seeker? Why did God, who is omniscient, suddenly feel the need to ask for directions from Sage Bharadwaj?

Being the Supreme God himself, Lord Ram has full freedom in setting and deciding the path for Himself. But still, He rejects His divinity and privileges. The sole purpose of His human Avatar is to set benchmarks of principles and values that steer beings towards a perfect life. He knew that generations to come would follow His mannerisms, and therefore He must be very cautious in all his actions. By asking from the Sage, Ram wants to convey the message to the beings, that guidance and mentorship of a wise and enlightened Master or 'Guru' like Sage Bharadwaj is a must in life.

Importance of SadGuru

'Hari Anant, Hari Katha Ananta.'

God is One, but His manifestations are infinite. Similarly, the target is One, but the paths or 'Yoga' to reach Him are countless. It is not advisable to select the spiritual path by the seeker by himself. Guidance is essential in worldly life, but in spiritual life, it is mandatory. Saint Tulsidas says that 'Sadguru' is higher than God and affirms that even Brahma and Shiva cannot swim across the 'mundane ocean of maya' without the guidance of 'Sadguru.'

Lord says 'that only the one who surrenders to Me can rise above Maya.' But the question here is, is the seeker wise enough in self to understand the true meaning of 'Surrender'? Only when the seeker accepts his ineptitude in understanding it, he feels the need for an enlightened and knowledgeable Teacher who can guide him. This is a universal principle. Ram's inquiry for direction from Sage Bharadwaj was in acceptance for the same principle.

Now the question is why a seeker, in himself, is not self-capable in deciding the right path? The reason is that mind-ego makes him believe that already he is very accomplished. Because of past conditioning of many previous births, the mind-ego had been heavily polluted with elements of greed, anger, fear, and violence. So mind-ego not only makes the being feel overconfident but also misdirects and detriments him. The same happened with Ravana. Though he was profoundly knowledgeable and had done great penance, yet he turned evil just because of this one crucial flaw. He was too conceited to accept the guidance of a Guru and, therefore, did what his mind-ego prompted him to do. We all know the end result. Only the Lord knows the functioning of mind-ego in entirety, and hence, He sends the message across, that seeker must follow an enlightened Mentor to progress in life righteously.

In some seekers, the sense of logic dominates, while some are action-oriented. But in many, emotions are predominant. It isn't that easy for the seeker to properly identify and apprehend what is his natural orientation, that is, is it logic, action, or emotion? Therefore a specialist is needed who has studied the human mind rigorously and clearly understands how life and the world function. Guidance from such a specialist or a Sadguru like Sage Bharadwaj is imperative for a well-organized and meaningful life.

The Four Disciples

Sage Bharadwaj, by virtue of his enlightened vision, knew that 'Sakshat'

God is sitting in front of him. But to participate in the Lord Ram-destined Leela, the Sage didn't let others perceive the reality. He wittily replied that whichever way Ram walks becomes the right direction for the beings to follow. The fact that Lord, despite being Supreme power and Omnipresent, is not at all hesitant in seeking his guidance, made the sage feel blessed and overwhelmed. He then sent four of his disciples with Lord to guide Him to the right path.

Saint Tulsidas says that these four disciples are the symbols of the four Vedas. Vedas are the Rule-Book that even God is expected to follow. It is like a President of a nation, who, despite being the most influential citizen of that nation, has to abide by the rules laid down in its Constitution. He further advises that the seeker must not follow anyone blindly, be it God or Guru, and must critically check on the criterions of Vedas. Lord Ram followed the four disciples and acknowledged the significance of Vedas. In the present times, the study of Veda may sound impractical to certain people, but that doesn't devalue their purpose in any way. Beings who have a Teacher of Veda in life are blessed. Beings who have a mentor like Sage Bharadwaj in life are also very blessed. But the one who has wholeheartedly surrendered in the lotus feet of Lord Ram is the most blessed of all beings.

Chapter 2.18

Meeting with Sage Valmiki : Hooligan becomes Holyman

O Maharishi, please advice, which place is right for us to reside,
O Ram, tell me, which place in this world you have not subtly occupied.

The People's Hero

For several days Ram, Sita, and Laxman with King Nishaad and the four disciples of Sage Bharadwaj walked in the countryside. Whoever came to know about the arrival of the Prince of Ayodhaya, would rush to meet and greet Him. Wherever Lord Ram would step, the people out there felt blessed applying the sacred dust of that spot on their foreheads. Wherever Ram would stop, a crowd of thousands would flock and assemble as if there's a popular fair going on. Hesitant Lord felt uneasy and so hurriedly kept on moving without halting. After a while, He requested the four disciples, who signify the four Vedas, to return. It denotes that the significance of the Vedas in a being's life is only up to a certain distance. With the advent of 'Vivek' and 'Bhakti' in life, the 'Vedas' are not a requisite any more.

After some days, Lord insisted Nishaadraj to return as well. It signifies that friendship can bring comfort and security in one's life but only to a certain extent. After that, being needs to face the challenges and deal with life himself. However, one must always be loyal to a friend, so the Lord didn't forget to invite King Nishaad at His crowning ceremony after the exile and forever remain indebted to him. Lord Ram, Sita, and Laxman proceeded and reached the beautiful ashram of Sage Maharishi Valmiki.

Story of Valmiki

In his early life, Valmiki was a violent dacoit who used to loot and murder the passersby. Once a wise traveler advised Valmiki to ask his family whether they would become his partner in his crimes. To Valmiki's utter dismay, his family refused straightforwardly. Their logic was that it's his job to feed the family, and how he does that is not the concern of a family. It didn't take Valmiki long to understand that in this world, society and relationships are all self-seeking. With such a realization, he felt very guilty and remorseful for his evil acts and feared the karmic repercussions. The wise fellow asked him to chant 'Ram' to attain peace and liberation. But it was difficult for Valmiki's immensely violent mind-ego to utter the holy word 'RAM' properly. He instead started chanting the word 'RAM' inversely that is 'MAR,' which means 'to kill.'

Word doesn't matter in 'Sadhana' or spiritual practice; it's the commitment and perseverance that ultimately matter. And it worked for Valmiki as well. For years, Valmiki kept on chanting and one day attained the pinnacle of enlightenment. Although, by chanting 'MAR-MAR,' Maharishi Valmiki progressed in his spiritual journey, it doesn't mean that seekers must also chant 'MAR' for the same purpose. His story only signifies that in the path of spirituality, there are no hard and fast rules. Spiritual practices can be done in any way; what is important is the focus and determination with which one treads the path of spirituality. Secondly, whatever may be the state of mind of the seeker, violent or rogue, it cannot become a barrier in spirituality. Valmiki wholeheartedly accepted his ignorance and incapability, and like a small child, surrendered to the Father Supreme. Later Supreme God, being satisfied with his practise or 'Sadhana,' gave him the most precious gift and the greatest privilege that a seeker can ever ask. It was the intellect and intelligence to ideate and bring to life the greatest epic - 'Ramayana' in words. It is quite interesting to note that the one who once could not even utter the name of the Hero of Ramyana became the greatest devotee and speaker of the tales of Lord Ram. It thus proves that being can be anybody with any past background, but it is only with the Grace of the Lord, that he can attain a higher level of consciousness.

The Two Creators

Meeting of Lord Ram and Sage Valmiki was the meeting of two Creators. By chanting Lord's divine name, Valmiki underwent a radical transformation. Similarly, it was only the epic Ramyana of Valmiki that helped spread the glory of Lord Ram in all 'Disha' or directions, and in all 'Yuga' or ages. By touching the feet of Sage Valmiki, Lord Ram sent the message to the world that one must always follow the commands of his Creator. Lord asked the

Sage a place where He can reside with Sita and Laxman for some time. Sage smiled and replied that there is no place in this eternity where the Lord is not present. However, from the perspective of worldly play or 'Leela,' he must settle at 'Chitrakoot,' a beautiful place for Yogis.

This small episode of Sage Valmiki is very insightful for new spiritual seekers. Commonly a seeker feels that to progress in spirituality, he needs to transform and refine himself. But, in reality, such transformation is not an easy thing to do, and therefore, many feel helpless and get disappointed. They become hopeless and consider themselves incapable of becoming eligible for the love of the Lord. Sage Valmiki declares with conviction that anybody, no matter how corrupt and polluted he may be, is eligible for the Grace of Lord Ram. His life is the testimony to that fact.

Being must never lose heart and keep trying to progress in spiritual life religiously. All that the Lord sees in a seeker, is the intensity, urge, craving, faith, and of course, the thirst. Just one noble thought, one firm belief and one strong hope that no matter what, one day, the Lord will come to me, can do miracles for the seeker. Sage Valmiki is a great inspiration for every being that surrendering in the lotus feet of Lord Ram is the only purpose of life.

Chapter 2.19

What God Wants

Devta and Sages want to give themselves credit,
They believed that the Lord's 'Darshan' is because of their merit.

Lord Ram with Laxman and Sita arrived and settled at the beautiful and sacred hill of Chitrakoot. Soon everybody around the region came to know about the Lord's arrival, and they flocked to visit him. Each one of them had their own mindset when they paid a visit to the Lord. While most went there driven by their 'Swartha' or selfishness, there were some who went purely out of 'Prem' or unconditional love. Not just Sanatan Dharma but every religion of the world has talked about selfishness or 'Swartha' and have always advised being to get over it. Yet self-obsession is embedded in the mind-ego and conscience of human beings so profoundly that for beings to manage it becomes very difficult. Saint Tulsidas has differentiated Swartha into three main categories. First are those who, for others' interests, don't bother about their own interests. Second, are those who look after others' interests but at the same time don't compromise on their own interests. Finally, the third are those who, for the sake of their selfish interests, don't refrain from harming others' interests.

To be 'Swarthi' or selfish to some extent is natural. But the problem arises when beings pretend to be concerned for others but stab at their backs. Devtas had delayed the advent of Ram-Rajya and schemed for Lord Ram's forest exile to eliminate Asura Ravana. Devtas wanted to enjoy all the pleasures that Heaven could provide, but Ravan had put restrictions on them by capturing Heaven. But at what price? Supreme Lord Ram had to face the adversities and suffering of forest exile for their unrighteous interest. However, deep inside Devtas felt guilty for Lord's sacrifice, and therefore, they were the first to arrive at Chitrakoot. It is quite amusing to note here that although Devtas wanted to show their gratefulness to Lord, they were not at all prepared to forgo their addiction for pleasures.

Lord Ram is the only perfect example who doesn't care about himself and serves others. Although He was fully aware of the swartha or interest of Devtas, He still greeted and blessed them, lovingly. He knew that for making someone realize the fruitlessness of pleasures and swartha, desires need to be fulfilled to some extent. Therefore for the sake of the welfare of Devtas and to stop Asura, He wholeheartedly accepted the sufferings of forest exile. He strongly believed that eventually, they would understand the vices of Swartha and tread on the path of 'Dharma' in absoluteness.

After Devta, the 'Sants' or Sages arrived to have the holy 'Darshan' of Lord Ram. Earlier, when Devtas came, Lord just greeted with folded hands, but when sages came, He prostrated at their feet. He knew that sages are pure souls whose only purpose is the welfare of humanity and, therefore, they must be highly revered. Sages, on the other hand, believed that the attainment of Lord Ram is the outcome of their spiritual penance or Sadhana.

However, at a very subtle level, even the Sages are affected by 'Swartha' or selfishness. They wanted to give credit to their dedicated spiritual practise. They believed that the Lord has arrived at Chitrakoot because of their hard penance. Although it sounds tad egotistical, yet Sages always hold a much higher position than all others as they never think of giving trouble to others. Instead, they serve the society forgoing materialism and pleasure. And therefore, Lord Ram had immense regard for them and ensured their security from the attacks of Asura.

'Kol-Kirat' the schedule tribes of the jungle were the last to come. It is quite understandable why they came after waiting for so long. Because of poverty and suffering and to manage their bread and butter, these tribes got involved in violence and loot. By discarding them, society had left no other option with them to survive. Out of natural guilt for their misconduct, they were initially reluctant but somehow gathered the courage to meet the Lord.

Pleasure seeking Devtas believed that the arrival of Lord Ram in Chitrakoot is the outcome of their master planning, whereas the enlightened Sages perceived that His arrival is the reward of their Sadhana or spiritual practices. As the innocent tribesmen couldn't claim anything of such sorts, they only considered themselves as 'most fortunate.' When one attains something he doesn't deserve and without any effort, he usually gives credit to the Luck. But the question is, out of the three, whose belief is true?

Let us try to find the answer with the help of an example. A long-time back, a householder invited a wise person at his home. For a cool and fresh breeze, he opened the window. As the atmosphere inside became pleasant, he praised himself for how intelligently he has placed the window in the right place and direction. To which the wise man replied, "It's you only who has blocked the breeze by building this wall, and it's you who has made the window for the breeze to flow in." The problem actually lies with us. First, we create obstacles and then work to make a passage and then expect appreciation for our little success. In all this, we forget to acknowledge the wind that is blowing and comforting us selflessly.

For Devta, Ravan is the wall, and Lord is the window, which they believed that they had smartly opened. For Sages, the wall is their Ego and window is their spiritual practice or 'Sadhana,' through which the Lord has arrived. Both Devta and Sages were like that householder who only gives credit to himself, forgetting the selflessness of the breeze, that is Lord's grace. But tribesmen are like those who neither build the wall nor the window; instead, they are just grateful. Lord Ram's Grace is like a divine cool breeze, which selflessly flows by its own will and eases everyone's soul, irrespective of their status, caste and creed. Care and compassion are definitive and innate attributes of the Lord. Beings, by virtue of their ignorance, create the wall and block the grace from flowing in their lives and later cry for solace.

One must understand that it's neither planning nor practises nor luck; Lord Ram arrives only at His own divine will. Being may think whatever he feels like, but Lord is unconcerned about it. All He wants is only and only pure and unconditional love from the being, which is neither a material nor an effort but a true emotion, a soulful feeling. Lord is never impressed with class, wealth, glory, intelligence, or practise. He becomes overwhelmed with just love. However, our mind-ego is so conditioned that it cannot accept only 'love' and be satisfied. Beings want the material, the body, along with love. In fact, the mind is unable to comprehend true Love, which is always unconditional and intangible. Therefore the circus of giving & taking continues in human society.

But being needs to know and accept that the Lord only wants Love and nothing else. As flowing and refreshing is the nature of the breeze; similarly, love is the innate nature of the Lord and also beings. Therefore knowing & accepting this aspect of the Lord is the best thing people can do for themselves.

'Lord only likes love, know to love, whoever wants to know Lord.' - Tulsidas

Chapter 2.20

Salvation of Dasaratha

The King realized that life without Ram is a waste,
What use does this body have if it cannot be with Him?

Despite his earnest efforts, Minister Sumantra had to return to Ayodhaya alone. With a heavy heart and moistened eyes, he reluctantly informed King Dasratha that Prince Ram has refused to return and is adamant about completing the fourteen years of forest exile. The moment Dasratha heard about Ram's denial, memories of the past flashed in Dasratha's mind. That day for the first time in his life, he revealed that bitter past episode of his life to Queen Kaushalya that tormented his soul the most. He was utterly disappointed and intuited that his time has come.

It all happened in front of Dasratha when Queen Kaikeyi had wrongfully commanded Prince Ram for forest exile. Dasratha didn't even try to intervene and witnessed everything as a quiet observer. He very well knew that what had happened was not right, yet he didn't speak a single word against the decision. Hence the public perception was that Dasratha is in agreement with Kaikeyi. But the truth was that he was filled with guilt and indecisiveness. As soon as Ram set out for the forest exile, Dasratha asked Sumantra to go with Him and convince Him to come back.

While in Ayodhaya, Laxman didn't criticize his father for such injustice against Prince Ram. But when Sumantra revealed the actual reason **for** coming with them to the forest, he couldn't hold himself back and burst out in anger. **Nowwhat made Laxman react in such a manner?** Dasratha let Kaikeyi exile Ram only on the basis of Dharma or honour. And now when he's affected by fatherly 'Moh' or attachment, he wants Him to come back. Laxman was infuriated on his father's indecisiveness and **flickering** mind. He strongly believed that once being has decided something, he must have the courage to stand for it. If Dasaratha is the epitome of **'Dharma,'** then he must bear the pain of separation; and if he is so attached with Ram, then he must have not bothered about righteousness and didn't let Ram leave at all. If he didn't stop Kaikeyi when he could, then why is he asking for Ram's return now? Not standing on your decision is also cowardice, which Mighty Laxman cannot tolerate.

Dasratha kept himself alive on a fallacious hope that Ram will return soon. But when Sumantra arrived empty-handed, this last hope also ended. Kaushalya tried to pacify him **but without any result, as** he now couldn't see the meaning of life anymore. That very moment his ugly past, his worst nightmare, the episode of Shravan Kumar came alive in his mind.

Long-time back when the unfortunate blind parents of Shravan Kumar expressed their interest in going on a pilgrimage, he readily decided to carry them on his shoulders and started the journey. On the way, to quench the thirst of his parents, he left them at a safe spot and went to a nearby pond to fetch water. It was during this time that Dasratha was out there in the forest for hunting. On hearing some noise from behind the bush, **he, guessing it as an animal, at once shot an arrow.** But to his utter dismay, he was shocked to hear the painful cry of Shravan Kumar. He immediately ran towards him, but it was too late. After knowing the reality, Dasratha felt very guilty and remorseful for his act of killing an innocent being. Before dying, the 'parents-devotee' Shravan Kumar requested Dasratha to at least carry water and quench his parents' thirst. To fulfill his last wish, Dasratha came to the parents with water who though blind, were able to figure out that some mishap has occurred. Dasratha divulged them the truth. On hearing about the death of their beloved and dutiful son, the parents couldn't bear the shock, and they too died on the spot. But before **breathing their last**, they cursed Dasratha that one day he will also die in the agony of separation of his son. This episode happened before the birth of Ram, and never ever did Dasratha spoke about it to anybody. In his last moments of life, this dark chapter flashed in front of Dasratha's eyes. He felt that the time has come when he has to pay for his sin of murdering the great Shravan Kumar. He revealed the story to Kaushalya and accepted his death.

Though the story of Shravan Kumar is the greatest symbol ever of a son's unparalleled devotion for his parents, yet it raises many questions. Dasratha dug his own grave by speaking the truth to Shravan Kumar's parents and trapped himself in the curse. So what is the practicality of truthfulness? There's no denying the fact that Dasratha made the gravest mistake, but that happened, **purely** unknowingly. Also, he sincerely and honestly apologized to the parents. Yet he was cursed. Aren't the parents unjust? Shravan Kumar, on the other hand, led a life of purity, devotion, and selfless service, but, in return, he **experienced** a painful death. So what is the point in being righteous in life if the outcome is so gut-wrenching?

For a being, it is not always possible to practice all aspects of Dharma that is duty, righteousness, and honour. It is precisely the reason why Lord speaks about Self-Duty or Swa-Dharma that is the 'defined' Dharma or duty, separately for every being. No matter how great a **particular** duty is, but if the being is incapable of practising it, then by accepting it, he will definitely land into trouble. Parents of Shravan Kumar ignored this aspect of Swadharma that is they failed to assess their capability and limitation and tried to practise Dharma of pilgrimage instead. A travel **journey,** be it pilgrimage in that era, which encompasses dense and dangerous forests, needed one to be mentally and physically fit. Therefore, such a travel was totally unsuitable for handicapped, blind parents like that of Shravan Kumar's. Yet they didn't hesitate to burden their son to fulfill their wish. Moreover, the parents did not consider the fact that their son would have to bear a lot of trouble and pain in carrying them on the pilgrimage. It, therefore, reflected unreasonableness and unintelligence on the part of the parents.

Despite being a King, Dasratha accepted his mistake honestly, fell at their feet, and apologized sincerely. He even offered to look after them all his life like his own. If the parents have had some level of tolerance and acceptance, which is **usually** expected from spiritual seekers, they would have forgiven Dasratha. But their attachment and dependence on their son was so intense that they couldn't tolerate his sudden demise and cursed Dasaratha in revenge. Their vengeance reflects that they lacked **both** 'Gyana' or wisdom and 'Vairagya' or worldly indifference.

Shravan Kumar read in the scriptures about unconditional service towards father and mother but didn't contemplate at all. No teaching, truth, verse, or rule, even if it comes from the Vedas, must be accepted without contemplating deeply about **its** relevance and practicality in one's life. **Also, not** every theory is applicable to everyone. Undoubtedly, 'Father and Mother are **next to** God,' this universal principle **is correct but not the complete truth.** 'The whole creation is God', is the absolute **and** ultimate truth. It is for us to understand the real and complete meaning of such scriptural principles and then perform duty as per our capabilities. Shravan Kumar didn't give a thought on 'devotion for parents' principle and instead confused the impractical job of carrying parents for pilgrimage with his **Swadharma**. He became so obsessed with the misunderstood Dharma that he didn't apply his logic and intelligence and took the **unjustifiable** step. His intention was not wrong, but his act was **utterly** impractical. He could have **thought** of other **viable** options like taking along more people with him, or he could have empathetically tried to make his parents understand the fact that they are not in a suitable **physical** state to travel such a long and difficult journey. Again, the point here is to assess capabilities and limitations before taking up an initiative.

King Dasratha had recently learnt the skill of sound-hunting that is hitting the target just on the basis of sound, without even seeing the target. He was eager to apply his newly learned skills and so shot the arrow in childlike excitement, believing the target as an animal and without assessing the possibility, if it is not. One must know that half-knowledge is more lethal than no knowledge. Jatayu and Sampati, the great vulture-brothers raced towards the Sun in excitement, and because of the heat of the Sun, Sampati's feathered wings got burnt. Their immature act resulted in tragedy. Either being must not venture, and if he does, he must have **thorough** knowledge of his goal. Had Dasratha waited and used his eyes to see what he was targeting at, and had he controlled his childlike excitement and acted patiently, then Shravan Kumar would not have lost his life.

With that said, we must understand that Shravan Kumar would still be considered as the greatest **icon** of an ideal son. It is some or the other little flaws which make us human. No matter how cautiously and intelligently one leads life, some errors are bound to happen. What is important to understand is the intention and sincerity of the being. And hence Shravan Kumar will always be considered as an inspiration and the epitome of Dharma and Bhakti.

More than external factors, being's own misunderstandings, and misjudgments are the biggest cause of his suffering and pain. Dasratha felt totally dejected when he found Sumantra arriving without Ram. The episode of Shravan Kumar flashed in front of his eyes. It didn't take Dasratha long to apprehend that today he was experiencing the repercussions of his **own** mistake he committed earlier. He accepted his misconduct and, in penance and remorse, decided to end his life. However, the curse turned into a blessing for him as he died longing for Lord Ram and proved the truthfulness of his love for Supreme God. And ever merciful and compassionate Lord Ram accepted the pure love of devotee Dasratha, and liberated and bestowed him salvation.

Lord has declared that whoever thinks of Him in the last moments attains Him. Dasratha **suffered the punishment** because of the curse, but at the same time, he got blessed for his sincere love for Supreme Ram. Saint Tulsidas says that no matter what mistakes one had committed in life, by surrendering to Lord Ram and loving Him truthfully, one will attain salvation, which is ultimate peace and bliss.

Chapter 2.21

The Great Bharat

Part 1

The integrity of Bharat was doubted by every other,
Even Kaikeyi mistook him as her co-conspirator.

After King Dasratha died of a broken heart longing for Prince Ram, Sage Vashisht immediately sent messengers to bring back Prince Bharat from his maternal-grandfather King Kaikey's kingdom. The messengers were categorically instructed not to disclose the news of King's demise to Bharat. It was essential because the sage knew that this tragic news would be tootraumatic for Bharat to undertake such a long journey. As soon as Bharat entered Ayodhaya, he was surprised to notice that the citizens didn't greet him as warmly as earlier times. The prevailing situation somehow made Bharat apprehensive about some tragedy. He first reached Queen Kaikeyi, who very enthusiastically rushed to greet him. Once inside, Bharat became aware of the happenings in the palace behind him. His heart was at once shattered in agony and pain. However, he managed to regain his composure, and with a deep sigh uttered the most shocking words that a son would ever say to his mother, 'O wicked woman, you have brought complete ruin to our family. O malicious woman, how is it that your heart did not break into pieces yet?'

The citizens of Ayodhaya had always loved Bharat so much so that they demanded Bharat's presence at Lord Ram's crowning ceremony. For them, without Bharat, no ceremony of Ayodhaya was complete. However, the turn of the events that led to the exile of Prince Ram shook their faith in Bharat. Most of them even started believing that Bharat was also involved in Queen Kaikeyi's ploy. While some of them were unsure, very few still believed in the nobility of Bharat. The skeptical citizens didn't stop here and questioned why didn't Dasratha wait for Bharat's return? They now thought that probably the King was no more confident of Bharat's loyalty and therefore wanted to execute the ceremony hurriedly in his absence. They also argued that hadn't Kaikeyibeen so sure of Bharat accepting the crown, then she wouldn't have played such a bold and devastating game of conspiracy.

The loyalists of Bharat, however, discarded all these misconceptions and eventually were proven right. They were dead sure that the heart of great Bharat only beats for his brother Ram. 'Logic' is a mathematician, and'Heart' is a poet. Only those who don't ever let the mathematics of doubts overshadow the poetry of love can only understand the dignity and truthfulness of Bharat. Mathematical and calculative minds can never appreciate true emotions. The odd response of citizens was surprising for Bharat, but he was too tense to interact with them. He was desperate to know the occurrences, yet his heart in anticipation of a mishap was afraid to ask because Bharat knew that 'Truth is not always joyous.'

Driven by their mind-ego, the undecided citizens again questioned why Bharat first went to Kaikeyi and not anyone else? According to royal customs, he must have first visited the eldest Queen Kaushalaya. Understandably, they assumed that since Kaikeyi was the root of the conspiracy, so he went to her first because he is also an active participant in it and wants to discuss the future course of action with her. But this doubt of the citizens was totally baseless. Firstly, Bharat never believed in any formality and customs. He was always a person who follows his heart and not the mind. Only a pure and noble one like Bharat can remain indifferent towards formalities. In fact, Bharat was most eager to meet his brother Ram first, and everybody knew that Ram had always spent more time with Kaikeyi than other queens. Therefore, to meet brother Ram, he went to her palace first. Also, if Bharat had visited someone else before Kaikeyi and had taken the decision of not accepting the crown, then Kaikeyi could have got the opportunity to falsely blame that person for brainwashing Bharat, against her. It is exactly the reason why the far-sighted Sage Vashisht instructed the messengers to take Bharat straightaway to Queen Kaikeyi.

Kaikeyi had been feeling very lonely of late. All the citizens and royals had discarded her. Even her close friends and relatives were maintaining a distance from her. Therefore, her only hope was her own son, Bharat. She very well knew that once Bharat becomes the King, then all these people would have no option but to bow down to her, and she would rule the grand kingdom of Ayodhaya happily ever after. The never-ending hunger for the throne had destroyed all her sensibilities. On hearing the arrival of Bharat, she got exhilarated as now all her dreams would be fulfilled. But in all this chaos, she had forgotten one important fact that *'Power may bring respect but not real love.'* Moreover, for a bereaved wifewhose husband's dead body is still lying there in the palace, to welcome Bharat cheerfully with typical royal customs seems to be highly inappropriate. But the ever-ambitious and self-obsessed Kaikeyi was empty of feelings and was filled with greed.

No sooner did Bharat enter Kaikeyi's palace than he inquired about the things. She fabricated the whole story, crediting herself for the master-stroke. It is interesting to note here that although the whole idea was that of Manthra, she even avoided mentioning her. This shows the naked reality of a greedy mind, which speaks a different language when it needs others' help and different language when the objective is successfully accomplished. Greed always pushes others away and wants to put itself in the forefront as the winner.

All this while unlike others, Kaikeyi was in high spirits, as she wasn't living in the present but was obsessed with the future. Every single moment she had been designing future plans which she will execute as soon as Bharat arrives. She intentionally ignored crediting Manthra to ensure that Manthra doesn't get any special importance from Bharat after he becomes the king. Had Kaikeyi even a little bit of sense that Bharat would literally hate her after knowing about her truth and conspiracy, then she would have put all the blame on Manthra. But as of now, the beautiful dreams of future had blinded her to such an extent that she even mistook her own son, the great noble Bharat, as wicked and greedy as herself.

Kaikeyi now felt that Ayodhaya had always been partial towards Ram and ignored her son, Bharat. Bharat was at his maternal grandfather's place for many years and was kept away from the due honour and love, which he deserved. She thought that probably, for this reason, Bharat would be upset with his father. But she was wrong. Hearing the news of his father's death, Bharat, in extreme agony, dropped on the floor. But even then, the mind-ego-blinded Kaikeyi didn't see a son's pain in Bharat; instead, she felt that Bharat is putting on an act to prove that he is actually very disturbed with his father's death.

From the night of asking for boons till that day, Kaikeyi was living a fake life. She was so engrossed in her theatrics that she believed that Bharat was also faking his pain, like her. Had she truly knew her son Bharat's heart, she would have divulged the tragic news with at least some pretentious seriousness, but she spoke as if nothing of much concern has happened. The greedy and self-obsessed in small successes tend to lose the farsightedness. Kaikeyi, in great detail, explained to Bharat how shrewdly she had outwitted the scheming of Dasaratha against Bharat by crowning Ram as the king. Her shallow mind had created an illusionary world where she presumed everyone is against Bharat and her.

All this while, Bharat was patiently listening to his mother. But a huge storm of anguish was growing inside him. He couldn't believe what had just happened. The great Bharat can accept anything, even the death of his father, but can't tolerate anything against his brother Ram, the epitome of righteousness. That very moment, the overwhelming wave that is Bharat uprooted the vices of wickedness, greed, and evilness that is Kaikeyi, leaving no scope for it to emerge again. Bharat, the symbol of Dharma, set an example which can never be erased till the end of time. Bharat was the most progressive step towards Ram-Rajya. This is the story of great Bharat, in front of whom even the Sanatan Dharma bows down.

Chapter 2.22

The Great Bharat

Part 2

You have drained the water to keep the fish alive,
Why did you not kill me as soon as I breathed life?

A drowning man makes the best of his efforts to save himself, but once he sinks deeper, he stops struggling and becomes lifeless, not knowing what to do. Similarly, Bharat was mourning loudly hearing about his father's death, but he still had hope in brother Ram. But as soon as he came to know about brother Ram's exile, all his hopes and strength shattered at once. He sat on the ground, lifeless and thoroughly disillusioned, not knowing what to do and what to say. Nobody other than the wounded one can experience and feel the magnitude of pain inside. The cunning words of Kaikeyi were like salt on wounds, which made it even more unbearable for Bharat. He burst out in anger and shook Kaikeyi to the core.

Although such harsh words from a son are not at all acceptable for a mother, nobody can label Bharat unjust. There was not an iota of greed or desire in him. Kaikeyi had offered him the reigns of the grand Ayodhaya Empire. He could have easily accepted it on the pretext of his father and mother's command, and nobody could have dared to raise a finger against him. But, for him, serving Dharma was way too greater than self-serving interests. Not just he rejected the offer, but he eliminated the conspiracy from the root. Mother is undoubtedly greater than even God, but after committing such a heinous crime, Kaikeyi no longer deserved to be called a mother. Although Lord Ram insisted a lot, Bharat never spoke a single word with his mother again. As soon as Shatrugan heard about the matter, he dragged Manthra to his brother Bharat's feet accusing her of corrupting Queen Kaikeyi's mind. In a fit of rage, mighty Shatrughan punched and kicked Manthara and broke her spine. Blood came out from her nose and mouth at once. One lethal attack of warrior Shatrugan could break a wall of concrete. So, one can easily visualize the condition of Manthra, who's just an old rotten piece of flesh. She was crying in severe pain aloud. Largehearted Bharat intervened and pacified Shatrughan and let Manthara escape, never to be heard or seen again.

No matter what Kaikeyi did, but some people still objected to Bharat's offensive words for his mother. But for a seeker, on the level of Bhakti and Dharma, it was totally justifiable. In a way, Bharat played the role of a Sadguru who gives bitter treatment to his disciples only to free them from the egoistic traps that come in the path of devotion or 'Bhakti.' Kaikeyi was trapped in her motherly attachment, 'Mamta' for Bharat. Sweet counselling, instead of freeing, would have intensified the trap even further, and therefore an intense shock was needed. Had Bharat tried to politely explain, Kaikeyi would have never realised her mistake. Words like bright sunlight are essential to remove the darkness of ignorant minds. The infection of greed had reached such a stage where cure by medicine was not possible. Now only by painful surgery can the rigid mind-ego trap be removed from the core of Kaikeyi.

Kaikeyi was feeling very conceited as everything was happening as per her planning. Bharat, with his harsh words, in a way, helped remove this artificial pride and benefitted Kaikeyi. She at once got liberated from the clutches of mind-ego that had been polluting her for long. After realizing her mistake, she did intense penance in guilt and remorse and surrendered in the lotus feet of Lord Ram. This incident also brought the truth of the greatness of Bharat in front of the world. Since then, Bharat was revered for his righteousness by every being forever.

This is one of the many ways by which Lord Ram ushers His grace and divinity for the welfare or 'Mangal' of the beings. Incidents, good or bad, will keep on happening in life. Pleasure and pain will keep coming and going. What we need to realize is that a difficult situation may appear unfair or unkind to us. But, there is always a life lesson and a solution hidden in it. The only purpose of those unwanted experiences is to free us from the vices, that is, the traps of mind-ego, just like Kaikeyi got free from her vices of attachment and greed. But the most important point is that until the being learns and internalizes these lessons, these ordeals of life keep coming back. Lord's commandment is, 'Learn and free yourself or be trapped and suffer.' *What you resist will persist.* Accept it or not, the ultimate choice always lies with us.

Lord always rewards 'Viveki' devotees like Bharat,

bycreating a situation wherein their greatness is automatically brought in front of the world to witness. Nobody in this universe can measure the magnitude of God's divine play or 'Leela.' But what everybody can do in life is to identify and realise that repercussion of greed is Kaikeyi, cunningness is Manthara, and reward for righteousness is Bharat. The role of the great Bharat doesn't end here. From here till the end of Ayodhaya Kand, Bharat, through his noble deeds, not only enlightened the Manushya and Devta but also Asura about the true meaning of 'Dharma.'

Chapter 2.23

Determined Bharat

When the stars are not in favor,
You are not only infected with sickness and disorder,
But also get stung by a poisonous scorpion,
And injected with high intoxication.

After a royal funeral ceremony, Prince Bharat religiously executed the cremation of King Dasratha. Following that, Sage Vashisht called a large assembly of royals, ministers, and citizens to decide the future of the Ayodhaya Empire. Vashisht and ministers were in favor of Bharat becoming the successor to the throne of the kingdom. Even Mother Kaushalaya insisted the same from Bharat. But the great Bharat had his own point of view. He very politely but assertively replied on their proposal. Until now, everybody knew how righteous and gentle he is, but today they realized how knowledgeable and enlightened Bharat is.

On hearing the unanimous wish of Sage Vashisht and mother Kaushalaya, Bharat was taken aback because despite being wise ones, they were actually though unknowingly, defending a crime. According to him, by allowing what Kaikeyi and Manthara conspired, to happen is actually encouraging the evil endeavors. When the wicked ones find that after an initial struggle, even the wise and sensible ones yield to them, then what could be more rewarding for them? And what will happen to human society when 'Adharma' or unrighteousness is allowed to dictate terms in this manner?

Bharat thoughtfully explains that Manthara is like 'Sardhe Satti,' an unlucky planetary position of seven and a half years which took Kaikeyi, who is like 'Shani,' the powerful but insensible planet, in its control. As per astrology, Sardhe Satti Shani destructively alters being's intelligence symbolized by planet 'Jupiter' or 'Guru.' In an unfavorable position of celestial stars, wise ones usually loses their sensibility and can even lose their life, like what happened with King Dasratha. According to Bharat, the deadly influence of 'Sardhe Satti Shani' is not over yet and that it can bring the destruction of the glorious Ayodhaya Empire.

The sickness and disorder Bharat is talking about are actually 'Vaat Rog' or Delirium, which instigates 'Kaam' that is passion, ambition, and obsession arising out of mental and emotional confusion. The intense greed for the crown in Kaikeyi and lust in Dasaratha created this disorder, which first forced Lord Ram to leave for exile and is now trying to disrupt the whole of Ayodhaya.

The poison of a scorpion always moves upwards from the bite-wound, giving excruciating pain to the human body. The forest exile of Lord Ram is like a wound in the hearts of Ayodhaya people. It is now rising and reaching the highest point that is 'mind,' making them go insane in agonizing pain.

Doses of weed intoxication may help one forget all sufferings, but as soon as its effect ends, the pain comes back again. By making Bharat the King, the intoxication of power may, for a while, relieve Ayodhaya's present state of pain, but soon its illusionary effect will be over, and they will again plead for relief. Delaying the problem is not the solution to the problem.

Prince Bharat didn't just explain the problem in great detail but also gives the solution to it. He said that the only solution is the jewel of Ayodhaya that is Lord Ram, whom he'll bring back soon. It is because Ram is the Sun in front of whom no planetary position like 'Sardhe Satti Shani' can stand. Ram is the Supreme Creator whose intervention can remove any disorder and sickness from the body at once. Ram is the only sweet antidote that can neutralize the most lethal poison and gives instant relief to the affected. And Ram is the 'Vivek' or the supreme conscience, which awakens being from the intoxicated state of mind.

This is a highly significant and insightful dialogue from Bharat. Most of the Beings in all times, especially today, are suffering from deteriorated intelligence, passion, confusion, pain, and intoxication. Although each one of us is a sufferer, we don't want to accept it. And then we look for solutions in this material world, but because of its impermanence, it fails us always. Our selfish ego even prevents us from opening up and speaking our hearts out about the suffering, and so one day, life ends in dissatisfaction and pain.

The cure recommended by Bharat worked miraculously. Every being of Ayodhaya stood with Bharat and accepted his verdict. Even Sage Vashisht, Mother Kaushalya, and all ministers agreed to Bharat. At that very moment, thousands of them got prepared to go with Bharat and bring back their very own Lord Ram. Although Lord didn't return then, still Ayodhaya got pacified. But why? Because they had unwavering faith and hope that after fourteen years, Lord Ram will return and glorify Ayodhaya once again.

However, the problem is that unlike the citizens of Ayodhaya, beings of present times, lack the 'faith' and 'hope,' and that is precisely why they suffer. Greater than the advent of Ram Rajya and intervention of Lord Ram is the faith or 'Vishwas' that the Omnipresent, Eternal and Most Powerful Lord Ram is there for us, who loves us and looks after us. Faith that the Lord is with us always and we are under His refuge illuminates the way just like Hanuman, Sugreev, Vibhishan, and more found the solutions in their lives. They spent the rest of their lifetime under the aegis of Lord Ram and excelled in life. In this context, God Shiva beautifully said to Mother Parvati-

'Uma kahun main anubhav apna,
Sat Hari Bhajan, Jagad sab sapna.'

I am telling you with my experience, only the Bhajan of Lord Hari is true, rest everything is inutile.

Chapter 2.24

Bharat meets Nishadraj

As soon as he heard that Nishaad is a dear friend of Ram,
Bharat gladly rushed to embrace him with open arms.

Prince Bharat, with mothers, ministers, and his full-fledged army, left Ayodhaya and ventured out into the forest in search of Lord Ram. The sudden news that Bharat with his whole army has entered the forest region bothered Nishadraj, the chief of Nishaad tribe and devotee-friend of Lord Ram. It made him doubtthat probably Bharat wants to attack Lord Ram to **establish** control over the kingdom of Ayodhaya. He immediately called upon his companions and readied them to stop Bharat and his army. Just then, one of the wise tribesmen suggested what if his judgment about Bharat is incorrect? What if, Bharat is a friend and not an enemy?

Considering the thoughtful suggestion, Nishadraj decided to personally go and meet Bharat and try to assess the acceptability of his intentions. Accordingly, he reached near the formidable convoy and prostrated in salutation. As soon as Sage Vashisht told Bharat that Nishadraj is a dear friend of Lord Ram, Bharat got overwhelmed with emotions. He felt like he is seeing Laxman in Nishadraj. With teary eyes, Bharat immediately got down from the **royal** chariot and hurriedly rushed to embrace him. Nishadraj too reciprocated with pure love and honor. All the apprehension in Nishaad vanished at once, and Bharat was now fully assured that soon they will be able to meet their beloved Lord Ram.

Now, Bharat essentially set out to find Lord and not to wage war against anyone. Then the question arises why did Bharat take such a huge army along with him? This can be confusing for anybody, and hence, Nishadraj's skepticism was logically not wrong. Only a great and enlightened soul like Bharat, the one who only thinks from the heart, has the vision of transforming a means of violence into the soothing medium of love. As hopes started becoming brighter, Bharat immediately planned to crown Lord Ram in Chitrakoot. He also thought that if Lord Ram decides to shift the capital from Ayodhaya to Chitrakoot, then all of them with the army will settle there.

Nishad's misjudgment of Bharat's intention is quite understandable. What is amazing to note is that Nishadraj, who's the chief of a small village with just a handful of warriors, still dared to challenge and battle the humongous army of Ayodhaya. The secret behind this fearlessness is his **relentless** faith and love in Lord Ram. It is the only reason why he was able to attain the highest wisdom**, andhe also very well** knew that the impermanent body is not the truth. To fulfill your Swadharma or the purpose of life, which is nothing except the service of Lord Ram, being must not hesitate **to offer** his everything, including life.

Not only that, his speech for his people was so inspiring that they too fearlessly stood **by him** to fight, though each one of them clearly knew that death in this battle is inevitable. Nishadraj announced that if they survive, the world will not only be pleased but also admire their loyalty, and if they attain martyrdom, Lord will ensure them ultimate bliss and salvation. So either way, they will benefit. Only an extraordinary benevolent heart can think in such a way. **Nishads,** who were discarded by upper castes of the society**, are,** in actuality, the real heroes and a true inspiration for all the ardent followers of Lord Ram.

It is quite interesting to see how Nishaadraj scrutinized Bharat's intentions. He purposely took with him two sets of food offerings for Bharat, one w**as a v**egetarian, and the other was non-vegetarian. His idea was that if Bharat would first accept the non-vegetarian one, then he is probably more inclined towards war. It **alsomade sense** because ancient sages have also declared that non-vegetarians are relatively more violent than their vegetarian counterparts. Nobody in this mortal world can be totally perfect**, and** therefore, the ancient sages have suggested to wisely hand-pick options, which have a comparatively lower degree of flaws.

Secondly, Nishaadraj intentionally first saluted Sage Vashisht, though the tradition is to first salute the Prince. Had Bharat been high on ego, he would have readily taken an offense for this act of Nishadraj. It is because the probability of threat is always higher in ego-driven ones. Simple Nishaadraj did not try to do anything extravagant but did what best suits his level. The Great Bharat, on the other hand, is beyond the realm of such trivial testimonials and trials. He is a picture-perfect reflection of divine consciousness, having totally eliminated the mind-ego from the core. He neither accepted the food offerings, nor did he notice the calculative salutations. As soon **as** he heard that Nishad is Lord's friend, he rushed to embrace him with true emotions. A royal prince coming in such close contact with a scheduled tribe was something the then beings had never seen or heard before.

In ancient times, 'Varna Vyavastha' was essentially a class-system designed to bring order in the society. But instead, it became more of an instrument to manipulate and control beings. It seems like the so-called upper caste has purposely used 'Dharma' like a jailor, who in the prison of 'Vedanta,' have shackled innocent beings in the guise of 'Varna Vyavastha.' So how can they expect due respect for Dharma in the hearts of imprisoned beings? Following the footsteps of brother Ram, Prince Bharat too instantly demolished the prison and freed the prisoners forever.

For Bharat, Nishad was a 'dearie' of Lord Ram, and therefore, he was equivalent to Laxman. Bharat always considered Laxman as the symbol of devotion and sacrifice. After the eventful meeting, Bharat was assured that with Nishadraj, he will definitely find Lord Ram soon. With this incident, the world came to know how devoted and great Nishadraj was. Also, the world witnessed the depth of Bharat's love for Lord Ram and His devotees. What we can see is that whosoever had dedicated his life in the service of Lord Ram has attained the epitome of respect, fame, reverence, and of course, the honor of the world. Saint Tulsidas asserts-

The one who has not been reckoned among the sages
And is not even counted as a devotee of Lord Ram,
Lives in disarray and is a burden on this earth.

Chapter 2.25

Warning to Devta

The one who thinks of troubling His devotee,
Is mercilessly destroyed in His Fire of Fury.

The royal march of Prince Bharat and his formidable army on the path of Chitrakoot scared Indra, the King of Devta clan. His mind at once, became full of apprehensions. What if Lord Ram accepts Bharat's heartfelt insistence and decides to return to Ayodhaya? And what if that somehow stops or delays Ravan's destruction? Then how will Devta clan be free from Ravan's ever-growing control? Indra very well knew about Lord's soft-heartedness. He was also aware of the fact that it's almost impossible to ignore the love of Bharat as it is holiest in the world. Therefore, the probability of the Lord accepting Bharat's request is quite high. All this and many more prompted the Devta to conspire to somehow prevent Bharat from meeting Lord Ram.

Last time the Devta approached Mother Saraswati for help, but this time, the self-serving Devta decided to consult their Teacher, Guru Brahaspati, for a solution. As expected, the **immensely**learned Brahaspati rebuked the Devta for such an unrighteous appeal. He also **admonished** Indra that Lord Ram can accept and tolerate any injustice, hatred, offence or crime against Himself, but if anybody tries to upset His beloved devotee, then he cannot escape **His wrath**. He further counselled that this whole cosmos worships Him, but Lord Ram worships Bharat, so **none is closer to** Lord other than Bharat. He firmly concluded, saying that the pleasure-seeking and selfish Devta must not even dare to create any hurdle in the union of **the greatest** Devotee and Lord.

Guru Brahaspati then pacified Indra, reminding him that once Lord takes up a task, it is bound to succeed, that is, the end of Ravan is certain. From a pure and sacred devotee like Bharat, there cannot be any harm to Devta clan. A great devotee like Bharat is always absorbed in thinking and doing good for others, and he is even unhesitant in sacrificing his own life for the well-being of others.Devta must come out of their selfishness and stop doubting Bharat as he had never ever spoiled others' interests in his lifetime. The inspiring words of wisdom of their Guru alleviated the Dev**ta, and in salutations, they showered flo**wers on the **holy** path of great Bharat.

Mind-ego's attachment towards selfish interests is so intense that it creates enemies just out of anybody, **without having** any solid grounds. In present times too, we can find many entities at international, national, organizational, religious, regional or business levels unnecessarily considering others as a threat or competition. Without having any solid grounds, a selfish, ambitious, and unsecured entity tries to harass a guiltless. In fact, the more the being is attached to self-pleasures, the more he fears. Since he is unable to deal with his apprehension of loss of pleasure, he tries to harm others. One can only get free from this ignorance by 'Vivek' or words of wisdom of **anelevated** one. However, for a materialistic-selfish one, it is also very difficult to accept somebody's sound advice, no matter how helpful it may **be, because** polluted mind-ego has a tendency to consider even the learned one as a self-seeking entity as itself. Considering that, the way the Devta handled their mind-ego trap and accepted the righteous advice of their Guru Brahaspati wholeheartedly is quite inspiring. Of course, they got diverted for a while but soon reinstated their faith in Lord Ram.

A true seeker or devotee is always free from the tricks of mind-ego and so doesn't get easily bothered like selfish beings. The reason is that what a seeker is seeking is infinite and available to everyone. One gets insecure only for things that are limited in nature. For example, 'land' and 'gold' are objects which have a limited supply on this planet, and therefore, there is so much yearning and chasing for them. But Lord is infinite beyond the boundaries of human imagination. A devotee doesn't need any other being or object to attain what he is seeking. And since there is no intervention from any external sources, he leads a contented and happy life. Lord **has declared that He will take care of all life needs of His devotee**, and the devotee doesn't need to bother himself in worldly affairs. All he needs is to serve the Lord unconditionally with pure love and dedication.

Just like great Bharat, the one who aims just Lord **attainsnot only** His endearment but also admiration and reverence of the world. Imagine how peaceful life becomes, which doesn't require you to work on earning, chasing, securing, and defending objects. Once the being surrenders to Lord, everything in his life gets sorted automatically. Saint Tulsidas also says to the seekers - *Jahi vidhi rakhe Ram tahi vidhi rahiye* - Live the way, Lord Ram wants you to live.

Chapter 2.26

Misunderstanding of Laxman

Never expected this, but can't blame Bharat alone,
Anybody can become bonkers after getting a throne.

Lord Ram with Mother Sita and brother Laxman were residing at Chitrakoot when they heard from locals that Prince Bharat is coming their way with a full-fledged army. Lord knew Bharat very well, and He at once understood thatBharatintends to crown his brother Ram as the King of Ayodhaya then and there in Chitrakoot and therefore is coming with the army to execute the ceremony as per royal customs. Now, Lord Ram was in a catch twenty-two situation. On the one hand, there was father's order of forest exile, and on the other hand, it's going to be brother's insistence to crown Him the King. Needless to say, He got very anxious pondering over how to deal with this 'Dharam Sankat' or the dilemma of duty versus love.

However, Laxman was of the opinion that as Bharat is coming to wage war, which will lead to violence between brothers, Lord Ram is feeling troubled. With bloodshot eyes, he at once declared that if anybody tries to trouble his Lord Ram, be it brother Bharat, then he will not pardon him. The fierce reaction from Laxman was quite natural because the service of Lord Ram is the only purpose of his life. Although Laxman apparently misread Lord's presumptions, the arrival of Bharat accompanied by a huge army naturallysignals a potential war. Therefore, Laxman's sudden rage is also justifiable. Laxman then concluded that ultimately Bharat could not be blamed for 'power hunger' because what he is doing is out of the influence of mind-ego traps of greed and control.

Saint Tulsidas aptly explains that in the history of human civilization, there is only one reason behind the failure of everyego-driven being and that is he has only considered himself as the doer and his skills and efforts as the only cause of his achievements and has totally ignored Lord's 'Grace.' Such a being expects appreciation for himself for his every success but puts the blame on others in adversities. He further clarifies his point with a very good example. In 'Swati Nakshatra' or constellation, the dewdrop that falls on an oyster transforms into a pearl. The oyster that receives this grace, therefore, becomes of immeasurable value. There are millions of oysters lying in oceans, but only on a few selective ones, the dewdrop falls. So can any of the chosen ones claim that because of some special quality, the dew specifically dropped on it?

In reality, there is absolutely nothing in the hands of oysters, and beings are also no exception to this. Everything that happens in life is strictly governed by the universal intelligence based on being's past karma and, of course, Lord's Grace. In fact, nobody could fathom the functioning of this intelligence. Accepting this truth, whenever one experiences success, then instead of being conceited and carried away, he should rather get more humble as God has selected him for His special grace. Even the worst dipsomaniac has a certain limit tointoxication, but no matter how much appreciation one gets, mind-ego is never satisfied. To endlessly seek credit and appreciation for self is actually a trap of mind-ego, which has been seen as the primary cause of grand failures in human history.

Laxman had the illusion that Bharat has taken a step forward in arrogance and hatred than even the most egotistical rulers of history, as he is the only one ever who has directly dared to confront God. He says that there is none other like Bharat who has misused Lord's brotherly love this way, and therefore, he wants to avenge and seeks brother Ram's permission to attack and punish Bharat.

What we are observing here is an utter misunderstanding of Laxman towards Bharat? If partial knowledge, impatience, fictitious assumptions, and insecurity of mind-ego can delude the most learned one like Laxman, then what is the capacity of ordinary beings to escape that? However, when Lord Ram is there, no mishap can ever occur. Lord is the 'Vivek,' which controls the irrational thoughts and makes one assess the situation wisely, thereby eliminating chances of misunderstanding and mishap. The one who always treasures the ever-gracious omnipotent Lord in his heart and sees himself mirrored in the heart of the Lord cannot become the cause and effect of any trouble. Both Laxman and Bharat are pure devotees of Lord Ram, and therefore, no misunderstanding can spoil their divine love and bonding.

Chapter 2.27

Truth Shines

The one who gets high, in the intoxication of power,
Has never been in the company of learned ones ever.

Seeing mighty Laxman fuming in anger, the Devta clan panicked again. Their apprehension was that instead of the Ram-Ravan's battle, there might be a war within the Raghukal family itself. Considering the grave consequence, they immediately cautioned Laxman through 'Akash-Vaani' or 'Announcement from Heaven' - "No doubt you are a great and undefeatable noble warrior but before reacting impulsively, you must think wisely about the merits and demerits of every action. Remember, the one who impatiently indulges in violence without reflecting ends up repenting his action."

Hearing the warning from 'Devlok', Laxman at once realized his misjudgement and was embarrassed for his harsh words for brother Bharat. To ease the situation, Lord Ram lovingly explained to Laxman that from a political perspective, his threatened feeling about Bharat was not totally wrong. Whoever drinks the wine of power does get high on its intoxication. It is almost impossible to deal with this trap of mind-ego. However, the wise one who has attended 'Satsang' of enlightened sages cannot get influenced by the intoxication of power. Bharat is a wise and pure soul, to whom, even the thrones of 'Brahma-Vishnu-Mahesh' together, let alone worldly attractions, cannot inebriate.

Saint Tulsidas says that mind-ego always remains dissatisfied with the present and, therefore, desperately looks for opportunities to change it into something beautiful. It is the reason why being is always found to be busy changing his perspective for himself and others' perspective for him. Driven by mind-ego, he endlessly looks for acceptance, recognition and honour for himself. To get rid of this never-ending craving, a thoughtful change is needed. And that change can only come from 'Gyan' and 'Bhakti.' But for ego, both knowledge and devotion are unacceptable, and therefore, mind-ego trapped being finds it very difficult to tread on the path of spirituality.

Instead of correcting mind-ego's dysfunction, ignorant beings make every possible effort to change their surroundings in accordance with their delusional perception of perfection. As a result, they usually fall victim to deadly addictions like drugs and wine to make themselves and the surrounding more acceptable. Being feels elated and cheerful and finds life enjoyable under the influence of intoxications. But like every worldly thing, these intoxications also have a temporary effect, which soon ends, and the being again faces truth and reality, which are repulsive to his ego. And again to evade the present, he starts consuming intoxications. This vicious cycle keeps on repeating, and that is how one becomes an intoxicant-addict.

The urge for intoxication is not the same for every being. Beings who have denser ego seek a stronger and permanent dose of intoxication that has a lasting effect of keeping them in the state of euphoria. Power is one such intoxication which gives a longer state of joy even to the most benighted being. With the attainment of power, the one who was unimportant earlier suddenly becomes the most sought-after. And he starts seeing others as miniscule and insignificant. The one who was standing there alone yesterday surprisingly finds a huge mass of people following him today. Such is the influence of Power.

However, in this circus of power, he is unable to figure out the real truth of the people following him. While some of his so-called followers keep him intensely intoxicated with their adulation to abuse his power, there are some who try to stand close to him so as to earn respect and honour through his position. And then, there are the shrewd opportunists hidden in the guise of loyalists whose only intention is to dethrone him one day and acquire his position. In reality, he, who is highly intoxicated by the wine of power, is never able to see this truth.

But not all powerful ones are like this. The one who has attended Satsang or has learned from enlightened ones, neither gets intoxicated nor is influenced by fake followers. 'Satsang' is that divine wine, the effect of which is eternal and most satisfying, in front of which no other intoxication can stand. The exquisiteness of Satsang lies in the fact that it makes every being live, believe and appreciate the present moment. It is Satsang that brings being back in the beautiful present moment, from the flights of egoic fantasies. Satsang shows him the truth that is 'Vasudeva Sarvam' or Lord is in every object and being. It thus puts an end to the tendency of compulsive judging and seeing others as lesser or superior. Being realizes that all his power, status or throne is because of the Grace of God and not because of his abilities.

After annihilating Ravan, Lord Ram gave the throne of Lanka to Vibhishan. From a diplomatic standpoint, it was a smart move by King Ram of crowning his loyalist. But from a devotional point of view, it was purely the Grace of Lord Ram on Vibhishan. However, in the sense of justice, it was as per Lord's vision of Ram-Rajya wherein whosoever misuses power will be eliminated, and the responsibility will be delegated to the most deserving one. Vibhishan was a real qualified one who had always given Ravan, his brother and king, righteous advice. But the highly-conceited and power-influenced Ravan insulted and ousted him. Even then, Vibhishan never thought ill of him and took the righteous step towards Supreme Ram.

Lord Ram expresses that Bharat is way beyond the clutches of mind-ego. He is like an ocean of divinity where there always remains stillness of purity. Waves of negativity are impossible to arise in this ocean. Lord then openly declared that even if the universe topples over, then too, Bharat was and he will always be the purest and greatest. Hearing Lord's highly inspiring words, Laxman got overwhelmed and elated. Weird imaginations and uncontrolled thoughts of mind-ego, which had disturbed him now, got dissolved by the Lord's words of wisdom. Laxman was deeply absorbed in the beautiful thoughts of Bharat's love, and it was just then that he heard a familiar voice from behind.

Chapter 2.28

Reunion at Chitrakoot

Only the Lord's name can make one free,
Chanting it, being finds peace & self-victory,
In every breath, I utter your name,
To live life, this way is my only aim.

With a mixed feeling of happiness and surprise, Laxman informed Lord Ram that brother Bharat has come to meet Him. As soon as Lord heard Laxman, he hurriedly got up and forgetting everything rushed to hug His dear Bharat. The spectators out there were overwhelmed seeing the reunion of two heavenly bodies and one soul. Although Bharat had reached the entry point of Lord's hermitage, **he seemed q**uite hesitant in meeting Him. It was primarily because he felt that he had lost the credibility to face the Lord.

He then recalled Lord's declaration that every being is welcome for His love, but the e**vil one cannot come cl**ose to Him. **But a**s soon as the self-serving materialistic being decides to discard jealousy, greed, cleverness and hatred, Lord frees him from all worldly negativities and then embraces him. That day Bharat was feeling very guilty inside and he even considered himself the**evilest**of all because he was the reason why Lord had to bear the trouble of forest exile. He felt as if he was having all the**villainous** traits in himself, and he didn't know how to **present himself in front of** the Lord? **These thoughts** inundated him despite the fact that everyone knew Bharat was not at all responsible for that unfortunate episode.

Bharat being a true devotee, then thought to himself that if the being cannot come face-to-face with Lord, then forever merciful Lord himself comes forward to embrace His devotee. Here Bharat makes us familiar with one of the most common traits **of a seeker**, and that is inconsistency. At times **the seeker** feels deeply devoted to the Lord, while at other times, he remains obsessed with materialistic affairs. But unlike**him**, when Lord accepts the seeker, for even on**ce, He then forever looks after him.** These insightful thoughts gave Bharat the **courage** to call his brother Ram.

It is interesting to note here that although Lord saw Bharat at once, He didn't respond intentionally. He was purposefully waiting for Laxman to inform him about Bharat's arrival. Earlier, Laxman had doubted Lord's ability to recognize the **true nature of the** people in the context of Bharat. Laxman had said that the Lord is very simple-hearted and trusts anybody **without giving a thought**. Lord didn't reply to Laxman then and waited for him to realize the greatness of Bharat by himself, which he did. This way**, Lord also** wanted to show the world the innocence of Laxman, who just a few minutes back was anxious to battle Bharat but was now eager to welcome and embrace him wholeheartedly with brotherly love & emotion.

The mothers, brothers, sage, ministers and citizens of Ayodhaya, who accompanied Bharat to the forest, finally got the opportunity to meet their Lord Ram. Lord greeted them individually with great love and warmth. Mother Kaikeyi was also there, but she was standing behind, deeply ashamed with guilt, and was hesitant in facing her dear son Ram. Lord at once understood mother's predicament and **He** himself went to her and touched her feet for blessings. He consoled her that whatever happens is because of Time, Karma, and Will of Supreme, **in front of which no human being has any control.** Lord also ensured that mother is totally free from guilt, which she has been carrying so far. Lord **also made her understand** that whatever had happened in Ayodhaya was not her fault. Therefore, by quoting the principle of Karma, He clarified that every being reaps what he sows, t**hat is, the forest exile is the Karma of Lord Ram, for which none else can be held responsible.** One has to face the outcomes of past deeds.

Now, the question is, why **a seeker even** after knowing about the eternal Karma principle, still indulges in acts of unrighteousness and cleverness? Goswami Tulsidas clarifies that **because of the influence of mind-ego, human-being** traps himself in evil endeavors. If the **seeker** is righteous, but at times falters and indulges in unrighteous acts, then it is because of his 'Sanskar' or Habits-Memories of past lives. It is also seen that **sometimes not just one individual** but a **group of individuals or even the entire society** gets involved in one same evil act. For example, female infanticide is **one of the most evil acts known, but still,it is** practised by a large part of society. Goswami elucidates that for such collective acts of evil, the blame game goes on transcending 'Kaal' or Time. Time is very powerful **as it governs the**

morality, ethics and conscience of ignorant beings and pushes them towards evilness. Based on **this** influence of Time, the **Yuga system was designed by the ancient seers.**

Next question is then in the present time, that is the era of Kaliyuga, where negativity is continuously rising, how can the being practise righteousness? Goswami nicely explains that in Kaliyuga, being has no power and no option whatsoever in his hand. He can **protect** himself from the evil influence of these self-destructive forces only by taking refuge in Supreme Lord Ram. Else he will just float aimlessly in the web of Maaya and continue committing sins **for which he has to face the painful repercussions.**

Kaliyug Kewal Naam Adhaara,
Sumir-Sumir Nar Utrahi Paara.

Queen Kaikeyi is enlightened with a clear, innocent and pure heart having surrendered to Lord Ram. Now it's Lord's responsibility to restore the safety, security, dignity and happiness of the mother. From that day onwards, nobody talked about or accused or labelled or even judged Mother Kaikeyi ever. That day the greatest burden was offloaded from Kaikeyi's shoulder by her dear son Ram. It was after a long time that her heart found little peace. And that is why Goswami Tulsidas repeatedly keeps saying that **in Kaliyuga** no doing is greater **than chanting 'Ram Naam.'**

Chapter 2.29

Declaration of Bharat

Life of a being in worldly dilemma is understandable,
But for the seeker, only the rule of black or white is applicable.

At Chitrakoot, Sage Vashisht, with a view to quicken the process of Ram's return, immediately called an assembly of Royals, ministers and elites of Ayodhaya to discuss the matter. Every citizen of Ayodhaya, including Bharat, wants Prince Ram to return to Ayodhaya and take over the throne as the King. On the other hand, there's Lord Ram, who wants to fulfill father Dasratha's order of fourteen years of forest exile diligently. But now that King Dasratha is no more, his orders cannot be revoked. So it is now the primary responsibility of the assembly to find the solution to the problem.

In the assembly, many members put forward their own suggestions. Sage Vashisht suggests that Lord Ram and Laxman can return to Ayodhaya, and Bharat and Shatrughan would fulfill King's order of exile on their behalf. Vashisht tries to convince Bharat saying that in worldly affairs, those who are ready to let go half of their possessions when they anticipate the loss of everything, are able to save themselves from many complications. It is quite natural and evident that there will be a conflict of interest between the entities, but one has to deal with it responsibly. Also, if every entity just thinks of its own interests discarding others, then nobody can leave peacefully. Therefore for the welfare of many, one must not be reluctant to compromise.

History always reminds us that whenever two formidable entities have clashed on the same interest, then it has only routed them to struggle, war and utter destruction. The same thing occurred in the epic of Mahabharata. Although the righteous Pandavas were ready to compromise with just five villages instead of half of the empire, mind-ego trapped Duryodhan was not ready to let go even an inch of land. Had he accepted Lord Krishna's proposal for settlement, the war of Mahabharat and the destruction of Kauravas wouldn't have happened.

Sage continued and said that the only purpose of Bhakti is to make the human-being detached and indifferent to the material world. If this change doesn't come naturally, then any claim of a spiritual seeker on knowledge and enlightenment is misleading and baseless. An ignorant being lacks the insightfulness and fails to recognize the truth behind an occurrence. He wears glasses of his own limited perspective and tries to see everything through it. Conversely, the wise one always takes others' perspectives into consideration while he tries to understand the actual cause of an occurrence. It also helps him to realize that the clash of interest is just based on human-being's belief system and therefore holds no grounds. In fact, clash of beliefs is actually the most useless activity humankind has relied on since ages and spent its precious time, energy and resources that have resulted in nothing other than losses.

Goswami Tulsidas says that a broad-minded person understands the futility of stubbornness or rigidness. Knowing and understanding the inefficacy of such clashes, he is always prepared to compromise for a larger good. Lord Ram himself practiced the same and was successful in making friends with beings havingdifferent belief systems. On the other hand, the self-destructive stubbornness of prejudiced Kaikeyi, Ravana and Bali made them enemies of their own folks. Despite Dasratha's repeated request to remain satisfied with the first boon that is crowing of Bharat as the king, mind-ego trapped Kaikeyi continued to be stubborn on her second demand, that is, the exile of Ram. Dasratha had no issues in crowning Bharat, but he very well knew that he cannot survive without Ram. Had Kaikeyi been sensitive and had accepted Dasratha's plea, then so much chaos would not have taken place in Ayodhya. The point here is to understand how the stubbornness of one individual like Kaikeyi can result in a problem of such a large magnitude.

Needless to say, Great Bharat was more than happy with Sage Vashishta's suggestion to complete the forest exile on behalf of his brother Ram. Bharat's greatness clearly reflected when he replied to Vashisht that in worldly affairs, the compromise on the half is a good deal, but on the path of spirituality, there can be no compromise. The principle of spirituality is totally different as compared to worldly disciplines. It is interesting to note here thathere too, the seeker that is Bharat was very adamant, but notfor personal gains rather to sacrifice his everything.

On the path of truth, it is only after complete renunciation that the seeker can attain completeness. So Bharat proposes that instead of just fourteen years, he will spend all his life in forest exile. There can be no space for compromise for Bharat, especially in the service of Lord Ram. Saint Tulsidas explains that in a worldly perspective, compromise on half definitely makes the being unhappy, but still, he accepts because of limited alternatives. But the attainment of Supreme Consciousness Ram is not half and not even a neuron lesser. It is absolute, and therefore for it, the seeker needs to renounce everything which he believes as 'I' and 'Mine.'

Only the one who is pure, beautiful and holy like the great Bharat can understand this reality. Practically it is very difficult for common beings to accept that everything that they have so far considered as their own, that is 'I' and 'Mine', is untrue. Therefore since time immemorial, enlightened ones have always advised beings to give up 'Ifs' & 'Buts' and just surrender to the Supreme Lord and practice Bhakti. Only then it becomes Lord's responsibility to liberate the being from the traps of untrue beliefs and show him the truth of peace, bliss and perfection.

Chapter 2.30

Duty Versus Love

Your order is my command,
I will look after the throne on behalf of you,
But if you return late even by a day,
I will immolate myself for true.

Lord Ram puts Bharat in a quandary when he announces that whatever Bharat decides will be final and acceptable to Him. But forever humble Bharat found it disrespectful to become the judge of the assembly and pass the verdict. He always considered himself no more than a petty servant of Lord Ram, and therefore, he cannot even think of giving an order to hisbrother. He could find no words to reply and remained silent. In fact, he was waiting for the Lord to decide the fate of Ayodhaya. While the assembly was trying to find a solution to the tricky situation, it was just then that the news of King Janaka's arrival reached them.

Everybody at the assembly sighed in relief that now the problem will be solved. So far, everybody present in the assembly was utterly confused and hence was not coming forward with their opinions. Despite being a wise and enlightened one, Sage Vashisht, too, found himself incapable of making the decision. With the arrival of King Janaka, he finally felt at ease as now the onus which was on him, being the senior-most, will be shifted to King Janaka. The entire assembly knew that no person in the world was better than Janaka in solving the problem.

The situation was indeed very complicated. On the one hand, was 'Dharam' or duty of Prince Ram as a son of Dasratha, and on the other hand, was 'Prem' or love of Prince Bharat as a brother-devotee of Ram. Bharat intensely wants Lord Ram to return, but Lord is helpless as He is bound by the order of their deceased father, Dasratha. If Lord stays in the forest, then it would be as per Dharma, but then it would also mean disregarding the pure and unconditional love of Bharat. And if Lord Ram accepts Bharat's love and returns to Ayodhaya, then it would be considered against Dharma, and that also means disobeying father's order.

In the present times, it is very difficult for the 'Swarthi' or self-seeking beings to accept that a situation like that of Ram-Bharat can arise between the brothers. In this highly conflicting clash of duty and love, there are no self-interests, but only selflessness of the brothers. There were other options open for Ram-Bharat like Lord Ram could have returned, and Bharat would have completed the exile on his behalf. Alternatively, Bharat could have stayed with the Lord for the exile and sent Laxman back. Ram-Bharat could have decided to do whatever they felt like, andno one in the universe could have dared to stop them from doing so.

This was Chitrakoot's prevailing situation, which for us, the selfish human-beings of present times, may seem to be hard to digest. Our logical minds would have argued that what's the point in all this drama? Raghukul would have simply terminated the orders, and everybody could happily return back to Ayodhaya. Queen Kaikeyi had withdrawn her orders, and King Dasratha was no more then why Lord was so adamant to complete the exile and for whom?

But there is also a good reason behind Lord Ram's adamancy. Saint Tulsidas says that one should live life in such a way that his every action through body, wordof mouth and thought of mind, is being watched by Supreme God. So whatever one has committed to, for even once, no matter if there is any mortal eyewitness or not, should be honored by him because it's the supreme consciousness in every being which is always watching. Remember, one can fool anybody, even himself, but not his consciousness. And this was the same rationale behind Lord Ram opting for completing the forest exile. For the Lord, words are much more significant than life. Once He has committed to something, it doesn't matter if the witnesses are there or not, He is going to fulfill it.

Raghukul Reet Sada Chali Aayi,
Pran Jaye Par Vachan Na Jaayi.

In present times, most of us can only think about our own interests and don't bother others' concerns, welfare and interests. Why is that, that wecan't think and act selflessly like Ram-Bharat? Why is it that we are so blindly obsessed with selfish motives? Why do we fear so much about the loss of wealth, pleasure, possessions and honour? Why are we unable to love unconditionally?

The answer to all the questions is one, and that is 'Ego'. Trapped in the temptations and clutches of ego, beings believe that the only purpose of life is to accumulate and secure material objects until their last breath. This urge for accumulation is so intense that even when one realizes that his material endeavors are wrongly directed, he still justifies his acts with the idea that this is how society and the world function. 'When everybody is mean and shrewd, why should I be noble and selfless?' Human beings have long forgotten to care for what is right and wrong. Immorality has become so widespread that now care, compassion and empathy are buried deep under the huge dump of selfish interests.

However, there are also exceptions. Wise beings though much lesser in number, have known to successfully free themselves from the traps of mind-ego and have realized the wastefulness in the Egoic belief system of 'I' and 'Mine'. These wise ones also have the ability to assess the situation in a larger perspective where individual identity, pleasure, reputation and wealth are of very little or no significance. Their only purpose of life is to work tirelessly towards the greater good of humanity. One universal principle, which only the enlightened understands and ignorant being finds it impossible to accept, is that the quantum of joys and sorrows is predefined. No matter how ambitious, desperate, selfish and insensitive one becomes, he cannot alter the destined quota of happiness & unhappiness in his life. One who accepts this fact is in a better position to discard selfishness.

King Janaka was considered the epitome of Dharam, Gyana and Bhava that is righteousness, wisdom and love. Therefore Sage Vashisht was very confident that Janaka would surely be able to resolve the issue, understanding the perspectives of both the brothers, Ram-Bharat. As expected, King Janaka, after carefully hearing the whole incident, speaks his mind. He says that in the clash between Dharma (duty) and Prem (love), the victory is always of Love. There is nothing in nature, not even the Supreme Creator, who is not under the azure of love. Therefore based on this ground, the exemplary brotherly love of Bharat wins. Hearing this, Bharat smiled and everybody felt elated that now their Lord Ram will be returning to Ayodhaya.

Janaka then elucidates that love is greater than duty, but the principle of love is that the lover has no say, no choice and no will of his own. A lover only acts as per the will of the one he loves. Herein Bharat unconditionally loves brother Ram more than anything in the world, and therefore Janaka advises Bharat to ask his brother Ram to share His thoughts and what He wants? And then whatever Lord Ram says must be accepted by Bharat unquestioningly and will be the final and sealed verdict.

Bharat accepts Janaka's judgment and, with joined hands, requests the Lord to tell him what he must do. Lord Ram, with great affection, asks Bharat to look after Ayodhaya for the next fourteen years on His behalf. After completing the exile, Lord says that He will return and take over the throne. Bharat finally accepts Lord's verdict, but then he also gives his final verdict. In fact, he warns that after fourteen years, if the Lord is late even by a day in returning to Ayodhaya, then he will immolate himself.

The beings of Heaven, Earth and Hell were awestruck, witnessing the greatest love of two brothers. Everybody knew the greatness of Lord Ram, but that day they realized the overwhelming stature and magnificent qualities of Bharat as well. This is the beauty of Dharma, Bhakti and Ramayana, which cannot be found anywhere else. This is the beauty of love that only a pure and sacred heart can understand and relish. This is the glory of Lord Ram, which only the great one like Bharat who surrenders in His lotus feet can understand.

Chapter 2.31

The Stage is Set

Bharat returns to Ayodhaya, but not empty-handed,
Because of him, the seeds of Ram-Rajya were planted.

Even the puredevotion, love and efforts of Prince Bharat could not change the final decision of Lord Ram. So utterly disappointed, Bharat and his entire entourage started preparing to leave Chitrakoot and return to Ayodhaya. With a heavy heart and tears in eyes, the citizens of Ayodhaya saluted and bid goodbye to their beloved, Lord Ram. The situation was equally testing for the Lord. The heart-wrenching moments of separation even made the One who is beyond the periphery of union and disunion very emotional. Bharat didn't want to return empty-handed. So while departing, he humbly requests Lord Ram to give him His holy sandals or 'Paduka' as a memento. Lord understood the reason and readily agreed to give His Paduka, which Bharat then carried on his forehead and walked back. When everybody left, Lord Ram with Sita and Laxman also returned back to their hut. Lord also had plans to pack up from Chitrakoot soon as he wanted to enter the Dandakaranya forest to start neutralizing the evil Asura.

After returning to Ayodhaya, the first and foremost thing Bharat did was to place Lord Ram's sandals or 'Paduka' on the throne or the 'Rajya Singhasan' of the Ayodhaya Empire. Thereafter every single day, Bharat would worship the paduka and sought permission from it before starting his day. Secondly, just like brother Ram, he toodiscarded the royal luxury and started living like an ascetic in the outskirts of Ayodhaya in the area of Nandigram.

As per the royal customs, a King was free to give any of his proud possessions to anybody without being questioned. King Dasratha, though out of being subject to manipulations by Kaikeyi, had appointed Bharat as the next King of Ayodhaya, which Bharat should have accepted as his responsibility. But it was no less than a curse for Bharat. For him, the owner of the whole empire was one and only Lord Ram. Lord's paduka on the throne essentially signified and reminded everybody that the King of Ayodhaya is none other than Lord Ram and Bharat is just a caretaker who is looking after the kingdom affairs on his master's behalf.

By opting to live an ascetic life in Nandigram, Bharat intelligently stayed away from power and pleasure, which is associated with the throne of Ayodhaya. He very well knew that power is connected to the mind, and pleasure is connected to the body. Mind and body are interdependent on each other. Once the mind becomes habitual of power, it constantly craves for pleasures, and once the body becomes habitual of pleasures, it seeks more power to ensure the continuity of these pleasures. Over time, this mind-body game becomes so dominant, that 'Vivek' or the intelligence feels helpless in curbing the influence of power and pleasure. Although at times, intelligence tries to caution the being about it, the pleasure-hypnotized being fails to read the message. Bharat was also well aware that there is no mortal or immortal being who has not been bitten by the snake of power.

Bharat was wise enough to understand that to protect oneself from the never-ending addictions of power and pleasure, mere 'Vivek' or intelligence is not good enough. Instead, strict discipline or 'Niyama' of mind and body is needed to curb such addictions. Therefore he gladly rejected the throne and the luxurious life of the royal palace and led a life of strict discipline and order.

In this context, there is an incident of 'Samudra-Manthan' wherein God Shiv requested God Vishnu to reveal to Him, His beautiful feminine form which infatuated the demons so much so that they just let the 'Amrit' or nectar slip off from their hands, for which they were battling ferociously and aggressively with demigods or Devta for such a long time. God Shiv couldn't believe how the attraction towards a female form can be so overwhelming. Although God Vishnu was somewhat hesitant initially, He later revealed His feminine form to Shiv. Surprisingly, Supreme Lord Shiv got so mesmerized by the divine beauty that He too forgot the reality and started chasing that female form, driven by the influence of attraction and lust. The incident bears a clear and important message for human beings. That is to be very 'cautious' in life.Such is the attraction of beauty and influence of lust.When even God Shiva can lose control, then how can self-discipline be expected from mortal beings?

Although Bharat was the epitome of Vivek or intelligence, he still considered himself incapable of dealing with forces of beauty, power and pleasure, which were attached to the throne of Ayodhaya. And therefore, he, by living like an ascetic and by practicing austere penance, wanted to instill that discipline in his life which is expected from a true devotee of Lord Ram. Although for practical reasons of administration, he would visit the palace and the city, he always remained detached. To ensure that nothing comes in his way, Bharat had already given the responsibility of the family to Prince Shatrughan, the youngest brother. Out of all the Raghukul brothers, it was only Shatrughan who led a regular domestic life during that exile period.

Goswami Tulsidas also firmly believes that along with 'Vairagya' or indifference, discipline or 'Niyama' is essential in a seeker's life. It is not necessary that every seeker goes to extremes like Bharat, but he must at least incorporate some measures which keep on reminding him to lead a disciplined life and not get swayed away by the evil influence of power and pleasure.

Bharat set a perfect example of dealing with power and pleasure outstandingly. Instead of becoming the King, he chose to look after Ayodhaya like a devoted servant of Lord Ram. When the administrator looks after the wellness of others by keeping himself detached to the influence of power and pleasure, then that 'Rajya' or country is bound to become a symbol of God-Governed country as then, there is no influence of Maya or temptations.

Bharat's great deeds were also in tune with the principle of 'Karma Yog' or Yoga of Action, wherein the seeker must surrender all actions to Supreme without having the least attachment for his actions or the fruits of his actions. As a matter of fact, a seeker can analyze any situation and act accordingly, but he must not expect favorable outcomes. The reason is very simple, and that is all actions of the world are happening and performing with the sole will of the Lord. We have to accept that our body, mind and intelligence are not intrinsic but given to us by the Lord.

Ignorance makes beings believe that it is they who decide the course of their life.And because of this ignorance, they experience pain and suffering. Remember, Lord doesn't intervene in the belief system of beings, rather gives the being complete freedom to reason and decide. Whether onewants to live in ignorance or work on his awareness is solely his own choice.

Again, Bharat is a great example of a Karam Yogi who had most sincerely practiced Lord's principles. After fourteen years of exile, the establishment of Ram-Rajya in Ayodhaya was not just the result of Lord Ram's simply taking over the reign of the empire. In fact, the stage for Ram-Rajya was already set by Bharat right from the moment when he refused to become the King and, without assuming the royal power and pleasures, executed all his responsibilities with immense sincerity and dedication. It is the same reason why Lord Ram, after returning from the forest exile, gives Bharat all the credit for the establishment of Ram-Rajya in Ayodhaya.

With this, the 'Ayodhaya Kand' or the chapter of Ayodhaya comes to an end. It also marks the beginning of Lord Ram's real challenges and the war against the evil Asura. One evening, Lord Ram was standing alone on the hilltop of Chitrakoot and gazing at the Sunset. In front of Him, the boundary of the Dandakaranya forest was disappearing in oblivion. So far, His devotees have learned about ethics, values and honour and have understood the real meaning of relationships and love. Now they will witness Lord Ram's ever-inspiring words of wisdom from the great enlightened sages who dwell in the forest. Also, the beings would witness that no life, not even the life of Maryada Purushottam Lord Ram, is free from adversities and pains. It is not about how challenging His life is; rather, it's all about how He dealt with life in the face of those challenges.

Ayodhaya Kand started with King Dasratha thinking about retiring and handing over the control of the kingdom to Prince Ram, and it ended with the death of Dasratha and forest exile of Prince Ram. All this happened very quickly and with bewildering twists and turns. This is how life actually is. This is the beauty of the unpredictable and unexpected attributes of life. This is the tale of Ramayana, the story of the simplest personification of a divine incarnation who led life in the most ideal and perfect manner, which, even after so many millenniums, still resonates in the heart of mankind.

ARANYAKAND

Chapter 3.1

Foolish doubts Divinity: Story of Jayant

Only two things are infinite, the universe and stupidity,
And I'm not sure about the former, but the latter is a reality.

It's always a divine spectacle for Heaven and Earth whenever Supreme Lord Ram and Mother Sita spend time together in solitude to enjoy the serenity of nature, beautiful mountains and pristine rivers. However, one such delightful moment didn't last long that day when Jayant, the son of Indra, sneaked on the heavenly couple like a thief in the guise of a 'Crow.' All of a sudden, the crow hit hard on the feet of Sita with its pointed beak and fled from the place. No sooner did the delicate lotus feet of Sita suffer the painful blow than it started bleeding. Sita didn't say anything, but the moment Lord discovered the bleeding injury, He got really furious. Lord plucked a grass blade or 'Tinka' from the ground and threw it towards the culprit. Immediately after the release, the Tinka transformed into a Brahmastra, the deadliest weapon ever known, and started chasing Jayant. To save his life, Jayant, back in his real form, started running away from the weapon.

He first went to his father, Indra, the Chief Lord of Devta, who, after knowing the stupid act of his son, at once refused to protect him. Utterly shocked, Jayant then rushed to God Shiva and God Brahma respectively to save his life. Knowing that he had infuriated Lord Ram, they too refused to give him shelter. With that, Jayant's last hope got crushed. He was scared to hell and understood that his end had come. Just then, divine Sage Narad Muni appeared before him and advised him to stop running around and that he must go back to Lord Ram and surrender in His lotus feet. Jayant realizing his grave mistake surrendered to the Lord, who pardoned his life, yet punished him by destroying one of his eyes.

Saint Tulsidas says that it was only due to the ever-kind and merciful nature of Lord Ram that Jayant could escape the dire consequences of such an offense. Otherwise, Lord would have surely slayed him just like He slayed Ravan. Now the question is why in the first instance, Jayant acted so foolishly and hurt Sita? For a long time, all that Jayant heard in Devlok was talks and praises of Lord Ram. Being the son of King Indra, such devotion of Devta for Lord Ram and not for him triggered feelings of insecurity and jealousy in his ego-driven mind. Like many others, he considered King Dasratha just a mortal friend of his father, and so perceived Prince Ram, the son of Dasaratha as an ordinary being. He always wondered what was so special about Prince Ram that everybody in the devta clan was so eager to devote their lives at His feet. Jayant's ego-trapped mind was not letting him accept the fact that Lord Ram is Supreme God in the human avatar, and therefore he took the imprudent step to verify Lord's might by himself.

Jayant had his own justifications behind such an act of imbecility. By hurting Sita, he directly wanted to challenge the Lord, to prove that he is no lesser. Also, he believed that in the guise of a crow, the Lord won't be able to recognize him. And this will prove that Ram is not the omnipresent and omnipotent God, but just an exiled prince of Ayodhaya. Supreme Lord Ram understood everything at once, and not finding his bow and arrows nearby, He used the grass blade as the weapon. Here the message is clear, that with the Grace of Lord, even the most delicate and harmless object like a grass blade or 'Tinka' can become the deadliest and the most lethal weapon that is 'Bhramastra'.

Next question is why Indra refused to save Jayant, though he was his own son? Firstly, Indra knew quite well that Lord Ram was going to annihilate Ravan and free devlok from his evil control. It was exactly what selfish Indra desperately wanted. Secondly, Indra could never dare to challenge the Lord as he was very well aware that Lord Ram is invincible God or 'Param-Bhram' himself. So he purposely decided to remain quiet instead of fighting for his son's foolishness.

Now the question is, why didn't God Shiva and God Brahma give protection to Jayant though he had surrendered to them? When one doesn't give refuge to others because of his own selfish reason, then such acts fall in the category of Adharma or unrighteousness. But when one refuses to give shelter to the seeker for the seeker's own benefit, then it becomes a noble and righteous act. It is precisely what happened in this case. Shiva and Brahma wanted Jayant to surrender to Lord Ram and not to them. It was because they knew that he could only benefit in Lord Ram's refuge.

Real Bhava or feeling of surrender stems only when the seeker is clueless about how to deal with the world, and he finds no choices left for him in anticipation of his helplessness. For a seeker to reach the epitome of surrender or 'Sharanagati,' he needs to experience zero capability in egoic-self and put all his faith in the Supreme. He also needs to understand and realize that other than Lord, there is no peace. An enlightened sage shows the seeker the path that leads to God, and therefore, Sage Narad Muni rightly advised Jayant for his own good. The message here for the seeker is to first seek the grace of a Saint Gurudev because none but he can guide a seeker to the ultimate truth.

'Gurukripa Hi Kevalam'

Ultimately, Jayant, like a true seeker, was able to realize his grave mistake and also the might of Lord Ram, in front of whom no other entity of the Universe can stand. Lord has already stated that once the seeker attains this level of realization, then He immediately comes to his seeker's rescue and frees him from all his sins and negativity.

But then the question is when Jayant already qualified as a true seeker, why did Lord still punish him and destroy his one eye? Saint Tulsidas nicely explains that the mistake of the sinner is dealt with by the Lord with both kindness and punishment. By punishment, not only do the Karmic effects of the wrong deeds are neutralized, but it also sends a message to others, warning them to refrain from doing the wrong action. The purpose of kindness is to give another chance to the sinner to correct his wrongdoing and not repeat it in the future.

Only punishment and no kindness results in sheer pessimism and hopelessness for the sinner, and the ever-merciful Lord never wants such outcomes for His beings. Again, only kindness but no punishment will simply give encouragement to wrongful deeds, as then there is no fear of harsh repercussions. Jayant had apologetically accepted his mistake and surrendered to Lord, and therefore Lord didn't kill Jayant, although his offense was no lesser than that of Ravan. The difference between Ravan and Jayant was that Ravan couldn't free himself from his untamed mind-ego and arrogance till the end. But Jayant's punishment was necessary, as the Lord wants the entire Universe to clearly know that whoever indulges in any wrongful act or hurt His 'Yog-Maya Shakti' Sita, in any way, cannot escape His wrath and the lethal repercussions.

Benighted beings may see Siya-Ram as two different entities, but they are One and the same 'Param Bhram' or Supreme Consciousness.

If Ram is the ocean, Sita is the wave,
If Sita is the voice, Ram is the meaning.

Jayant, in his utter stupidity and ignorance, didn't realize this truth and saw Sita as a desireful mortal and did the foolishness of injuring her. In another version of Ramayan, it is said that before hurting Sita, Jayant met her once in the isolation of the forest and extended his proposal. Princess Sita refused him and also counseled him to not be carried away by his mind-ego. Such advice from a perceived mortal woman penetrated within, hurting his ego, and he decided to hurt Her.

In today's times also this corrupt mentality is seen in those maniacs who, after being refused by a female, intend to hurt to make her suffer, even for life. It has also emerged as the primary cause of crime against women. Actually, this is the perverted male Ego, which forces these maniacs to think and act in the most horrible and imaginable manner. Ego's villainous trait is - 'What I cannot have, I will destroy'. Ego cannot accept a 'NO'. For Ego, survival lies in extending its influence by overpowering whatever is considered as desirous, beautiful and tender. Any sort of defeat or failure is 'death' for Ego. And Ego very much fears death.

Through this episode, Lord Ram warns these maniacs to refrain from thinking or acting in horrible manners, failing which will lead them to repercussions they will repent forever, during and after life. Also, the message is that the sinner must surrender to the Lord and accept whatever punishment is given. In this way, they will liberate themselves from all sins. The 'Bhramastra-Tinka' destroyed Jayant's one eye, which symbolizes evil so that he is only left with the other one that is the eye of wisdom. And it was wisdom which ultimately freed Jayant from the self-destructive Ego, and led him to ultimate peace.

Chapter 3.2

A Devotee's Dilemma : Who is eligible?

Compassionate Lord has an unusual and mystifying quality,
The one who solely depends on Him is loved by Him dearly.

While leaving Chitrakoot, Lord Ram with Mother Sita and Laxman meets many Sages and Devotees along the way. One such was Saint Sutikshan. He was a simple, humble forest dweller and a true devotee of Lord Ram. Although he was desperate to meet the Lord, he was stuck in a dilemma. He believed himself to be ineligible and unqualified to come face to face with Lord Ram as a devotee and therefore was hesitant in approaching Him. Also, the sage had the opinion that only those who are highly knowledgeable, elite and elegant are fit to meet Lord and not ordinary unimportant ones like him.

Commonly, it is seen in today's world that the one who is labeled as able and materialistically successful, is somewhat insensitive towards the weaker section of the society. Such a person believes that the weaker section is like a parasite on society that wants to feed itself without putting in any effort and intention. Whereas it is often observed that the ones who are compassionatefor the underprivileged section are those who actually see some sort of inadequacy in themselves. **Troubled with inferiority complex they seek solace in lessers's gratitude for helping them**. This egoic sense of paucity makes them sympathetic **but not in totality.**

In this context, Saint Tulsidas says that there is only Lord Ram, who is all-capable, omnipotent, and also infinitely compassionate. Considering his attributes in a worldly perspective, we can say that He is super-successful, who doesn't feel any sort of inadequacy and yet is very empathetic. This is one of the many great qualities of Lord Ram, which is loved and admired by all His devotees. And this is essentially the trait, Lord Ram wants every being must inculcate in self. But the question is, why only a true devotee and not a self-proclaimed religious person understands this message of the Lord?

Saint Tulsidas aptly explains that although many label themselves as religious, in reality, there exists just one in a million who truly have absolute faith in the ísness of God. What the stories, scriptures, vedas and sages say about God, these so-called religious fellows accept them just for the sake of it. In actuality, they are very much unsure of the existence of the Supreme Entity and don't really bother much to unearth the truth. Unlike a spiritual seeker, they depend on the world to satisfy their desires and to get rid of their insecurity. Therefore the experience of the divine, though not impossible to seek, yet seems extremely difficult for them. Most of the **religious ones**come under this category.

Everyone in this world faces some or the other problems in life, and there are three ways to tackle them. One, is that hefeels confident enough to deal with the problem by himself. Other is with fabricated humility, he seeks help from those who are considered as capable by society. **Third is, he just cannot face the struggle and so gives up**. Point is **that either by not putting an effort** or by dependingon self or in others, doesn't allow the being to tread on the path of spirituality.**So the question is if all these methods are incorrect then what is the right way to deal with life struggles?**

Lord is the sole giver of sweet or sour fruits for all our good or bad deeds. 'Lord is ever-compassionate,' means that He can give sweet fruits to the being, even without him doing anything virtuous. In order to properly understand this unique quality of compassion, the seeker needs to have Bhava or feelings, which is beyond the gamut of logic. The one, who sees himself helplessand yet doesn't expect help from anybody else in the world, also never gives up butputs all his faith and hope only and only in Lord, can experience this divine virtue of compassion and love. Such a being can be truly termed as 'Ananya-Bhakta' or an Unwavering devotee. Lord declares that although beings believe Him to be just, fair and impartial, He has a special soft corner for a devotee, who solely depends on Him and not on anybody or anything else.

Saint Sutikshan feels that he has done nothing good, noteworthy or significant in life and so he is reluctant to approach Lord Ram. But then he recalls the declaration of Lord Ram, 'the one who solely depends on me, is dear to me.' This gave Sutikshan the courage and confidence that even though he lacks anymerits, yet his unwavering faith in Lord Ram qualifies him to be called as His devotee.

This is Bhava or true inner emotions of a real devotee, which is not easy for ordinary, ignorant beings to comprehend. The common perception is that the one who talks about Bhajan-Bhakti-Vairagya and is not indulging in worldly affairs like others is actually a lethargic being, who wants to escape from his duties and responsibilities. Well, this can be the perception of the mortal beings, but for Lord Ram, if such a seeker wholeheartedly relies on Him, then He will ensure his well being. And that is why Saint Tulsidas repeatedly affirms that the one who wants to prosper in life must only and solely depend on Lord Ram and nobody else, not even on his own self.

'Ek bani karunanidhan ki, So priye jaike gati na aan ki.'

I bank on one characteristic of the all-merciful Lord. He holds the devotee dear who depends exclusively on him.

Chapter 3.3

Intuitions of a Devotee's Heart

If God is perfect and present everywhere,
Then how come evil also thrives in the same sphere.

Though you are in every Being and not apart,
Yet I pray to you to make your abode only in my heart.

That day Sutikshan got the fruit of his prolonged and dedicated spiritual practice or 'Dirghakalin Sadhna' to unite with Lord Ram. It was like a dream come true for Sutikshan, and he couldn't think of losing Lord Ram ever again. He therefore earnestly requests Lord Ram that although He is present in every particle and in the heart of every Being, He must particularly reside in his heart. This was a strange request by Sutikshan because Lord Ram is the SupremeElement, then it is implied that He is present in every particle of the Universe, at every dot of time, space and life. The entity which is found here or there, alive or dead, or then or now, cannot be eternal and omnipresent. Also, if the entity exists more somewhere and lesser somewhere else, then it's certainly not equanimously all-pervading. Moreover, if the entity is selective in nature, that is, present in the heart of some Beings while absent in the heart of other Beings, then the entity is no different from an ordinary mortal object.

But all these presumptions cannot be held true for Lord Ram, and Sutikshan knows this better than anybody else. Then why is Sutikshan so keen on wanting the Lord to reside in his heart, particularly? Does this mean that the devotee is not satisfied with the omnipresence of Lord Ram? What more can be insulting for Ram, if He, though residing in the heart of all His devotees, is still not able to quench their thirst? Question is that, if Lord Ram claims to be everywhere, then how come is He lesser in Devotee Sutikshan's heart? Lord Himself claims that He and the heart of the devotee where He resides are everlasting, then why is Sutikshan asking?

Here we have a contradicting situation, that is, either Lord Ram is not God or Sutikshan is not a true devotee. Well, what Sutikshan actually means is that a devotee always longs for that God, who, by residing in his heart, not only makes His presence felt, but also cures the flaws in devotees. A devotee doesn't want that God, who, despite residing in his heart, remains indifferent. It is said that Supreme God is absolute and complete, but a devotee won't discover this truth until he has realized God himself. But a seeker who is still on the path to realization and yet to attain enlightenment wants 'that' God or Ram, who without delay interacts with him and looks after him in joys and sorrows.

We all yearn for 'that' Ram, who is not unresponsive to us, instead who consciously interacts with us whenever we need Him and makes us feel loved, privileged and cared for. But usually, for a very long time or 'Dirga Kal' on the path of spirituality, the seeker doesn't get any response from the Lord. It is because of this perceived indifference of Lord Ram that there are doubts, complaints, grievances, jealousy, frustrations, anger, greed and anxiety in the seeker's heart. A true devotee assumes that either there can be Ram or there can be flaws in the heart, as both can never exist together.

Second question is if God is perfect and He is within us, then why is He allowing flaws to stay with us? But the truth is that both Ram and flaws together dwell in the Being's heart, and thisis the grievance of Devotee Sutikshan. He complains what's the use of Ram's presence when these flaws, negativities and ego are still manipulating Beings and making them suffer? Lord Ram is all-capable, omnipotent, and so whenever He wishes, He can purify the devotee's heart and remove all its shortcomings.

To be indifferent and dispassionate is the choice of God. A 'Jigyasu' or inquisitive seeker wants to know the reason for this, whereas a 'Bhakt' or devotee doesn't question and simply accepts it as the will of God. A 'Sansari' or ignorant being, on the other hand, is least bothered about it. Had Lord ventured in the forest exile all alone, then He would have apathetically spent the time and returned to Ayodhaya. Considering His indifferent nature, anyone can predict that He would have never bothered to attack and destroy Ravan. And then, there would have been no Ramayan. It was only due to Ravan abducting Mother Sita, which infuriated Lord Ram and because of which He pledged to slay Ravan. Also, Laxman, all the time, prompted Lord Ram to use the weapons and show His mettle to the world. Hence unconditional love for Sita, punishment for Ravan and reminders from Laxman prompted Lord Ram to respond and take action.

We must also understand that 'the God,' who is without any compassion or anger, cannot make His followers to either love Him or fear Him. Hence, both compassion and anger play a vital role. It is only by seeing the beautiful, compassionate nature of Lord Ram that an ordinary mortal being gets attracted towards Him and inculcates Devotion or Bhakti. Now, to ensure that God's compassion is not misused by evil beings, fear of God also becomes a must. Fear makes beings cautious towards not doing anything unrighteous. Fear makes ignorant worldly beings refrain from evil acts. Lord Ram helping Sugreev by hunting down Bali, was an act of pure compassion. Again, Lord Ram sending Laxman to threaten and remind Sugreev of his promise though was an act of generating fear but was also out of pure compassion. The outcome of it was that Sugreev became an ardent loyalist of Lord Ram forever and was able to attain the highest level of devotion. So both love and fear of God are necessary for the seeker on the path of spirituality.

By requesting Lord Ram to forever reside in his heart, Sutikshan specifically wants the Lord to not be apathetic, unresponsive, stoic or indifferent. Not just that, but he also wants the Lord to guide him on every step of his life with both love and fear. That way, devotee Sutikshan can also, like Sugreev, attain the highest level of Bhakti. Goswami Tulsidas mindfully indicates that it hardly matters whether the Lord is perfect and omnipresent because it's only when you are able to firmly establish Him in your heart, that you will experience ultimate bliss in life.

Chapter 3.4

Pride in having Lord Ram as Master

Tulsidas lives, breathes and thinks, only Lord Ram.
His one trust, one faith and one strength is Lord Ram.

In addition to his urge to make Lord permanently stay in his heart, Sutikshan now talks about one more aspect of devotion to Lord Ram. He humbly asks Lord to ensure that His devotee never gets deprived of the ultimate pride or 'Abhiman' of being the most loyal servant of Lord Ram. Lord Ram was utterly surprised with this unusual request of Sutikshan. Normally, all spiritual seekers ask God to free them from the clutches of pride and ego or 'Abhiman & Ahankar Mukti,' but this uncommon devotee wants to live with a devotee-servant's ego forever.

To deeply understand the rationale behind such a request, we need to first figure out what actually the ego of worldly identity denotes? Guided by his inherited behavior, a worldly person usually introduces himself with his name, position, relation, caste, religion, nationality and so on to create a good image in the inquirer's mind. But when such an ego-trapped person couldn't attach an identity which makes him superior in others' eyes, he tries to 'drop names' that is, he links himself with a known and important personality of the society. On the other hand, that same known and important one may think that by linking his name with that 'lesser' person, his reputation will diminish, and so he tries to offload that useless burden from his shoulders. Just imagine how weird and embarrassing a scene it creates when one wants to shamelessly link to the other while the latter tries to repudiate such an association.

Next we must try to comprehend what the ego of spiritual identity refers to? For the desire-driven society, a devotee is inconsequential, while for the devotee, the society appears insignificant. He is essentially an innocent child for the One whom he proudly wants to link himself to, and that is Lord Ram. The child-devotee has every right on his father, and the father-Lord also feels happy and honored in carrying the child on His shoulder. The child-devotee knows his limitations and capabilities very well, so naturally, he doesn't have that worldly ego of superiority governing him. But, at the same time, he is well aware of the infinite power and capabilities of his father-Lord, and therefore, he always feels proud of Him. One of the most interesting facts about devotee-ego is that it's not easily comprehensible for all seekers because, at the core of this ego, there is actually no ego. Sutikshan is, in fact, seeking this same devotee-ego from Lord Ram.

From a worldly perspective, we have learned that a devotee-servant's primary responsibility is to serve his master-Lord unconditionally. The great devotee-Bharat had pledged and announced that there can be no Master like Ram in this eternity and that he wants to serve Him till oblivion. But instead of taking his service, Lord Ram seemed more eager to serve Bharat, His most loved devotee. There is no one like Ram, who is always worried that His devotee might hesitate in accepting His service and care. This quality of Lord is indeed totally opposite of how things work in our regular world.

Every being in this world, sooner or later, realizes that in every single step of his life, he is always dependent on one thing or another. Be it people, material, name, fame or relationships, all are mere objects of the mundane world. It is the world which the ignorant being believes so strongly. In fact, a life without these objects becomes absolutely unimaginable for him. Then there are some, who despite attaining success in these objects of the world, are still unsatisfied and want to role play Master-Lord with other beings. The more the count of their followers, the more ego-gratification they experience. Although almost every human being has learnt from his Religion that the attachment with material is the only cause of suffering, he is neither willing nor able to accept this truth and, therefore, continue to suffer all his life.

Saint Tulsidas assures that mere realization of just one connection or egoic identity that Lord Ram is my Master frees the human being from all dependencies of the material world and hence, from all pain and worldly suffering. Even in his own life journey, Goswami Tulsidas encountered many big and small names who wanted to know what was so special about him. Emperor Akbar was one of such names. But that didn't change the Saint's reply. For everyone, it was one and the same - *'Tulsidas is a famous servant of Lord Ram.'* This powerful divine association with Immortal Supreme was the reason why there wasn't a single day in life when the Saint had to ask for anything from this mundane world.

One must always remember that God Ram is the Supreme Divine who is watching everything, everywhere and every time. How can He give a chance to anyone to underrate His devotee? How can He spoil the divinity of His name? How can Lord Ram's devotee ever be dependent on anyone or anything else when Lord Himself has taken all his responsibility? Tulsidas reiterates that when my every need, desire and want is fulfilled from my Lord's forever-open door, then why must I ever knock on the doors of this selfish world? Sutikshan wants the same devotee-servant identity and pride so that he neveragain has to depend on anything other than his Lord Ram.

Chapter 3.5

Significance of Pativrat Dharma: Unwrapping the Misconceptions

Even if the husband is old, sick, pauper, unfaithful, abusive or a fool, a wife who disregards him will face many types of suffering in the afterlife. - Sagemother Anasuya

Lord Siya-Ram and Laxman had the privilege to meet many eminent sages and saints during their stay in the Dandakaranya forest. Once they decided to visit Sage Atri's ashram to enlighten themselves with his words of wisdom. After a pleasing initial exchange, Mother Anasuya, the wife of the Sage, shared with Sita, the significance of 'Pativrata Dharma.' The great Sagemother explainedthat 'Pativrata Dharma' essentially relates to chastity, loyalty, surrender and a wife's headstrong devotion towards her husband.

Still today, these values hold great importance, especially in Hindu households. But in contemporary times, where males and females are considered at par at all levels of society, the term 'Pativrat' is presumed to bear a controversial connotation. Many believe that Veda, Ramcharitmanas and particularly Goswami Tulsidas are sexist and male chauvinists. Understandably, there is resentment in the hearts of feminists against the practice of such perceived 'Pativrat' Dharma. For them, Pativrat is a disciplinary instrument by which males, for ages, have suppressed and dominated the female kind.

Saint Tulsidas is often criticized for his thoughts concerning the female kind. One of its most undesirable outcomes is that just because of this one misunderstanding, the wonderful creation that is Shri Ramcharitmanas is often rejected or discarded by the critics. But after thoroughly studying Ramcharitmanas, I can confidently say that Saint Tulsidas is definitely not anti-feminist but is just misinterpreted. The fact is that the lines which apparently seem unacceptable in the first glimpse usually have a much deeper and compelling meaning and it is only after mindfully delving into it, that one can truly absorb the meaning.

Almost in every religion of the world, the concept of 'Vrat' or fasting is very much in practise. In Sanatan Hindu Dharma, one can find plentiful ways of fasting mentioned. Now, what does fasting actually relate to? The real meaning of fasting is to religiously practise a fixed set of rules. Most common forms of fasting are food-related. As per the occasion, customs, country and period, the criteria of this food-fasting custom also keep changing. As such, the fasting rules, especially those related to consuming or avoiding rice, wheat, salt, fruit, water and so on, tend to vary vastly.

Here the underlying idea is that whenever a human-being is strongly determined on a particular resolution, which in this case is 'fasting,' then his spiritual power increases, which the being can use for the fulfilment of a desire. This clearly means that fasting is nothing but an age-old methodology to attain higher energy. 'Pati-Vrat' word is made of two different words, where 'Pati' means husband and 'Vrat' stands for fasting. So Pativrat Dharma means a wife's absolute devotion towards her husband, to gain greater spiritual power.

A scientist generates energy using forces of nature. Electricity, Nuclear and Gasoline are some of the many forms of quantifiable energy. Vrat or Fasting is the process by which one can generate and obtain qualitative spiritual energy in life. If Pativrat is given so much importance in almost all types of Vrat, then there ought to be valid and sound reasoning behind it. Most of the fasts are done for a set time-frame, whereas Pativrat is for a lifetime. In other fasts, the focus is primarily on inanimate objects or God's idol, whereas the focal point of Pativrat is an alive and conscious human being, which is 'husband.' Moreover, while in other fasts, the doer has to build a relationship with the object using imagination, Pativrat is a two-way expressible relationship. Only Pativrat Dharma has a sense of tangibility in comparison to other prevalent fasting customs.

One cannot expect God's idol or picture to reciprocate to his fasting instantly. No matter how much the emotional seeker worships God with sheer love, enthusiasm and devotion, he still doesn't easily get a response from Him. But the seeker never loses hope. He strongly believes that one day God will definitely reciprocate, and therefore, he continues with his Sadhana and Bhakti with even stronger conviction. The seeker mindfully accepts that all his ardent efforts, dedication and hard work put during the difficult years of spiritual practise, are a testimony to attain spiritual fulfilment. For a true seeker, these testing years are extremely painful where every moment his heart pains, longing for the divine love of his Lord.

One must note that the faults and flaws associated with the medium of Vrat must not affect the Bhakti Bhava or Devotion of the seeker in any way. And in the spiritual practices of Pativrat, the seeker is the wife. A good example is 'Matru-Pitru' Bhakti that is Devotion for Parents. Does any child consider physical attributes, behaviour or mannerism of his parents as essential parameters for such Bhakti or devotion? Is there any child in this universe who rejects his biological parents and looks for good looking, well mannered or wealthy parents just for the sake of Bhakti? What Sagemother Anasuya wants to make us understand is that, just like in other devotion forms, in Pativrat Dharma too, the flaws of the husband must be accepted.

Will a Deshbhakt or a Patriot ever reject his motherland or the country where he is born just because there is poverty, unrest, corruption or backwardness? Can any patriotic citizen think of doing Bhakti of another country just because it is more beautiful or developed than his motherland? The answer to all of them is a big 'No.' Ayodhaya was never as prosperous as Lanka. In fact, it is Lanka, which is called the Kingdom of Gold and not Ayodhaya. But despite defeating Ravana and conquering Lanka, Lord Ram was least interested in Lanka. Hewas very much eager to return back to His home. It is clearly reflected that night when He touchingly spoke to Laxman - 'Brother, even though Ayodhaya is not advanced like Lanka, but this place doesn't attract me. I am missing my home'. What Lord intended to say was that the basis of Bhakti and love cannot be good or bad attributes. True love can never be conditional, and the same also applies to Pativrat Dharma.

Unconditionality doesn't mean that while searching for a suitable matrimonial alliance for the bride-daughter, the family must not act judiciously and just accept any proposal right away. But the point is that even when matrimonial alliances are fixed with extreme caution and care, there always remains a possibility that the outcome may not be as expected. For example, after marriage, the husband may lose wealth or status or beauty. Or, if he turns out to be uncaring, unfaithful or abusive, what choice does the daughter and her family have then?

Either the marriage can be ended by divorce or else it can bedragged on with dissatisfaction for life. Pativrat Dharma is to joyfully accept a good or bad relationship, not because of choicelessness but considering it as the will of God. Wise people have said that the one who keeps on changing tracks will most likely, never feel settled in life. This means that the urge to switch relationships by continuously rejecting the previous and hunting for better prospects can never give one satisfaction.

Having said that, we must be very clear that Vrat or fasting of any kind, including Pativrat, is a matter of choice and not compulsion. If a married woman doesn't want to practise it willingly, then her spouse, in-laws or the society has no right to impose it on her. In fact, Vrat is a spiritual practise which is totally based on individual willingness and choice. Nobody can be forced to practise Vrat, Bhajan, Sadhna, Tapasya, Yoga or Tyaga. In my spiritual quest, I have not read or heard anywhere that somebody was forced, and so he became a seeker, devotee, saint, sage or yogi. Spirituality is an individual's own choice and not a directive. In the same way, Pativrat Dharma cannot be enforced but to be accepted.

People also condemn the Pativrat Dharma because they believe that it is meant just for females and not for males, thereby encouraging gender bias. There is no denying the fact that male species have misused this practise for selfish and egotistical interests since ages. One of its evil branches is the practise of 'Sati.' Therefore its condemnation is not at all surprising. But just like Pativrat, Patnivrat, that is, commitment, service and devotion of a husband towards his wife is equally valid and applicable. Moreover, in both Pativrata and Patnivrat Dharma, the criteria are absolutely the same. But the practise of Patni-Vrat was purposely ignored and, in fact, never even spoken of.

Though Mother Sita's second forest exile is not included in Ramcharitmanas, still without going in further details, I would like to point out that after Her exit, Lord Ram never ever even thought of second marriage in his whole life, though the concept of many wives or polygamy was not uncustomary in Kshatriya class in those days. He had taken the oath of Ek Patni Vrat or One Wife, at the time of marriage and forever practised it religiously. The point here is that if Pativrat Dharma is expected from the wife, then Patnivrat Dharma is also expected from the husband. There can be no exception to this rule.

Needless to say that Mother Sita is an ideal wife and Lord Ram is the most perfect husband one can ever think of, and they complemented each other the way nobody ever did in the history of the world. Those who surrender and devote their life to the lotus feet of Siya-Ram will be bestowed with great values, and they will learn the true meaning of a perfect relationship. A sincere, committed and devoted relationship of the lifetime is a great spiritual practise or Tapasya. 'Dharma can be dismissed, but Karma is inevitable.' It is easy to escape from adverse situations in life but difficult to accept them unconditionally. Escapism is regressive, whereas acceptance is progressive. Ram-Leela is an eternal love story of two divine lovers who embraced Dharma, no matter what the situation of life was.

Chapter 3.6

Time in Dandakaranya: Meetings and Sermons

The Labyrinthine Maya is like the endless ocean,
Traversed only in the divine yacht of Ram's devotion.

During their period of stay in the forest exile, Lord Siya-Ram with Laxman met many great Sages and Saints who inspired them in those years of hardship. It was also in tune with Lord's proclamation that His primary purpose of incarnation is to unite with His devotees. Thus, the destruction of Ravana was secondary to Him. Logically speaking, God has and is everything, and there is absolutely nothing which He needs to do. All He longs for is the unconditional love of the being. He only seeks the true affinity of His creation. In return, Lord is forever ready to bless and bestow His true lovers with knowledge, peace, prosperity and security, which they yearn for throughout their lives. It was the same reason why both Lord Ram and Laxman slayed many Asura who were troubling the forest dwellers.

Before settling in Panchvati, the Ram-Laxman duo left no stones unturned to clean sweep the Dandakaranya forest from the evil presence of demons, ensuring the well-being of devotees. Lord is always equanimously compassionate. In fact, Kaal or death was Lord's Grace, which freed the Asura from their painful demonic existence and united their consciousness with Supreme. All of them were highly grateful to the Lord for His profound compassion. It was the magnetic experiences of Satsang (Discourses), Gyan (Knowledge) and Bhakti (Devotion), which made Lord Ram so eager and restless to leave Ayodhaya and interact with the great learned ones of Dandakaranya. Secondly, through the Leela of these meetings and sermons, Lord wanted the future generations to understand the meaning and purpose of life.

Maharishi Agastya

It was a dream come true occasion for Lord Ram that day when He finally reached the ashram of the great Sage Maharishi Agastya. Just like Maharishi Vishwamitra was the most revered Sage in North India, Maharishi Agastya was the most honoured and reputed Sage of South India. In the meeting, Lord, like a curious disciple, asked Sage Agastya - 'What is the right way to slay Ravan?' Lord Ram firmly believes that the motive behind the war, be it against Ravan or anybody else, must not be personal but the establishment of Dharma or Righteousness. Lord wanted to deal with His would-be feud with Ravan with absolute righteousness. Lord had taken the resolution to put an end to the atrocities of Ravan. Therefore, instead of staying back at a pleasant place like Chitrakoot, He kept on moving in order to come closer to His target. So far, the target is unaffected because Lord didn't witness any direct evil act of Ravan; otherwise, it could have given the Lord a valid reason to wage war against him. Therefore Lord went to Sage Agastya for consultation as to what should be His future course of action.

Having said that, we must clearly understand that Lord Ram is 'Param Bhram,' that is Supreme God Entity. The resolution to end evil or to do good doesn't rise in 'Param Bhram' by self. It is the resolution of His seekers and their earnest prayers, which is the primary cause of His incarnation and action against evil. It was when Mother Earth, Sages, Devta with Lord Brahma came to Narayan for help, that He took the pledge of destroying Ravan. Although God is indifferent towards His creation, He always has one universal purpose, and that is the well-being of His devotees.

Sage Agastya couldn't help smiling when he heard Lord's query and said - 'With what perception have You asked me this question? It is by virtue of your Bhakti that I could know a little about your infinite Glory. You, the suzerain Lord of all Lords, are asking from me as if you are an ordinary mortal. Instead, I humbly pray to You to dwell in my heart with Sita and Laxman forever and give me Bhakti of Your lotus feet. But I know that because of worldly play or Leela, You have asked me how to destroy Ravan, and so my advice for You is to settle in the most charismatic and holy spot that is Panchavati and sanctify the forest of Dandakaranya. There you will find a strong reason to wage war against Ravan.' Thanking the sage for his valuable suggestion, Lord left the ashram and again started travelling.

Vairagyavan Laxman

More than a decade had passed by of the forest exile when Lord Ram had settled in Panchavati. There He befriended Jatayu, the king of vultures and an old acquaintance of His father, King Dasratha. Panchavati was an amazing place on the banks of the river Godavari. Laxman was so moved by its scenic beauty that he built a beautiful Ashram near the river. As soon as Lord Ram took up His abode there, the sages and the forest dwellers of the Panchvati region were freed from the threat of evil Asura.

Once upon a time when He was sitting at ease, Laxman asked guilelessly - 'Instruct me, oh my Brother-Lord how to internalize spiritual wisdom (Gyana), dispassion (Vairagya) and illusion (Maya). Also, discourse me about the intricacies of devotion (Bhakti). Explain to me the difference between God (Ishwara) and Being (Jiva), so that I may have unwavering devotion in You and my sufferings and delusion are uprooted from the core forever.'

Lord Ram smilingly replied - "My dear brother, listen with your mind, intellect, concentration and reasoning fully absorbed. I will explain everything to you in a nutshell. The very feeling of 'I' and 'Mine,' and 'You' and 'Yours', is Maya, which shadows the ultimate truth from mortal beings. Whatever is perceived by senses and that which lies within the domain of mind is Maya. Maya has two divisions, one is ignorance (Avivek), and the other is Knowledge (Vivek). Ignorance casts Being into the sink of worldly existence. Knowledge has no strength of its own but is directed by Me only. It brings forth the true understanding of Creator and Creation.

Spiritual wisdom frees the being from the clutches of mind-ego (Ahankara) and blesses him with the divine eyes, which sees the Supreme element in all animate and inanimate objects. Dear brother, he alone should be called a man of ultimate dispassion who is beyond the supernatural attractions or Siddhi of Maya and discards the/such attractions like a grass blade. Mortal being doesn't know the truth of Maya or Ishwara (God) or Jiva (Self). Only the Supreme God is the Knower and the One who gives bondage and bestows liberation based on beings' Karma. He transcends everything and is the controller of Maya."

"Dispassion, intelligence and spiritual wisdom are necessary for spiritual progress, but that which melts My heart, without any delay and effort is only Devotion or Bhakti, which gives immense happiness right from the beginning to My devotees. Dear Laxman, devotion stands for itself and is independent. It is incomparable and the very root of all bliss. It can be acquired only and simply by the kindness of Sages and Saints. Being must cultivate deep devotion and should sincerely remain engaged in his own duty or Dharma. Devotion brings aversion to worldly pleasures and increases fondness in Sravana (Listening) of My Leela (Worldly play)."

"The Bhakt or devotee should be extremely persistent in Bhajan (Adoration) and must recognize Me alone as his guru, parents, kinsman, lord and deity. Whenever the devotee speaks of My glories, a thrill runs through his body, his voice gets choked, and tears flow from his eyes. He is then free from lust, vices, ego and hypocrisy. I am ever available at the beck and call of such a devotee. I am always illuminating like a flame, in the heart of the one who depends only on Me and worships Me without any selfish purposes."

Laxman was greatly delighted to hear his Brother-Lord's invaluable discourse on the discipline of Devotion (Bhakti) and, like a true devotee, bowed his head in the lotus feet of Lord Ram. With elevated talks on Vairagya, Gyana, Karma, Dharma and Bhakti, the royal Raghukul trio peacefully spent many days in Panchavati.

Love is an endless journey, which on each step unleashes infinite joy and bliss, which one has never experienced before, and which increases manifold with time. In love, the onus is not on the devotee but is on the deity. What does God want from us? There is absolutely nothing that the being can give to Him except his pure 'Bhava' or Love.

The one you are looking for is only looking for you.
You and Him are one but portrayed as two.

Chapter 3.7

SURPANAKHA: GENESIS OF LANKA DESTRUCTION

Pervert Surpanakha acted immorally to fulfill her illicit desire,
Because of her, the entire Asura clan had to face consequences, dire.

Although Lord Ram had pledged to destroy the evil Asura King Ravan from the face of the earth, He had still not found an adequate reason to wage war against him. Being the epitome of righteousness, Ram couldn't just resort to bloodshed right away without having a sound justification for the same. However, the free-spirited character and perverted act of Surpanakha actually helped solve this problem. The destruction of Lanka Empire had its genesis in Ravan's sister Surpanakha.

Once when Surpanakha, the self-proclaimed Duchess of Dandakaranya, was passing by Panchvati, she had the unique opportunity to witness the divine grandeur of Lord Ram and Laxman. Being deeply mesmerized to see the Raghukul duo, she disguised herself as a very beautiful lady and tried to shamelessly seduce Lord Ram and Laxman successively. However, she couldn't succeed in her evil motive as both of them refused her. Also, their satirical replies offended her greatly. This enraged her so much that she at once transformed herself back into her real ugly demonic form and attacked Sita, considering Her to be the actual cause of the refusals. In order to defendSita, Lord signalled Laxman to chop Surpanakha's ears and nose, as punishment. Highly embarrassed and humiliated, Surpanakha immediately fled from the scene but threatened that they will have to pay a heavy price for such a heinous act. Although she deserved the treatment, Princess Sita felt really sorry for her.

With an intense fury of revenge, Surpanakha first approached her and Ravan's cousin brothers Kharr and Dushan, who were guarding the southern border of the Dandakaranya forest with a formidable army of fourteen thousand Asur soldiers. Due to her tactical provocation, all of them rushed to

Panchavati along with their army to avenge their sister Surpanakha's insult and humiliation.

It didn't take long for Lord to sense the impending danger. As soon as He saw the Asura army marching, He asked Laxman to take Sita in a nearby cave and guard her. Waging war against the mighty Asura, Lord destroyed Kharr, Dushan and all Fourteen thousand soldiers single-handedly. They all got liberated from the inferior Asura yoni and attained peace in the lotus feet of Lord Ram. But Surpanakha was still not ready to accept the defeat as she was yet to realize the might and divinity of Lord Ram. She was desperate for revenge, and hence she rushed to Lanka to approach her brother, the mighty Ravan.

Undoubtedly, Surpanakha was totally unrighteous in shamelessly approaching Lord Ram, and therefore she got the punishment she deserved. But it's highly uncommon to see a female, although of the 'Tamoguni' Asura species, being so unapologetically seductive. So what could be the reason for Surpanakha's such overtly debauching intentions?

Scriptures beautifully state that a female in childhood is the responsibility of the father, in adulthood is the responsibility of the husband, and in old age is the responsibility of the son. Under no circumstances, a female must be left unattended and unprotected. Surpanakha was one female who was not ready to accept any relation, be it brother or husband, which limits her freedom even by a bit. What is 'Maryada' or dignified modesty for other females, is a prison for Asuri Surpanakha.

In the first glimpse, it may appear to us that the opinions of holy scriptures for female kind are outright regressive and restrictive. Not just that, but the scriptures also seem to impose boundaries, snatching away female freedom. None, be it human, animal, fish or bird, likes dependence and captivity. In fact, the urge to absolute freedom and independence is inborn in every living being. So despite knowing the real essence of life, how come the scriptures appear to be against female freedom in particular?

A common belief is that whatever is dear and valuable to us must be cared for and kept secure. Nobody keeps a piece of glass inside the locker unless it is as precious as a diamond. The inherent freedom of glass-piece in comparison to the dependence of diamond is because of its zero worthiness. In ancient times, females were primarily considered symbols of beauty and tenderness, while males symbolized vigour and gallantry whose responsibility was to give protection to others.

While talking about 'Maryada' or Boundaries of Modesty, Sanatan Dharma, Ramcharitmanas or Tulsidas do not intend to propagate exploitation or control of female kind. Here 'Maryada' does not signify prison captivity; instead, it means safety, security and protection. The purpose of prison, therefore, is punishment, but the purpose of locks, bolts and guard in the house is only safety. Hence the arrangement talked about in scriptures does not call for disciplining females but providing them due security.

Now we need to understand that all limits, boundaries, dependence or 'Maryada' were meaningless to Surpanakha. Lord Ram immediately understood her character and so He satirically yet politely excused himself by saying that his wife is with him and that he has taken the oath of one-wife. But He purposely pointed toward his brother, saying that Laxman is single here, so she could ask him. Encouraged by Lord's suggestion, she then proposed to Laxman, who also satirically replied - 'O beautiful damsel, I am Lord Ram's servant, I am myself dependent on him, and therefore life with me will not suit your sensibilities. Lord Ram is the mighty emperor of Awadh, and so whatever he will do, it will be accepted by all, gracefully. So you again try to persuade him.'

What Laxman actually meant to say was that a free-spirited demon like Surpanakha cannot accept two setsof restrictions. First, marriage, in itself, is a kind of social constraint. Second, when that marriage is fixed with a servant, such inhibitions tend to double. Laxman's apt reasoning convinced her so much that she again overtly proposed to Lord Ram. Her idea of 'my life-my rules' was to be unapologetic, disorderly, immodest and shameless. What impression does that female give if she proposes two royal brothers repeatedly and simultaneously?

Surpanakha was a widow, and her husband was killed by none other than her own brother Ravan. Ruthless Ravan had his own reasons and didn't even hesitate to end the life of his own brother-in-law. After the momentary agony, this loss actually turned out to be a boon for her as she can now enjoy her 'my life-my rules' policy without any 'Maryada' or implied social stipulations. Whenever Ravan, as an elder brother, tried to discipline her, she would shut him up, accusing him of making her a widow. Therefore understanding her distorted mind state and to avoid embarrassment, Ravan deliberately settled Surpanakha at Dandakaranya, a place far away from Lanka along with her brothers Khar and Dushan.

Falsely and unabashedly, she says to Lord Ram - 'There is no suitable match for me in this universe, and so I am still a maiden. Now, after seeing you, I am content.' Due to her untamed character, Surpanakha was not interested in living in Lanka, which was surrounded by a vast ocean. Instead of civilized society, she preferred to live in wild forests like Dandakarnya. It, therefore, seems like anything that obstructs free movement like water or society, was not acceptable to her. Surpanakha, whose fingernails were like winnowing blades, was evil-hearted and was labeled as She-Snake or 'Sarpeni.'

Sarpeni is considered to be the culmination of cruelty. She even reckons her own offspring as a threat to her survival and can eat them to satisfy her hunger. The one who is a cold-blooded murderer is always very insecure about his own life. A mother may die hungry, but till her last breath, she will feed her children first. But Sarpeni or Surpanakhais far from this great woman attribute. A selfish and greedy person like her doesn't bat an eyelid in destroying her own people just to quench her thirst for selfish desires. Because of Surpanakha's obstinacy, her family got destroyed.

Surpanakha is the symbol of 'Avidya-Maya.' A few days back, Lord Ram was explaining to Laxman the two forms of Maya. One is Vidya or knowledge, and the other is Avidya or ignorance. While Vidya is the energy that creates life, Avidya creates disorientation and pushes the beings farther away from Dharma. A human being is like a lost traveller in the desert who is dying out of thirst. Avidya first gives him a sip of water and then tempts him to follow her to the cascade of pure and refreshing water. The disoriented and jaded traveler in the desperate urge of pleasure follows her, and just when he reaches the edge of the cliff, 'Avidya' pushes him in the dark pit of death and suffering.

Surpanakha tried to lure Lord Ram and Laxman but got defeated in her own trick. Both are men of ethics and principles, and therefore such temptation could not disorient them. Lord Ram is the symbol of 'wisdom', Lady Sita is 'devotion,' and Sheshnag Laxman is 'stoic dispassion.' Only a wise and dispassionate being, who is submerged in the nectar of pure devotion can save himself from the temptation of 'Avidya-Maya.' Such one easily understands the ploy of Avidya and neutralizes it. With this incident of Surpanakha, followed by Khar and Dushan's attack, Lord Ram found a solid reasonto destroy Ravan. Also, that was the day when Surpanakha penned the chapter of 'Kaal' in the life book of Ravan.

hapter 3.8

Ravan, the simpleton

If He is Narayan Himself,
I will battle Him and get liberated by His arrows with pride.
If He is a mortal prince,
I shall defeat Him in the battle and carry off His bride.

Overtly humiliated Surpanakha looked desperate to wreak vengeance on the Raghukul brothers as she barges into the court of Ravan and berates him in front of the full assembly. She reprimands her and shouts, 'You drink and sleep, day and night and take no heed of the enemy, who is now at your very door.' In distress, she threw herself down and said, 'Should I be tortured to this state even though you, my brother, the King of the world, is still alive?' Ravan in great bewilderment asks, 'Who has dared to strike off your nose and ears?'

She then superficially narrated him the whole episode, but purposely omitted the part of her perverted behavior. To instill the fire of hatred, she falsely portrayed Lord Ram and Laxman as slayers of Asura species. Not just that, but also to ignite Ravan's carnal desires, she further says, 'The elder one has with him a young belle. The Creator made that woman the very embodiment of loveliness. Her charisma seems even greater than a hundred million Goddesses of beauty.'

On hearing about the violence and mockery with his sister by Laxman and destruction of his brothers Khar and Dushan by Prince Ram, Ravan burned all over with rage. Although he tried to console Surpanakha by bragging about his strength in many ways, the incident left him in a pensive mood. It became obvious when he retired to his palace that night, full of anxiety and couldn't sleep. He thought to himself, 'Khar and Dushan were as powerful as me, who else can kill them other than Supreme God Narayan Himself?'

Since time immemorial negative characters have always appealed to human minds more than their positive counterparts. Whether it's an ambitious dictator of real-life or a ruthless villain of reel life, people have always liked and shown a lot of interest, though out of sheer curiosity, in these eccentric personalities. For Hindus, Ravan is an eternal symbol of the most evil entity. And yet still today, there are some intellectuals who believe that Ravan was actually a devotee of Lord Ram and that he was aware of the true identity of Prince Ram as the Supreme God. But then there are also different groups of people who angrily question how a devotee can ever dare to kidnap 'Jag-Janini' Mother Sita and also use 'Shringar-Ras' or flirtatious expressions for Her? So the question remains, is it right to call Ravan a devotee?

That night Ravan's mind was crowded with thoughts and assumptions. First, he felt that 'Only God Narayan and no mortal being can kill Khar and Dushan, and if that's true, I must use this opportunity to liberate myself. I cannot practise 'Bhajan' in this demonic and Tamoguni body, and therefore I must intentionally create enmity with Lord Ram in order to get executed by His arrows. And in this way, I will easily attain peace and salvation.' It's interesting to note here that although Ravan never thought of seeking God, not even in his dreams, in his lifetime, that night, he did. His corrupt, selfish, and careless lifestyle didn't ever let him think in the right direction. The loss of Khar and Dushan shocked and made him feel so insecure, although for a moment, that the Supreme-Power flashed in his thoughts. But quite predictably, this rare noble feeling or Bhava in Ravan was momentary, and he was again overtaken by his untamed mind-ego. He eased his vulnerable mind, reminding it about the blessings of God Shiva and God Brahma and got assured of his indestructibility.

The possibility of divine intervention in his life through the incident of Surpanakha doesn't excite Ravan at all. It was clearly reflected when the very next moment, his self-destructive ego wakes up and makes him perceive Lord Ram as a mere mortal being, and therefore, taking away all his fear for Supreme Narayan. Now Ravan thinks, 'In revenge for Surpanakha's insult, I will defeat the two princes in the battlefield. And I will abduct the beautiful lady and make her my queen.' If we call a person with such an evil and unsettled mind like Ravan, a devotee, then it would overtly contradict the 'Bhakti-Shastra' or Principles of Devotion.

There was absolutely no relevance of 'faith' and 'love,' in the life of Ravan. He was the epitome of immorality and indiscipline. Then how can such a sinful character ever realize his true self and participate in Lord's Leela? Lying on the bed in a highly intoxicated state, Ravan starts planning the 'Sita-Haran' or abduction of Lady Sita that night. He decides to take the help of his fellow 'Asur Marich,' who possesses the extraordinary skill of changing guise and make him his partner in crime. Ego, conceit, and ignorance take us far away from the truth. It's also the reason why the possibility that Lord Ram is God Narayan Himself never again struck him all his life.

Just to remind the reader, this is the same Asur Marich who got caught while troubling Sage Vishwamitra years back, and Lord Ram spared his life by just throwing him away, not killing him along with Tardka and Subahu. That episode made the terribly frightened Marich recognize Supreme Ram to the core of his heart. After that, living alone on the island of Maldweep in the Indian Ocean, the Asur started practising spirituality or 'Bhajan' and sought the Grace of Lord, discarding Tamogun or his natural instincts. Unfortunately, being an Asur, Marich was never able to express his devotion or Bhakti. Rather, he had to disguise himself as a guile-golden deer to face Lord Ram. But the surety that he will be slayed by Supreme God Himself gave him great excitement and hope, despite the fear of impending death. Deep within, he knew that death by the Lord is a blessing of liberation from his demonic or Asuri body.

On the other hand, Asur Ravan, who although was scared and anxious from inside, always pretended to be fearless and brave. This is another prominent attribute of mind-ego. Beings who cook up stories about their boldness and courage and leave no opportunity to blabber those fancy tales to others are actually the ones who are most insecure from inside. Fear and pretentiousness are absolutely not the attributes of a Devotee, and so this Ravan of Shri Ramcharitmanas is most definitely not a Devotee. He is just a big fool who, despite receiving innumerable reasoning, warnings and hints from many enlightened ones, including Lord Hanuman, could not understand the ultimate truth, that is, the purpose of his and every being's life is to surrender in the lotus feet of Lord Siya-Ram.

Chapter 3.9

'Jag-Janini' Sita enters Fire: Twist of Manas

Until I destroy the demons, You abide in Fire,
Your reflection will play the Leela and inspire.

After the eventful Surpanakha incident, **life at Panchvati** was again back to its **normal** course. One day, when Laxman went into the forest to collect fruits and bulbs as part of his daily responsibility, Lord Ram found it the ideal time to speak to 'Jag-Janini' Sita. In seclusion, Lord said to Her, 'Dear, I want to play some humanly leela and so till I destroy all the evil Asura, You abide in Fire-Element.' As per Lord's direction, Mother Sita calls the Agni-Devta (God of Fire) and goes with him as **his** daughter. With Lord Ram in Her place, She, with her inherited godly power, magically created Her identical reflection body, who looked absolutely like Her in appearance, grace and, of course, divinity. It, therefore, reveals to us a very interesting fact, that is, in Ramcharitmanas, Ravan had never actually abducted, touched, misbehaved or even interacted with real Sita. **Even Laxman came to know of this secret only at the time of 'Agni-Pariksha'.**

The first original version of Ramayan was written by Maharishi Valmiki in Sanskrit, **which** was considered to be the language of highly knowledgeable ones **and was not accessible and understandable for commoners. As such, this Ramayan turned out to be more of an intellectual and historical treatise. On the other hand, Goswami Tulsidas's Ramcharitmanas, a spiritual and devotional poetic saga of Ramayan, was written in the 16th century in Awadhi,the language of commoners and became hugely popular among both intellectuals and masses.** It is believed that Valmiki reincarnated as Tulsidas to bring out the 'Bhakti' attributes of Ramayan, for the benefit of mankind. **In Ramayan,episodes of Agni-Pariksha** (Fire Test) and Sita-Paritagya (Sita Second Forest Exile) are two such distressing incidents that have forever intensely **agonized** the hearts of the followers. Unlike Valmiki's Ramayan, Saint Tulsidas has omitted the 'Sita Forest Exile' episode in Manas and **heended the storywith Siya-Ram returning back to Ayodhaya.**

In Ramcharitmanas,Saint Tulsidas, though not openly but in subtlety, mentioned citizens of Ayodhaya as sinners for doubting the character of Mother Sita.**He considered** 'Ayodhya Vasi' worthy of mention only because they are loved by Lord Ram whole-heartedly. It is evident from the fact that **though Lord Ram was totally broken after Sita'sExile because of their baseless suspicion, He still didn't exhibit hard feelings for them, and always took care of them like a father figure.**

Right from the very beginning, Goswami Tulsidas **was more inclined to show/reflect/mirror the character-building, spiritual-understanding and devotional-attributes ofRamayan.**He purposely introduced **theturning** point of 'Sita Entering Fire' in his work. This unique take on the epic overtly demarcates Ramcharitmanas from Valmiki Ramayan as the **latter's Ram appears to be insensitive, having doubted Sita's character and send Her for forest exile.** Understandably, the reader feels more connected and a very emotional affinity with Tulsidas's Ram. This twist of Tulsidas also gives a **new logical meaning** to Agni-Pariksha**and** satisfies the heart of **Bhakta becausedevotees of Siya-Ram could never tolerate Ravan misbehaving with Mother Sita.**

What we need to understand here is that there can be many different versions **with unique new twists, but fundamentally the core storyline of Ramayan remains the same.** The difference of **beliefs and thoughts** is primarily because each writer-devotee has his own unique perspective. **A true devotee is always free to see and depict God in his own way, and there is no authority that can stop him from doing so. This is the liberty/ level of freedom Sanatan Dharma gives to the devotee. Having said that, out of hundreds of unique Ramayan versions, Goswami Tulsidas's** Ramcharitmanas is the most accepted and loved version of all times (period).

Saint Tulsidas beautifully says that just like Sunshine cannot be separated from the Sun, similarly, it is impossible to separate Siya-Ram from each other. In fact, they are One Element but play as two for human leela. On the contrary, both Ravan and Surpanakha are totally egoistical body-identified beings. Most of the human beings are like them, though not in totality but to quite an extent. Hence, it is beyond the cognitive abilities of ego-trapped ordinary beings to fully comprehend the oneness of Siya-Ram. Ravan and Surpanakha **had their selfish interests**, and they both believed that by separating Siya-Ram, they could fulfill their individual motives. Looking at the forever-attentive and protective nature of Ram for Sita, Surpanakha concluded that it's impossible to win and manipulate Prince Ram till Princess Sita is around. Similarly, Ravan believed that as long as Prince Ram is there, he won't be able to win Princess Sita with his proposals.

Mother Sita knew very well that a strong reason **had**to be generated for Lord Ram to destroy Ravan. Siya-Ram separation was the only suitable reason to triumph over evil. It is Mother Sita who brings Ram to His devotee, and again it is only Herself who can be the reason for Ram, slaying evil. **Therefore,'Param-Brahm' Ram is indifferent and dispassionate in whom emotions are invoked by 'Jag-Janini' Sita.**

As per Vedantic science, Energy is in all 'Five Elements' or 'Panchamahabhutas' that are Earth, Fire, Water, Earth and Space, but then why **Lord asked 'Shakti-Swaroopa' (Energy) Sita** to abide **particularly** in the element-Fire? King Janak found baby Sita from inside the earth, and so she **is considered as** the daughter of Mother Earth. From Her birth till this episode, the qualities of element-**Earth that are creation and tolerance** were needed from Sita. But for Ravan's destruction, the qualities of element-Fire that are fury, illumination and destruction were **needed**. It is because the darkness spread by evil demons could only be eliminated, and Peace reinstated **only with the Light of Fire**.

Just as Ravan gets slayed, the **lethal** role of Fire-Element ends, and through the gimmick of Agni-Pariksha (Fire-Test), Sita's reflection dissolves, and real Sita reunites with Ram. Later in Ram-Rajya, **Sita plays the role of 'Maha-Lakshmi,'who is the Nourisher and Preserver of Life**. In this entire Ram-Leela, Mother Sita played the three roles of Creator-Earth, Destructor-Fire and Preserver-Mahalakshmi successively. **Scriptures have given the sequence as Creation-Preservation-Destruction, but Mother Sita's sequence in Ramcharitmanas is Creation, then Destruction and finally ending with Preservation.**

The message here is that Destruction, be it of any kind, must never be the end of the story. Her belief is that the Cycle of Life must not end with destruction but with nourishment and preservation. Mother Sita is the cause, effect, energyand consciousness. A million Ravan cannot face Her, even for one single moment. But Ramayan Leela of 'Sita-Haran,' **where Ravan apparently seems to have overpowered Sita,is absolutely necessary to make ignorant beings understand the lethal repercussions of disturbing 'Shanti-Swaroopa Sita' or Divine Peace.**

Chapter 3.10

Liberation of Marich: Transformed Thinking or 'Chintan'

He realized that either way he goes, his end has come,
Therefore gladly, he accepted the command of the demon.

As part of his conspiracy, Ravan wanted to divert the attention of both Prince Ram and Laxman so that once they were away, it would be easy for him to abduct Princess Sita. In fact, Ravan had carefully chalked out every single detail to make his conspiracy a success. Accordingly, to execute his plan, he went to his Asur kin Marich who was an expert in changing guise. After a little brainstorming, Ravan came up with the most brazen and evil idea. Looking at the delicate humane nature of Lady Sita, he wanted Marich to become an enchanting golden deer. He was sure that the Lady would be tempted, and so She would ask Her husband to catch it for Her. After hearing Ravan's master plan, Marich was in an immense dilemma. He was sure that once Lord Ram chases him, he will not survive. On the other hand, if he refuses to play this role, then Ravan wouldn't spare him, and he will have the same fate. Nonetheless, it didn't take Marich long to make the decision. He graciously chose 'Bhakti' and preferred to die through the divine hands of his Lord than the wicked Ravan.

Just a reminder, this is the same Marich, who, with his mother Tardka and Subahu, was bothering Sage Vishvamitra in the forest region near Ayodhya. In reply, the two Princes Ram-Laxman attacked them. While Lord Ram killed the other two, surprisingly, He spared the life of Marich but threw him far in the ocean on the islands of Maldweep (Maldives). We come across so many diverse devotees-characters in Ramcharitmanas. They are interestingly distinct, yet we see a striking commonality in all of them. However, Marich's story is totally different and uncommon. He is one such ardent devotee whose spiritual journey started with enmity with his own God.

All the flaws in the life of a human being are sowed by the way he thinks or 'Chintan'. Constant thinking of comforts and pleasures gives rise to the desire to acquire them. Unfulfilled desire leads to anger, which then destroys 'Vivek' or intelligence, ultimately ruining the peace and happiness of life. A human life that is no less than a powerhouse of infinite possibilities goes in vain because of insane and injudicious thinking, and the irony is that this insanity is considered normal by human beings, who, unfortunately, don't even realize this fundamental flaw of mind throughout their lifetime. Marich, who symbolizes 'Chintan,'had a very focussed mind, but it was functioning in the wrong direction. Unlike his mother and brother, he was well aware of his evil thinking, yet he considered it warrantable because of his family background.

Lord Ram killed Tardka and Subahu but spared Marich. Lord knew very well that if it's the 'Chintan' that creates flaws, then it's also the same Chintan, which inculcates love and devotion in being. So thinking or Chintan is a medium that should not be destroyed but orchestrated in the right direction. By throwing Marich far away, Lord actually paused and diverted 'Chintan' from negativity, thereby giving Marich time to think meticulously and introspect. Like Lord's every act, this also worked and Marich, though out of fear, was now only thinking about Lord Ram. And in this way, his spiritual practise or 'sadhana' got initiated. To be able to see and think of your Lord continually is Sadhna, the reason for which can be anything - love, fear or hatred. Marich even shared this fact with Ravan that from that day onward, wherever his sight goes, he, out of extreme fear, only sees the two divine brothers Ram & Laxman with bow and arrows. All this while, he lived all alone on the islands, consuming only fruits and bulbs and chanting 'Ram-Naam.'

Because of a lack of faith in divinity, beings seek satisfaction in mundane objects and therefore get deflected from the truth. The upbringing and the family culture play the most important role in instilling right or wrong values or 'Sanskar' in the being. The same thing happened with Marich. Earlier because of his unjust upbringing, he used to believe that joy is only in worldly pleasures, and therefore he resorted to violence to satisfy his desires. But Lord's treatment gave a new meaning to his life and completely changed his thought process and perspective. This sequence again validates that the intention of wellness always accompanies Lord's punishment. It was only then that the connection so created in the heart of Marich for the Lord was devoid of worldly expectations and filled only with surrender or 'Samarparn.' Worldly relations, be it with your close family, thrives only on "give and take" but the relationship of the being with the Lord is outright selfless and unconditional.

Although the insistence of Ravan prompted Marich to take the form of golden deer, he was pretty sure that today he was chasing his own 'Kaal' or death. It's interesting to note that even though Lord's deadly arrow pierced his heart, yet cascades of love and joy flowed in every cell of his body. By sacrificing his life, he played an important role in Ram Leela, though apparently, it may seem to the world that he was a loyal servant of Ravan who played a wicked role in 'Sita-Haran' or the abduction of Sita. It's also evident from the fact that still today, people in general, label the wicked ones as Marich. However, a thoughtful understanding of his character would reveal that he was actually a true devotee-servant of Lord Ram.

Initially, there was a lot of apprehension and uncertainty in the mind of Marich. But as he came closer to Lord, all his fears evaporated, and he realized the ultimate bliss of 'Atman' or self, in front of which, life and death, do not hold any value. Now with immense joy, he was playing the 'Swaran-Mrag-Leela' or the running and chasing game of the golden deer. Instead of getting executed by evil Ravan, he found it to be noble and infinite times better to get liberated in the hands of Lord Ram. He therefore proudly chose to give away his 'Pran' or life as an 'Ahuti' or oblation in the 'Ýagya' or resolution of Lord Ram.

Story of Marich immensely inspires us with the truth that no matter how negative a person's 'Chintan' or thinking is or was, he can still transform himself and direct his thinking on the path of righteousness. We must understand that the Lord, at times, gives harsh treatment but only to those in whom He sees potential. It is solely up to the being to learn from those events and mend his ways, like Marich or continue with self-destructive idiocy, like Ravan. In fact, there is no human being on this planet who, at least once, doesn't think of the wastefulness of his insane, injudicious and wrongful thinking or Chintan. But unfortunately, this realization is soon lost because of mind-ego's compulsive thinking of desires and insecurities. Saint Tulsidas asserts that freedom from obsessive, wasteful and compulsive 'abnormal' thinking can be attained only when the being unconditionally surrenders in the lotus feet of Lord Ram. And like Marich, it's only then that the 'Chintan' is focussed in the right direction, and the being realizes the ultimate success, bliss and peace.

Chapter 3.11

Sita Doubts Laxman: The Greatest Hurt

One wrong reaction gave a regret of a lifetime,
Karma is inescapable even for personalities, divine.

In the history and literary works of the whole world, there is none other than the great Laxman who has proved such unconditional and selfless love, service and renunciation. Laxman had devoted his entire life to the service of Lord Siya-Ram. He had unconditionally offered his everything that is Guru, Parents, Wife, Family, Wealth, Comforts, Name and Fame. Mother Sumitra had inspired Laxman to go to forest exile as a son-devotee of Siya-Ram. She reminded him that accompanying Siya-Ram for forest exile is by no means renouncing or losing anything but gaining everything. It became evident when she said to him, 'What trouble can that child have in a forest, desert or Hell, who has the most compassionate and powerful Siya-Ram as mother and father?'

Buthis pure love couldn't prevent the most agonizing mishap from occurring. The intention of the same great Laxman was doubted and that too by his own God-Mother Sita. Though later realizing Her mistake, Mother couldn't forgive herself for a very long time. The hurtful words She had spoken to Laxman, didn't let Her be at peace. Sheaccepted that the evil act of Ravan and Her untold sufferings in Lanka was a punishing repercussion for hurting Laxman. But the question is, how come that day, such inappropriate words slipped from the Mother of Universe? One day at 'Ashok Vatika' in Lanka, She revealed to Trijita that it was as if something unexplainable had compelled her to blurt out such harsh words for Her brother-son Laxman.No matter what the reason behind that unexpected incident was, the truth is that nothing in the world, not even Lord Ramcanperturb the most dispassionate or 'Vairagya Van' Laxman, other than his Mother Sita.

Lady Sita knew very well that nothing else, but Her distressing words could make Laxman disobey Lord's orders and leave Panchvati. Lord Ram with Sita had already planned the Leela or Divine-Play for the destruction of Ravan. Laxman was not part of that stratagem. Therefore, for the sake of Leela, Ravan had to be given the opportunity to abduct Sita. But the point is that if Laxman had stayed with Lady Sita, this cannot be made possible. Readers must keep in mind that complete Ramayan, including the war of Lanka is just a Lord Ram's Leela, and Laxman was just playing his role as per Lord's instructions. So Laxman getting injured, unconscious or tied up was all part of this unforeseeable Leela. The truth is that one strike of 'Sheshnag' Laxman can destroy Ten thousand Ravans.

Before going after the Golden Deer Marich, Lord Ram ordered Laxman, 'There are many ferocious demons who roam around in the forest. As per the need of the situation, use your intelligence, power and skills, to ensure the safety of Sita.' As per the order, Laxman was fully committed to his job with high alertness. No threat, fear or temptation could divert his focus. On being hit by Lord's arrow, the golden deer Marich deceptively called out loud Laxman's name in Ram's voice for help. But Laxman outrightly rejected this fake call of help and continued guarding Sita. Seeing his unwavering stance, Mother Sita wondered, what could be the possible way to send him away? Accordingly, She staged a very worried look and ordered Laxman that he must rush for his brother's help immediately as He is probably in big trouble.

But Laxman was unaffected by Mother Sita's apprehensions. The thought that Supreme Lord Ram is in trouble was pretty amusing for him, and so he couldn't stop himself and laughed. Seeing his reaction, Mother Sita got really agitated and yelled at him with harsh words. She also gave him an ultimatum that if he doesn't go, She will destroy herself. Finally, Her doubting his intentions for Herself,tore up his heart and soul. He couldn't believe his ears and the words, he just heard from his Mother. Ultimately he could not stand it any longer and went away from Panchvati, frantically looking for Lord.

This whole episode was the starting point of Lanka-Leela. It all started with a mere desire for golden deer. For a Bhakt, to use Lord for his desires is like selling a hard-earned golden trophy for the fulfillment of a stale pleasure. Believing Marich's voice as Lord's voice was again an act of sheer ignorance. And to think or believe that the Supreme Powerful Lord can be in danger was doubting the might and prowess of Supreme. When God is away, then the company of a Saint is the biggest savior for the being. But doubting the character of Saint Laxman again shows being's distrust in the holy words of Saints. All these flaws of mind gave the evil-ego that is Ravan who was in the fake guise of a Sage, the opportunity to abduct the 'Bhakti-Shakti-Shanti-Laxmi' Sita and cage Her in the prison of greed, that is Lanka. By playing this role of ignorance and intentionally becoming mean, Mother Sita showed what happens when desires, doubts and distrustfulness govern the mind of the benighted beings.

Though everything was staged, yet from a behavioral perspective, Laxman also didn't act wisely and responded inappropriately with laughter to Lady Sita's deepest concerns. Love brings apprehensions, and Laxman knows this very well. When in Chitrakoot, he heard that Bharat is coming with an army, he doubted Bharat's intention and immediately stood up to confront him. Though later, he repented distrusting Saint Bharat. Our mind becomes possessive and insecure for those it loves the most. The same logic applies to Lady Sita also. In the episode of Golden Deer Leela, a wife's concern that her husband could be in trouble was very natural and logical, especially when She could hear cries for help in Ram's voice. In such a seemingly grave situation, a more mature response with some wise convincing was expected from Laxman. Instead, he started laughing mockingly. Laxman's lack of seriousness followed by laughter infuriated Mother Sita. And in such a rage, loose words and harsh reactions from a wife, are not surprising at all.

Whatever may be the reason, Laxman had to pay the price of this behavioral immaturity. Laxman regretted and lost his smile for a very long time. The pain of separation from Sita, on brother Ram's face, always made Laxman feel guilty. He could not forgive himself. Mostly human beings are very casual in behavior. For them, a thoughtful and careful response is not something of serious consideration. But the selection of words, timing and appropriate reply, as per situation, does make a huge difference. In Leela's perspective, Sita-Haran had to happen, but from a worldly perspective, the ugliness of this unfortunate incident could have been avoided. But this is how life is.

Only by conscious evaluation of self conduct, one can learn from past blunders. And this is the lesson that needs to be grasped from this episode. Just one casual reaction can change the course of the future, and therefore one must take utmost care and think judiciously before speaking. This is the lesson Goddess Sita and Laxman intend to teach the worldly beings. But there is one thing more. Laxman's dedicated service to Lord and Sita's unwavering love for Lord reflects that even after making a blunder, one can re-attainGrace and peace through steadfast devotion in the lotus feet of Lord Ram.

Chapter 3.12

The Fickle Ravan: Dysfunction of Mind

Hearing Sita's fiery warning, Ravan burnt with exasperation,
But in the heart, he worshipped Her feet and got satisfaction.

The news of the demise of Khar, Dushan and of fourteen thousands Asur soldiers, single handedly by Lord Ram shook Ravan to the core. In those moments of intense anger and revenge, a sudden fear arose in his flickering mind - "Khar and Dushan were as powerful as me and no mortal being, but only God can slay them. Has Narayan actually incarnated in the form of Prince Ram?" But soon, his self-destructive mind-ego again interrupted this thought. The great scholar of Vedas, Ravan knew very well that God is not only the Supreme Power, but He is also Omnipresent. He then intentionally planned to create enmity with Lord Ram as he wanted to die through God's arrow and attain ultimate salvation. But he wanted to be absolutely certain. The conspiracy of Swaran-Mrag or golden deer was his plan to test the reality of Prince Ram. As per Ravan, if Ram would have recognized the truth of the deer and didn't have chased it, then it would have proved that He is 'Sakshat' Narayan Himself.

However, Prince Ram failed the Swarn-Mrag test. For Ravan, the one who runs after a deer like an ordinary hunter cannot be God. Now misbelieving the Supreme Trinity that is Ram, Laxman and Sita as mere mortals, Ravan focussed on his ploy of abducting Sita. He was sure that hearing the fake Ram's call for help, utterly perplexed Sita would have no option but to send Laxman to His rescue, and the same thing happened as well. Just as Laxman left, Ravan disguised as a holy sage entered the Panchvati premises and indulged Sita in a fabricated conversation. But for highly enlightened Sita, it didn't take long to sense that something fishy is going on. She scolded him in a stern voice, "Although you are in sage attire, you are talking like a fraudster."

Ravan at once got back to his real form and divulged his evil intentions.

Lady Sita gave him a fiery warning, "You an ugly rodent is desiring a Lion's bride. Lord will be here anytime. It seems like your end is near." Saint Tulsidas says that hearing those true but pinching words, Ravan got enraged, but deep inside the heart, he prostrated in the lotus feet of the 'Jag-Janini' Sita. So the point is, was the anger shown by Ravan real or overtly pretense? Does Ravan, in actuality, a true devotee of Lord Ram but acting as evil?

The only constant attributes of ego, in a villainous being, are Fear and Anger. Ravan's inner worship of Devi Sita may appear so, but it is not real devotion or Bhakti. In fact, it was the compelling, divine voice of Supreme Sita, which suppressed the functioning of his mind-ego for some moments and inspired the Asura to worship Her feet. We often hear people saying that they felt very pure and peaceful in the company of a knowledgeable Saint. The reason for this realization is not the being but the divinity of the Saint. The same applies to Ravan.

Ramcharitmanas speaks about the mental illness of 'Sannipat' or Delirium that arises in those who have a high degree of Kaam-Krodh-Lobh that is Lust, Anger and Greed. Let's say if a mentally disturbed person touches someone's feet or does 'Namaskara,' then does it signify that he is well behaved and composed? The truth is that just like at one moment, he is nice with others, at the second moment, he can hurt others. Nobody can take responsibility for an insane person.

Mind, like a mentally disturbed and unpredictable entity, keeps on wandering in the infinite universe of ego, habits, memories and thoughts. Sometimes the mind is alert like a Yogi, and in the next moment, it's lusting like a Bhogi or pleasure seeker. Sometimes it hurts others while other times, it shows great sympathy. Sometimes it sees itself as a broke and pauper while at other times it glides in self-pride. Intellectual or imposter, righteous or unrighteous, friendly or abusive, the unstable mind changes its roles ceaselessly. No matter how unconvincing it may sound but the state of delirium, that is, instability, abnormality and flickering of mind cannot be cured without the Grace of God. I agree that today Science and it's stream like Psychology is very advanced and that it must be applied in clinical mental disorder cases. Science can give temporary relief but cannot permanently cure the dysfunction of abnormal minds of normal people. Nothing can bring Peace to mind unless the being doesn't surrender his life in devotion or Bhakti.

Ravan is the symbol of 'Sannipat' or mind dysfunction. Sometimes he is deeply engrossed in Tapasya of Shiva and Brahma while other times, he is busy abducting beautiful females from all over the world. In the urge to conquer the world, he mercilessly engages in acts of violence with others. While in the Ashok Vatika episode, he shows kindness by asking Meghnad not to kill Hanuman but just bring him to the court. That day he greeted Marich with immense respect while the very next minute, he called him an idiot and stood up to slay him. Sometimes like a cowardly petty thief, he plans to steal, while other times, he boasts of his valor and courage. Sometimes he foolishly misinterprets the wise counselling of his wife Mandodari while on the death of his son Meghnad, he comforts and speaks intellectually on life and death to her. Again, despite already capturing the kingdom of Lanka from Kuber, he again goes after him in the Himalayas and fights again. There are several instances that clearly reflect the unpredictable mind of Ravan.

Ravan aptly symbolizes the state of Delirium or 'Sannipat,' the mental illness mentioned in the 'Uttra Kand' of Ramcharitmanas. In Ravan, lust, anger and greed or Kaam-Krodh-Lobh had reached their epitome, and so losing the stability of his mind was inevitable. And therefore, in one moment, he got mad with anger with Sita's insulting words, while in the very next moment, he worshipped Her feet in his heart and considered himself most fortunate.

The most lethal disease that affects human beings is not biological but a dysfunctioning mind. This virus is not only highly contagious but is also the root cause of all human sufferings. That's not all, but an even bigger problem is that the being is not ready to accept that he could suffer from this virus. One must understand that recognizing the Ravan element and finding a cure for this dreadful dysfunction is only possible if one is mindfully conscious and commits his life to 'Bhakti.' Ramcharitmanas is not just about Bhakti, but it also builds moral character and provides the solution to all mind dysfunctions. However, not many will succeed in curing themselves because, in mankind, there is a hopeless attachment with insanity or the Ravan. But those who will, will undoubtedly shine bright in the aegis of Lord Ram and achieve everything they aspire for.

Chapter 3.13

Martyrdom of the Great 'Gidh-Raj' Jatayu

For ages, infinite beings have died, are dying and will be dying in future,
But there is not a martyrdom like Jatayu in world's history and literature.

It didn't take Lord Ram long to apprehend the mischief of the Marich disguised in Swarn-Mrig or the Golden Deer. Lord, after slaying and liberating Marich, rushed back to Panchvati. On the way, He was utterly surprised to see Laxman running towards Him, as He categorically had entrusted him with the safety and protection of Mother Sita in Panchavati. Sensing a conspiracy, both of them immediately got concerned for Sita's safety and dashed back. As soon as they reached Panchvati, they frantically started looking for Her but could not find Her around. Looking at the unexpected turn of events, they hurriedly ventured into the forest, searching for Her. Not very far, they found the great Gidh-Raj or the Vulture-King Jatayu helplessly fallen on the earth and badly injured. Lord rushed to him and rested Jatayu's head on His lap. Jatayu then remorsefully informed them that the King of Lanka, Ravan had abducted Sita, and though he battled vigorously with him, he could not help protect Sita. In the fierce fight against Ravan, Jatayu had lost his wings, and so he fell from the sky. With every passing moment, his chances of survival were sinking.

Knowing about the dastardly acts of Ravan, Lord Ram got furious and announced aloud, *"O Great Jatayu, when you go in Heaven, don't tell My father King Dasrath anything about the happenings. If I am Ram, then very soon Ravan with his whole clan will himself tell him the story of their own destruction."* The Earth trembled, and the Devta finally sighed in relief. The Kaal or death warrant of Ravan was sealed.

Lord earnestly wanted to save his life, but the enlightened Jatayu replied with a smile, "The One, whose mere recitation of name at the time of death, delivers even the gravest sinner, is in front of my eyes. O Lord Ram, what else I need from life? For what purpose must I keep this body now?" Very few have the guts to refuse the offered immortality and embrace death. Jatayu is undoubtedly one of them. He, although being very old in age, had the valour to combat the deadliest warrior of the world, that is, Ravan. Here, on the one hand, is Jatayu, who happily rejects immortality for getting liberated by the Lord and, on the other hand, is Ravan, whose only purpose of life was to attain immortality and power.

While abducting and carrying away Sita in his flying-machine or Pushpak-Viman, the warning and the challenge of Jatayu, really surprised Ravan, especially when the challenger was an old and vulnerable bird. Ravan thought that probably this vulture had lost his senses and so had dared to challenge Ravan. But he totally misjudged and underestimated Jatayu. It became evident when in the fierce battle, Ravan got badly injured and almost got killed by the brave old vulture. However, Ravan luckily evaded death and got alive again because of the boon. Even after putting up a great fight with Ravan, Jatayu finally got defeated. He was on his deathbed in unendurable pain, but before departing, his last wish was to inform Lord Ram about 'Sita-Haran,' that is, the abduction of Sita.

Like a dutiful son, Prince Ram rested Jatayu on his holy lap. Knowing and acknowledging the great sacrifice of Jatayu, Lord couldn't control his tears. He rested His palm on Jatayu, and his pain vanished. Lord insisted him to live so that He could get the opportunity of serving the great Jatayu whom He considered equal to His father. Although Jatayu knew that Lord has the ultimate healing power and can give him immortality, he still refused His insistence.

Most human beings believe that death is a painful end, in which the most precious object that is 'Dehá' or 'body' is lost. But for enlightened ones like Jatayu, death is only a golden opportunity leading to the door of liberation. One, who believes only Deha as truth would naturally get terrified whenever there is a threat to Deha. For him, death is losing his entity forever. But the one, who truly believes and considers Atman as his real identity and Deha as a vehicle, sees death as the end of one chance and doorway for the next one.

Suppose, if somebody is given all the pleasures of the world, anything that he asks for but with a rider, that he cannot leave the house, then it's actually a punishment. The Deha should not become a cage, and so God has given the Being an exit in the form of death. Had God not created this exit, then the Deha would have become the prison and a punishment for the being.

'Death would not be called bad, O people, if one knew how to truly die.' - *Shri Guru Nanak Dev*

However, this doesn't mean that one must intentionally end his life. In fact, no being has the right to do so. Every human life has a unique purpose, a Swadharma, which he needs to diligently fulfil irrespective of the odds of life. The one who doesn't accomplish the purpose of life cannot be in peace before or after death. Jatayu had successfully accomplished his Swadharma, which is fighting Ravan for protecting Lady Sita and informing Lord Ram about the incident.

A devotee like Jatayu firmly believes that at the time of death, if one recites the name of God, then even the gravest sinner gets liberated from his bad Karma and attains freedom. No matter what the situation is, being cannot lie, fake or fool at the time of death. Natural thinking and uttering the name of God in the last moments only prove that throughout his lifetime, he has fully depended on God and His Name. The worthiness of life is in detaching self from material and rediscovering the connection with the infinite. 'Mukti' or liberation means to rise above the worldly dependencies.

For Jatayu, there was no unfinished business in the world, and so for him, there was no point in just living for the sake of it. A business traveler visits a city and stays in the hotel. Why should he continue living in the hotel after his business meeting is finished? By sacrificing Deha in the service of Lord Siya-Ram, Jatayu believed that the true purpose of his life was accomplished. On the basis of Arth (Gain & Loss), Dharam (Righteousness), Kaam (Desires) and Moksha (Liberation), leaving the body was the most appropriate choice for Jatayu.

Arth - Jatayu would get rid of a low existence of vulture with an old, worn-out body and would get that position, which is difficult even for the King of Devta, Indra.

Dharam - He was dying with honour for righteousness fulfilling his Swadharma, and there could be no better use of life than this.

Kaam - Being can desire the whole World and can even achieve it. But what about the one who has achieved the Creator of Billions of Worlds? This is the end of desires.

Moksha - This was a good opportunity for him to attain liberation in the most comforting, divine lap of Lord Ram. Who knows if he could ever get the same opportunity again?

Finally, Lord Ram was speechless and accepted the will of Great Jatayu. To live by chance and to die without any purpose is not the objective of life. Just one in a million knows how to properly utilize the resources, which he is born with and has attained. The incident of Gidh-Raj Jatayu shows how to righteously use the resources that is Deha, even if it means death. Swadharma or the purpose of life is, therefore, more important than life itself. Ravan all his life was desperate for immortality, but the great Jatayu rejected it willingly, even though it was offered by Supreme God Himself. King Dasratha died with an unfulfilled intense desire to see his son Ram, but Jatayu closed his eyes in the arms of Lord Ram. There is no one as saintly, courageous and fortunate as Jatayu. Jatayu closed his eyes, and thatvery moment, his Atman merged with Parmatman, and he became one with his Lord Ram.

Chapter 3.14

A Tribute to SHABARI

Butterflies can't see their wings, they can't see how truly beautiful they are, but everybody else can.

All three Loka were bustling with excitement and happiness; a great soul had arrived; everybody was her fan.

'Why is this cheering? What's happening?' Parvati asked Shiva curiously,

'It's the great Shabari,' Rudranath replied to Parvati overwhelmingly.

The ardent devotee of Lord Ram, and the symbol of endless love, Shabari finally got liberated.

Hearing about her, the epitome of patience, devotion and purity, all faces with Sunshine were painted.

Though born in a low caste of hunters, for devotion and knowledge every moment, Shabari would pray.

At her wedding, as per their custom, her father brought a thousand cattle for sacrifice; blood was on the way.

The slaughter was unacceptable to her, and to evade those innocent killings, in the middle of the night, she secretly escaped away,

Her quest for truth led her to many ashrams, but being from a low caste, she got badly treated and pushed away.

Against all the odds, Sage Matanga willingly accepted her as daughter-disciple, unconditionally,

Gave her the shelter and wisdom, while she served her Perceptor, earnestly.

Many years passed by, once the Sage said, 'My time is over, I am leaving this body, is there anything I can do for you?'

'Lord, what will I do here, take me with you to the highest abode, as the body is not me, only the soul is true.'

He asked her to wait for the day when Lord Ram will give Darshan to her,'Till then you do Sadhana and clear the karma, due.'

For countless years she eagerly waited for the arrival of Lord Ram, and each day for Him she prepared oblations,

She would roll herself on the path to clear it from thorns and beautify the surrounding with decorations.

She waited resolutely each day, but when the Sun went down and Ram was not around,

She would brace herself again for the next day and the next round.

One day she went to the village pond to fetch some water,
Seeing a low caste, a sage got furious and with a stone, hit her,

The blood drops from her wound turned the pond's water red.
'Witch,' the fake and frightened sages shouted and fled.

The ignorant sages did Yagya, Havana, Puja and Vrata, but the pond color won't change,

The next day, they got the news that Lord Ram with Laxman, searching for Sita, is in nearby range.

The sages approached Lord and requested help, for they can't live without the water of the pond.

To find a solution, Lord took a dip in the pond, but the color red didn't respond.

'Tell me how it happened?' Lord Ram questioned the sages and got to know of the real situation.

'Oh sages, you have broken my heart, nothing will change, until I meet Shabari', was His declaration.

Hearing the news of Lord Ram's arrival, Shabari was overjoyed and rushed to the spot hastily,

The wait was finally over; today is the big day, in excitement, even the earth forgot to spin momentarily.

The dust from her feet fell in the pond, and by itself, the blood color turned back to pure water,
The shallow sages were ashamed, but Lord Ram smiled, meeting the Creator's own daughter.

She embraced Ram tightly, and thanked Guru Matang for the prophecy he had made,
'Ram, I was waiting for this day for so long, Please come to my hut,' she prayed.

Lord picked up the 'Shabari ke Ber,' but Laxman cautioned, 'These berries are wild and half-eaten, not good to eat,'
But Lord didn't stop and announced, 'Anything that is offered to Me with Love, I accept it, other than this, nothing is sweet.'

Lord was touched by Shabari's innocence and purity, 'Mother, I am pleased with your devotion, ask anything you ever wished,'
'You have given Darshan, my Ram, I just pray for Bhakti,' and with tears, Lord's feet she washed.

Lord proclaimed, 'What the small child is for mother, a devotee is for Me,
But if he stops relying on Me, then he is no longer My responsibility,
You are the greatest devotee; surrendered to you is Me and My divinity'.

Ma Parvati's eyes moistened, listening to the great Shabari's saga of true devotion, from God Shiva,
It doesn't matter to Lord Ram, the caste, class and gender of the seeker; He only sees the love of the 'Jiva.'

Chapter 3.15

Shabari: The Epitome of Pure Love

"I don't see caste, kinship, lineage, reputation and physicality,
Wealth, honour, name, resources or honour of the family,
Also I am not impressed with achievements and ability,
Only the one who loves me is dearest to Me, in this eternity." - Lord Ram

Lord Ram and Laxman cremated Gidhraj Jatayu and moved ahead. On the way, they encountered a weird demon named 'Kabandh' (meaning Torso). Its head and legs were shoved inside the trunk of the body. It only had miles long hands for movement, through which it captured any passing by being and satiated his hunger. Though Kabandh was condemned, its strategic position at the southern border of Dandakaranya Forest was a lethal barrier for Asura. In a way, it was guarding the forest. He attacked Lord Ram-Laxman while they were crossing his terrain. They defeated him in the fight, and he surrendered.

In his past life, Kabandh was a 'Gandharva' or beautiful heavenly being, who, for his misbehaviour, was cursed to have a demonic and ugly life by Sage Durvasa. Lord Ram scolded him for his misconduct, but then the ever-compassionate Supreme forgave him. A pit was dug by Laxman, and Kabandh was cremated in it. This was the only way to liberate him from his lowly demonic existence. Following after that, Kabandh appeared in his beautiful Gandharva form, thanked the Lord and pointed towards the path that led to the ashram of Shabari. Lord Ram and Laxman moved forward and reached Shabari's ashram. On seeing them, Shabari was overwhelmed with joy, remembering the prophecy of her Guru, great Sage-Father Matang.

Shabari, the symbol of love, is one of the greatest characters of Ramcharitmanas who is very famous for her sweetness of berries that Lord Ram could never forget all His life. When Lord had returned to Ayodhaya and was crowned as the King, many grand buffets were organized in His honour. But every time He used to frankly mention in public that no delicacy in the whole world could match the sweetness of *'Shabari ke Ber.'* Those were actually wild berries that are fatal for the human body, but the true love and unparalleled devotion of Shabari transformed them into heavenly sweet fruits. Those berries are even spoken of today, remembered as 'Shabri ke Ber' or half-eaten berries of Shabari. It is believed that only after tasting each berry's sweetness, Shabari offered it to the Lord. Such love of a simple-hearted devotee is undoubtedly rare to find in Sanatan Dharma.

Shabari is also revered for one more reason, and that is, Lord Ram sought her guidance to know the whereabouts of Mother Sita. He humbly inquired only from her the way to get Sita back. It was on the advice of Shabari that Lord befriended Sugreev. Shabari was not an ordinary devotee but an enlightened Yogini who, despite having all the 'Siddhi' or Supernatural powers at her disposal, never used them. Although she was at a very high degree of Consciousness, there was no trace of arrogance or pride. She was always meek and humble to everybody. She was on the topmost position of human evolution after traversing the mammoth ocean of hardship and difficulties of life. Seeing Lord Ram at her doorstep, she could not believe her eyes. Goswami Tulsidas says that in the whole of Ramcharitmanas other than Prince Bharat and Mother Shabari, such level of Bhakti could not be found in any other devotee.

It is well known that every fruit has its unique flavour. Fruits are compared on the parameters of freshness, quality and taste. In some, the skin is thicker, while in others, the seed is larger. Shabari's fruits had neither the shameless skin of pretension nor the egoic seed of desires. That is why Lord Ram says that these fruits of love had given Him absolute satisfaction for the very first and only time.

Ravan is 'Moha' or attachment, who had abducted 'Bhakti-Devi' or Goddess of Devotion, that is Mother Sita. 'Vivek' or intellect that is Jatayu, tried his level best but could not save Her. He informs Lord Ram about the 'Sita-Haran' but could not tell Him how to get Her back. Therefore the Lord asked 'Prem' or Love, that is Shabari for the solution. The point is that every being's aim is Bhakti, but the Moha in his life confiscates his life's aim and purpose and disillusions him. By using Vivek, every being tries hard to fight Moha, but fails. Only Prem or unconditional love for Supreme can help the being to get rid of all worldly Moha and attain Bhakti. Just as Lord Ram killed Ravan, the Supreme slays Moha and gives the seeker Bhakti.

'Prem-Murti' Shabari replied, 'Lord, You are omnipresent and knower of all hearts, then why are You asking me about Sita? But since it's Your Leela, please go towards Pampasar lake. There you will find Sugreev and befriend him. Further plans will be set there only.'

Lord Ram was pleased with her and discoursed on 'Navdha Bhakti' or the Nine attributes of Devotion and declared that only Shabari has all of them. With this, Shabari ignited 'Yoga-Agni' or 'Fire of Concentration' and immolated herself. She completed her cycle of mortal existence, and finally, became one with Supreme Consciousness. Lord Ram and Laxman gave obeisance to her and marched ahead. It was only after meeting Shabari that Lord regained some peace, which He had lost after losing His beloved Sita.

Like mortal beings, even God sometimes needs encouragement, love and guidance. Every being who treads on the path of Bhakti plays an essential role in His journey. Unlike mortals, Lord Ram's earthly journey is not for settlement of his Karmic accounts but to set high morals, instances and ethics for the beings to follow. Shabari belonged to a low caste 'Bhilini' and was of 'Istri' or female gender. In those times, these attributes were considered secondary characteristics and, therefore, also ineligible for spirituality.

Women are secondary,
My caste is lowly,
And I lack intellectuality. - Shabari

Mother, I recognize no other kinship,
Except that of Devotional fellowship. - Lord Ram

Her solemn and unwavering dedication towards her aim proved that nothing could deter you if you hold the spirit of perseverance. Lord Ram has Himself said, 'I only recognize Devotion and Love and nothing else.' We all face regrets, frustrations and obstructions, because of which life, which is a collection of beautiful poetry, becomes terrible suffering. Only love, purity, and surrender in the lotus feet of the benevolent Lord Siya-Ram can help us come out of the anima and find peace and bliss in life.

Chapter 3.16

Narada questions Lord Ram : Narayan-Narayan

Lord, You took avatar and got married Yourself, but you didn't let me do so; why?
Narada, how can I let you spoil your Sadhana, as you are the jewel of my eye.

Lord Ram-Laxman, after seeing Shabari, reached Pampasar and took a dip in the pure water of the holy lake. Goswami Tulsidas writes that there He acted like a heartbroken lover, singing emotional love sonnets of separation in His beloved Sita's memory. His mannerisms were like that of a mortal human being who is in a very miserable state. This part of Ramcharitmanas is one of the finest poetic masterpieces, aptly expressing the real pain of separation. Narad Muni, a Vedic Divine Sage and a great devotee of God Narayan, who sincerely witnessed the whole Leela, couldn't hold himself and arrived at the scene.

In the early part of Balkand, before Ravan's story begins, there is an interesting part of Narad's desperation for marriage, and God Narayan is not letting it happen. That day at Pampasar, Narad questioned Lord Ram *(Avatar of Narayan)*, "If marriage is such a wrong thing that You didn't let me do it, then why did You get married because of which you are now experiencing the pain of separation? That day I prayed to you to give me a beautiful form. Instead, you gave me a monkey face, and so I got rejected by the bride." That time, Narad got uncontrollably furious after knowing God Narayan is responsible for the bride's rejection and cursed Him that He too will face the pain of separation one day. Today that curse had come true.

Today, seeing the sorry and remorse state of the Lord, Narad was bewildered and asked Him that if He hadn't allowed anybody to get married, then Narad would not have complained. But Lord intentionally and specifically didn't let Narad enjoy marital bliss. Lord Ram smiled, hearing Narad's complaint and lovingly explained, "Let's say God has two sons, one is grown up and matured while the other one is young and childish. The elder is 'Gyani' or the practitioner of Knowledge Yoga, whereas the younger is 'Bhakt' or the practitioner of Devotion Yoga. Generally, even if the elder son of the family doesn't seem to be interested, then also the family members are eager to get him married first and at the earliest."

"But the younger one, who isn't mature enough to understand the meaning of marriage, and yet insists on it, believing it to be an occasion of celebration and pleasure, then obviously the parents reject his demand and smile at his childishness. Naradji was acting in the same way." Seeing the bride Vishvamohini's beauty, he acted immaturely, like what a small child does on seeing a toy and rushes to grab it, chucking other things in his hand. Out of infatuation and temptation, even the one who had spent years in spiritual practices can act like an immature child and spoil his spiritual merits. Had Narad not lost focus on his aim, that is, Supreme Narayan, he wouldn't have become so desperate to get married and would not have faced rejection.

Lord considered Narad like His own little child and dealt with him like a parent. Just as a small child who becomes uncontrollable, argumentative and furious on the refusal of his desired object, Narad cursed his Father-God Narayan. But God, like a loving parent, accepted the curse with much patience and tolerance. Lord explains that lust is like a snake, and anger is like fire. Both older and younger sons are vulnerable to the threat of the snake and fire. Parents know that the elder one can deal on his own while they always need to be cautious about the safety of the little one. And therefore, Lord had to make sure that Narad was not stung by the snake of lust.

What Narad meant was that if the Lord had not allowed him, why did He Himself get married, even after knowing that the 'pain of separation' is an intrinsic part of the mortal relationships? Lord beautifully replied that when a small ignorant child gets tempted to touch fire, then a mother rushes to save him from getting burnt. But many times, she burns her own fingers in this act of protection. And therefore, Lord wittingly said that in the course of protecting Narad from the snake of lust, He Himself got stung by that snake.

A child is and must always be grateful to his mother for being the protective shield in his life. But at times, the small child, by hitting or screaming, takes a kind of revenge from his own mother for not fulfilling his demands. That is exactly the reason why Narad cursed God Narayan. If today the Lord is facing the pain of separation from Sita, this is the repercussion of protecting Narad. With this discussion, the illusion of Narad ended at once, and he prostrated in the lotus feet of his ever-loving and caring Parents-Lord Siya-Ram.

Chapter 3.17

End of Aranya-Kand

The attraction of the female self is like a lamp-flame,
O Mind, discard lust and make only Siya-Ram your aim.

Goswami Tulsidas ends 'Aranya-Kand' with the advice that the female kind is a Deep-Shikha, a lamp flame hence a seeker's mind must not become a 'Patanga' or Kite insect, which easily gets attracted to this flame, and on coming closer to it, burns itself and dies. Instead, the mind must discard this attraction and practise 'Bhakti' or devotion and 'Satsang,' that is, the sacred discourses on Ramayan.

In scriptures, many a time, we find a common advice that is to stay away from womankind. While some have used this as a reference to degrade the females, others have criticized scriptures for being so irrational and regressive towards females. This 'chaupai' or advice of Tulsidas appears to be following the same women-degrading ideology of scriptures. But if we delve wisely into the matter, we will understand that the accusation on Saint Tulsidas for speaking against the female kind is not correct. To better comprehend this, we must recall the transformation story of Tulsidas's own life.

It was a stormy night in the month of *Shravan* when rain-lashed and lovelorn Tulsidas was standing on the banks of the holy Ganga. He just had to get across. He yearned to be with his beloved young wife Ratnavali, who went to visit her family. But in that wild weather condition, no boatman would dare to take him across the river.

Understandably, he was advised to go back home. But for Tulsidas, home is where the heart is, and that was with his beloved wife. As he stood there undecided, completely drenched and pondering, he suddenly saw a dead body floating nearby. At that very moment, his passion clearly had scant regard for the departed. So Tulsidas, with his intense craving for union with his wife, desperately took the support of that stiffened cadaver to row himself across the swollen waters. He also fearlessly climbed up the window of Ratnavali's room on the first storey, using an alive, venomous snake as rope. Ratnavali was taken aback and asked how he had even got there. "On a dead body and an alive snake," her loving young husband answered.

"If you could love Ram as much as you love this body of mere flesh and bones of mine!" Ratna murmured. The taunt had found its mark. The raging storm outside became a mere breeze compared to the terrible storm of guilt that arose within him. At one fell swoop, it decimated the lustful man into a resolute devotee. He then turned and walked away, never to return.

After the turn of the event, Tulsidas had realized that Lust in the human body is the biggest hurdle on the journey to attain perfection. In fact, Lust is a mind-ego trick to trap intelligence in an immensely pleasurable activity, making it forget the purpose of life. This way ego diverts the intelligence away from itself towards futility, ensuring its own survival and expansion.

In the original verse or 'chaupai,' the word 'Deep-Shikha' has been used to describe the female beauty, meaning a lamp's flame in the English Language. Some critics consider 'Deep-Shikha' as a derogatory word used for women. However, the truth is that in earlier literary works, 'Deep-Shikha' was used as a metaphor for pure and exquisite female beauty by great writers. Tulsidas has also used the word 'Deep-Shikha' to express the divine beauty of Lady Sita. In all his works, he has expressed devotional inclination in his works towards Mother Sita even more than Lord Ram. So is it possible for Tulsidas to use a derogatory word for his own God-Mother Sita?

Tulsidas doesn't say that this 'flame of beauty' or Deep-Shikha must be extinguished or destroyed. He just asks Mind not to become a Patanga or Kite insect, which is to refrain from the lustful attraction. In romantic literature, Patanga symbolizes a lover who has an unwavering affinity with the Deep-Shikha; that is his lady love.

From ancient times, the romance and love tales of literature and history, no matter how great and popular, are not free from the egoic trap of attachment. In unconditional love, there cannot be any expectations. True love is not what happens between two forms, but true love is that attachment which only happens with the formless, who is present in every form. Had the Patanga or the lover truly loved the Deep-Shikha, had he genuinely had appreciation and respect for her divinity, beauty and exquisiteness, there would have been no expectations and urge for attainment. There would just have been caution in not acting ungraciously. Deep-Shikha is neither inviting nor approaching anybody. It is the Patanga that draws himself to her. The urge to come close and touch her is not 'love,' but 'Vasna' or 'lust.' The culprit is the Patanga and not the Deep-Shikha.

Vasna not only destroys the Patanga's life but is also the cause of the spoilage of life and honour of the Deep-Shikha. Often, we see that when a desperate and one-sided lover (psychopath) knows that he cannot own her honourably, he tries to destroy her. Like Ravan, when there is only desperation for abducting beauty and no honour, then it becomes the root cause of destruction. But the mind-ego of the masses is such that instead of seeing the fault of the Patanga, they criticize the Deep-Shikha. Even Goddess Sita was not spared by the same ignorants.

The reason for this foolishness is that the mind is one entity, which cannot be easily directed towards righteousness. Strong determination and perseverance is needed to pull the mind from worldly attraction and fix it on the Lord. It is only by the Supreme Grace and not human will alone that mind can be drawn away from the magnetic effects of 'Vasna' and leads it to 'Satya' or truth.

To a certain extent, in such quotes of scriptures wherein it is advised to stay away from females, there is an element of female objectification. Secondly, it appears that the scriptures are written only from the perspective of males and that they don't acknowledge that a female can also be a great saint, a Maharishi or a Mahatma. That is probably because most of the scriptures in that era were only written by males based on their own life experiences. Comparatively, there is less volume of spiritual works by females. Having said that, Sanatan Dharma and Indian civilization are full of great female Mystics and Saints like Gargi, Maitreyi, MeeraBai, LalDed, Janabai, Sakhubai, Muktabai, BebeNanki, Sarada Devi, Sister Nivedita, Annie Beasant, Anandmayi Ma and many more. In fact it is foolish to see an Enlightened Saint or Mahatma on the tangent of a male or female body. It is the knowledge and grace that matters and not the form.

In this part of Ramayana, we see that it was the same lust that made Surpankha act pervertedly with Lord Ram and Laxman, and it was the same lust that made Ravan act foolishly with Lady Sita, sealing his 'Kaal' or death. At times, worldly temptations influence the mind to be 'Surpanakha,' while other times, they make it act foolishly like 'Ravan'; therefore, Saint Tulsidas advises to discard the seed of the evils, that is Kaam. The whole of Lanka got burnt and destroyed by the Holy fire of Deep-Shikha' Sita.' Who should be blamed for this destruction-Heavenly, pure 'Deep-Shikha' or evil and desperate 'Patanga'? Goswami Tulsidas says that the only way to get rid of this self-destructive vice of 'Kaam-Vasna' is 'Bhakti' of the lotus feet of Lord Siya-Ram.

KISHKINDAKAND

Chapter 4.1

Fear in Sugriv: Story of the Human-Being

O Hanuman, these two warriors look angelic and yet deceptive to me,
You find their real identity and if they are a threat, then just signal me.

Lord Ram, with brother Laxman, had reached the valley of Rishyamukha mountain, where Sugriv with his four ministers that is Hanumanji, Jambavan, Nal and Neela, has taken refuge from the threat of Bali. Sugriv got very frightened the moment he saw Lord Ram-Laxman and expressed his concern to Hanumanji, "They appear to be majestic and divinely powerful. You guise as a Brahmacari (Religious person) and check on them. If there is any trouble, just signal me. I will escape from here."

In Ramcharitmanas, Saint Tulsidas has wonderfully explained a step by step sequence for Bhakti-Marg or Path of Devotion. And in this sequence, the first and most important step is '*Knowing*', your deity. Unless one doesn't have good knowledge and understanding, it is very difficult to develop faith. And, without trust, love cannot blossom. Devotion without love is as impossible as extracting milk-cream from water. It is only because of the lack of knowledge of the truth of Lord Ram that Sugriv got scared seeing Him.

Bali was cursed that if he climbs on Rishyamukha Mountain, then his head will be destroyed, and therefore Sugriv found it ideal for making it as his ambush. Despite that, he never felt at ease. In fact, anything that is worldly or materialistic can never make one at ease. The one and only solution is 'Samparpan-Bhav' or Absolute Surrender to the Lord. "Although Bali himself cannot come here, he can send someone to attack anytime," this very thought always made Sugrivfrightened for his life.

Seeing the two heavenly charismatic brothers, he at once feared that they were his 'Kaal' or death, sent by Bali. He thought, "Since they are carrying bow and arrow, they can hit me, even from a distance. The best option for me is my friend, the most knowledgeable, fearless, intelligent and powerful, the great Hanumanji. Only he can protect me from this threat." Therefore Sugriv asks Hanumanji to check if there is any trouble and to signal him.

Like an ordinary mortal human being, Sugriv is also surrounded by problems, to the extent that even his wife, family and home have been snatched away. Even though he had lost everything, he had one thing which worked for him, even in such troublesome times. And that one thing was none other than the great Lord Hanuman, the epitome of 'Supreme Faith.' Saint Tulsidas has said that "In the times of crisis, when the world seems to have fallen, the one who holds on to his faith in Hanumanji, will, without any doubt, get free from all the worries.Shiva, the God of Faith, has taken the avatar as Hanumanji to serve Lord Ram".

Sugriv may have lost everything, but he never let go of his faith in Hanumanji, and this resulted in putting an end to all his problems, and this eventually helped him become the undisputed King of Kishkindha kingdom. If one contemplates thoughtfully, he will realize that the Present moment is never the actual problem. Problem is endless and compulsive analysis, anticipation and apprehension of the future, which is the root cause of all joy and sorrows in our life. Some beings ignorantly imagine a beautiful future and try to escape the present moment. They don't put in the necessary effort and commitment required to make that beautiful future materialize, thereby resulting in spoiling the present, resulting in unhappiness.

The one who has absolute faith, trust and confidence in the Lord remains indifferent towards the future. None, but God knows the future accurately. God is infinitely compassionate and human-Being is the responsibility of God. Even when two beings put in the same effort for the same task, the outcomes are never the same. There is no certainty of the fruits of actions, so Tulsidas Ji firmly advises tosurrender every expectationto God.

Whatever Ram has decided will happen.
Why unnecessarily bother analyzing? - Tulsidas

Goswami Tulsidas says that just this one thought gives tremendous strength to face the worst of situations and deadliest threats. The ultimate symbol of 'Faith' that is Lord Hanuman was there with Sugriv, and therefore, in this situation of uncertainty, Sugriv wisely left the decision to him. When one is unclear, unsure, uncertain and thoroughly disillusioned, then the being must trust a true friend's opinion and must have complete faith in his decision. In such a situation, the friend-guide becomes even more alert and cautious because now not one but two lives are dependent on him. Sugriv trusted the symbol of 'Faith' that is Hanumanji and ultimately attained Lord Ram. Tulsidasji affirms that whosoever puts his trust in Hanumanji like Sugriv, will attain the 'Kripa' or Grace, in the lotus feet of Lord Ram.

Chapter 4.2

The Wait is Over: Hanumanji meets Lord Ram

The meeting of the Two was a game of hide and seek,
Both of them are pundits in conversational technique.

On the request of Sugriv, Hanumanji, disguised as Bhramacari (Pious person), approached Lord Ram-Laxman. It was a very significant moment for both Lord Ram&Hanumanji, the divine actors. Each one of them was immensely witty and expert in hiding their true identity. Hanumanji was sure that the two divine personalities he is seeing are not just two mortal princes, and there was more to this than meets the eye. Avatar of God Shiva, Hanumanji didn't try to speculate or test; rather, He made Lord Ram Himself the medium to know about His own identity. He simply and very politely asks for His introduction. But Lord Ram was in a playful mood and didn't want to reveal the truth so easily to His Param-Bhakt or Greatest Devotee. He wanted to enjoy the game of hide and seek. It seemed as if He was hinting - "It's not so easy to recognize Me, try harder."The Lord wanted to check the depth of Hanumanji's devotion.

But Hanumanji was no less and cleverly put up many questions back to back to win this word game. He curiously asked, "Who are you, blue and fair-skinned ones? Appearing as Kshatriya (Warrior Class) but dressed like sages, roaming in the forest, who are you? Travelling with soft feet on this difficult and wild terrain, who are you? Despite such a beautiful and delicate body frame, you are withstanding hot, cold and stormy weather, tell me who are you? Are you one of the trinity that is Brahma-Vishnu-Mahesh? Or, are you Narayan Himself in human form? Are you the liberator of beings from the clutches of mind-ego and Maya? Or, are you the eradicator of evil from the face of this planet?"

In this game of hide and seek, the clever devotee actually had hit the bulls eye and rightly identified Lord, but Lord was still in the mood to play a little more. The 'creator of illusion' or Mayapati Ram again tried to create an illusion or Maya to hide His reality. He replied, giving His earthly introduction, "I am the son of King Dasratha of Ayodhaya. With his permission, I have ventured into the forest. My name is Ram, and he is my younger brother Laxman. My wife, Sita, was also with us, but she has been abducted by an evil demon. Now I am desperately searching for her. O great Bhramacari, I have told you about myself, now you too kindly tell me your story."

For an ordinary being, this introduction may appear to be plain and simple, but it has more to it. Also, it's quite amusing to note here how Supreme Lord Ram has crossed the limits of His acting or Leela by innocently asking about Hanumanji's identity. But every statement in His introduction has a deep hidden meaning. By introducing Himself as Dasratha's son, Lord is trying to prove that He is a Creation and not, The Creator. Again, by saying that with His father's permission, He has ventured into the forest, He is negating Hanumanji's presumption that He is the cause, reason and effect of the Universe. Instead, He is just a puppet in the hands of destiny.

Lord Ram meant that God is indifferent, formless, immortal and blissful. Then how could someone, standing in front of Hanumanji in the blue and fair human bodies form with the names Ram and Laxman, who are in distress of losing Princess Sita, be God? How come the One who is born in the mortal Raghukul family can be the eternal Supreme entity? Here, Lord means to say that Hanumanji's guess that He is God does not seem to be correct and that Hanumanji must re-evaluate his assumptions. Finally, if Lord Ram is God, the knower of every particle of this Universe, then did He need an introduction of Hanumanji or anybody, for that matter?

However, Lord's tricky talks didn't work, andHanumanji immediately recognized Him as Narayan, the Supreme God of the Universe. Lord Ram had lost that game of hide and seek from His greatest devotee. Hanumanji immediately dropped to his knees and prostrated in the lotus feet of his Lord Ram. He always knew that God has incarnated as Prince Ram in Ayodhaya. Undoubtedly, God is the greatest, but the eyes of devotees, which cannot be baffled and immediately recognise their master, are even greater than God himself.

In Krishna Leela, Lord Krishna lifted the entire Girraj Mountain on the nail-tip of His little finger. The citizens of Gokul took refuge under it from the heavy downpour and proudly praised, "See how great and strong is our friend Krishna, who has effortlessly lifted this mountain." But the Gopis, the great Cow-Maid Devotees of Gokul, replied, "See towards our friend Radha,

She in Her eyes has lifted Krishna, along with Him lifting the mountain." The greatest of everything are the eyes of Shri Radha. So who is greater - 'Bhakt Drishti' or 'Bhagwan,' that is 'Eyes of Devotees' or 'God'? This meeting of Lord Ram and Hanumanji reinstates the faith in the hearts of seekers that for God, nothing is dearer than a true devotee. Therefore, the seeker must not lose hope and carry on with his practise for 'Dirgha Kala' wholeheartedly without counting days, months or years. It is because the Lord will Himself come to him one day, but as per His will. All that a devotee needs is the 'Drishti' or Eyes to recognize his Lord.

Great are the eyes of eternal Devotee Hanumanji, from which even Lord Ram could not escape. Hanumanji is and was Lord Ram's servant, devotee and companion of childhood, who, on the instructions of Lord, left Ayodhaya and settled in Kishkindha. His mentor, the Sun God, had asked him to look after his son Sugriv. Since then, Hanumanji became a close ally and friend of Sugriv and was eagerly waiting for the day he would reunite with Lord Ram.

With the advent of Hanumanji, the dark clouds of suffering subsided, and the golden rays of hope enlightened the cosmos. More than the story of Shri Ram, it is the story of Devotees that inspires and makes us feel connected to Shri Ram. No wonder Hanumanji has the maximum number of temples, more than any other Hindu deity or God. He is the medium, messenger and the divine link between Being and Lord Ram. Saint Tulsidas created Hanuman Chalisa, which is the most recited, chanted, listened and sung devotional hymn in the whole world. Just a small iota of faith in Hanumanji can make an ordinary and weak human-being move even a mountain. All Hanumanji wants is the well being of Lord Ram's devotee. His one message is that nothing in this eternity is worthy, except for surrendering in the lotus feet of Lord Siya-Ram.

Chapter 4.3

Lord Ram-Hanuman 'Milan': God is not Unbiased

Hanumanji prostrated to Lord but He didn't respond,
O Lord, your indifference is against the rules of Bhakti-Bond.

Despite being prostrated and wholeheartedly wished by His great Bhakt Hanumanji, Lord Ram remained indifferent and didn't react at all. He instead asked for his introduction. There was not an iota of excitement of meeting His old friend-devotee, Hanumanji. This was quite unlikely of the Lord, who always takes the first and the final step towards His devotee. Hanumanji was still on his knees and yet the Lord didn't lift him up onto His divine shoulders, nor did He bless him by placing His palm on the devotee's head. In all of Ramcharitmanas, this is probably just one notable incident where the Lord appears to be somewhat insensitive. As was expected, Hanumanji could not bear it any longer and he said out of deep grievance, "Lord, in a worldly perspective, Your asking about my introduction is understandable but on the tangent of Bhakti, this is no less than injustice towards me."

He remorsefully continued, "Is it because I am dimwit, materialistic and manipulative, that you have forgotten me and hence, such a cold shoulder? Lord, it is only because of your extremely baffling Mayathat Beings are lost in this material world. And it's only through your Grace, that Beings can escape this never-ending trap. And for that, 'Bhajan' or spiritual practice is a must, which I am incapable of doing. I swear on You that I am telling the truth. But having said that, a servant and a son live at ease and with certainty, depending on the Grace of his Father-Master and so the Two Supreme Divinities Ram-Sita, have to ensure and honor this strong belief of the devotee."

Now, there was a valid reason behind Lord's such indifferent behavior and it took a while for Hanumanji to realize it. Hanumanji was in the guise of a "Brahmachari" (a Religious person), to whom Lord Ram regards even superior than Himself. Therefore, if He blesses a Brahmachari, then this would be against the rules of His worldly 'Leela' or play. Dueto this reason, the Lord had to contain the great excitement and love inside, while meeting His greatest ever devotee, Hanumanji. In fact, it was none other than the Lord, who was eagerly waiting for the moment when Hanumanji transforms back into his real form, discarding the Brahmachari form.

Here, the message for the seeker is simple and straight-forward. One has to attain the love of the Lordonly throughdiscarding his egoistical worldly attire. Failing to do so, he will not be able to recognize the Supreme, even if God Himself comes to him. Moreover, God will also be unwilling to embrace a seeker, unless he accepts and reveals his true self. Perhaps, this was one of the most significant reasons why many characters of Ramayan, be it Ravan or the whole of Asur clan, couldn't recognize God Ram because they were not able to come out of their worldly egoic identities. Modestly realizing this and his mistake, Hanumanji immediately discarded the 'Brahmachari' guise and now in his original form again prostrated in the lotus feet of His Lord. The very next moment, the Lord, with great love and joy, lifted him up and hugged him dearly. Lord couldn't control His tears and in those drops of divine nectar, all the obstructions between Ram-Hanuman, Lord and Devotee, Bhagwan and Bhakt washed away.

Lord thenheartily spoke, "Dear Hanuman, don't feel bad and don't fill your heart with pain-feelings. You are dearer to Me, twice more than Laxman is dear to me." Hearing this, the holy heart of Hanumanji was blessed with profound solace. But the question here is, can love of Supreme God Ram be ever quantifiable as twice, thrice and so on, when since, it has been declared and is universally accepted truth, that God is even-handed for all beings? A clarification was needed from Lord Ram about what does He exactly mean by giving twice more love to one devotee (Hanuman) than another(Laxman)? Lord then clarifies that the world may say that He is impartial & even-handed with all His Beings, but the truth is that the one, who has, unwavering and absolute devotion or 'Ananya-Bhakti' towards Him is dearer to Him, always.

This clarification is of paramount importance and **is** needed to justify the Principles of Devotion or 'Bhakti-Sidhant'. Because if God is unbiased with all His Beings then what is the purpose of Bhakti or religion or spirituality? What is then the inspiration or the special hope for the seeker for leading a life of righteousness? There has to be some incentive for seekers, committing their whole lives in seeking the Supreme. Else then, there would be just fear and reverence forGod, but no love for Him. Relationship of 'Bhakt' and

'Bhagwan' is unconditional but is expressed purely on the basis of "give" and "take" of love. And hence, if God will not respond to His devotee's love, then one day the devotee might also give up, which God will never want to happen. Therefore, the principles of Devotion or 'Bhakti-Sidhant' state that although God believes in parity yet through love, He can be compelled to respond and act in Devotee's favor.

For Lord, 'Ananya-Bhakti' means that, for the devotee, there is no other dependency or reliance on anything or anybody in this whole universe, except Lord Himself. "This whole world and each and every being is the manifestation of my Lord", and strongly believing in this principle the 'Ananya' or 'unique' devotee must serve everybody but all his love must be dedicatedto the Lord, only. Only Hanumanji has attained the highest position and perfection in 'Ananya-Bhakti' and therefore Lord Ram recognizes him as the ultimate symbol of Bhakti or Devotion and gives him a status twice as superior as Laxman.

Nonetheless, Lord Laxman is also a great 'Ananya' devotee and so we must not consider him any lesser. This is just an expression of love of Lord Ram for not just Hanumanji but all His devotees, which gives them hope that one day they can also attain the position like that of Laxman in the heart of the Lord. Every being must understand and believe that there is nothing unachievable in this cosmos, for the one who has attained Lord Ram's love. Andtherefore, Saint Tulsidas again and again proclaims that nothing is worth doing except surrendering in the lotus feet of Lord Siya-Ram.

Chapter 4.4

Milan of Lord Ram & King Sugriv: The Bond of Friendship

Knowing the ordeal of His devotee,
The Master of Universe got angry.
O, my dear Sugriv! I will do the remedy,
And I pledge to punish Bali, your enemy.

After the holy reunion (Milan) of Lord Ram & Hanuman, when Hanumanji suggested that Lord Ram and Sugriv must unite and help each other in these difficult times, Lord readily affirmed. Hanumanji then carried both Lord Ram and Laxman on his divine shoulders and flew to the top of 'Rishyamukh' mountain, where Sugriv had taken refuge with his companions. Seeing the two warrior sages arriving with Hanumanji, Sugriv got assured that they were friends and not enemies. It was a propitious moment when they met each other and their strong bond of friendship was sealed by Hanumanji, the arbitrator, with Element-Fire as Witness (Agni-Sakshi).

Here it is interesting to note that other than this incident, nowhere else in Ramcharitmanas can we find any involvement of a witness or an arbitrator in the union of a Devotee with Lord Ram. In Sugriv's character, there is indeed the element of devotion and service, but along with it, there is also an element of equality with the Lord. Only he could dare to sit on the same level as that of Lord Ram. Their stories were also similar as both of them are royals who had lost their kingdoms and wives.

Element-Fire is the greatest symbol of true friendship. 'Wood in fire' and 'fire in wood', symbolize 'Togetherness.' Arbitration of (Pawan-Putra) Hanumanji, the son of Wind-God was imperative because, without element-air, fire cannot manifest. Therefore Wind is a friend of Fire. Not just that, Wind is also considered the epitome of selflessness as it continuously plays its part in giving life to the Beings without any expectations. And this precisely depicts the nature of Hanumanji, which is, serving others without any expectations. He is undoubtedly the one who can be called a 'Karma-Yogi.' If Sugriv is like 'Wood,' then Lord is like 'Fire.' This Devotee-Lord union was significant because that day, both wood and fire needed the help of each other and also of wind for the success of this collaboration.

Sugriv was the eyewitness to the kidnapping of Lady Sita. So without wasting any time, he quickly narrated the whole incident to Lord, "I along with my ministers was sitting on this mountaintop when we heard Her voice. A Demon forcefully took a Heavenly Lady on a flying chariot. She was weeping and screaming the name 'Ram' again and again. At once, the Lady saw us and dropped a torn cloth piece towards us." Seeing it, Lord immediately understood that the Lady was no other but His beloved wife Sita and that the demon was Ravan.

Later Sugriv narrated his painful story, "Bali and I are brothers who had always loved each other. One night a demon named 'Mayavi' arrived in our city of Kishkindha and challenged Bali. Out of rage, Bali at once jumped to fight. Seeing the might, valor and aggression of Bali, Mayavi got scared and ran away. Bali and I both ran after him. Seeing Mayavi entering a dark cave, Bali asked me to wait for him at the mouth of the cave for fifteen days and said that I should consider him dead if he doesn't return till then. After that, Bali entered the cave to destroy the demon."

"Fifteen days passed by, and I decided to wait for another fortnight to take action. Then one day, a stream of blood gushed out from the cave", he anxiously continued, "I thought that Bali was dead and got scared for my life. So I covered the mouth of the cave with a huge rock and rushed back to Kishkindha. I was never interested in the throne, but on the insistence of ministers and Bali's wife Tara, I accepted the crown of the King of Kishkindha. But Bali was alive, and he had executed Mayavi. When he returned after many days and saw me on the throne, he got mad with anger. He felt cheated by me and so attacked me. Considering me as an enemy, he took over all my assets and abducted my wife. As I couldn't face Bali's might, I escaped from there and reached 'Rishyamukha' Mountain with my close friends and ministers to save my life. My Lord, every moment my heart is burning in anger, fear and sorrow for not being able to save my wife."

Hearing the ordeal of Sugriv, the sympathizer of the meek and weak, Lord Ram boiled with anger. Flexing His potent muscles, He proclaimed angrily, "Listen, my friend Sugriv! I will execute Bali in just one arrow. Even

God Brahma and God Shiva cannot save Bali from my attack." Those words from the Lord comforted Sugriv and his companions at once. After a very long time, they breathed a sigh of relief and bowed to Lord Ram.

Later on, Laxman narrated the story of Lord Siya-Ram, knowing which Sugriv realized that Lord's problems are much greater than his own. Sugriv's feud with Bali was purely a family issue. On the other hand, the conflict between Lord Ram and Asur Ravan was at a different level where millions of lives of Manushya or mankind, Devta or demigod and Asura or demon were at stake.

In today's world, most people usually mock or make fun of others' weaknesses. It is an attribute of the mind-ego to prove others lesser in order to make itself feel superior. But a compassionate and enlightened person, after knowing others' weaknesses, never mocks and becomes even more caring and sympathetic instead. Seeing her ailing child, a mother gets genuinely worried. She sees it as her own shortcoming and puts in her best efforts to cure the problem. Similarly, Lord Ram is like a mother figure to all Beings. Inevitably, He takes up the responsibility of curing Sugriv's weaknesses.

When somebody openly divulges the weaknesses of another, then instead of doing any good, he unknowingly destroys whatever self-confidence the other one is left with. For example, if somebody says to a patient who is suffering from a life-threatening disease that his condition is incurable and there is no hope, then he is actually prompting the patient to die. Mutual encouragement, motivation and compassion are the need of the hour. Even if it means telling a lie, then too, a statement that inspires an ill and weak is very much required.

By intentionally avoiding confrontation with Bali, Sugriv may seem to be a coward and escapist but Lord sees his weaknesses from a totally different perspective. Lord expresses his brotherly love and concern to Sugriv like a truly caring guardian. He openly says that Sugriv is as dear to Him as His brother Bharat. And this one encouraging statement totally changed Sugriv's personality and confidence, forever. After that, never again did Sugriv feel weak or frightened. It was clearly reflected later at Lanka when Sugriv all alone jumped and fought with Ravan fearlessly. That is how unconditional care, trust and encouraging words do magic in one's life. Such is the power of Lord's love and assurance.

When Princess Sita had seen Sugriv's group on the mountain top, She didn't call for help. She very well knew that, like Jatayu, they too could not face the might of Ravan and perish. The throwing of cloth piece towards them and repeated calling the name 'Ram' was like a trail of evidence used by Mother Sita to make Lord reach Her because She knew that only He could destroy Ravan and rescue Her. Also, She knew that there is always a right way to deal with problems, and for that, patience is a must, else there is only loss and no success.

When Sugriv handed over the cloth piece to Lord Ram, He at once held it to His heart and felt even more anguished for Lady Sita. But He didn't lose His composure, nor did He get desperate to begin the work of searching Sita immediately. Instead, He asked Sugriv to narrate his story. Such is the great benignity of Lord Ram, which attracts everybody towards Him. Every being of this world is dealing with some or other problems. Mostly, we show our happiness to make others feel lesser. Lord says that we must use our happy times to work even harder for others' service and benefit instead. In bad times, a selfish one always seeks others' shoulder to depend on, which he himself had never offered to others in their bad times. Hence Lord says that the bad times are meant to make us realize the pain others go through in a similar situation. And this realization helps us nurture compassion.

Seeing a great noble personality like Lord Ram going through such a troublesome phase, many people may question the relevance of Dharma or righteousness. Lord's journey gives them the impression that treading the path of truth is very painful. An obvious question that the mind-ego keeps asking is that what is the point of practicing Dharma when it is full of hardship? But the wise one knows that the answer to this question lies in life's experience and not in words. So the right question to ask here is what lesson did this world had learned and gained for ages through that towering noble personality 'Ram' and His great journey of 'Dharma'?

Had Lord been like ordinary beings, then He too would have desperately chased his desires, rightfully or wrongfully or hid Himself from fears. But He never deviated from His path of Dharma, not even for a single instance. No one in this material world is free from pain, although the reasons can differ. Even Lord Ram had to suffer the pain of separation from His beloved wife. Lord Ram very well understands this predicament of human beings; therefore, after listening to the painful story of Sugriv, He immediately decides to solve his problem first, forgetting His own problem.

Now, if we observe carefully, we will find that Sugriv, while narrating his story, was trying to paint a picture of his own innocence. He says that out of love for his brother Bali, he selflessly ran with him after the demon Mayavi. But, on the other hand, Bali asking Sugriv to wait for him at the mouth of the cave actually reflects Bali's concern for his younger brother Sugriv. Sugriv waited for not fifteen but thirty days, that's good on his part, but seeing the bloodstream flowing out from the cave, his bluntly running away, is nothing but sheer cowardice. If he was really concerned for Bali, he should have gone inside the cave to check his well-being. By saying that ministers forced him to take over the reins of Kishkindha, Sugriv tried to show his selflessness. But had he not wanted the throne, who could have forced him? Although Bali's son Angad was a highly qualified and deserving candidate for the throne, Sugriv intentionally overlooked his nephew and made himself the king.

One can label Sugriv as selfish with flawed characteristics, but he can, in no way, be reckoned a wrongdoer. It is evident when Lord Ram took Sugriv's side, although Bali was also His ardent follower. Between Sugriv-Bali and Vibhishan-Ravan, Lord favored and endorsed the righteous brother. He always expects maturity and forgiveness from the elder brother. Hence, Bali should have overlooked Sugriv's mistakes and accepted him with love and warmth, setting a perfect example of brotherhood. But the fact that Bali had committed such a heinous crime of capturing his own brother's wife and property was not only unimaginable but also intolerable.

Lord willfully flexed his biceps (Gesture of a Warrior) and pledged the destruction of Bali with great conviction. He didn't want to waste a single moment towards solving His devotee's problems. He comforts Sugriv by saying, "So far to save yourself, you had to run helter-skelter, in this world, but Bali will not be able to save himself even if he runs to other worlds." This eventful 'episode' of unification of Lord Ram and Sugriv gives immense hope, strength and courage to the devotees that no matter how bad the times are, no matter how difficult the problems are, and no matter how wrongfully they have acted in life but if they seek His refuge, then Lord Ram will stand for them and support. There is absolutely nothing insurmountable for Him in this whole universe. And it is the reason why Saint Tulsidas repeatedly says that to solve their problems, Beings must devote their lives and surrender themselves only and wholly, in the lotus feet of Lord Siya-Ram.

Chapter 4.5

Justice of Lord: Liberation of Bali

For all the beings, Lord Ram has an equal affinity,
Then why did the Lord attack me deceivingly?
Why did Lord befriend Sugriv and consider me as a villain?
History will not forget the unfair treatment Ram has given me.

After hearing the entire incident of the kidnapping of Mother Sita, Lord Ram comforts Sugriv, saying that he must not grieve anymore and fully rely on Him. However, Sugriv was still in fear and doubt, and so he replied, "O Hero of Raghukul, Bali is a staunch warrior; he possesses immense strength and is invincible in the battle." To convince Sugriv, Lord agreed for a test, and He effortlessly struck down seven palm trees in one single shot of an arrow. Witnessing Lord's immeasurable strength, Sugriv was relieved and got assured that Bali could be defeated now. Lord then asked Sugriv to go and challenge Bali for combat and assured him that while they engage in the fight, He will execute Bali and free Sugriv from all sorrows.

Sugriv duly followed Lord's instructions, but because of the very close resemblance between Bali and Sugriv, Lord Ram got confused and didn't shoot. As a consequence, the mighty Bali thrashed Sugriv, who then had to escape to save his life. Lord told him about the problemand also the solution. He then asked Sugriv to challenge Bali again but this time, Lord purposely wore him a string of flowers for identification. Understandably, Bali and his wife Tara were utterly surprised to see Sugriv come back again and challenge. Sensing something tricky, the prudent Tara advised Bali not to fall into the trap and ignore the challenge. She also explained that a scout in Kishkindha has informed her that now Sugriv has the support of Lord Ram, the Prince of Ayodhya.But Bali's mind-ego didn't let him listen to her, and he again accepted Sugriv's challenge. They started fighting again and finding the right opportunity, Lord, hiding behind a tree cover, shot an arrow at Bali, who at once collapsed.

Even today, the way Lord Ram ambushed Bali and killed him is considered inappropriate by many people, and the question that arises in our minds is, '*why didn't Lord come face to face with Bali and challenge him openly?*'This question has always bothered many people. Therefore a detailed explanation is required to understand the Justice and Dharma of the Lord.

First and foremost, please note very carefully that unlike historians of other civilizations, empires and religions, the practitioners of Sanatan Dharma do not modify or manipulate the original facts in order to showcase their icons and idols as totally flawlessto suit the sensibilities of their followers. The sages and the speakers of Ramayan could have easily altered the facts of Bali's execution, leaving no scope for criticism and the people over the period of thousands of years would have accepted it without any doubts and questioning. However, the fact is that the enlightened sages wanted the future generations to know and realize the deep meaning hidden behind this convoluted act of God and thereby understand Dharma.

To do or not to do, that is 'Antar-Dwand' or an undecided state of mind, is applicable for mortal beings and not for God. Lord Ram very well knew that His way of executing Bali would become an object of criticism for the society, yet He didn't try to avoid it; rather he happily welcomed the scrutiny. One of the most striking facts of Ram-Rajya was that there was not only freedom of fundamental rights but also freedom for fearless scrutiny, even against the King. Thus, the precious Jewel of today's Democracy, that is, the Freedom of Speech and Expression, was, in fact, the most ordinary right of the citizens of Ram-Rajya. To give Bali the chance and time to condemn, criticize and question, Lord Ram intentionally hit him in such a way that he didn't die immediately.He could have executed Bali in a blinking of an eye, but He gave him extra breaths instead so that he could question Lord for such retribution.

Lord Ram with Laxman and Hanumanji stood in front of mighty but stumbled Bali. Out of rage and agony, Bali put many allegations on the Lord. He said, "O Lord Ram, You have incarnated to restore righteousness, and yet You hit me deceptively like what a hunter does while hunting an animal. For You, both me and Sugriv are equal, but you took his side and rejected me." He wanted clarifications from Lord Ram but had failed to realize his own unrighteousness. Bali's ignorance lies in the very fact that although he is accepting Lord Ram as Eternal God, he is challenging His verdict. Here we must understand that God is not because of Beings; instead, Beings, Birth and Death are because of God. Although He doesn't need to explain anything to anyone, Lord Ram duly justified His stand out of pure compassion and rectitude.

The rules of Warfield and the Court of Justice are different. In a war, two warriors combat each other face to face but the Judge of Court, while sentencing capital punishment is not expected to fight and execute the guilty. Bali has himself acknowledged Lord Ram as God who has incarnated for the establishment of Dharma, which means Lord Ram is the Supreme Justice of the entire universe. He had neither enmity nor friendship with Bali, so there was no relevant reason whatsoever for Him to challenge Bali. Sugriv had put some allegations on Bali in front of the witness Hanumanji, the epitome of Truth. It was only afterhearing the whole case that Lord concluded Bali was guilty.

Again, the question arises why didn't Lord give Bali a chance to defend himself? The answer is simple and straightforward.Lord is not like an ordinary mortal Judge who only gets to know what is put forward as evidence in front of him,and after hearing the case from both sides, he gives his final verdict. But when the Knower of All, the Eternal God himself, is on the Judge's chair, the need for such judicial formality ends. When He declares someone guilty, there cannot be any objection, disagreement or appeal. Therefore Bali was bound to face the punishment, sooner or later. Like a hunter who shoots his target, Lord secretly shot an arrow to kill Bali from behind a tree. By shooting Bali deceptively, Lord was simply punishing him. Also, he wanted to shock Bali in such a way that he comes out of his mind-egoic trap and realizes his mistake. It was indeed God's Grace; He treats every wound uniquely to heal it permanently. Lord replied in anger, "Bali, the younger brother's wife is like sister and daughter. Whosoever forces her for the fulfillment of carnal desires will be executed."

Hanumanji, Bali and Sugrivall belonged to the 'Vanar'race. Don't confuse Vanar with those small and restless monkeys we see today, jumping here and there on the trees and buildings. Vanar were like Neanderthals, a human-like race having ape-like physical attributes. Although the pre-existence of Vanar is not known, it is believed they lived along with the human race. They had their own civilization, culture, society and rules. They lived in urban centers and were highly knowledgeable, intelligent and developed as humans. The sense of right and wrong may not be applicable to animals that don't have reasoning power. However, Vanar were far ahead of time and much evolved and hence, the Dharma was as much applicable tothem as it was to the human race. Therefore Bali being a Vanar was very well aware of right and wrong, and his crime couldn't be overlooked on the basis of the plea that righteousness cannot be expected from a Vanar.

Even after knowing the wrongdoings of Bali, if He had not taken action and executed Bali, then He would be blamed for not fulfilling His duty. Bali complained that he was not given a chance to defend himself, and therefore, Lord's judgment was unfair and lacked leniency. To this, Lord replied, "You are a fool! You think yourself very intelligent, and yet you didn't listen to the warning your wife Tara gave you". Omnipresent Lord was aware that Tara had tried to stop Bali from confronting Sugriv. Never before did Tara interfere in Bali's affairs, nor had she spoken against his will, then how come now suddenly she intervened. Secondly, who was that scout of Kishkindha, who had informed the presence of Lord Ram-Laxman first to Queen Tara and not to his King Bali? When the King is looking after all the affairs, then it's quiteobvious that the scout will go to him first and inform. The point is that there was no scout, but it was Lord himself who inspired Tara to give sense to Bali. God's Leela is neither explicit nor transparent because it is intermingled with Maya or 'Illusion.' One has to apply the virtuous mind to know and understand, and such 'Vivek' or sharp intelligence was expected from Bali.

Previously, Bali had himself acknowledged to Tara that Lord Ram, the Supreme God, is the one who had arrived in Kishkindha and was supporting Sugriv. So after knowing that Lord has arrived, Bali should have thanked his destiny, and himself should havesurrendered in His lotus feet and accepted his mistake. Instead, Bali complained that the Lord should have come face to face with him, but then the question is, what is the primary principle of spirituality? Does God need to approach Being, or must the Being approach God? Does the master pursue the servant, or does the servant follow the master? Bali's main problem was hisarrogance of power as well as the ego of 'Gyan' or knowledge. Remember, the knowledge that doesn't liberate the Being from the mind-ego is worthless.

Bali was so engrossed in his vanity that he had no consideration for God's supremacy. The Relationship of Being with God is of both love and fear. The emotion of fear is deeply embedded in the psyche of Beings. The sole purpose of fear is to make the Being strive for God, which ultimately proves to be very useful in spiritual advancement. But most of the ignorant beings, instead of understanding this spiritual application, baselessly fear this impermanent world and waste their precious lives. Bali confidently tells Tara that God is equal or 'Sam-Drishti' with all, and neither will He favor Sugriv nor Bali. Indeed God is equal but does that give the right to someone to be unrighteous? The Lord is definitely impartial and indifferent. To Him, all are His children, but when He sees that one of His children is troubling others, then He doesn't hesitate to give harsh punishment. Everybody must clearly understand the fact that God is the architect of the Law of Karma, which clearly states that - to every action, there is an equal and opposite reaction. And nobody can escape his Karma.

Seeing the non-discriminatory attributein God, beings must strive to incorporate the same quality in their lives. But the bitter truth is that all of us are very weak as far as tolerance and acceptance are concerned.One good news and we dance in ecstasy, admiring ourselves for the achievement. On the contrary, one bad news, and we start crying, complaining about the injustice of God. That is precisely what happened in the case of Bali. Whatever Bali achieved in his life, he considered that as his own accomplishments. And now, on his deathbed when he is reaping what he had sown, he is crying foul. He ignored the will of God. Also, he had ignored the fact that in the past, Lord had executed Tardka, Subahu, Marich, Khar, Dushan and many other evildoers. Despite that, how could Bali expect to escape His justice?

There is a reason for every character of Ramcharitmanas strongly believing that Lord Ram is forever kind and compassionate. Lord didn't intervene in the first fight between Bali and Sugriv. When Bali arrogantly rejected Tara's intuitive advice and came rushing for the second fight, Lord again gave him a clear hint to stop and surrender. The string of flowers on Sugriv clearly indicated that Lord is with Sugriv. Had Lord wanted, He could have easily executed Bali in the first fight itself, but He wanted to give that ignorant Bali another chance to rectify his faults. But when he still didn't realize and took God for granted, then the Lord decided to punish the arrogant.

Such ignorance and arrogance need to be addressed and, of course, executed. All allegations and complaints of Bali are baseless. After knowing Lord's answers, Bali was speechless and accepted his grave sins. He conceded his defeat and surrendered to the Lord. He sincerely apologized to Sugriv and his wife, Roma. Devoid of all flaws, Bali is now a completely transformed man. He, with immense humility and remorse, pleaded, "Lord! Now that I am dying in your lotus feet, am I still a sinner?" This one true and pure thought transformed Bali from a wicked villain into a victorious yogi. The ever compassionate Lord Ram was content seeing the radical transformation and offered Bali to cure his wounds and pardon his life. But being a satisfied and peaceful soul, Bali now wants to get liberated. He feels extremely fortunate to be dying through the arrow of Ram, which also opens the door of salvation or 'Moksha' for him, andhe doesn't want to lose this golden opportunity.

No decision, no judgment and no justice of the Lord can or must be challenged. He is infinite and Supreme. Goswami Tulsidas affirms that one who criticizes Lord's action cannot find purpose and peace in life. Bali was fortunate that God, Himself clarified his doubts, but not every being can be as fortunate as Bali. Therefore Beings must be very careful about their karma. Like Bali, they too must surrender in the lotus feet of Lord Siya-Ram without any questioning and attain ultimate peace.

Chapter 4.6

Lord Ram enlightens Tara: 'Sankhya Yog'

Seeing her dead husband, Tara was in extreme distress,
Lord then revealed to her the Yog of Jiva's progress.

The shocking news of Bali's execution was a major blow for the whole of Kishkindha. The news of his unfortunate demise spread like wildfire everywhere around. Even though Bali acted cruelly with Sugriv, he was always revered for his Kingly greatness. There is no denying the fact that the entire Vanar race was living fearlessly under the aegis of Bali. The very thought that when the most powerful Ravan couldn't dare to bother him, then who else in the world had the guts to face Bali, had always made the Vanars of Kishkindha feel safe and protected. Losing such an able King was undoubtedly terrible news for them. But all of them were also aware of his unrighteous act towards Sugriv. So this loss didn't ever convert into hatred or aggression against Sugriv and the slayer of Bali, Lord Ram.

On the other hand, they had already got the news that Sugriv had befriended the Supreme Lord Ram, who had killed the invincible Baliin a single arrow shot. They at once rushed to the spot and collected around Bali's dead body with deference and respect. And among them, Bali's wife Tara was the one in most distress. For the first time, they saw their Queen Tara, the wisest person of their kingdom, so uncontrollable and shattered. It was not unexpected as she had lost her beloved husband, and losing a dear one is always the most shattering tragedy for anybody.

Since the beginning, Beings have been tirelessly trying to figureout a permanent solution for all their suffering and unhappiness. They want uninterrupted and lasting happiness and peace. Beings want to hold happiness firmly and don't want it to escape away, no matter what. Even a mere thought of adversity panics the vulnerable mind of human beings. But as per the spiritual principles, in this material world, permanent and continuous happiness is nothing but an illusion. Every seeker is well aware of this irrevocable limitation, yet they ignorantly believe that they can control joy and sorrow. Hence they keep on trying till the end of life but with no result.

Science today, irrespective of any field, is primarily focused on making our lives more and more comfortable, convenient and secure. Every year trillions of dollars are lavishly spent just to make mankind feel better. But the question is, has allthis advancement and spending been able to increase even an iota of happiness in mankind? Certainly not! As a matter of fact, Beings are still living in immense insecurity and frustrations, even more than before, that is, the pre-scienceera. Although the tools, instruments, technology and fashion are constantly changing, man's expectation for a permanent solution hasn't changed a bit. And this gives rise to many questions in our minds. Has science reduced the death rate? Has poverty lessened radically? Does the new-age finances and economy able to reduce our worries and stress? Ultimately the question is, is today's mankind satisfied being blessed with multifaceted offerings of Science? And the answer to all of these is a big "No."

But it's not like we don't have the solution to this mankind's never-ending expectations. The age-old 'Vedantic' and Spiritual sciences know the root of this problem of human beings and therefore offer a permanent solution. Spirituality aptly explains that the problem and solution are connected to the mind of the Beings and not with external objects or situations. The material objects do give us pleasure, but it is always short-lived. For most of us, the world's richest man with billions of dollars may seemto control the economy of millions of people. But we must not forget that today it is him; yesterday it was someone else; tomorrow it will be someone else! It is because only 'change' is permanent in this world.

Also, people's memories are very evanescent. It's a common fact that the respect one is enjoying today will be handed over to someone else tomorrow, and then the life of the previous one will become just a bundle of frustration of memories of the good old days. This may sound unconvincing to the one who is running in the worldly rat race, but the one who has thoroughly realized the emptiness inside will understand and accept this truth. Another best way to realize this truth is to find out and know about the end days of those who the world had acknowledged as richest and greatest.

The manifestations are endless, but the most basic problem of human life is one and only, and that is unhappiness. This fact also holds true in the case of mighty Bali. It was a difficult moment for Tara, who was weeping for her deceased husband, Bali. Lord Ram, knowing that Tara is wise, explained and consoled her through 'Sankha-Yoga' or the analytical study of soul and body. Both Lord and Bali knew that Lord could stop death and extend the life of the 'Jiva' or Being. But in his last moments, Bali, too, realized the futility of an ignorant and materialistic birth and so embraced the death of his body. Now,a few more valid queries crop up from this incident. What is the meaning of Grace of God? Is it just about wellness, prosperity and happiness? If the answer is 'Yes', thenhow can both an egoistic one who always believes success is his and not because of Grace and an atheist one who doesn't believe in God at all, prosper in life?

A Favorable and unfavorable situation is a state of mind. The mind has been programmed with major flaws by an ignorant society over thousands of years. There is nothing good or bad; God's Grace is in every moment. It, therefore, means that every moment is an opportunity for the being to come closer to his real purpose in life. The difference between a spiritual and non-spiritual person is nothing but the acceptance of this truth. The universal fact is - What God has decided for the Being, only that will happen. Even if the Being doesn't accept God's Grace, he has to accept what is destined for him. The difference will be - he will cry, complain and crib, whereas a believer of Grace will always keep smiling. One should not expect immediate success in Faith as soon as he stepsinto the spiritual domain. We must understand that 'Faith' is a journey,and it takes its own course. Hence we must not expect every spiritual seekerto become mature right away. It takes time to decrypt the deeply embedded incorrect programming of the mind. It's not an easy job for a benighted being, and only one in thousands truly practices it. But we need not feel frustrated because, with time, change does occur.

One of the greatest enlightened masters, Goswami Tulsidas has himself faced unimaginable ups and downs in life. At one time, as a four-year-old orphan child, he even had to beg to fill his stomach. Also,there was a time in his life when Kings and Wealthy people would line up to see him. But never ever did he accept good times as Lord's love and bad times as Lord's indifference. All his works and life boil down to just one idea, 'I would only accept that your Grace is with me when my mind is totally free from worldly thoughts and only filled with your devotion.'

When Lord offered life to Bali, he questioned, 'Lord, who can be so foolish to cut the 'Kalpatru' or 'Tree of Life' just to build a fence around an ordinary Babool Tree?' Here we can witness two extreme traits of Maryada

Purushottam Ram. Just a few moments back, Lord, with bow and arrows in His hand, was displaying His rage to Bali, and now He was placing His hands on Bali's head and showering Hislove and affection. Bali doesn't want Lord's anger or His boons; instead, all he wants is 'Bhakti' or devotion, which is the one and only solution for all human beings' problems and issues. Needless to say, Lord readily understood Bali's earnest wish and granted him the same.

Lord really admired Tara. Fromthe very beginning, she acted wisely and tried to mend Bali's wrongful ways. He implicitly explained to Tara that even if Bali was given a new life then also, he will again die one day and thatshe will be mourning in the same way again. It is totally futile not to accept and live in the present; it doesn't work at all. Non-acceptance of the present unfavorable consequences can never be the solution. Moreover, non-acceptance of the present situation intensifies fear which in turn exacerbates the unending unhappiness in life. Lord neutralized the core of all these flaws, which is the mind-ego, in Tara and said, "Tarathat what is lying in front of us is just Bali's material body made up of five elements. If this body is the cause of your distress then why don't you take it back with you? And if you are lamenting for the Soul or Atman, then remember that it is eternal and never dies."

Mind-ego cannot survive just on the soul orthe body. It wants an alive Being with both soul and body, with which it can identify itself and which it never wants to let go of. It is not easy, even for a few advanced seekers, to accept 'Sankhya-Yog' or spiritual knowledge in completenessbecause Beings are very much emotionally attached to the body and with its relationships. Just knowing doesn't necessarily mean accepting. In Shri Bhagwad Geeta, during the 'Dharma-Yudh,' Arjun was in an utter dilemma. How can he attack and kill his own cousins and relatives, that is, Kauravas? Lord Krishna then explained to him, first with the lessons of Sankhya Yoga, that relations and body are untrue, and only the soul or Atman is true. Therefore, it is the duty of each and every human being to fulfill his Soul's Dharma. Bali's end was in accordance with Dharma which his prudent wife Tara alsoaccepted eventually. Ultimately she got solace and attained peace. Above all, she may have lost her loving husband, but she has attained the indestructible knowledge of 'Sankhya Yog' by surrendering in the lotus feet of Lord Siya-Ram.

Chapter 4.7

Tulsidas Perspective on Female Freedom: Orthodox or Sensible

Like heavy rains destroy the formations of plants-bed,
Freedom doesn't nurture but spoils females, instead.

Even in this 21st century, where gender equality is a burning issue, Saint Tulsidas's stance on "Female Freedom" in Ramcharitmanas undoubtedly creates resentment in many people. It is criticized as a male-egoic thought to suppress female kind. Saint Tulsidas even had to face condemnation from a large section of society and was labeled as anti-feminist and, of course, judgmental. Althoughapparently, the lines seem to be inappropriate for many, a careful and patient study would unveil the hidden meaning and relevance of such a seemingly contradictory perspective.

After the end of Bali, Lord Ram contentedly declared that Sugriv with Angad would take over the reins of the kingdom of Kishkindha. Now since it's the disturbing rainy season, all of them will have to wait till it gets over. After that, Sugriv will initiate his formidable Vanar army to expedite the search operation of Lady Sita. In the meantime, it was a very special moment for Sugriv and all his associates as they were blessed with the companionship of Lord Ram. While waiting in a mountain cave, Lord spends some quality time describing the various attributes of rains along with giving life lessons to Laxman. Saying these lines on the female kind, Lord must have been thinking about Surpanakha since she had purposely misused her freedom and acted without any modesty. Hence she became the genesis of the Lanka War, which destroyed millions of lives.

Just before 'Sita-Haran,' Laxman had solemnly marked his 'Territory' in Panchavati, popularly known as 'Laxman-Rekha' for protection of Lady Sita. Laxman-Rekha was not a command but a request from Her for Her own safety, and she was not bound but was free to cross the line anytime at her will. Thought is that, lines or boundaries are needed to protect ourselves from the dreadful life consequences symbolized as 'Ravan.' Such a Ravan has the capacity to manipulate and fraudulently convince its vulnerable targets so much so that they themselves jump out of Laxman-Rekha and become its prey. Remember, Ravan or evil consequences are actually incapable of jumping inside the "Line" unless we let them in.

In ancient societalpractices, the primary responsibility of males was to look after external affairs. Females, on the other hand,were liable to look after the household, family and internal affairs. The resources for the household were arranged by the male and handed over to the female to use impartially for the well-being of every family member. Lines or plant-beds or 'Kyaari' are drawn to create a safe zone where the sapling can grow to its best potential. Thus "boundaries" are there not to curtail freedom but to safeguard and sustain wellbeing. Through these lines what Goswamiji meant was thatif water from rains is not distributed properly in the field, it will accumulate in one zone only and will spoil the crop of that particular zone, thereby triggering the leftover area to starve. This water or resource accumulation at a single zone signifies selfishness and partiality. Similarly, if the lady of the house stocks more resources for herself than what is required and does not distribute them fairly, then the whole farm field with its entire crop, that is, household and family members, will get spoiled. Therefore just like a plant-bed or kyaari, the female is expected to fairly distribute the resources (water) throughout the household (family).

Suppose the roles, which nature has designed for males and females, get interchanged, that is, females looking after external matters and males taking care of internal household affairs, then also the probability of household arrangement getting spoiled becomes very high. Here we need to understand that each being is born with an innate 'Swadharma' or individual duty. This is not just applicable for females but also to males. In the modern era, people are openly vocal about women empowerment so much so that any injustice against women could result in worldwide movements. However, there are questions that also need to be addressed impartially- Is the life of males totally free of trouble and difficulties? Is the management of worldly affairs easy and rosy? Isn'tthe arrangement of resources and fulfillment of family expectations a difficult job? And last but definitely not the least - Is the struggle in the life of males any way lesser than females? In this debate of male-female equality, what is needed is not a cry for rights but deep understanding and tolerance. Nature has designed male and female differently for a purpose. So do we need to blame nature and ask for our preferences? Procreation is a divine extension of Supreme God's attribute of Creation, which is gifted only to females. In that case, should males too complain of inequality and demand the same gift?

'Mind-ego trapped Being doesn't like limitations,' and it applies to both males and females, equally. But if we contemplate thoughtfully, then we will realize that boundaries become the problem only when they are enforced. If the male tries to force and prove his control over the female every time, then the struggle is bound to happen and persist. The issue of female freedom and inequality exists because of those sadistic males who had misused their authority and privileges. In fact, no female is a fool who, out of thin air, would just get frustrated and take a stand on freedom and equality against her own family. Having said that, like Surpanakha,unjustified exceptions can surface out of intense selfishness, making her act unrighteous.

Being a firm believer of 'Gyan & Bhakti Yog,' Saint Tulsidas strongly feels that the one and only permanent solution for freedom is the Knowledge of 'Self.' The human body can be categorized on a gender basis but, in reality, the Being or 'Jiva' is neither male nor female. Till the time Beingidentifies itself with the physical body, it will not be able to experience absolute freedom. In the history of Sanatan Dharma, although it might appear that the 'Gyan & Bhakti Yog' is dominated by males, there are many great females who have transcended from gender & body identity or 'Deha-Abhiman' and attained enlightenment. However, that doesn't prompt the enlightened mothers or masters to complain; they know very well that the 'male-female' factor actually doesn't matter.

It is the worldly beings, who are trapped in the clutches of mind-ego and are always busy finding faults with everything in the world, exceptthemselves. When God is there for every Human-Being, male or female, every moment, then why should one worry and depend on anything else? Lord Ram and Mother Sita are most compassionate and the epitome of knowledge. Goswami Tulsidas earnestly says that only by devoting and surrendering 'Self' in Their lotus feet can the Beings attain absolute and permanent independence and freedom. Those who still don't believe in this truth will continue struggling for freedom and empowerment but would never attain the peace they need, which their 'Self' is yearning for. We ignorantly fail to realize this simple fact and therefore suffer throughout our lives. Through Ramcharitmanas, Goswami Tulsidas is teaching us that Struggles do end, and clarity is attained by leading a life of 'Dharma' that is 'righteous-boundaries.'

Chapter 4.8

Punishment for Devotee: Irresponsible/ Ungrateful Sugriv

Attaining throne, treasure, kingdom and wife,
He has forgotten his promise.
With the same arrow that has executed Bali,
Tomorrow I will kill him, without a miss.

As soon as the rainy season was over, Lord Ram and brother Laxman became a bit impatient. **Both of them were eager to initiate the search operation without any further delay. In fact, Lord was waiting for Sugriv's message, but things didn't turn up the way He expected. It appeared to Him as if**Sugriv had totally forgotten his promise of initiating the search **for** Princess Sita through his Vanar army. As a result, Lord at once got infuriated. It was evident since Lord was getting desperate to somehow trace the location of Lady Sita. He was firm that once He gets this information, He can single-handedlydefeat even the 'Kaal' or Death and free His beloved wife, Sita.

Not just that, but He also had a brother like Laxman who alone could destroy millions **of**Asur. Although the forevermerciful Lord could have forgiven anything, He was extremely astonished at the turn of the event and especially Sugriv's behavior. How could one who was once discarded by his own brother and was living in **the forest like a fugitive**, the one who was empathetically talking about commitment and renunciation, change so much after attaining the throne?How could Sugriv forget that he recovered his lost throne only because of Lord Ram?

On one hand was thankless Sugriv, who after getting back all the pleasures of life, has forgotten **thepromise he made to the Lord** while on the other hand was great Laxman who **had discarded** his everything including home, family and luxuries and dedicated his entire life in the service of Lord Siya-Ram. All that Lord wants from Sugriv is to help Him find out Lady Sita's location and nothing more. Sugriv has a large number of Vanars who could spread in different directions, and therefore, they can facilitate and quicken the search process. Lord knew that Laxman would do the rest of the jobwithout the help of even one Vanar. While saying these lines to Laxman,Lord also showed an important aspect of human nature. When a Being does a favor **to**another, he also expects something in return, and when the expectations are not fulfilled, then 'Anger' originates in his heart. **That day Lord was executing the 'Anger-Leela'.**

Lord, for the sake of Sugriv, had even accepted the infamy of killing Bali. For simplification of discussion, we may consider that He took such a step for Sugriv but for Dharma at large. Similarly, to protect the same Dharma, He also would not hesitate in punishing Sugriv. Now if we carefully observe the event, we will find that Sugriv's 'Adharma' or unrighteousness is even worse than Bali. The reason is simple and straightforward. Bali didn't listen to the words of his wife, Tara, but here Sugriv has knowingly ignored the order of Supreme God. Moreover, Bali didn't witness Lord's Supreme Power but Sugriv had not only witnessed it but also tested it. Despite knowing Lord's reality, when someone acts like Sugriv, then he is actually the biggest fool on this planet. Also, seeing Lord punishing Sugriv impartially, at least Bali's soul will get some peace, if not anything else.

According to our holy scriptures, there is no sin greater than ungratefulness. Ungratefulness reflects insensitivity in the being. Regretting his mistake, Being tries **to correct** it and **he** must also apologize for it. But in the mind-ego of an insensitive being, there is no guilty consciousness, no regret and therefore no remorse for his wrongdoing. And that day, it clearly appeared that devotee Sugriv is no exceptionand that he also belonged to the samecategory. As per the rules of justice, Lord's punishment for Sugriv was apt and was pleasing for Laxman.

Laxman had never liked Lord's excessive large-heartedness as he had seen undeserving ones misusing this liberty over and over again. Compassion is undoubtedly a great attribute for the giver but in the receiver,it also entails **a highpossibility** of becoming complacent. The nature of the mind-ego is such thatif it gets to know that even for grave crimes, it would not be punished and pardoned easily, then it shamelessly schemes for even more hideous acts. Therefore, mind-ego simply believes that whatever it does is right and justified andcontinuously tries to justify its immorality until the end.

Laxman too wanted to give Sugriv the proper treatment for **his**

ungratefulness. He felt satisfied hearing the Lord's decision of punishing Sugriv, **but**he was well aware of the fact that the word 'Tomorrow' in Lord's linesis an intentional escape window opened by Lord Himself for His loving devoteeSugriv to survive. Also, he knew Lord's heart very well. So he wanted first to close this window of 'Tomorrow.' And therefore he himself picked up his bow and arrows immediately and spoke, "Lord, Sugriv must be punished not tomorrow but right now and not by great 'Yourself' but by me. Please give me permission. The one who has dared to take Lord for granted, needs to be executed at once".

Although Lord Himself had shown His wrath before, He didn't want Laxman to punish Sugriv. However**, on the insistence of Laxman, the ever-forgiving Lord Ram only asked him to scare Sugriv and remind him of his promise but without harming him, even a bit.** That is why Goswami Tulsidas repeatedly says that the Lord is forever kind and compassionate to the one who for once commits himself to His 'Bhakti,' even falsely. **In fact,a devotee is pardoned by Lord even when he commits the gravest mistake.** Remember, there is none more loving, caring, and infinitely powerful than Ram, and therefore the purpose of life is not in this **untrue** material world but in surrenderingto the lotus feet of Lord Siya-Ram.

Chapter 4.9

Hanumanji pacifies Laxman: Perceptive Sugriv

Sugriv shivered in fear, knowing angry Laxman's arrival,
Hanumanji handles the situation, ensuring ***Kishkindha's*** *survival.*

Seeing Lord Ram upset, Laxman got infuriated, and he made up his mind to execute Sugriv at once. But the forever merciful Lord asked him to calm down and instead ordered him to intimidate Sugriv and bring him there. Laxman entered Kishkindha city and thundered in anger. Seeing this, thousands of Vanar citizens trembled in fear. None had the guts to face the wrath of the Super Powerful Laxman. The news reached Sugriv in no time, and he too shivered in fright. Although he was the King himself, he couldn't find the courage to face the might of Laxman. However, he played intelligently and asked Hanumanji to take Tara along and handle the situation.

From the beginning of Kishkindha-Kand till now, it has become apparent that Sugriv had many faults, but he had one stellar quality, which not only ensured his safety every time but also helped him progress. He had the vision to foresee the right person for the right purpose. Not just that, but he also had the rare ability to bring out the best use of an individual. Needless to mention that by virtue of these impressive leadership qualities, he managed his army in the Lanka war very efficiently and that impressed Lord Ram. It is clear from his instructions in complex situations that he was an expert in understanding the human psyche. But most importantly, he had the 'Vivek' or intelligence to befriend Hanumanji, the greatest ever devotee of Lord Ram. The first time he proved this acumen was when he first met Lord Ram-Laxman. Out of his group of ministers, he only asked Hanumanji to find out the truth. This resulted in his close friendship with the Lord, who executed Bali and gave him back the throne of the Kishkindha kingdom. And that day, when death or 'Kaal' was at his doorstep in the form of Laxman, he again sent Hanumanji along with Tara to deal with the matter.

The readers often question what prompted him to send Tara along with Hanumanji? Also, how could Tara, the widowed queen of Bali, be of any help in this matter? There was nothing common between Hanumanji and Tara. Although a woman has the ability to lure a man in her favour, the one they were going to deal with was none other than the great Laxman, who is known as the epitome of 'Vairagya' or 'Dispassion.' Therefore, it is inevitable that Sugriv would not dare make such a mistake. The involvement of Tara may seem to be uncustomary, but in the end, this maneuver proved to be helpful and quite successful for Sugriv. If we consider the gravity of the situation that day, Hanumanji was an obvious choice. Besides, he was the mediator and the cause of Sugriv's alliance with Lord Ram-Laxman. Moreover, there was none like Hanumanji as far as wit, politeness and convincing speech were concerned. Considering all aspects, the choice of Hanumanji, therefore, was perfect.

The perceptive Sugriv had observed Laxman's disinterest, reluctance and detachment from the female kind. For the last thirteen years, Laxman had only andsolely looked towards the lotus feet of Mother Sita, let alone interaction with any other female. Sugriv very well knew that Laxman was an honourable Prince of Raghukul. Although he would not let the offender escape, he can never be harsh towards a female unless it's an order of his brother-Lord. Sugriv was also aware of the fact that no female could entice Laxman. But at the same time, he was sure that Tara would help foster the feelings of sympathy and compassion in the large-hearted Laxman. In addition, there was another valid reason behind sending Tara to deal with enraged Laxman. A couple of months back, Tara had suffered a great loss, and that was her husband Bali's death. Lord not only gave her a discourse but also consoled her and accepted her as His disciple.

Tara's husband Bali was executed because he conflicted with Sugriv. In such a scenario, she had all good reasons to hate Sugriv. But the wise and enlightened Tara had forgiven him and forgotten that incident. If she had hated him, her hatred would have proved a non-acceptance of the Lord's act of punishing Bali. Of course, it is a fact that Sugriv is the reason for Bali's death, but Lord Ram is not an ordinary one who can be easily manipulated and misused at one's own will. He is Supreme Intelligence, and His judgment and decision cannot be questioned, challenged or disapproved. Tara was beyond the attribute of 'Raag-Dwesh' that is personal 'Likes & Dislikes.' She was now in full support of her son-like brother-in-law, Sugriv.

Everyone, including Laxman, had revered her for her benevolence. Being a shrewd diplomat, Sugriv purposely sent her as a symbolic reminder to Laxman to forgive and be kind to him. Also, Sugriv analyzed that by seeing Lord Ram's disciple Tara, His brother-devotee Laxman would probably come out of his anger and, therefore, not become violent with Sugriv. Sugriv had very intelligently and perceptively played this card to save himself from the wrath of Laxman. Hanumanji and Tara went together and clasped Laxman's feet. Seeing a lady and that too a Queen, Laxman got startled. He stopped there, and his anger lines also vanished from his face shortly. Sugriv's gambit had worked. Sensing it as the right opportunity, Hanumanji, too, with his sweet speech, politely tried pacifying Laxman. But he knew that all such tactics could not distract a great devotee like Laxman.

But as soon as Hanumanji started 'Ram-Katha' or recitation of Lord Ram's Life, devotee Laxman at once sat down mesmerized, forgetting his purpose and rage. By the way, his purpose of intimidating Sugriv was already fulfilled. Even before his arrival, the far-sighted Hanumanji had already cautioned Sugriv and called the Vanar soldiers to assemble in the court of Lord Ram. Thus, the assignment of Mother Sita's search was also initiated. Such is the devotion of Hanumanji that whatever 'Vritti' or feeling surfaces in the heart of Lord Ram, he would know instantaneously and work towards its fulfilment. This is the true connection between 'Bhagwan & Bhakt' or God & Devotee.

Now Laxman, too, realized the commitment of Sugriv and Kishkindha kingdom towardsLord Ram. Sugriv then came and saluted at Laxman's feet. Laxman smiled and embraced Sugriv. Although both Laxman and Hanumanji are remembered as the epitome of Lord Ram's 'Bhakti,' the story of Sugriv also inspires mortal Beings with flaws and faults as they often make mistakes in ignorance and reminds that the door of the Lord's love is always open for them. Once the seeker **starts thinking** of surrendering in the lotus feet of Lord Siya-Ram, then he becomes Lord's responsibility, and **the** correction of his flaws **also** becomes Lord's **accountability**.

Chapter 4.10

An Unusual Excuse: Sugriv blames Maya

No matter how hard Being tries,
Yet 'Bhakti' doesn't rise.
Only those few progresses,
Whom Your Grace blesses.

After an eventful day, Sugriv, accompanied by Laxman, arrives in front of Lord Ram and prostrates in His lotus feet. Before the Lord could utter a word, Sugriv straight away started making excuses for forgetting his pledge. Sugriv says, "I am not at fault. You are the Creator. You have created Maya, which has such a strong influence on the Being, that only with your divine Grace can the Being free itself from it. Even the great enlightened ones get trapped in Maya. I belong to the Vanar-kind, who are considered lesser than Human-kind, especially in terms of cognition and intelligence. When Humans cannot evade the invincible trap of Maya, how can we Vanar conform to absolute 'Dharma' or righteousness?" Sugriv had forgotten his pledge to help Lord Ram in His search for Mother Sita as he got engrossed in the royal pleasures. By giving such a philosophical excuse, he was simply trying to prove his innocence. Undoubtedly, Sugriv'sploy worked but it was rather amusing and surprising for everyone present there.

Lord was thoughtfully listening to all of Sugriv's excuses since no other devotee has ever said such a thing to Him. But what surprised Lord the most was that, not once, unexpectedly, not even falsely, did Sugriv apologize or show any sign of regret for his ungratefulness. Not only that, but he didn't even intend to promise that he would not repeat such a mistake. Instead, he put all the blame on Maya. It was evident when Sugriv cleverly said that it's the God who frees the Being from Maya as the Being cannot free himself on his own. He, therefore, indirectly puts all the responsibility for this whole mistake on Maya and, of course, on Lord as well.

What Sugriv was trying to establish here was principally opposite of 'Bhakti-Shastra,' which clearly states that the devotee should only see flaws in Self and never blame his Lord. But the onlookers were surprised to see the Lord smile at this weird excuse of His devotee. And more shocking for them was when Lord compares Sugriv with His brother, the great Saint-Prince Bharat. Nevertheless, what Sugriv said pleased Lord because though he was playing smart, he was actually telling the truth about the mayhem created by 'Maya', the divine illusion.

Now, since Sugriv had been given the position of a 'friend' or 'Sakha' by the Lord, he believed that why should he apologize like a servant or 'Das' in front of the Lord? For simplification of the discussion, we can consider Sugriv Bhakti as 'Sakha-Bhav' and Hanumanji Bhakti as 'Das-Bhav'. Being a friend,he believed he had all the right to reason or question the Lord. What Sugriv intended to ask the Lord is that when He is the one who confuses the Being through Maya, then how can He punish the same Being for his forgetfulness and ignorance? Also, when Lord Himself cannot prevent Maya from barging into His Universe or 'Srishti,' how could He expect the mortal being to deal with it? And if the Lord is omnipotent and still not helping the Being to come out of the trap of Maya, then who is to be blamed, Being or God? It may sound bold,but the relevant logic of Sugriv worked and pleased Lord as well. Consequently, it also made the Lord think that, like his brother Bharat, Sugriv is a very knowledgeable devotee who truly loves Him.

'Bhakti' or devotion is essentially the path of faith and connection. Unlike other spiritual disciplines, the devotee doesn't just mug up the various 'Vidhi' or age-oldworship methodologies given by scriptures or priests and practice it mechanically like a robotic machine. Instead, the devotee worships with true feelings and emotions that arise from a pure heart, and hecan unhesitatingly and unapologetically communicate to the Lord. Lord, too, doesn't assess or analyze the words of His devotee merely on the basis of some pre-established notions. He only sees the "Love" with which a seeker connects with Him. Sugriv can speak like this because he is a true devotee whose connection is pure and unconditional. Very few devotees can match Sugriv's level of dedication and purity. Also, that day Sugriv had raised an important question through his excuse, which is relevant for every seeker. Spiritual methodologies or 'Sadhan-Bhajan' is a spiritual exercise prescribed to every spiritual aspirant, but the question is, is there a fixed format of 'Sadhan-Bhajan' through which the seeker attains Enlightenment? Are there any protocols or boundaries in Bhakti? Can a seeker who doesn't diligently follow the prescribed format of Sadhan-Bhajan, not be eligible to seek the Lord?

Dirty clothes are washed with soap and water. What if the water used is itself dirty? Can it then wash and purify clothes? Every seeking activity, be it Karma, Gyan or Bhakti Yoga, is polluted with one or the other flaws of Maya. For instance, one needs money for activities like a pilgrimage, decoration, feast, charity, etc. So, can anybody claim that the money used for these activities is absolutely righteous without an element of cleverness or dishonesty? Besides, in business activity, not one but many are involved. Can anyone claim that each stake holder played fairly when participating in it? Even the fire ignited in a 'Yagya-Havan' burns living insects and microorganisms that dwell in the atmosphere. Therefore, the one answer to all the claims is 'No.' Every 'Sadhana' or seeking activity does get polluted; the reason could be any because it is initiated by human beings, who are under the influence of three primary modes of nature, namely Satogun or purity, Rajogun or passion and Tamogun or negativity. Only that which is beyond the modes of nature is perfect. Therefore, an imperfect activity cannot fetch perfect results.

Lord knows this limitation, and therefore, He has given the window of 'Sharanagati' or the Yoga of Surrender to the seeker. A real devotee accepts and understands this limitation and knows that he is not capable of attaining Lord through the various seeking activities. He just tries to intensify his intention to attain Lord and requests Lord to rescue him. We can only deal with our flaws by surrendering the same ego to the Lord.

Sugriv forgot his promise to serve the Lord and got indulged in material accomplishments. Similarly, we also set big spiritual targets but soon forget and again get indulged in family affairs in the material world. So, when the seeker truly and genuinely wants to progress but somehow fails, what option is he left with? Saint Tulsidas affirms that there is nothing to be ashamed about or to feel guilty about in forgetting or diverting from the path of attaining God. The seeker can complain authoritatively to the Lord, "If You do care for me, then help me."

That day Sugriv did exactly the same,and his complaint,which was actually a great prayer,pleased Lord a lot. His appreciation was clearly reflected as He simply smiled back and said that every true devotee and seeker is as dear to Him as Bharat. Goswami Tulsidas also confirms that no entity in this universe is as understanding and caring as Lord Ram. Therefore, Beings must realize that the one and sole purpose of life is 'Bhakti' of Lord Siya-Ram.

Chapter 4.11

Search for Sita Begins: Journey of every Seeker

When Lord knows that Sita is in the South direction,
Then why did He send the Vanars to different regions?

And when Lord knew that only Hanumanji would find Sita's location,
Then why did He send others to face challenges in this mission?

The formidable Vanar army of Kishkindha led by Sugriv assembled in the forest court of Lord Ram. Lord wanted to ensure that everything was in place and decide the course of action. Accordingly, Sugriv divided the army into four parts for better reach and effectiveness. He sent three search parties in the three directions that are North, East and West. The fourth party was assigned for the South direction under the leadership of youthful leader Prince Angad accompanied by senior Jambavan, brother duo Naal& Neel and most importantly, the Great Hanumanji. However, readers may find certain elements in this planning pointless. First, why was the search executed in other directions, especially when Jatayu had already told the Lord that Ravan had abducted Lady Sita and went to Lanka, which is in the South? Also, the fact that Sugriv had witnessed Ravan's flying chariot going towards the South justifies the assumption.

Second, sending other members along with Hanumanji also seems to be ineffectual. The reason is simple. Lord Ram is the Supreme God, and He already knew that only Hanumanji would be able to find Sita. This was also proven when He gave the Ring or 'Mudrika' only to Hanumanji and nothing else to any other members. The question then arises: What was the point in engaging so many of the Vanars when the Lord already knew that this task was only to be fulfilled by Hanumanji in the South direction?

God Ram is the Knower of everything. The real Goddess Sita was never kidnapped, and yet from 'Aranya-Kaand' till 'Lanka-Kaand', the greatest initiative of Her search that mankind had ever witnessed was undertaken. First, finding Her location, then marching the humongous Vanar army, then planning the Lanka attack, then building the legendary 'Ram-Setu' bridge, then fighting the great war of Lanka and finally execution of mighty Ravan. Ultimately, putting an end to the whole episode with the divine reunification of Lord Siya-Ram. Was there any need for all these events to take place at all?

Ram-Rajya is the vision of Lord Ram where each and every Being must be made to feel like co-participants, where effort or 'Purushartha' is given great importance and where there is a spirit of inclusiveness and teamwork. Goswami Tulsidas also emphasizes that although the occurrence of the events appears odd, this is the truth of life. The truth of existence is simple, but it seems to be or is actually most difficult for the Beings to realize. God is the closest entity to the Being and yet appears to be far away. Although we are able to understand this truth by virtue of our knowledge and intellect, we fail to accept it because of our mind-ego conditioning.

God has a permanent solution to eradicate this perplexing illusion of the Beings. He believes that the best way is to make the Being himself see that he is in illusion. Human psychology is such that it easily believes what it sees and does and not what it is told. Let's try to understand this interesting fact with a very popular example. On an extremely hot day in a desert, suddenly a thirsty traveler sees a water body at a far distance. His companion advises him that it's not what he thinks it is and warns that all his efforts are going to be futile. But he doesn't listen to any of the advice and rushes towards it to quench his thirst. Only on coming closer does he realize that what he mistook as a water body was, in actuality, the Illusion of 'Mirage'. So, for ordinary minds, it is seen that it's always better to experience the truth yourself because you don't accept others' advice. Similarly, although this whole Lanka War exercise did absorb extra time, energy and resources, it ensured 'acceptance' of Truth and demystified illusion. And therefore, for Vanar-seekers, the spiritual effort that is the pursuit of Mother Sita, who is the Goddess of Peace, Energy, Wealth and Bhakti, was imperative.

The realization of truth, be it of the illusion or the mirage, though it seems to be in the reach of the seeker or traveler, is in actuality in the hands of God. Remember, without His will, the seeker cannot move an inch towards his target. Grace of God is the 'Pran' of every life. Grace is not an object which can be attained or lost. God is unconditional, and He doesn't seek a reason before manifesting Grace to His Beings. Here one may ask, if Grace is available to everybody, then what is the point of treading the path of spirituality? Then what special miracle can a spiritual seeker witness in life?

The answer is simple and straightforward. Being can know about Grace through scriptures or sages, but unless the seeker puts his own efforts or 'Purushartha' in spiritual endeavors, he cannot comprehend by himself that Grace is already with him. Therefore, no spiritual 'Purushartha', be it in the wrong direction, is futile, but it is always rewarding. When a seeker works tirelessly to the best of his capability and yet fails, a feeling of humility and surrender arises in him and only then does he become eligible for Grace. This is nothing but the act of breaking free from the egoic sense of 'Doer-ship' or 'Kartapan'.

Again, the spiritual efforts are only meant to give ventilation to the seeker's thirst and unease. A thirsty man in the desert cannot sit patiently. He will try his best and search for water before finally giving up, putting his everything at stake. The Seeker situation is also similar to this. To attain 'Bhakti', the seeker becomes very impatient and does his best to achieve it. In fact, a spiritual-thirsty soul cannot simply sit at ease. All these seemingly inefficacious spiritual efforts actually help cleanse his 'Antaha-Karana' or the Inner-Self, to become eligible for Grace. Worldly Karma can go waste or give negative consequences, but Spiritual Karma only gives progress and facilitates the evolution of consciousness.

To achieve a target, moving in the right direction is imperative. But who can say which direction leads to God? Here Lord Ram wants us to understand that all directions lead to Him. Each and every Vanar, no matter in which direction he ventured, ultimately attained the blessings, love and affinity of Mother Sita. What can be more promising for the Being is that no matter in which direction he goes to quench his spiritual thirst, whether he is successful or a failure, he ultimately becomes eligible for the divine love of Mother Sita. Kids rush to jump on the lap of their mother. Some reach while some fall on the way, but the mother, no matter what, leaps forward to get hold of her child herself. And therefore, rushing and falling are not futile for the seeker-child because Goddess-Mother does come forward to hold and embrace us.

Vanars were not polished or well-equipped with sophisticated weapons, and yet they defeated the mightiest Asur army on this planet. Such war cannot be fought unless there is no inner connection with the cause. The Lord wanted the participation of each and every Vanar, not out of command of their King or out of any compulsion, but to quench the thirst of the Vanar devotees.

All the Vanars participated equally with full enthusiasm; they together built the 'Ram-Setu', fought the Lanka war and finally attained the 'Darshan' and Grace of 'Jag-Janini' or Mother of Universe that is Sita. The worldly identities of Sita, namely, a Princess of Mithila or Queen of Ayodhya, were not important to the Lord. For Him, the most important thing was that even the most inferior Being be it a Vanar, must truly connect with Her.

When the efforts of the Being are invested in a project, then the success or failure of that project becomes his own endeavor. To invoke the same feeling, Lord engages all Vanars in this elusive quest. When Vanar groups were departing for the search of Mother Sita, only Hanumanji was the only one with whom Lord Ram divulged his feelings. The great Devotee knows the heart of his visionary Lord. The alliance of Bali-Ravan and other contemporary leaders of those times was purely based on 'give and take' or 'Raj-Neeti'. Conversely, the vision of Ram-Rajya is totally different. Here the satisfaction and benefit of every citizen are more important than the vested interests of a few leaders. Ram-Rajya is based on mutual Love or 'Prem-Neeti'. Goswami Tulsidas says that like Vanars, anyone who wants to enter the domain of Ram-Rajya must, with the core of his heart, surrender to the lotus feet of Lord Siya-Ram.

Chapter 4.12

Lord Hanuman Leads: Power of RAM-NAAM

Tired and dejected Vanars seemed difficult to stay alive,
Only by keeping faith in Hanumanji, they could survive.

On the command of King Sugriv, the long-awaited mission for the search for Lady Sita was going to happen. As soon as the decisive meeting was over, all the Vanars dispersed from Lord Ram's assembly and proceeded as per they planned. Hanumanji was standing last in the 'South' group, which was led by Angad. But just in a few days' time, after the group had left, the circumstances were changed, and Hanumanji had to lead from the front. Here 'Last' and 'Front', these two words signify 'Following' and 'Leading,' respectively. Most people's mind-ego always provokes to be in the front and to be acknowledged as the leader. Needless to say, it is only because of the attachment to the position 'Leader'. Conversely, there are some people whose mind-ego fears come in front, and they always prefer to stay back. These people also lack the confidence to lead and are anxious of uncertainty and mishap. Hence, standing 'Last' essentially signifies zero confidence and cowardice. Besides, there is the mind-ego of some other calculative people who, merely for the sake of recognition and respect, rush to stand in front, but the moment they see a tough challenge and threat comes their way, they don't hesitate to hide in the last line. Such an attitude signifies impersonation and baloney.

However, Hanumanji, who has defeated all his immortals of mind-ego with the Supreme power of Ram-Naam, is beyond the tricks of 'Last' and 'Front'. He doesn't care whether he gets the credit or not and whether the situation is intimidating or rewarding. His sole purpose in life is to serve Lord Ram. A true devotee is the one whose only purpose is to please his master without bothering about the consequences. Although it was the Great Hanuman who was most enthusiastic in this journey to seek Lady Sita, he never demonstrated it loudly like others. Instead, he maintained his composure and was always quiet and stable. He was the closest to his master Lord Ram, yet he would patiently wait in a corner until all other Vanars got their share of blessings. There was not a speck of 'me first' feeling within him but just pure love and patience, and this is what 'Bhakti' is all about.

In the worldly aspect, the one who comes last is labeled as a 'failure,' but in 'Bhakti', the one who stands at the last is always extra special. When Hanumanji heard that his master Lord Ram called him to come near, he got very emotional, deeply felt that the purpose of his birth was fulfilled on that very day. Hanumanji, the avatar of Supreme God Shiva, took the form of a Vanar only to serve His dearest Lord Ram and held back for a very long time, just for this epic moment. Lord Ram gave him Lady Sita's ring embedded with 'RAM' and blessed him. Hanumanji, along with the group, then left in/for the search of Goddess Sita, the Mother of Bhakti (Devotion), Shakti (Energy), Laxmi (Wellness) and Shanti (Peace). Ramayan is not only a past historical event but also the story of every Being. Every human being, including you and me, is looking for Mother Sita in our lives. In this eventful episode, the Vanars represent the heart of every seeker, and Lord Hanuman is the 'Sadguru' or Teacher for every seeker.

For days, the Vanars searched every nook and corner of forests, hills, rivers and lakes with full dedication and perseverance, forgetting sleep and hunger, but they couldn't get any clue about Mother Sita. Already they were very upset about not getting any clues and being hungry, thirsty and weary, also added more and this discouraged them very much. Under the dynamic leadership of Angad, the son of Bali, although the Vanars started off very enthusiastically, they couldn't maintain the momentum. Even after trying very hard, they didn't find any progress. All these made them thoroughly discouraged, and they started feeling as if their life journey was coming to an end.

Even in this difficult time, it was only Hanumanji who was totally balanced, focused and composed. When every Vanar in the search group was more concerned for his own life, the great Hanumanji was not at all bothered for his own but worried very much for the survival of others. A smart traveler always carries necessary things before starting the journey to deal with difficult, unforeseen situations. No spiritual endeavor and no life are free from difficulties. Out of all Vanars, only Hanumanji had the stamina and strength of 'Ram-Naam', which is imperative for every seeker to survive and sustain till the end of every life journey.

Hanumanji was keen to help the Vanars and was constantly thinking of possible solutions. When he noticed something at the top of a nearby hill, his instincts clued him positively. Trusting his gifted instincts, he quickly reached there and found a cave opening, through which many birds and animals were entering and exiting. He immediately understood that the food and water source, which was needed to save his fellow Vanars, was inside the cave. On the other hand, the leader Angad was dejected, and he was reluctant in leading the group forward. Moreover, he felt frustrated for failing in Lord Ram's purpose. Although he was in no way incompetent, he felt that he didn't have what it took in those stressing and crucial moments. In Mahabharata, Lord Krishna came to the rescue of Arjun and gave him the divine knowledge of the Supreme Shri Bhagwad Geeta. Here, Hanumanji came forward and led the army from the front to boost the morale of Angad.

Saint Tulsidas proclaims that by just remembering the great Hanumanji, all problems of Beings can get resolved. This principle is like a diamond-edge made/cut inerasable line engraved on a granite rock. The great Pawan-Putra Hanumanji has the unique power to swap impossible to possible for the success of Lord Ram's devotees. It is the reason why Tulsidas solely depended on Hanumanji throughout his life. There occurred many happenings in his life where he witnessed the divine blessing of Hanumanji manifested to protect and guide him. Undoubtedly, Hanumanji is the ultimate symbol of 'Trust' and 'Faith'. Without faith, even a mundane job cannot be accomplished, now think of how the 'Faith' should be in the case of 'Bhakti'. This fact became evident when the Vanar group propped their faith in Hanumanji and entered the cave chanting RAM-NAAM.

The food and water source is actually the Grace of Lord Ram in any seeker's life. As long as the seeker is not able to experience Grace in his life, he, like Angad and Vanars, fears to enter the cave of Faith. Also, as the seeker progresses in Faith, the mind-ego purposely gives rise to intense life-threatening anxious thoughts to stop his progress. As a result, many people who initially get excited to walk first, after a while, find it difficult to move and in course of time, they even hesitate to carry on. Thus, the trap of mind-ego is so influencing that the first goers soon lose their momentum and fall apart.

But when a Being puts his utmost faith and trust in Sadhguru Ram-Bhakt Hanuman, then he is led by Hanumanji himself. Therefore, no fear, no anxiety and no problem in this universe can stop him from attaining the Grace of Lord Ram. Let's try to understand this truth with a good example. Every human being is the traveler, Hanumanji is the vessel, and Lord Ram is the destination. Of course, the one who is not initiated in spirituality yet will find it difficult to comprehend the meaning and value of Trust, Faith and Grace. Through 'Sadhan-Bhajan' or spiritual discipline, one should first need to make all possible attempts to purify his inner self. Only then, he will experience the manifestation of Grace in his life. Remember, in the most challenging times of our lives, Trust and Faith only gives us the much-needed control, hope and the courage to keep moving.

Hardly the one who doesn't know where to find the 'light' is the one who fears to the dark. Hanumanji is that light which cannot be put out even by the darkest forces like Ravan; one just needs full faith to attain him. Hanumanji has the supreme power of 'Ram-Naam'. Goswamiji says that today, right now, no matter where you are and in what state, just start chanting 'Ram-Naam' and, with absolute guarantee, see how the world transforms in your favor. That day, while entering the cave under the leadership of Hanumanji, the Vanar group too realized this truth and started chanting 'Ram-Naam' altogether. Consequently, they attained the divine Grace of the Lord and also the solution to their hunger and thirst. They even got the direction and regained the lost energy to pursue their mission with full vigor and courage. Saint Tulsidas repeatedly says that whosoever put his unconditional faith in RAM-NAAM can procure the love and care of Hanumanji and become unstoppable just by defeating all his sufferings.

Chapter 4.13

Cave of Swayamprabha: Universal message

She showed the Vanars the way to Lady Sita,
Attaining salvation she then unified with her 'Ishta'.

Hanumanji, followed by the Vanars, set foot in the cave and found a beautiful fruit orchard and a fresh water spring. There they also saw Tapaswini Swayamprabha, a female saint who was in deep meditation. Before eating fruits or drinking water, they first searched for her permission. Swayamprabha already knew the mission of Vanars, that is to find Lady Sita, she very compassionately first asked them to quench their thirst and hunger. Then she revealed to them that she herself is a devotee of Lord Ram and was told a long time back that a group of Vanars who are in the duty for Lord Ram would arrive at her. She also added that she will help them and only after then her Tapasya or penance will end; also she will attain salvation in the lotus feet of Lord Ram. Today was that great day, () which she had been waiting for a very long time.

Life of Swayamprabha is filled with the nectar of Bhakti. She was not doing Tapasya or penance for blessing or for supernatural powers. She knew that more important of having Bhakti was to ensure that the vessel, in which holy nectar of Bhakti is kept, must always be pure. A devotee purifies Self or Antahkarana through the fire of Tapasya or intense penance. So that she becomes eligible for the Grace of Supreme. The Vanars realized that Swayamprabha was an essence of love and compassion. So they narrated their story and failures to her. She comforted them and said that they must not feel dejected and that they will certainly find Lady Sita. She further said, now that they have given her the vicinity of her 'Ishta' Ram and so she must also show them the right path.

The seekers of same intent when coming together, then there will always be a favorable happening. They get to know the issues, problems and experiences of each other. They share their insights among themselves and do acquire very much benefit. But not all seekers are at the same level. Swayamprabha was way ahead than Vanars on the path of spirituality. Only she and Hanumanji had realized the truth of Lord Siya-Ram. But what she said was not just for Vanars but also very useful for the seekers of today's times. Her message is -

Firm Determination

The seeker must be tightly intent towards his target. The one who is in doubts, suspicions, hesitation and jeopardy cannot succeed though he may try a lot. Without firm determination, a seeker cannot get rid of his bond with the mundane worldl. He has to drag his mind away from ignorance and through it towards his intent.

Don't be Remorseful

In the roots of remorse are locked the memories of past mistakes. Remorse is useful to a certain extent in self-contemplation and cautiousness, but too much of it gives hopelessness. If, on his way, a traveler falls in a hole and hurts himself that doesn't mean he must keep looking back at the hole and feel remorse, endlessly. Instead, the traveler must look forward on his path with alertness so that he doesn't descend again. If the Vanars keep on repenting that more than a month has passed by and we have got no clue of Lady Sita, then it's a wasteful remorse. The seeker's mindset must be - 'No matter so far I have wasted my life, but now onwards, I will not waste even one moment more. With the Grace of Lord Ram, the dark night of ignorance is over and I am awakened. I shall never again back off. With my mind, speech and heart, I will be focused only on Lord Ram.'

Discard Calculativeness

Vanars appraised and understood their situation. Firstly, they were not sure whether they could ever find the vicinity of Lady Sita. And secondly, they thought that, if they return without any information about Lady Sita, then their King Sugriv would punish them for sure. So, they thought that since the cave, presently they are in, has a conducive environment with food and water source, they must neither move forward nor return, but to stay right there inside the cave forever. Every seeker faces such a situation in his life. Initially, the seeker faces uncertainty or 'Sanshaya' and then comes 'Pralobhan' or temptations. On the path of spirituality such temptations are really a great impediment. And to discard these temptations and continue to move forward is indeed very difficult for any seeker. From ancient times till today, we see this happening. All the celebrated and worshiped Godman fall in this category who after attaining wealth, name and success stops their seeking and gets fascinated in the pleasures. But the sincere seeker cannot stop mid-way. This same 'Pralobhan' or temptation in the form of the throne of Ayodhya also came to Prince Bharat, but he abandoned it and instead, continued to be just a humble devotee-servant of Lord Ram. A seeker must not cease because of suitable conditions rather continue the striving for where he has to reach with utmost sincerity and serenity.

Close your eyes

This is the most important and precious message of Swayamprabha which is reflected in almost every other verse or 'Chaupayi' of Ramcharitmanas. Here, closing your eyes means to contemplate and assess on one's own self. Eyes can only see what is outside, the materialistic world. When the seeker closes his eyes and focuses on inner-self, then eventually he finds out that the source of all bliss is very much inside him and not from somewhere outside. Closing of eyes also means becoming 'Udaseen' or indifferent towards the worldly play. Again, closing eyes means acceptance of insufficiency in self and surrendering in the lotus feet of Lord Siya-Ram.

Swayamprabha in indirect means gave these precious lessons through her encouraging and heartfelt words. Vanars had tried hard but had failed. Devi Sita, the 'Goddess of Bhakti' is not attained by 'Purushartha' or some special efforts. She can only be attained by faith and surrender. The message of Mother Swayamprabha is eternally inspiring for every seeker of any 'Marg' or Spiritual-path.

In Ramayan, there is not much said about her in detail. Through her episode Goswami Tulsidas wants to explain to the seekers that on the path of spirituality, nobody can ascertain how, when and through which medium, the help and the grace can manifest. Who or what will come, how and when it will come is not predominant. What is important is to expect the most unexpected. What is even more important is to know that the grace of Lord is always with the seeker and ensures his progress. A seeker, like Vanars and Swayamprabha, must not give up; rather assess himself, that whether he has truly surrendered in the lotus feet of Lord Siya-Ram?

Chapter 4.14

Transformation of Angad: Value of 'Satsang'

For human beings, Satsang is life's most valuable reward,
'It is My reason for incarnation', says the Supreme Lord.

As per the instructions of Tapaswini Swayamprabha, the Vanars winked hurriedly and in a flash found themselves outside of the cave, on a deserted sea shore at the southern tip of India. For them, the prophecy of Swayamprabha didn't seem to be coming true, because they apparently couldn't find any way, where they could advance on that deserted beach, in search of Lady Sita. They again were completely broke and got dejected so much that they decided to end their lives. The words of Swayamprabha furnished them hope and they were expecting that as soon as they opened their eyes they would see Lady Sita right in front of them. They were like that small child who plants the seeds of carrots and out of curiosity, unearths the saplings to check the progress. Obviously, by digging in and out continuously, the plants cannot grow and will die, disappointing the child greatly.

Vanars symbolizes seekers and Swayamprabha the Preceptor. A seeker must have immense 'Shraddha' or 'Trust' in the words of 'Sadhguru' or 'Preceptor'. Shraddha demands great forbearance and unwavering faith in the heart of the seeker. Just like Mother Shabri, who for many years sincerely followed the instructions of her Sadhguru Matang with 'Shraddha' and didn't divert from her Sadhna or spiritual practice. Unlike Shabri, the Vanars were not that determined and dedicated seekers. Vanars signify an impatient and restless mind which is difficult to fix on a particular target. These Vanars were troubled more so because of the time limit set by their King Sugriv. As the days were passing by, they were losing hope and were getting/feeling fazed.

In the life of a seeker, a time limit can either become fruitful or can become an obstruction. There is no anything called as a fixed rule. Without a time limit, some seekers become complacent and lazy. While for some, if there's a time limit they become impatient and restless. A true and complete seeker must be very careful and must not get trapped in either of these situations. Therefore, a Sadhguru is a must who can give instructions after understanding the nature of the seeker.

The real reason for Vanars' hopelessness and despondency was the puzzled mental state of their leader, Angad. Till date, Angad couldn't yet trust Sugriv completely. On one hand, he believed Sugriv to be the cause of his father Bali's demise; while on the other hand, he considered the slaying of Bali by Lord Ram as justified. Angad was always in apprehension that whenever Sugriv would get a chance, he would wipe him off from the scene. Angad, being a leader of the group, was unable to accomplish the assignment in the fixed time limit and was entitled for punishment by Sugriv. Angad felt that Sugriv intentionally put this time limit condition so that the South Vanar group would fail and so Sugriv might get a reason to punish him. Although the truth was that Sugriv didn't have any such intentions as Angad was thinking. There was no conspiracy. Sugriv, under the order of Lord Ram, had become totally righteous. But, this is how mind-ego plays with the Beings, compelling them to distrust each other and live in insecurity and hatred. Resentment and skepticism are life lines for mind-ego, whereas trust and love are death for it.

Angad was tired, dejected and in a dilemma. On one hand, he was a devoted follower of Lord Ram; while on the other hand, he hated Sugriv. Strange is the trick of mind-ego. If he had absolute trust in Lord Ram, then how could he question Lord's wisdom? How could he think that a petty being like Sugriv could influence Supreme God Ram in his favor? For Angad, if Sugriv is the culprit, then the Lord is also to be blamed. But, he is in total surrender for Lord Ram and against Sugriv. This signifies a confused and doubting mind of a seeker. A seeker must be very clear in his head and must not allow mind-ego to play with his belief.

The one who believes Lord Ram to be a mortal being will always be in delusion. In Ramcharitmanas, Goddess Sati, Kakbhushundi, Garun and of course, evil Ravan, all of them had gone through the same delusion of misbelieving Lord Ram as a mortal being. This skepticism is not unnatural for Beings but then an enlightened mentor is needed who can throw light and clarify the doubts. The other three except Ravan had the good fortune of attaining 'Satsang' and therefore were able to destroy their ignorance.

The son of God Brahma that is Jambavan, the symbol of intelligence, understood Angad's delusion and counseled - "Dear Prince Angad, don't misbelieve Ram as a mortal being. He is formless, without attributes (Nirgun-Nirakar) and the cause of creation. He out of love for His devotees has taken the human form (Sagurn-Saakar) and has blessed our lives. He manifests purely out of His is own will and not because of the Karmic Cycle. A devotee must not get trapped in delusion and earnestly participate in Lord Ram's Leela with devotion and faith."

It was not like Angad didn't believe Lord Ram as God Himself but in the life of a seeker, swings between doubt and trust keeps occurring. The pure words of wise Jambavan removed the delusion and Angad got enlightened with truth. This is the power and value of Satsang or spiritual discourse. Satsang is like an influential wind that scatters the dense dark cloud of ignorance and allows the Sun of Knowledge or 'Vivek' to shine bright. Angad who was totally dejected earlier now was full of enthusiasm and fearlessness.

An old vulture named 'Sampati' from his cave-nest was overhearing the conversations of the Vanar group. He walked outside and caught sight of a large gathering of monkeys which was fragile and babbleing of ending their lives. The flesh of so many dead monkeys was kind of a royal feast for Sampati. He spoke, "Today gods are kind to me. I will eat all these monkeys and will satiate my long time hunger". Seeing the sheer size, ferociousness and intentions of the vulture, the Vanars got very scared. They realized that now their life's end is sure. This South direction group although had the bravest and strongest of all Vanars, yet they got scared from one old vulture who can't even fly and catch his prey. Though it seems uncommon, yet the play of mind-ego is such that, at the time of extreme despondency, even a small threat makes Beings feel very weak and hopeless.

But the great Angad fearlessly replied to Sampati, "There was one great vulture 'Jatayu', who for the cause of Lord Ram, sacrificed his life and here is you, Sampati, again a huge sized vulture but you becoming a barrier in the cause of Lord Ram. If in the search of Mother Sita, like Jatayu, we are ready to sacrifice everything, then even 'Kaal' or death itself cannot touch us." Vulture might not be a very adorable bird for human beings but for Bhakt, it will always be a symbol of greatness because of one great vulture, the'Gidhraj' Jatayu. Till date devotees of Lord Ram, seeing a vulture, remember Jatayu, who was the most important link in the love saga of Lord Siya-Ram. Angad was a diplomatic visionary and by quoting Jatayu martyrdom, not only motivated Vanars but also inspired Sampati to be a help rather than an obstruction.

Angad's one statement gave super energy to Vanars and also made

Sampati think about his younger brother Jatayu's selfless service to Lord Ram. Truly, the Satsang of Jambavan, totally transformed Angad's life and made him not only a lethal warrior with a very sharp political diplomat but also a Great Bhakt, who has surrendered his life in the lotus feet of Lord Siya-Ram. Wherever and whenever Ramayan will be recited, the name of great Angad will echo out loud and stay in the hearts of devotees.

Chapter 4.15

Sampati inspires Vanars: Never Give Up!

O Vanars, look at me, rise and work on a solution,
Nothing is impossible on the path of Lord's devotion.

The news of Jatayu's martyrdom for the cause of Lord Ram stunned Sampati and opened his eyes. He was saddened and also got ashamed for frightening Vanars who were working relentlessly in the service of Lord Ram, to find the vicinity of Mother Sita. He then revealed to them his past, "I and Jatayu are real brothers. Once when we were youths, we took a challenge to fly to the Sun; but because of the unbearable scorching heat of the Sun, Jatayu retreated half way back to Earth and I in my arrogance, although burning, continued to fly. Ultimately, because of the heat, my wings got badly scorched and I fell back on Earth, unconsciously. There, Sage Maharishi Chandrama took pity on me and healed me. I felt dejected having lost both of my wings. The Sage's teachings and discourses helped me to dis-identify with the body and come out of the agony."

"He foretold me that in future (Treta Yuga), the Supreme God 'Param-Brahma' will incarnate as King Ram, a human being. At that time, his Wife will be held hostage by Ravan, the Asura King of Lanka. A group of spies in search of Her will come to you. He assured me once I tell them the vicinity of Mother Sita, a new set of wings will appear and I will be able to fly again. Today, the words of Maharishi have come true". Using his (vulture's) sharp and unlimited sight range, he informed the Vanars that Mother Sita, plunged in grief, is lodged in 'Ashok Vatika' of Lanka. He declared that only the one who can cross eight hundred yojans (miles) of ocean and is a repository of great intelligence will be able to fulfill the task of Lord Ram.

Sampati asked the perplexed and disheartened Vanars to look at him and stand up now with enthusiasm. He wanted them to realize that with the

Grace of Lord Ram he had obtained a new set of wings and new strength to fly again. And so how can they, being the soldiers of Lord Ram, lose hope? They must rise now and accomplish the task. Grace of God, is everything and is with each and every being, but the problem is that many human beings don't believe in it. Hence, we don't let Grace manifest in our lives and so suffer. Sampati was restoring faith in Vanars in Grace.

A weak and defeated one cannot get inspired from a person who has always been powerful and prosperous. Rather than seeing a thriving person, he will get even more frustrated about his debilitated state. But, if he looks up to an achiever, who was in the indistinguishable or even worse, weaker than him and who by his efforts or 'Purushartha' and faith or 'Vishwas' rose to new heights, then he would definitely get inspired from such an Achiever. This 'If he can do, so can I' assurance and confidence is of paramount value in a person's life. The story of Sampati had the same effect on Vanars and gave them the needed push.

The story of Sampati is also quite significant for spiritual seekers. There was an intense urge in young and stubborn Sampati to reach the Sun and prove his mettle to the world. Just like egotistical and ignorant human beings, he also wanted to show himself superior. He as well involved his younger brother Jatatyu in this act of haughtiness. The mission began with much eagerness, but in the midway Jatayu sensibly decided not to fly further and return back. He had realized the meaninglessness of this ambitious flight. He realized that firstly, it is becoming very dangerous and secondly, even if they somehow achieve this impossible attainment, then also would achieve nothing worthy except ego gratification. No achievement is ultimate and final. Today it's them; tomorrow it will be someone else. So then, what's the point in putting lives in danger?

But, Sampati lacked this sensible perspective and foolishly tangled him with his impractical and worthless aim. In an ego driven worldly perspective, Sampati appears to be courageous and Jatayu a coward because of his withdrawal. But, when sense prevailed, Sampati realized that his aim and his not returning with Jatayu was simply an act of stupid vanity and arrogance. This realization proves that every being like Sampati has the potential to think sensibly. Fault finding in others comes naturally to Beings, but it is not so common to see us accepting our own faults. Sage Chandrama taught Sampati how to dis-identify with mind-ego and apply intelligence. Dis-identification from ego means to disassociate oneself from his Name and Physical Self.

Just like defeated ambitious human beings, Sampati was in extreme pain and fell unconscious on the Earth. But this fall actually proved to be the greatest blessing for him. This incident made him understand the limitations of physical self. On top of that he got the refuge of a great Sage, only who could have helped him to realize the truth. Sampati's story of the fall of physical self and rise of real self will always remind the spiritual seeker to be very cautious about the play of ego. An egoic and arrogant being initially seems to be successful and rising on the stage of the world but if he is not following an Enlightened one, his fall is inevitable.

Although Sampati had got a new perspective, yet he was still without his wings which he had lost in his race towards reaching the Sun. The wings are the most important and strongest body part of a bird. This sense of weakness, dependence and surrender laid the foundation of his ultimate spiritual progress. Though his ego and arrogance was smashed, he still was in need of the eligibility to become a true Bhakta or devotee of the Supreme. Sage Chandrama had told him that only after seeing or 'Darshan' of Mother Sita, the Goddess of Bhakti, he will get his wings back, which is his strength and eligibility to practice Bhakti. After listening to the story of service, commitment and martyrdom of his brother Jatayu for Lord Ram, the sapling of devotion sprouted in his heart. For Bhakti, there needs to be fluidity and not stiffness in the heart, which Sampati attained after knowing about his great younger brother.

For inspiration and realization, the study of 'Bhakta-Charitra' or 'Stories of Devotees' is essential for the seekers. Sampati realized that although Jatayu too lost his wing in his battle with Ravan, yet he rose to great heights and attained the lap of the Supreme God Ram, which is umpteen times greater than the Sun. He felt that just because of his ego, he had wasted that precious time so far. He was eager to rise from his low level of existence. Sampati had now understood the meaning of true and unconditional love. He again got a fresh and great perspective in life. This intense eagerness in the heart of beings is the actual cause for their spiritual progress.

He inspired Vanars to look towards him and said, "If an ignorant vulture like me could benefit from the Grace of Lord Ram, then how can you, who are following His command, be so disheartened? Just by chanting the Name of His, "RAM-NAM", even the gravest sinner gets benefited. Now, placing Him in your heart and leaving aside this cowardly thought of suicide, just work on a solution. Then nothing in this eternity can stop you in reaching Mother Sita." Saint Tulsidas says that only the one who doesn't give up in life, puts his faith in Lord Ram and is patient, is eligible for real success and reward, which is attainment of the Lord Siya-Ram.

Chapter 4.16

Lord Hanuman Regains His Lost Powers

O Hanuman, why are you silent,
In eternity, You are the only lion.

I can destroy Ravan with all his kinsmen and army
And uproot his palace which is just a worm's colony.

Sampati flew away after telling Vanars the location of Mother Sita. The Vanars then started discussing among themselves who has the ability to cross this vast ocean. Every Vanar voiced about his strength, but none of them had the confidence to cross it. Only Angad declared that he can do this seemingly impossible task, but he was doubtful whether he would be able to return back or not. Jambavan said to Angad, "You are totally capable of returning back also, but you're our leader and the prince of Kishkindha. We cannot risk your life. I could have done this but because of my old age, I feel incapable."

Even though Sampati had motivated the Vanars group very beautifully, yet they weren't really convinced. They forgot what he was encouraging and just remembered only the challenge of four hundred miles of ocean. In challenging times like this one, the real character and qualities of the Beings are known to the world. Same words of wisdom don't have the same perseverance and the same effect on every Being. That is every Being has a different level of awareness and intelligence and so not everyone gets inspired equally. No matter how much quantum of water is in the ocean, one can only fill water as much as the size of the container that he has. The Vanars already have the blessing and the Grace of Lord Ram with them, whose one cell is greater than umteem number of such oceans. Yet the Vanars couldn't see beyond their physical limitations. They were trapped in their mind-ego and so were not able to have faith in the Grace of all-capable and all-pervading Lord Ram.

This is not only Vanars problem but also every human being's problem.

The sense of separation with the Supreme Consciousness, which is exhibited by our ego, makes us feel limited and we are unable to put absolute faith in Grace. And therefore, throughout our lives, we live in insecurities and threats. A challenging and difficult situation panics us. Jambavan, the son of Brahma had served the Lord in His previous Avatars. He was also very much capable, but in this Tretayug, he felt incompetent. He spoke like those people who live in their past, and since they feel incompetent today; they just continue boast about their past achievements. Angad's worry was like those people who keep on thinking about the future. He was confident that he could cross the ocean but he felt uncertainty in dealing with Mighty Ravan, reaching Mother Sita and returning back. If he had realized the truth of the Mother of Energy, who is the Creator, Preserver and Destroyer, that is Mother Sita, he would have no apprehensions and fears. Saint Tulsidas says that Mother Sita is behind the cause and effect of every action. She is the subtle, invisible and silent Energy which empowers Beings and lets Hanumanji to destroy half of Lanka.

In challenging times, it is indeed difficult to maintain faith in Grace. We claim that we are surrendered devotees, but since we have not yet actually witnessed or trusted Him, we tremble in fear on seeing a difficult situation. Angad or other Vanars were not free from this seeker's dilemma. But in this world of ignorance, fears and incapability, there was one Super Powerful Entity, who was aloof from all this discussion and lost in his own world. Jambavan saw him and couldn't tolerate Lord Hanuman's silence.

The one who solved the thirst and hunger of His comrades through the cave of Swayamprabha, how come he is not participating in this challenge? He didn't even try to pacify the Vanars when they were frightened on seeing Sampati coming to feed on them. That time, Angad stepped in and handled the situation. He seems to be lost since their meeting with Swayamprabha.

The truth was that only Lord Hanuman was able to understand the teaching of Swayamprabha in totality. She had asked them to close their eyes, signifying to contemplate, to have faith and to surrender to the Lord Ram. Lord Hanuman, on closing his eyes, got so mesmerized in the devotion of his Prabhu Ram that he had lost the perception of the outer world. Throughout the Sampati episode, his gross body was present there but his subtle body was somewhere else. He had also missed what Sampati had told to the Vanars about Lady Sita's location at Ashok Vatika, Lanka. This we knew because when he landed in Lanka, he didn't know where to find Mother Sita and he was in search of Her everywhere in Ravan's huge palace. It was when he met

Vibhishan he got to know about Her location.

Lord Ram knew that Lord Hanuman is very unique and is quite unlike all the Vanars. In the beginning of the Ramayan, all the Devta had pledged to incarnate as monkeys, apes and bears to serve the Lord. God Brahma too sent his son Jambavan for the same purpose. Lord Ram's greatest friend and devotee is God Shiva, the symbol of Faith or 'Vishwas' and His avatar is Lord Hanuman. Thus, the Faith within Lord Hanuman was absolute which others had lacked. That is why, even after counseling of Swayamprabha and Sampati, the Vanars still couldn't find the guts to take up the initiative to find Mother Sita.

Jambavan recalled to him about 'Ram-Karya' the 'Work of Lord Ram' and there was an instant and astonishing magical effect. The golden body of Lord Hanuman expanded to the size of Sumeru Mountain, his whole persona changed; there was anger, extreme courage and enthusiasm in his eyes. He motivated his kinsman and climbed on a mountain peak. He roared again and again like a lion and all his fellow Vanars shouted and cheered for him. The message from Goswami Tulsidas is to -

Seek Ram, Love Ram, Surrender to Ram,
But work tirelessly to become like Hanuman.

Chapter 4.17

Leap of Lord Hanuman

The Enlightened One roared and jumped into the sky,
Crushing the vanity which the mountains signify.

Bidding adieu to his fellow Vanars, Lord Hanuman got up and climbed up the peak of a mountain. When he jumped, the whole mountain sank down under the earth. What is the message Goswami Tulsidas wants to give in this incident?

Here the mountain symbolizes stubborn, difficult and mighty ego, which is standing tall and stiff. This mountain-ego doesn't believe in bowing down. Nobody can ascertain the quantum of faults, flaws and foolishness one has inside. It is not easy to jump across or destroy this mountain-ego. Inside it, there is a dense dark cave of 'Moh' or ignorance. In the cave resides a demon like 'Chitta', cannibal like 'Mind', haunted memories and pleasure seeking snakes. There are many who try and succeed in climbing the peak of this mountain-ego, but their purpose is never to spring across the ocean; (here the ocean symbolizes egoic body identification). Forget to dare crossing it they can't even imagine trying it. They just want to show off their greatness by standing on heights to hide the shallowness within them. A midget becomes the tallest by sitting on the shoulder of a tall man.

The idea behind all these is to realize that anyone who is infected with a superiority-inferiority complex, do use the instrument of fake ego, just to prove and show off that they are bigger and greater than others. But Lord Hanuman is so great in himself that he doesn't need any mountain-ego to prove. Rather, he doesn't want to prove anything. Still it appears that he is taking support or help from this ego-mountain for his legendary leap. His grand statements about crossing the ocean, destroying Lanka and killing Ravan, a few moments back, seems to be indicating his ego, pride and arrogance.

But his purpose for doing so was to liberate his kinsman from egoic fears which they were carrying within themselves. Therefore, just after his seemingly egoic statements, Hanumanji asked Jambavan, "Please guide me and tell me what I must do." This seeking of sound advice from a learned and matured one is itself an evidence of non egoism. The sinking of the mountain under the earth signifies victory of great Hanuman, over his ego. He doesn't aspire to destroy Lanka. He doesn't want to compare himself with others and prove himself greater. He is just eager to bow down in the lotus feet of Mother Sita and attain the bliss of Her Grace. And that is why, the mountain of pride could not stand as it was before and that too in front of the force of his divine noble intent.

It happens very often in our lives that we assume the malicious one as our well wisher and benevolent one as our enemy. Similarly, we are very bad in recognizing the simple hearted one and a cunning one. What seems to be an act of demonstration can have a valid and noble reason and what seems to be an act of humility can be unreal for some selfish reason. This is something that our mind-ego fails to comprehend. But the noble executor cannot go to each one and explain the real intent. This endeavor can be taken only by the shrewd ones. Also, it makes no point because even if the noble ones tries, the sheer stupid and egoic people don't accept sense and can't end their prejudices. And therefore, like Lord Hanuman, the doer must only be focused on his intention and not on others' opinions.

It is the intent that matters. In Shri Bhagavad Gita - Eighteenth chapter, Lord says that no action in this world can be perfect. Every action has a flaw. And this flaw will always be pointed out by someone. But the doer must only think and act in great involvement and be indifferent to others. Only a mind which is free from ego can think selflessly and act righteously. And only the intent of an ego-free mind matters and nothing else. Only with the merger of Grace of Lord with the purity of a Devotee, can this stubborn and mighty ego be destroyed. The only purpose of all the epics, stories and scriptures of Sanatan Dharma is to educate the beings to watch the ego and free themselves from it.

SUNDERKAND

Chapter 5.1

Test of Sursa: Mighty & Wise Hanumanji

He can melt the heart of the cruelest entity,
His Heroism is unmatched in this eternity.

The 'Mountain of Gold' named 'Manak' was an old friend of Pawan-Devta, the father of Hanumanji. He was hiding under the sea since the threat of extinction. As soon as Hanumanji began his flight, Manak came out and offered him the best of pleasure servings on it's surface. But Hanumanji had no time to waste and so he politely refused the offer.

Seeing this, the Devta or Demigods, who were witnessing the Divine-Leela all this while, were assured that if this gold mountain couldn't lure and distract Hanumanji's focus, then no other gold of Lanka or any object of greed can corrupt him. But Ravan the ruler believed more in the instrument of 'Fear' than 'Greed' to get his task accomplished. From the beginning, just by showing the fear of brutal treatment, he would force others to bow down to his command. Therefore, the Devta wanted to test the courage, guts and intelligence of Lord Hanuman, to be absolutely assured of his success. They were desperate to get rid of Ravan than anybody. So to test Hanumanji's courage and valor, they decided to send 'Sursa'.

There is always a doubt that if the examiner is kind and sensitive hearted, then he would not like to fail the candidate. It was obvious to believe that the place where Hanumanji has to reach is not going to treat him with any sort of kindness or compassion. There will be risk and death at every step. And therefore, Sursa was chosen as she was the cruelest creature in the whole world. Sursa was the Goddess of Nagas or Serpents. What kindness can be expected from a mother-snake who can kill and eat her own offspring? The one who can be savage towards her own offspring, can she be sensitive towards anyone else, be it Hanumanji?

Sursa, the symbol of cruelty and death, stood in the way of Hanumanji and said, 'Today the Devtas have offered me a nice meal.' Along with the courage, she also wanted to test the intelligence of Hanumanji. Had she straightforwardly said that she was going to kill and eat him; then this would definitely test Hanumanji's strength but not his intelligence.

Demigods and Hanumanji are of the same clan. Hearing about the involvement of Devta in sending Sursa, Hanumanji could have got shocked and furious as he knew that by going to Lanka, more than Ram-Kaj or Lord Ram's task, he was doing Devta's task. A regular person would have felt very much cheated after knowing that the ones for whom he is risking his life, are giving him troubles. This was the tool of Bhed-Niti or Divisive Diplomacy, which Sursa used to provoke Hanumanji. She was aware of the mightiness of Mahaveer Hanuman and so by referring to Devta, she cleverly escaped the direct blame and ensured safety for herself. Not only did she prove herself innocent but also made Hanumanji think judiciously.

Hanumanji replied to Sursa in these words, "Mother, I am going to Lanka for the Ram-Kaj. There, I have to deliver the message of Lord Ram to Mother Sita. From Lanka, I will go straight to Lord Ram and deliver Mother Sita's message. Then, to satisfy your hunger, I will come to you and let you feed on me. This, I am pledging and therefore, I request you to kindly let me go now". Hanumanji, by addressing Sursa as Mother, showed immense regards because she was sent by the Devta clan, which was his own family. On seeing a child going on a difficult and dangerous path, a mother at times uses threatening words to stop the child. This she does only for the sake of the child's protection. Likewise, says Hanumanji, Sursa is obstructing his path to protect him from the extreme dangers of Lanka. In this way, he completely changed the meaning of the test.

In spiritual perspective, this was a very difficult test for Hanumanji's because the one who had obstructed his path was although insensitive but not an evil entity. She was just doing as asked by Devta. To feed a hungry is the greatest Dharma; and the difficult question or 'Dharam-sankat' in front of Hanumanji was to decide between the Lanka mission and Sursa hunger. It is easy to decide between evil and good but very difficult to make a choice between two goods or two bads. Ultimately, it depends on the wisdom of the Being to decide which of the two is for the greater good. Hanumanji was very clear that in this situation, nothing is more important than Ram-Kaj because the welfare of the entire world depends on this mission.

Sursa was already impressed with the reply of Hanumanji and she very well knew that there is no point in blocking his path anymore; but from a worldly perspective, she still wanted to toss a test. So she refused to accept Hanumanji's reply and put up a condition that if Hanumanji can enter her mouth and come outside safely, then she will let him go. Hanumanji accepted the challenge and she opened her mouth to one yojan (mile) to eat Hanumanji. But, on seeing this, he increased his body size to two yojan. This size doubling went on until Sursa spread her mouth to one hundred yojan. Sensing it as a favourable moment, Hanumanji reduced his body size to an atom and immediately entered her mouth and also came outside, before she realized anything.

This game of wit may appear strange but there is deep meaning hidden for human beings. When one engages himself in good deeds or Sat-Karma like social service, charity, helping or going out of the way for others' sake, then it is but natural that he is praised by people. This 'praise' or 'Lokeshna' can become an egoic addiction because if the being gets persist in the praises, then his mind-ego craves for more of it. And then, he expands his involvement in more good deeds, not out of compassion but so as to get more and more praise from others. In such a case, there is a high possibility that the seeker distracts from his original intention of being good and gets trapped in the never ending loop of cause and effect.

Let's say, someone contributes a small amount to a needy person. As a result, those in need start praising the giver publicly and because of this, so many other people who are in need also start approaching the giver. The egoic gratification of the giver compels him to now donate larger amounts to all the needy people so as to get more and more praise, respect and honor. The crowd of needy keeps on expanding. There is no end to this practice of donating and asking. So even the giver should fix up a limit for donation, else he would resort to unfair means of earning to give larger amounts or he would feel guilty for not being able to take care of all the needy people. In both of these conditions, a spiritual seeker is bound to fail on his journey.

The idea of Robin Hood may seem to be inspiring but the act of looting from 'haves' to give away to 'have-nots' is also an unjustifiable egoic trap. Hanumanji, not even for a moment forgets or gets deflected from his objective, that is to reach Lanka, to find Mother Sita and to convey Her the message of Lord Ram. The mouth of Sursa signifies the claws of an egoic trap of attention, appreciation, recognition and praise or 'Lokeshna'. It spreads its mouth vastly so as to eat the intelligence of the seeker and divert him from his actual intention . Hanumanji is not an ordinary spiritual seeker but a supremely powerful and enlightened God-soul who had the capability to enlarge his size infinitely. Sursa could have never defeated him in this game of size expansion nor could she have never had a chance in terms of powers. And yet to give a solution and message to the mortal beings, he didn't use force but used sense in this manipulative situation. When Sursa expanded her mouth to one hundred yojans, Hanumanji could have again expanded to two hundred yojans but he smartly became extremely small, unnoticeable for Sursa.

Point is that, till the time the seeker intentionally tries to come into notice of others, there is always a threat of getting trapped in the ego of recognition. And when he zeros himself, that is, makes himself invisible or undetectable to the society, he is free from the threat of egoic trap. If Hanumanji had even a bit of victory-defeat-ego, he would have definitely kept on expanding himself. But he already knew that it was silly to do so. He is going to Lanka like a spy who needs to cautiously and successfully exchange the information and not pursue an open war. With the huge body size, he would have come in the radar of the enemies. Only an egoic fool like Ravan, would do such stupidity but there was no scope of losing focus for Hanumanji in Ram-Kaj. His objective is Ram-Kaj and for that he can either become a godzilla or a microorganism, human or animal, male or female and anything. A true seeker is the one who is flexible, indifferent and is extremely focused on his objective.

Hanumanji had defeated Sursa in the challenge and yet he very humbly and politely requested her to let him go. Seeing his mightyness, intelligence and humility, the heart of the cruelest entity of the world, Sursa melted. She adored and blessed him, "You will definitely be successful as you are the essence of power and intelligence." On hearing these words, Hanumanji got excited because firstly, as this was the indication that in this journey a favorable behavior from opponents is possible. Secondly, packing down and expanding of the body sizes indicated that in this mission there will come many challenges wherein he would have to face them by changing his form as per the circumstances. Finally and most importantly, if the cruel Snake-Mother Sursa can bless him as her son, then most definitely he will attain the Grace and affection of Mother Sita. Hanumanji loudly announced 'Jai Shri Ram', the Devta admired and showered flowers and he resumed his journey with immense joy in his heart, knowing that there is no entity in this world which can defeat or harm the one who has whole heartedly depended and surrendered in the lotus feet of Siya-Ram.

Chapter 5.2

Lord Hanuman Slays the Shadow Hunter

Singhika trapped Hanumanji through his shadow,
But the Mahabali slayed her in one single blow.

On his journey to Lanka, Hanumanji had to face deadly obstructions on each and every step and these obstructions were quite different in nature with each other. But the 'Victorious-Vanar' Hanuman overcame each hurdle and successfully reached Mother Sita. One of the most fatal and unusual challenges was 'Shadow-hunter' demoness Singhika. She used to live on the ocean bed and had the magical power to snatch/trap the shadow of the beings that would cross her. She would drag the being through his shadow and feed on it. Hanumanji, unaware of this demoness, flew over her and she immediately caught His shadow and dragged Him to her.

A shadow is the follower of the body. It moves and stops with the body and has no choice or control of its own. This is really unbelievable how one just by catching the shadow of an object could manipulate the movement of the object. But Singhika had the miraculous power to do so. While Hanumanji was flying over the Singhika's region, he felt that something was pulling him and breaking his motion. He looked all around and didn't find anybody because the trap was somewhere deep and hidden from the eyes. But the unfortunate Singhika didn't know that this time she was dealing with the Incarnation of Rudra, the Great Hanuman.

In spiritual perspective, Singhika symbolizes the state of jealousy or 'Irshya'. Jealousy is a clever trap of mind-ego and is mostly found in those who appear to be large hearted like the ocean. On one hand, a being works hard to inculcate good qualities within him; but on the other hand, burns in the fire of jealousy after seeing others having the same good qualities. It is a confusing trick of mind-ego where one is actually a striver of higher qualities but from inside, he is against someone in whom he finds the same qualities.

Even though an aircraft is taking off the runway and rising in the sky, its shadow will always fall downwards on the ground. This means that no matter how cautiously and meticulously one is rising by inculcating good qualities within him, even then there will be a black spot in his personality which can become the cause for his downfall. A jealous mind-ego works hard in identifying the faults and flaws in others. And by blowing these faults and flaws out of proportion would try to bring them down in the eyes of the society. This circle of rise and fall is an endless happening. This egoic trap of jealousy is so indistinct that the performer is unable to recognize that what he is thinking and doing is unrighteous.

Singhika out of compulsion of her jealousy ego-factor catches the shadow of Hanumanji. Now, the question is, does Hanumanji also have a black spot in his personality? How can there be any flaw in the Great Hanuman? The golden colored Hanumanji has a pure heart which is more pure and precious than the entire gold of the world. There is not one fault or flaw in his personality, life and thoughts. But, yes! There is some wheatishness or 'Shyamata' (Complexion of Lord Ram) in his heart which makes Singhika confuse it to be his shadow. And this shadow is in actuality a reflection of his beloved Lord Ram. This wheatishness has the gleam of more than millions of Suns but the one who is blind cannot see it. Tulsidasji says that the one who doesn't have this wheatishness in his heart, that is love for Lord Ram in his heart, is always open to others' threats.

This wheatishness is the highest quality of a devotee. Through the story of Singhika, Goswami Tulsidas says that even Love or Bhakti for Lord, can become an object of jealousy for the other ignorant ones. Singhika misunderstood this divine wheatishness as the shadow of a body occupied with faults and flaws. Extreme bitterness, hatred and jealousy that come out of ignorance become the origin of foolishness and destroy the being. Ram-Bhakt Hanuman is totally free from the negative traits of hatred or envy. How can the one whose heart is filled completely with Siya-Ram, can accommodate anything else? The one who tries to conspire, attack or bring down a true devotee was just inviting his own death or Kaal. The same happened with Singhika. Mahabali Hanuman, after understanding her reality, slays her in a moment, dives out of the ocean and reaches the shores of Lanka.

The traits of jealousy, negativity and hatred will always be there but hidden from the others' eyes. One gets free from these traits just by first accepting its presence in self and then, requesting the Supreme to free him from it. A devotee is never bothered from the threat of the ignorant and jealous haters. Because the one who has surrendered himself in the lotus feet of Lord Siya-Ram knows that he is now Lord's responsibility and like Hanumanji the Supreme Lord Ram ensures the safety of His each and every devotee.

Chapter 5.3

Lanka: The City of Gold

The stupendousness of Lanka was amazing,
But tonight, its ego will witness itself burning.

Lord Hanuman had crossed the ocean and reached the shores of Lanka. He climbed up a nearby hill and took a complete view of the Lanka city, which was famous in the whole world for its power, prosperity and progress. This was a magnificent city which has been the world'scentre of attraction for ages.Its history was full of wars for its throne of gold.

This grand kingdom was called Lanka. Ravan was born in this city. Although he was the son of an Enlightened Sage, Vishra Muni, his ambitions and aspirations had made him a wicked person. He, after capturing the whole world, at lastapproached Lanka. Already, the fame of this kingdom had reached all the ears. On seeing the huge army of Ravan, surrounding the Lanka Fort, Yaksha King of Lanka (Kuber clan) got terrified. Without any retaliation, he surrendered his kingdom to Ravan and escaped. In this way, without any real efforts, Ravan became the world renowned impressive emperor of Lanka.

Saint Tulsidas sees Lanka as the body of mind-ego in human beings. Till the time, this body (Lanka) is not ruled by Vibhishan (Conscious-Being), the establishment of Ram-Rajya (Enlightenment) in Ayodhya (Self) is not possible. With the passage of time, the throne of Lanka had been occupied by ambitious, selfish and evil rulers; but now, it needed an ethical ruler like Vibhishan. The city, built by God Brahma, was first ruled by Devta (righteous), then Yaksha (Selfish) and then Asura (Evil). 'Satogunni' Devta clan are the symbol of justice and knowledge. 'Rajogunni' Yaksha clan are the selfish collector of wealth. 'Tamogunni' Rakshas are the symbol of brutality, cruelty, and negative qualities.

Ravan, the symbol of Attachment (Moha), with the companionship of Kumbhakarna, the vanity-ego (Ahankar) and Meghnad, the passion (Kaama) becomes super successful in slaughtering, torturing and ruling the whole world. Vibhishan, the Conscious-Being (Jiva), out of compulsion, is bound to live with these evil entities or negative attributes of mind-ego. To change this state of Lanka, the Avatar of God was imperative. When, through the union of Dasaratha (Gyan) and Kaushalya (Bhakti), Lord Ram incarnates, only then Vibhishan is able to take over the reign of this Lanka. That is able to overcome the negative attributes of mind-ego and bring righteousness in the society. The story of Lanka is actually the real reflection of every seeker's nature or 'Antaha-Karana'.

Hanumanji, the epitome of stoicism or 'Vairagya', was witnessing this Lanka of 'Raag-Dwesh' or personal likes and dislikes. He explored each and every inch of the city but there was nothing which could attract or tempt him. The burning of Lanka was not Hanumanji's impulsive act but a well thought idea to show and prove the impermanence of mind-ego, material pleasures and likes and dislikes. A life is a waste, if trapped in Lanka and is not able to seek the lotus feet of Lord Siya-Ram.

The Jiva that is Vibhishan, was offered all the pleasures that one can aspire for but his true calling was only for Lord Ram. Finally, he got that opportunity and was pleased with his spiritual practice or Sadhana; Lord Ram crowned him as the King of Lanka. Since then Vibhishan successfully looked after Lanka, the mind-ego and applied it constructively and progressively. Vision of Ram-Rajya is not to destroy Lanka but to destroy the attachment of self with Lanka. Hanumanji's role is to initiate this process for Vibhashan, the seeker, who has devoted his life in chanting the name-RAM.

Chapter 5.4

Lankini attains Wisdom: Punch of Saint Hanuman

She was the most reliable guard of Ravan's kingdom,
In one blow, she realized the truth and attained wisdom.

Hanumanji, after taking a good look at the city, then tried to stealthily enter the gates of Lanka fort. He had minimized his size to an insect, but was caught by the most vigilant, alert and trustworthy guard of Ravan, that was Lankini. She called Hanumanji a thief and like a true Asura, declared to eat him alive. But in the end of the meeting, she is found to have thrown herself down in the divine feet of Hanumanji. She feels grateful to her Karma and says that discourse from a Saint or Satsang is more valuable than Heaven. Quite surprisingly the reason for this miraculous transformation was a fist punch of Hanumanji. Nowhere else do we come across such an incident where a Satsang is practiced by a fist blow? Also we will notice that just coming in close proximity to a Saint doesn't mean it's a Satsang. Rather, with immense faith and reverence to absorb the teachings of the saint is an actual Satsang.

The said Saint was Hanumanji and the seeker was Lankini but She instead of giving respect to him kept on insulting Him. But who was Lankini? What was her story?

The exotic kingdom of Lanka was built by God Brahma and He appointed Lankini as the watch-guard. In the beginning, when Lanka was ruled by Devta, Lankini was pure and Satogunni in nature. With the passing of the Lanka throne from Devta to Yaksha (Kuber), she became desireful one and Rajogunni like Yaksha, the hoarder of wealth. But when the throne was occupied by Ravan, she got really upset thinking that now like Asura and demons she too would become evil and Tamogunni. God Brahma consoled her and promised that when a Vanar will punch her with fist and she bleeds heavily, understand that the rule of Ravan is coming to end. And then, she will be free from this vicious cycle of Gunnas (Sato-Rajo-Tamo) and will be liberated.

Lankini was given all the information by God Brahma but living with Asura for such a long time, she had herself become Asura like. Because of bad company her 'Self' was totally corrupted. A white cloth turns darkish because of dirt and after washing it thoroughly the dirt is removed and it glows pure white again. Similarly, with Hanumanji's blow of knowledge, her 'Self' got washed off from the impurity and became Satogunni and pure. Also, she regained her lost memory which was buried beneath the load of demonic and evil conditioning.

No Being is impure in its essential form. The 'factory settings' done by God are perfect and pure. It is the attachment or 'Moha' with the material which causes the Being to forget his reality. Also, the worldly relations with others appear to be so real that the Being totally forgets his true one relation with the Creator. Lankini and Ravan's relationship was that of Servant-Master. She had become so loyal to evil that she had lost her sense of righteousness so much so that she mistook Hanumanji as a burglar and rushed to destroy him. The blow of Hanumanji was actually the intense impact of 'Satsang'.

The blood that came out from her was actually the venom filled by Asura's company. Once the Being gets free from this venom of demonic qualities, he regains his sense of righteousness. To walk and fall is common. But to stand again after thousands of falls is the quality of a true seeker. Lankini was a seeker who had lost her way in this 'Maya'. Saint Hanumanji recognized her originality and gave her the treatment that she needed. She realized that actually the blow was for her mind-ego and ignorance. Now, in the new light of wisdom, she could clearly see the divinity of Hanumanji. Common people consider wealth and prosperity as a result of spiritual merits or 'Punya' and therefore they regularly stand in the queues of temples but a devotee knows that the outcome of spiritual merit is attainment of an Enlightened Spiritual Master.

Lankini's spiritual merits of the past gave the fruits that day in the form of Hanumanji. Only a Saint and His Satsang can guide the seeker towards the path that leads to ultimate bliss. Goswami Tulsidas says that seekers surrender in the lotus feet of Lord Siya-Ram and Siya-Ram prostrates in the lotus feet of Saints.

Chapter 5.5

Meeting of the Two Bhakts: Being Vibhishan is not easy

Hanumanji narrated Shri Ram-Katha and introduced himself,
The two hearts of Bhakti got elated and reached somewhere else.

After liberating Lankini, Hanumanji then entered the city of Lanka. He spent the whole night looking for Mother Sita in every house and building, but everything was in vain. In the end, he entered the palace of Ravan and searched every corner, but there too he got no clue of Her. Just when he was coming out of the palace, he saw a hermitage wherein the name, 'RAM' was embedded on top of it. The surrounding was also filled with Holy Basil plants (Tulsi) which are very dear to Lord Ram. On seeing this contradictory scene in the land of evil Ravan, Hanumanji was pleasantly surprised. He never expected to find a Saint or Devotee's hermitage in this land of mundane and carnal desires. He knew that Asuras were skilled at changing guises and so was not very sure about the authenticity of the hermitage. He said to himself, "How Ravan, the extreme antagonist of God Narayan, could allow somebody to worship Him in Lanka?" In this land of illusions and temptations, one needs to be extra cautious before drawing a conclusion.

Although logic and intelligence are must before taking an action and that too, when the repercussions are matters of life and death, but in the sphere of Bhakti, the Grace of the Saints and God is the instrument. While Hanumanji was still thinking, he saw Vibhishan, the younger brother of Ravan, who was chanting the name of Lord Ram coming out from the hermitage. That hermitage was actually the home of Vibhishan. The love that flowed from the chanting made Hanumanji believe that Vibhishan is no evil but a great Saint and Devotee of Lord Ram.

The relation of Hanumanji and Vibhishan is very different. Both of them considered the other one as a greater Saint and servant of Lord Ram.

Hanumanji believes that it is still easy to practice devotion or Bhakti in a favorable place and time. But for Vibhishan, in Lanka and especially in these times, it was almost impossible to practie Bhakti of Ram. He couldn't even imagine the existence of a Saint at such a place. But there he witnessed Vibhishan chanting Ram-Naam and so he concluded that there could be no one as great Devotee as Vibhishan. He immediately said to himself that only by taking the help of such a Saint, he could reach Mother Sita, the Goddess of Bhakti.

On the other hand, after seeing Hanumanji, Vibhishan felt that that day he had finally met a great Saint. One who can cross the ocean, face all lethal challenges and problems, to deliver Lord Ram's message to Lady Sita, cannot be an ordinary Being but the greatest Devotee of Lord Siya-Ram. Both of them came face–to-face and chanted Ram-Naam together. Both of them had already surrendered to the divinity of Ram-Naam. Vibhishan is the symbol of meek devotees and Hanumanji is the symbol of courage and faith in devotees.

With the union of meekness and faith, divine nectar of joy and love flowed in the hearts of both the devotees. With the arrival of faith in the life of meek, Vibhishan was assured that now, he too can attain the lotus feet of Lord Ram. Vibhishan asked Hanumanji, that being an Asura and brother of Ravan, will Lord Ram trust him? To which Hanumanji replied, "When a wild and lowly monkey like him, whom people don't even like to look at, can become eligible for Lord Ram's Grace, then this doubt must not arise in your mind." After getting the location and the way to reach Mother Sita from Vibhishan, Hanumanji got excited. He after bidding bye to Vibhishan, left to complete his mission. Vibhishan sighed in happiness. Finally, the time has come. End of Ravan has begun. And now, Vibhishan will be able to meet Lord Ram in Whose lotus feet he had surrendered his everything.

Whenever seekers are lost in the tunnel of darkness,
Hanumanji gives hope, courage, faith and alertness.

Chapter 5.6

The Grass-Blade or 'Tinka': Thrashing of Ravan

Princess Sita, I will give you everything, become my wife,
willfully,
O fool! save your life and surrender to Lord Ram,
unconditionally.

As per the directions given by Vibhishan, Hanumanji reached Ashok Vatika, the place in Lanka where Ravan had kept Mother Sita. Hiding behind the bush and looking at Mother, he was thinking, "How do I approach Her? How can I make Her to trust me?" While Hanumanji was figuring this out, he saw Ravan with his queens and guards entering the Ashok Vatika. The evil King of Lanka was wearing beautiful gold ornaments to evoke attraction in Lady Sita. By bringing along the entourage, he wanted to prove that every princess, who he desired for, had surrendered to him and had become his wife and that too willfully. And so Lady Sita should also follow the same footsteps. This was actually a full blown demonstration of wealth and desires. But the foolish Asura didn't realize that this time with whom he is dealing..

Mother Sita, the Goddess of Creation and the beloved of Lord Ram had the power to burn out, not just Lanka but the whole world with just in one blink. She is 'Love' and not 'Destruction'. She is 'Tolerance' and not 'Retaliation'. She is 'Mercy' and not 'Punishment'. We, the servants and the devotees, beg for 'Purity' of mind and self from Her.But an idiot like Ravan instead of worshipping, tries to lure Her to fulfill his carnal desires. Well, so is the nature of the wicked. In the company of the virtuous, the wicked ones appear to be doing some good endeavors, but the dirt inside their head doesn't get cleaned easily.

Actually, the most regretful and unfortunate thing about Ravan was that even after possessing the most magnificent things, this fool could never utilize them wisely. Even after attaining the Grace of Great Lord Shiva, he stupidly asks for immortality instead of His most sought Bhakti. Likewise, even after coming in close proximity to the Goddess of Bhakti Mother Sita, instead of surrendering in Her lotus feet, he wants to compel Her to move as per his accordance, and for that he tries to use decisive and crafty tactics.

Believing himself as a great scholar, he tries to show off his negotiation skills. He says to Lady Sita, "You are both beautiful and intelligent. An intelligent person makes a decision only after considering the pros and cons. Ask yourself, what use is this beauty of? Is it to be burned in the Fire of Tapasya? You are born in a prosperous and grand family, but unfortunately you got married to a wrong person, who doesn't value you. Why else had he brought you along in the wild forests? I respect your beauty. There is a palace of gold just for you. Your husband is incapable of even hunting and bringing a tender gold deer to you. This whole Lanka is built of gold. All this can be yours. But you should also know this, not only I can be caring and liberal, but I can also be brutal and ruthless whenever I need to. This whole world bows down in front of my muscle power. If you don't accept me, I will have to destroy you. For the one you weep day and night, is no match in front of me. If He had been worried for you, he would have reached Lanka by this time. Definitely, He had forgotten you and must have gotten involved with another female. In this situation, there is no point in wasting your life. And so, you must accept my proposal. All my wives including Queen Mandodari will be at your service."

The daughter of the Sage King Janak, daughter-in-law of the Mighty Ruler Dasaratha and wife of the Master of the Universe, Lady Sita who was silent so far, now replied, "Listen, O ten-headed monster, can a lotus flower ever prosper in the glow of a fire-fly? Carve this in your heart, you have no idea what Lord Ram's arms are like. O wretch, you abducted me off at a time when there was none by my side and yet you don't feel ashamed, O vile and impudent rogue! Lord Ram is the Sun and you are a worm that glows in the darkness of night. My Lord's arms are lovely as strings of blue lotuses. Hear this now, my solemn vow, you demon, either that arm or this sword in your hand will have my neck and nothing else."

She then picked a Grass-blade and held it between Herself and Ravan. To take the shield of a grass-blade or 'Tinka' by Lady Sita appears to be very strange. Ravan would have thought to himself, what good would this grass-blade be of? But Lady Sita knew the significance of the grass-blade. It was the same 'Tinka' which Lord Ram transformed into Brahmastra, the most lethal weapon the world had ever known and in punishment shot it at Jayant for his misbehavior towards Her. No entity in this whole universe could save Jayant from that grass-blade and ultimately, he begged mercy from Lord Ram and saved his life.

Her message for Ravan was, "This grass-blade can destroy you now. Knowing the might of Lord Ram and the story of Jayant, surrender at once and seek mercy for your sins. The ever-compassionate Lord will forgive you." Hanumanji who was witnessing the whole incident wanted to come out and attack Ravan, but his first priority was to deliver the message of the Lord to the Mother and so he waited.

The lovers of Lord Ram, for the sake of just one recitation of the name 'RAM' can discard all the pleasures of the world at once. What to say when everyone knows that Mother Sita is the dearest to Lord Ram? Nothing surprising to see, that for Her all the riches and gold of Lanka is like a grass-blade. King Dasaratha gave away his life for his son. To lure his daughter-in-law is sheer stupidity.

Point is that the one who is a true devotee of Lord Ram, who seeks His love, doesn't care for anything in the world. No temptation of wealth or fame or power can divert his path. He gives no value to it. And Lord Ram too reciprocates the love of devotees equally, in fact much more. Once the Being takes His refuge, then with the Grace of Lord even a grass-blade becomes a lethal weapon and protects the devotee. This is the assurance of Lord Ram. And this, Mother Sita proves by thrashing Ravan with a grass-blade. He, who calls himself the master of the Three Lokas, couldn't dare to even come closer to Her. Goswami Tulsidas says that for the Beings nothing should be more valuable than surrendering in the lotus feet of Lord Siya-Ram.

Chapter 5.7

The Declaration of Yogini Trijita

In Lanka, there was a pious Asur-Devotee,
Whose heart was filled with Lord Ram's divinity.
She assembled others and spoke about her dream,
Surrender to Sita and She is Entity-Supreme.

After being thrashed and scolded by Goddess Sita, the shamefaced Ravan left but ordered the Asuri-women guarding Sita to frighten Her, so that She agrees to his proposal. There was anger filled in Ravan against Lady Sita. Being insulted and thrashed in front of all his wives, he was embarrassed and agitated. He had also faked a sword attack on Lady Sita, but taking Queen Mandodari's insistence that not to do such a dastardly act and also taking that as an excuse, he put his sword down. Well actually, he knew that if he had tried attacking Goddess Sita, he would have been destroyed then and there.

It's not wrong to term Ravan a gluttonous dog, who just to satisfy his hunger, sticks his mouth here and there. And on being kicked away, shamelessly comes back again and again. This is also exactly the state of human mind-ego, which is greedy and shameless, doesn't have self-respect and keeps on sticking its mouth like a stray dog. The desire for wealth, power and name is the food of this egoic dog. And the funny part is that the herd of gluttonous dogs too gets inspired, in fact making the most shameless one as their leader. And when someday, the leader is able to grab a piece of flesh from the drain, the others applaud for his achievement. It is sounding derogatory, but this is actually the state of today's immoral people.

Ravan tries to prove that by tolerating the thrashing by Lady Sita, he is being gracious but actually it is not patience but priggishness. If somebody wants to call the stray dog who after being shooed away multiple times, as tolerant, then yes Ravan is also tolerant one. The truth is that every clever gluttonous Being puts up the mask of tolerance and patience. He too had this hope inside him that someday he will attain his desired object. Some Beings are born with this self-impertinence and Ravan was the flag-bearer of those ones.

Before leaving, Ravan orders to frighten Lady Sita, so that She Herself comes to him and accepts him, else he announces that he will kill Her after a month. His Asuri-women slaves wore an intimidating guise and tried to frighten Lady Sita. The foolish Ravan did not understand the fragrance of Bhakti or devotion and wanted to force Her to act as per his expectations. And if Bhakti is not fulfilling the cravings, then She is of no use and so he shows his resolution to destroy Her. On the other hand, Hanumanji who was witnessing the whole incident from behind the bush felt this as another Leela or divine act orchestrated by Lord Ram. But there was another great devotee of Lord Ram in Ashok Vatika and her name was Trijita.

Vibhishan, Mandodari and Malyavan got the courage to speak against Ravan only after Hanumanji had burnt Lanka. But Trijita is an incomparable and true believer of Lord Ram who spoke against Ravan and bravely stood against Ravan's order before the Lanka-Dahan (burning of Lanka). She stood like a mighty wall and didn't allow the demon-women to even come closer to Mother Sita. Such devotee of lion-heart is actually one in million. And therefore, Princess Sita too gave her the same reverence which She had given to Her Mother Sunena and Mother-in-law Kaushalya, only. Divinity personified as Lady Sita called Trijita as Mother, again and again.

In the extremely troublesome days, the melodious note of Faith resonated. Trijita had a vision and she very much believed it to be true. She, standing in the premises of Ravan, fearlessly mocked Ravan in front of others. She said to other Asuri-women who are asked to frighten Lady Sita by Ravan, "If you want your good, just serve Lady Sita. In my vision, I saw a mighty Vanar of golden color, single handedly putting the city of Lanka on fire. He also destroyed the huge Asur army of Lanka. Ravan was sitting naked on a donkey with a garland of mutilated skulls and arms around his neck, and was moving towards South, the direction of Kaal or Death. King Vibhishan is sitting on the throne of Lanka. I am totally sure and telling you all that very soon this vision is going to be true."

Trijita symbolizes 'Ritambhra' which means a Devotee in whom no other thought or Vritti can evolve except Truth. Well, every Being is a reflection of Supreme God and therefore, the qualities of Truth, Fearlessness and Omnipresence should also be there in every Being. These attributes are indeed in each one of us but because of our mismanaged mind-ego, we ourselves put barriers in experiencing them. The one who sincerely indulges himself in spiritual practices becomes the Yogi and witnesses these divine qualities as he had become one with Supreme consciousness.

Trijita was a Yogini who had by meditating on the lotus feet of Lord Ram had attained the higher state of consciousness. She had attained the divine vision where the lines that demarcate awake-state, dream-state and sleep-state and also past, present and future get erased. And therefore, she could confidently and fearlessly announce loudly about the end of Ravan. This was a warning from her to those who don't believe in her vision that this is for sure going to happen, and if they want to save themselves, then they must surrender in the lotus feet of Great Sita, the Mother of Universe.

"What you believe as true is a dream,
What you think of as a dream is reality.
Dreams appear to be true in present,
But in the morning they are forgotten.
But the dream that I am telling to you
It was true yesterday, today and tomorrow." - Trijita

These words filled with the power of purity and truth influenced the Asuri-women that they immediately dropped their guises and weapons, and prostrated in the lotus feet of Mother Sita. Goswami Tulsidas wants to tell us that what the Being believes in doesn't matter, the truth, that Siya-Ram is the Supreme Entity of the entire creation, cannot be challenged. And therefore, for your own good, give up away the doubts and queries and just take refuge in the lotus feet of Lord Siya-Ram.

Chapter 5.8

Bhakt Trijita: The Light at the end of Tunnel

O mother! Please set a pyre with me in it and put it on fire.
O dear! Be patient, on His way is the Supreme Highflyer.

The purpose of Lord Siya-Ram's Human Leela is to enjoy the earthly feelings, emotions and relationships. But more importantly they want Beings to learn about an ideal life. Trijita managed to set things in favor of Lady Sita but the storm in Her heart and the pain that She was feeling remained as it is. Lady Sita was feeling very low so much that life felt like a burden to Her and in those agonizing moments, She got desperate to end Her life. For this, she looked towards Trijita and insisted, "O mother! You helped me in difficult times, now do one more favor. Set a pyre and as soon as I sit inside, put it on fire. Please don't take my words in any other sense. Every living body gets destroyed one day. But by purposefully ending this body, my love for Lord Ram will be proved as true in the eyes of the world. It's better to end this life rather than hearing the traumatizing words of Ravan".

After being cheated by Ravan guised as a Saint, Lady Sita got so disturbed and pained that now She was not able to trust anybody. Probably, She had thought that just to save Her, Trijita had made up her dream story. Also, in Trijita's story, the part of a Vanar appeared totally fictitious to Sita, because yet She was not aware about Lord Ram's friendship with any Vanar. She might not believe the story but She had found love and care in Trijita. A mother to please her child tells fictitious stories and for this, can anybody call the mother a liar? Similarly, Trijita out of pure love for Sita, spoke her dream story to protect Her and also to give Her hope. But, Lady Sita had lost all Her hopes and instead of dying after a month at the dirty hands of Ravan, She wanted to end Her life today.

But, the great Asur-Saint Trijita had understood the pessimism in Lady Sita. She also understood that words cannot pacify Her at this hour.

And therefore, she didn't say a word except for replying, "Dear princess, it's impossible to find fire in the night." Trijita meant that even when a corpse is not cremated in the night then how is it possible that what Lady Sita wanted to do can be done?. Trijita meant to warn Lady Sita not to get trapped in this illusionary night of Lanka. That is, they must wait till this night passes by. And then, by tomorrow morning something so grand is going to happen that Lady Sita would awake from this dream of hopelessness. It appears that Trijita already knew that Hanumanji was around and therefore, her dream would surely come true. But then, revealing this truth to Lady Sita would spoil the meeting of Hanumanji with Her. And therefore, she quickly excused herself.

Ramayan is an eternal and legendary battle between Light and Darkness. On one side is nocturnal Ravan and on the other side is Scion of Suryavansh Lord Ram. Ending one's own life would mean accepting the victory of darkness. The daughter-in-law of Suryavansh cannot let the resolution of Darkness come true. She got to live to see the end of Darkness and spread of Light in Lanka.

Night brings depressive emotions and a sense of isolation. The deep darkness of night instills fear in the heart of Beings. It is seen that in the night, illness and suffering escalates. The psychological reason for it is that in the day time, the individual is surrounded by his well wishers. Their wishes and care elevates the mood and environment. The Sun light charges up the spirit of the individual and brings hope, whereas in the nights, the individual finds himself all alone. The despair increases and he loses patience. But, no matter how dark and depressive the night is, in the dawn, the Sun rays envelop the world and darkness elopes.

Lanka is a land of nocturnal and Ravan is the master of darkness. He had that ability of demolishing hope and positivity in others through his speech and actions. Princess of Mithila, Sita was seeing darkness in all four directions. She had lost all hope and optimism. But, Trijita could see the Light of the Dawn arriving very soon. She was pretty sure that tomorrow's morning was going to end the pain and bring tremendous hope back. And therefore, she insisted that Lady Sita must wait till tomorrow and not get impatient. Ultimately, Trijita's faith won.

Later Hanumanji had said to Goddess Sita - "Mother! With the rise of Sun 'Ram', the dark army of demons will get destroyed." Trijita truly loved Sita like her daughter and said that you have called me Mother and then you are insisting for fire. Can there be such a cruel mother who will agree to her daughter's immolation? Trijita sensed that now her role is up for the time being and so she left. Probably, she knew that now Hanumanji will arrive in the scene of Lanka and will turn the tables. The mountain-like unwavering and mighty faith of Trijita is an assurance and declaration to all Beings that whoever surrenders in the lotus feet of Lord Ram cannot be troubled by evil darkness. Just two things are needed - Faith and Patience.

Chapter 5.9

RAM MUDRIKA: The Ring of Lord Ram

Hanumanji seeing the right moment, dropped the Lord's ring,
Sitaji caught it and believed it as fire, which she was wanting.

From the time of Ravan's arrival to till the departure of Trijita, Hanumanji had to be just a mute spectator hiding behind the bush. Whatever was happening was painfully intolerable for him. In front of the greatest and strongest warrior that this world has ever seen, Hanumanji, an evil Asura Ravan had dared to be rude with Mother Sita and also tried to attack Her. What could be more defeating and insulting for Hanumanji? Hearing the wicked statements of Ravan, the fury inside Hanumanji was bursting like a volcano but remembering the orders of Lord Ram, he remained quiet. Probably, for the first time his patience was tested to such an extreme level. Ultimately, he was successful in that test. Things happen at the right time and at the right pace, and this fact was well accepted by Hanumanji. Also, he had a doubt that if he had intervened in between hurriedly, then it would have led to war with Ravan resulting in the end of Ravan and this outcome would have spoiled the purpose of Lord Ram's human Leela or earthly drama.

Under these circumstances, his decision to wait was perfect. Though later Hanumanji said to Mother Sita that letting Ravan speak at that hour and not stopping him, is a black spot on his face and tomorrow he would slay these demons and wash that black spot with their blood. And yet, there was another perspective which blossomed in the heart of Hanumanji and that was the play of Lord Ram's Grace or 'Kripa'.

Though the end of Lady Sita was in favor of Mandodari because Princess Sita was in a way replacing her position in the eyes of Ravan yet the way Mandodari stopped her husband at the right moment was actually divine intervention. Then, the presence of Trijita in that cluster of Asuri-women who were selected to harass Lady Sita was nothing less than a miracle. Hanumanji was also very surprised, overhearing the dream of Trijita wherein a Vanar would burn Lanka. Lord Ram had sent him to just deliver His message and return back, but Trijita's dream was giving different signals to Hanumanji.

He witnessed how the cruel hearts of Asuri-women transformed after hearing Trijita's dream and therefore, he was taking her dream very seriously. Actually, it was this dream that inspired Hanumanji for action and destruction of demons and Lanka. Was it the play of Karma or the Lord's Leela or the Trijita's dream or might be all? Whatever may be the cause, but Hanumanji did much more than what was asked to do by Lord Ram. However, later Lord Ram was very pleased with Hanumanji's brave deeds.

After Trijita left, the question in front of Hanumanji was how to approach Mother Sita and in what form? She was so depressed that She wanted to end Her life. A small mistake in dealing with this sensitive situation could lead to unwanted repercussions. Hanumanji could not take that risk. He saw Her emotionally asking 'Ashok' tree, under which shade she was living, to give Her fire so that She could immolate Herself. Hanumanji felt that actually what Mother is seeking is something else and that he was carrying with him, the 'Ram-Naam'.

In all four Sat-Treta-Dvapar-Kali Yuga, in Past, Present, Future and in Heaven, Hell, Earth, that to which every Being surrenders to and looks up to for refuge and attains peace is the name of Ram or RAM-Naam.

The fire that Mother Sita was asking was actually established in this Ram-Naam. Not just fire but the soul of all elements that is water, air, earth, sky and all celestial bodies that is Sun and Moon is established in this three-letter word - RAM. The signet ring which Lord Ram had given to Hanumanji to give to Princess Sita had RAM, embedded in it. Hanumanji climbed up the tree in a small monkey form and dropped that dazzling ring.

Hanumanji made sure that the drop-timing was perfect so that the ring must fall right in the hands of Mother Sita and not on the ground. And so it happened. Seeing a bright object dropping from the tree, Mother confused it with fire and caught it in in Her hands. Seeing this as another act of Grace, Hanumanji with tears in eyes thought that the Symbol of Bhakti or devotion, that is, the Ring is now safe in the hands of the Goddess of Devotion or Bhakti-Devi, Mother Sita. The period of sorrow and suffering had ended with this moment. Now, the end of Ravan had begun. Goswami Tulsidas says that Hanumanji comes to the rescue of the one, who surrenders in the lotus feet of Lord Siya-Ram. Condition is one, dependence only on RAM-Naam and nobody else.

Chapter 5.10

Mother Sita reattains Faith: Glory of Ram-Katha

Separation from Supreme gives doubts and apprehension,
Only the Faith of Hanumanji can give peace and liberation.

Goddess Sita was astounded seeing Lord Ram's Ring in Her palms. It was bewildering and at first, She was overjoyed but then she doubted, thinking, "How could this ring reach here?" Also She thought, "Has Ravan, to prove his victory, tried to throw this ring to me," but then immediately, She corrected Herself, "That day I doubted the mightiness of the Lord at Panchvati, and in consequence became a prisoner of Lanka. I am again making the same mistake. It is impossible to defeat My Invincible Ram. Probably, this ring is an illusion created by Asura? But then, even the best illusionist or magician cannot create a replica of this divine ring. I don't understand."

An illusion or magical trick can impress lesser intelligent ones, but people with higher intelligence, don't get impressed easily. Mother Sita is the cause and effect, Creator-Preserver-Destroyer of this whole Srishti or Creation. She, for Her love for mortal Beings, is playing an earthly drama or Leela. At Panchavati, She got tempted on seeing the golden deer and didn't act wisely. But that was a part of Her Leela. She intentionally did like that, as per the directions of Lord Ram, so that their Leela can move in the right direction. Ravan, a great illusionist, can recreate a thing which could confuse others. But as soon as it comes in the hand of Mother Sita, it reveals its truth.

There are certain contradictory statements in this incident which are actually confusing for the reader. On one hand, She is playing Leela and wants to immolate Herself, while on the other hand, She knows the truth and the future and has absolute faith in Lord Ram. Also, on one hand, she is submerged in the tears of pain and doubts, while on the other hand, She knows that Lord is insurmountable and the end of Ravan is nearing soon. An actor has to be very careful, the acting must appear natural and only then, the actor can expect applause from the spectators. Lord Siya-Ram are like actors who are playing Leela or drama on the stage of this world.

Joy, sorrow, ignorance and knowledge are the attributes of mortal Beings and not of the Creator Herself. If Mother Sita is enacting them, then this means that She is just addressing the problems of human beings through Her Leela. It is because of Moha or attachment with the physical self and it's identities, that the Being forgets his real true self and believes himself as a prisoner. The egoic traits like the Asuri-women which were surrounding Sitaji troubles and frighten Her. The temptation of power, pleasure and gold entraps the Ravan that lives in the mind-ego of Beings, in materialism. All these various facets of human life were reflected by Sitaji's Leela during Her stay as a prisoner in the Ashok Vatika of Lanka.

In this perspective, the role of Hanumanji is that of a spiritual preceptor or 'Acharya'. The ring embedded with RAM is a reminder of the existence of Omnipresent God. A seeker seeing and understanding the purpose of the ring, soon realizes the truth of Soul and Supreme. And thereafter, the illusion or Maya fails to confuse his mind.

Hanumanji understood Mother Sita's confusion and immediately, began singing the eternal Legend of Lord Ram or Ram-Katha. Such is the beauty and charisma of Ram-Katha that Mother Sita forgetting everything, got mesmerized in the divinity of Lord Ram. So far nothing, not even consolation of Trijita could pacify Sitaji but the divine melody of Ram-Katha by the greatest Bhakt Hanumanji, immediately relieved Her suffering and reinstated faith and peace.

There is no doubt that a mother sees only the beauty and good qualities in her child but she too gets real happiness when others appreciate her child. Sometimes, we too are not able to value our near-dear one. But when we hear appreciation from an outsider, only then, we feel proud and happy for our near-dear one. Sitaji had absolute love and faith in Lord Ram and She tried to pass Her days of suffering in Lanka in His memories and chanting Ram-Naam, but she couldn't relish the nectar of Lord Ram's Bhakti. It was when Hanumanji along with name, qualities and stories brought the light of intense faith or 'Vishvas' and 'Shraddha' to Her, She could re-attain the forgotten peace. Devotion or Bhakti has to be unified with Faith or Shraddha and only then, the seeker can experience divine bliss.

Listening to the glory of Lord Ram through the purest voice of Hanumanji, Sitaji regained Her strength and joy. While staying in the unfavorable environment of Lanka for ten months, the sprouting of apprehensions and doubts are natural. Hanumanji eliminated this skepticism. When Sitaji hears how much Lord Ram is impatient and eager to get some news of Her, She feels immense satisfaction and joy. There can be doubts but truth stands tall. Nobody can separate Lord Siya-Ram. Hanumanji is forever available for those unfortunate ones who have doubts in the Supremacy of Lord Siya-Ram. Goswami Tulsidas says that anybody at anytime can learn from Hanumanji, that the only purpose of life is to surrender in the lotus feet of Lord Siya-Ram and nothing else.

Chapter 5.11

Hanumanji meets Mother Sita: Message of Lord Ram

Hanumanji gave the news that the days of suffering are over,
Lord is coming with Vanar army, for Lanka takeover.

After listening to the story of Lord Ram, on the insistence of Mother Sita, Hanumanji jumped from the tree and stood in front of Her. As soon She looked at him, She turned Her face on him. She had expected a grand personality of the speaker, of such a beautiful and wondrous Ram-Katha and Hanumanji didn't fit in Her expectations. An animal that too a small monkey could be the orator of 'Ram-Katha', seemed impossible to Her. Yet She asked, "When and how did the Vanar species get together with Manushya society?" Hanumanji then narrated Her the story of Lord Ram's friendship with Sugriv and the Vanars.

Story of the Lord is incomplete without the story of His devotees. Just cooking and serving exotic dishes is not good enough. It is complete only when the person who consumes those dishes smiles out of satisfaction, then the purpose of those exotic dishes is fulfilled. The true consumers of the nectar of Lord's story are who else but the devotees. Therefore, without the harmony of Lord and Devotee, the Story of Ram or Ram-Katha is incomplete. After realizing the purity of Hanumanji, Mother Sita got convinced that he is indeed the greatest devotee of Her Lord Ram.

Throughout the narration, Hanumanji kept on highlighting how much Lord Ram loved and missed Lady Sita. And that, how much Lord is impatient to know about the whereabouts of Her, the proof of which is Hanumanji himself, who had risked his life for Lord's work or 'Ram-Kaj'. And yet Mother Sita sarcastically commented that Lord Ram had totally forgotten Her.

This sarcasm is beyond logical thinking and appears to be inappropriate coming from Mother Sita, but then it is filled with the nectar of love and affinity. We don't think much about saying things for the one who we truly consider as our own. And this whole cosmos is the witness of Oneness of Lord Siya-Ram. Sometimes, one wants to hear the same thing repeatedly because of the joy associated with those words. And then, to get it heard again and again, some or the other excuses are given. Mother Sita just wanted to hear Lord Ram's feelings for Her again and again. Her complaint for Him forgetting Her, was actually another excuse, to make Hanumanji narrate it again. The nectar of love is such that its thirst in the heart of the lover is never satisfied.

Mother Sita then asked Hanumanji the well being of Lord Ram-Laxman. Hanumanji replied that they are perfectly fine, but Lord Ram is sad because of Her sadness. Hanumanji spoke to the Mother,

"Lord Ram has said that, *Ever since I have been separated from you,*
Everything to me has become its very reverse, eyes have lost their view.
The fresh and tender leaves on the trees look like flames of fire,
And the nights appear to consume the cosmos entire.
Beds of lotuses are like spears planted on the ground,
While rain-clouds, pour boiling oil all around.

Those that were friendly before, have now become tormenting,
The cool, soft and fragrant breezes are now like snakes, hissing,
One's agony is assuaged to some extent by sharing it with others, frankly,
But there is no one who will understand the pain in my heart, sadly.

The reality about the chord of love that binds you and me is known to my mind alone,

And my mind is not with me, for it abides with you and not in my spirit or body zone."

Hanumanji then spoke his thoughts,

"Had the Hero of Raghu had any news about You,
He would not have waited and had reached You.

The moment Ram's arrows make their appearance like the Sun,
The Asura species like the shadows of night will find no place to run.

O Mother, wait patiently for some days more, till Lord arrives with His

Vanar army,

Trust the words of this servant; none can face His wrath, in this eternity."

As he uttered these words, his voice was choked with emotion and his eyes filled with tears. While talking with Mother Sita, Hanumanji was standing in the form of a small monkey. Hearing the declaration that Lord Ram will come with Vanars and defeat Asura, Mother Sita was surprised. She felt that this little Vanar is actually an innocent child and he doesn't know the mightiness of the demons. She very softly asked him, "Son, all are Vanars, pygmies like you? Demons are huge and ferocious. I don't understand how Vanars will be able to face them."

Hanumanji's heart, after hearing Mother calling him as son, danced with joy but his face was still expressionless. Mother then blessed him, "Let Lord Ram love you a lot." On hearing these words, Hanumanji's happiness knew no bounds. It is always the devotee who is desperately seeking Lord's love but when Lord Himself loves His devotee, then what can be more rewarding for the devotee. This is an ultimate example of 'Nirbhara-Bhakti' or 'devotion of absolute surrender'. This means that now the initiative of spiritual practice or 'Sadhana' is less on the seeker or 'Sadhak' and more on the sought or 'Sadhya'. A devotee is like a kitten, totally dependent on its mother-cat. This is the highest position in devotion, which Hanumanji was blessed by the Mother of Bhakti, Sita Herself.

Hanumanji then revealed his real form which was as colossal as a mountain of gold, terrible in battle, possessing great mightiness and full of valor. Mother Sita now took comfort in Her heart, the days of suffering have ended and now the destruction of Ravan has started. Assurance of Hanumanji of the arrival of Lord Ram, overwhelmed the Goddess of Bhakti. Goswami Ṭulsidas says that whoever has devoted this life in the lotus feet of Lord Siya-Ram, first becomes the beloved of Hanumanji.

Chapter 5.12

Challenge of Hanumanji: Disruption of 'Ashok Vatika'

Mother! There are nice juicy fruits around and I am very hungry,
Son! Fill your stomach, but be careful of the demons guarding the trees.

After being blessed by Mother Sita, Hanumanji looked around and spoke, "Mother, I am very hungry and there are nice juicy fruits on the trees around." The motherly affection flowed in Goddess Sita's heart. There is nothing more troubling for a mother, who cannot feed her hungry child. There are fruits that can satiate hunger but Mother Sita is also worried about the safety of Hanumanji as many ferocious demons were guarding the orchard. She knew that this orchard, that is Ashok Vatika, is very dear to Ravan. On seeing him eating the fruits, the guards would definitely attack him. She shared Her concern with him, to which Hanumanji replied, "Mother, if I have your permission, then I am not concerned about these demons." Mother Sita was pleased and confident, and so replied, "My dear son, keeping the lotus feet of Lord Ram in your heart, proceed to satisfy your hunger."

Hanumanji entered that part of the vast orchard, from where Mother Sita could not see the violence which was going to happen. The mighty Hanumanji then started eating the fruits but along with that he also began uprooting the trees, thereby spoiling the orchard. This may appear an act of indiscipline but there was a reason. By disrupting the orchard, Hanumanji was directly challenging Ravan in his own territory, declaring the unparalleled strength in the messenger of Lord Ram. A true devotee of Ram is fearless. To wake the sleepy ignorants, sometimes just the dialogues are not only enough but the action is also needed.

After, Hanumanji thought that if he returns quietly just like he came, then the vision of Trijita would prove to be false and the fear which it has/had created in the lady-demons who were guarding Mother Sita would evaporate and then they will again trouble Her. Therefore, to prove Trijita's dream as true and to ensure the safety of Mother Sita, Hanumanji decided to show his power.

The very beautiful Ashok Vatika is the symbol of 'Moha' or Enchantment. Ravan believed that the temptation of this grand orchard would change Lady Sita's heart and She would agree to his demands. But that fool didn't realize that what on earth can influence the Goddess of Prosperity. The one who is surrendered to the lotus feet of Lord Ram cannot be tempted by anything.

Hanumanji the epitome of 'Vairagya' or Stoicism attains the best fruits in this orchard of enchantment with the blessing of Mother Sita. He satisfies his hunger and uproots the trees, disrupting Ashok Vatika, the precious jewel of the crown of Ravan. For materialistic worldly Beings, it is not possible to defeat the strike of enchantment. But here is Hanumanji, who has all 'Siddhi' or supernatural powers and thus, all Yog or spiritual merits bow down in front of him. Goswami Tulsidas says that what can influence the one like Hanumanji who is surrendered in the lotus feet of Lord Ram.

Chapter 5.13

Meghnad Vs Hanumanji: 'Kaam' Vs 'Bhakti'

An ignorant one suffers because of desperation and obsession,
The awakened one flourishes because of his love and devotion.

The havoc created by Hanumanji made the Asura guards at 'Ashok Vaatika' to attack him. Some of them perished there and then, while some got badly hurt and few were able to escape. The escaped ones rushed to Ravan and informed him about the disruption of Hanumanji. Ravan sent his son Akshay Kumar to deal with the situation and he too got killed. The demise of his son broke Ravan's strength and then he asked his son Meghnad, the great warrior, to not kill Hanumanji but to trap him and to bring him. Meghnad was the greatest warrior of Lanka. He was renowned in the world for his victories in battle fields. Those who didn't fear facing Ravan, were also not confident to face Meghnad. The 'Swarg-Lok' that is the abode of Devta clan would shiver hearing the name of Meghnad.

The terror of Hanumanji and the demise of Akshay Kumar had shaken the core of Lanka. The citizens feared for their life. In such circumstances, Ravan could only trust Meghnad. He had absolute faith in the mightiness and skills of his son, Meghnad. Never did he fear for his courageous son. Ravan was totally confident of him. Meghnad himself always enjoyed defeating enemies and bringing them in chains in front of his father. He was a great son, actually a devotee of his father, Ravan. He desired to see the whole world bowing to his father. More than his own success, he had committed his life for the success of Ravan. His 'Pitra-Bhakti' or 'devotion for father' was unmatched. Everyone in Ravan's family had criticized him for abducting Princess Sita or 'Sita-Haran', except for Meghnad. Though he realized the wrong doing of his father and yet he stood with him till the end. War between Hanumanji and Meghnad was a clash between two great sons. Hanumanji is the devotee-son of Lord Ram, and Meghnad who was devoted to his father Ravan. Both of them are great devotees and both of them are great warriors.

Meghnad entered the battle arena of 'Ashok Vatika' on his chariot. Hanumanji, seeing him coming, immediately understood that this one is not going to be easy. He roared aggressively and broke Meghnad's chariot. The defeat of Meghnad had begun. The chariot of righteousness or 'Dharam-Rath' which Hanumanji was riding on was invincible. Lord Ram had taught that the real warrior is the one who defeats his inner enemies that are unrighteous thoughts, ideas and habits. And Hanumanji was, on this parameter, also the greatest one. The name 'MAHAVEER' given to Hanumanji was not just a formality; he is indeed the greatest and bravest one that this world has ever seen.

Meghnad got shocked with Hanumanji's attack. Before he could regain his senses, Hanumanji had slayed many of his troops. Now, dropping the weapons, both Meghnad and Hanumanji began arm wrestling. But this act of bravery again costed Meghnad very dearly. In one punch of Hanumanji, he fell flat on the ground and fainted. Hanumanji had the chance to kill him right there and then, but this was against his righteousness. He jumped and sat on a tree branch, giving him time to get up. Meghnad got up and realized that he cannot defeat Hanumanji. He then used the most powerful weapon he possessed, that is 'Brahamastra' or the weapon of Brahma. Though Hanumanji had the power to fail Brahamastra, yet he accepted to be hit by it, so as not to be disrespectful to God Brahma. Everybody is always very eager to safeguard their honor. But to ensure others' honor are the qualities of just two, Lord and Saint, that is Lord Ram and Saint Hanuman.

After being hit by Brahamastra, Hanumanji faked unconsciousness and fell from the tree, but it was very clever of him to fall where the demon soldiers were standing. And in this fall, surprisingly, Hanumanji didn't get hurt at all. However, many of the demons got crushed under his humongous body and perished.

Meghnad is the symbol of 'Kaam' or passion that is desire and the effort to fulfill the desire. The creation happens through 'Kaam' and that is why, although 'Kaam' is undesirable, yet is unavoidable. 'Kaam' is essentially in the core of every living being and that means the wicked 'Meghnad' element resides too, in every Being. Quite often the 'Vritti' or instinct of 'Kaam' or intense passion hits the human being and the one who doesn't know how to deal with it gets trapped in it. Human-Being then without assessing right or wrong, indulges in the acts of mundane desires, bodily comforts and pleasures, at the cost of others. Initially, this does give enjoyment but ultimately this act of 'Kaam' brings sorrow and suffering. This world is full of examples where 'Kaam' or ambitious individuals had achieved a lot but didn't care about righteousness and others' interest and then had faced a miserable end. They fell from so-called great heights and were never able to rise again.

After being hit by Brahamastra, Hanumanji too appeared to fall but he is a Holy Devotee and as per the Principles of Bhakti, nothing can topple a true devotee. His fall was actually intended to crush Asura soldiers. Though hit by passion, the devotee crushes the wrongful consequences signified by 'Asura soldiers'. This means that when the 'Kaam' or an evil tries to attack a 'Bhakt' then the 'Kaam' does get momentary pleasure of success, but ultimately he has to face the lethal consequences. On the other hand, unfavorable becomes favorable for the devotee of Lord Ram. And there are many examples, not only in Ramayan but also in recent times. Grace of Lord Ram or 'Ram-Kripa' chases an intelligent-knowledgeable-devotee or 'Viveki-Gyani-Bhakt', epitome of this is Hanumanji.

Meghnad used the Brahamastra and got satisfied with the victory. But this joy ended pretty soon. And then, he had to pay a very heavy price. The same night, the whole of Lanka got burnt by the fury and fire of Hanumanji. Hanumanji and Sundarkand is the proof that the one who has surrendered in the lotus feet of Lord Siya-Ram is invincible and unconquerable.

Chapter 5.14

Hanumanji counsels Ravan: Glory of Lord Ram

Sense of Doership leads to sorrow and arrogance,
Lord's Ram is the source of every movement and occurrence.

Hanumanji allowed Asura to chain him and march him to Ravan's court. The highly perceptive Hanumanji wanted to observe the Lanka city so that later this strategic information could be used at the war time. He also wanted to have a word with Ravan, and therefore, he decided to become a prisoner. Having no idea of what lies ahead, the demon-citizens of Lanka rushed to Ravan's court to enjoy the spectacle. Ravan's superb glory was beyond description but Hanumanji remained unfazed. Ravan laughed seeing a Vanar but the next moment got serious thinking about the slaughter of his son Akshay Kumar by Hanumanji. Ravan thundered, "Who are you and by whose order have you wrought the destruction of the orchard? What, did you never hear my name? For what offence did you kill the demons? Are you not afraid of losing your life?" Thousands of Asura eyes and ears were set on Hanumanji.

Hanumanji then announced aloud, "Know, O ten-headed monster! I am the messenger of Lord Ram, who is the cause of creation, preservation and destruction; the upholder of this planet and it's life; the one who takes avatar to protect Dharma and destroy wretches like you; the one who broke Shiva's bow which you couldn't even move; the one who single-handedly killed Bali, Khar and Dushan who were superior than you in strength. It's with just a small iota of His energy that you have been able to conquer this world and you dared to abduct His beloved spouse. Surrender now and return Lady Sita. The ever compassionate Lord Ram will pardon you."

Sadistic Ravan had always enjoyed giving pain to others, but today his 'Karma' and 'Kaal' were standing in front of him in the form of Hanumanji. Today Ravan, the destroyer of civilizations, couldn't protect his own grand orchard 'Ashok-Vatika', the conqueror of Devta couldn't protect his own son and the slayer of millions couldn't save his Lanka from burning and destroying. Hanumanji, the symbol of 'Vairagya' or 'Indifference', had shown a mirror to him. But the symbol of foolish mind-ego, that is Ravan, didn't want to accept the truth. He by showing off arrogance was hiding the fear and pain of losing his son. He had not learnt the lessons of the Past and he was unable to see the threat waiting for him in the Future.

The experiences of the past are the genesis of today's joys and sorrows. With each passing moment, the Present becomes the Past and the Future becomes the Present. Nobody sees the Future, but the average Beings stupidly thinking about the uncertain future, trap themselves in the 'Worry' and 'Fear' tricks of mind-ego. Then there are some who don't want to analyze their past, present and future, and therefore, they are never ever able to improve or change. Hanumanji wanted to counsel Ravan, make him realize his mistake and help him improve himself; but Ravan lost in the illusionary Past and the Present, was not ready to take the advice.

Ravan believed that a Vanar alone cannot be so brave, and so he was impatient to know the master, with whose inspiration, Hanumanji had brought havoc in Lanka. It was beyond his comprehension that somebody who knows him can stand fearlessly like Hanumanji, in his court, where the divine entities like Indra, Kuber, Surya and more Devta shiver in fear.

Hanumanji's reply is the most prominent advice that was not only for Ravan but also for every egoic and selfish individual. "While performing action and while feeling proud of your achievement, Ravan, you must question - Is that you who is making the things to happen? Who is orchestrating every happening of your life? What is the cause of success and failure? You take pride in building structures, kingdoms, businesses and empires but you are unable to see the Supreme energy working behind the curtains which is creating and destroying innumerable entities in this infinite universe. Think, is everything happening as per the intention of the human mind? Is nature an inert entity? Can this whole concept of 'Life' and 'Death' be possible without a Conscious intelligence? You can take pride in fathering many sons and nurturing millions of people. Again, you can believe yourself as the ultimate terminator after slaying thousands of warriors. But, is your achievement stands anywhere close to the three functions of the conscious intelligence or Consciousness, that is - Creation-Preservation-Destruction that is Brahma, Vishnu and Shiva?"

"You took pride in lifting Mount Kalisa, the abode of God Shiva, but you couldn't move an inch of that old discarded bow of God Shiva at 'Sita-Swayamvar'. There have been greater evil entities that existed before you who had achieved much greater things than you. But, did, even one of them able to escape their Karma or consequences of their actions? These words are for a perceptive mind which can contemplate deeply and so if you have it, then think about your life pattern. There is only One intelligence, energy or consciousness that is working behind every action and occurrence."

"Similarly every success, action and thing which makes up a Ravan is just a reflection of that Supreme Intelligence. Who can be more untrustworthy and treacherous than you who had abducted the same energy that is Mother Sita, who has bestowed you so much? If you are an honorable and courageous warrior, then you would have challenged Lord Ram, openly. But your actions were worse than a petty burglar. And this Ravan wants the world to honor and salute him. Shame on you!"

Hanumanji concludes, "A messenger has no opinion of his own, he is just the medium of his master's thoughts. Return Mother Sita to Lord Ram and He will pardon you." That day Hanumanji showed the mirror of truth to Ravan and by speaking the glory of his master proved the depth of his devotion.

Chapter 5.15

Hanumanji punishes Lanka: Asur-ego goes up in smoke

The sadistic demons had always enjoyed torturing the weak and helpless man,
But this time, they had to pay a heavy prize by bothering the great Hanuman.

Ignoring the valuable words of Hanumanji, Ravan ordered his troops to execute the Vanar intruder. Just then, Vibhishan entered the court and reminded Ravan of political diplomacy, "Executing a messenger, even if he is of an enemy, is against the order." The courtiers who went mute after hearing Ravan's death-punishment order, now suddenly in one voice whole-heartedly supported Vibhishan's advice.

Question is why the courtiers, the shameless loyalists of Ravan, his Asur-courtiers neither utter a word nor showed pleasure on hearing the death sentence of Hanumanji but so encouragingly supported Vibhishan's advice? The destruction of 'Ashok-Vatika' the orchard, slaying of Akshay Kumar and fearlessness of Hanumanji had actually shook the core of each and every citizen of Lanka. They had so far felt that Lanka is an invincible and impenetrable gold city of Ravan where they are totally safe and secure. But, their age-old belief was disrupted that day and they were now unsure of their safety. They now believed that this Vanar will not remain quiet on his executory order and will again create havoc, also injuring and killing them. And hence, it's better not to provoke him. But they also feared Ravan and so couldn't oppose his orders. The sensible advice of Vibhishan was an opportunity for them to protect themselves and their families from the wrath of Hanumanji. Their agreement with righteousness was not out of mercy but purely out of fear.

Lord Ram is Supreme God, Mother Sita is Goddess of Creation, Hanumanji is the Saint-Messenger of God and Vibhishan is a true devotee of God. That day, Vibhishan played his devotee role aptly by rescuing the Selfless Saint, Hanumanji. But the other Asura-courtiers who symbolize the selfish instincts of mind-ego wanted to play calculative by keeping both Ravan and Hanumanji happy. Ego driven human beings are like these Asura-courtiers who live out of fear of God but also cannot discard the pleasures and security which they believe their manipulative selfishness provides them. They want to seek Lord Ram, but at the same time they don't want to discard Ravan. Their life becomes an arrangement of unlimited compromises. But there cannot be any compromise with unrighteousness and selfishness in the life of a devotee. Vibhishan didn't care for his life, let alone the pleasures and security which Lanka had given him and did not compromise with the order of Ravan.

Then there are ego driven clever Beings who seem to be adjusting and welcoming. They at times accept others' viewpoint, although it is contradictory to their own intention, just to show off their fake respect and affinity towards them. Ravan or every wicked human being lives a two-faced life. On one hand, when needed, he becomes an authoritarian, unmerciful, determined and harsh leader; while in front of his own Lanka people, he shows his caring, loving and sensitive side. But in reality, in both the cases the driving force is his selfish motives and not bravery or consideration.

Ravan wanted to demonstrate his love for his brothers. For Kumbhakaran, he had arranged luxuries so that he may sleep peacefully for six months, and also for Vibhishan, for whom he had built a temple where he can worship God Narayan peacefully. Well actually whenever needed he had used Kumbhakaran's invincible mightiness and powers to win battles. And since, Vibhishan was specially blessed by God Shiva, therefore Ravan didn't want to upset Shiva, his 'Ishta' or personal God, by troubling Vibhishan.

Ravan laughingly agreed to Vibhishan and changed his order not to execute Hanumanji but to set his tail on fire and let him go. Sadistic Ravan had always enjoyed inflicting pain on others. But this time, it was different because this time he was dealing with the Great Hanumanji. This was the last laugh in Ravan's life. Hanumanji smiled in his heart as he was up to mischief.

As the demons tried to implement Ravan's order, Hanumanji started extending his tail. Trijita's dream was actually coming true. Whatever stuff was needed to burn Lanka, Ravan himself had arranged it. The demons with cloth and oil were trying to tie the ever growing tail but were failing repeatedly. It was a funny scene. Hanumanji's sarcasm towards Ravan was,

"First measure the vastness of my tail, then think of assessing the glory of my Lord Ram. When all the resources of Lanka are insufficient to tie the tail of just one Vanar, then how can Ravan even think of challenging Lord Ram?"

But the question is, is it justifiable to punish the whole of Lanka for the crimes of one person, Ravan? Especially, when the courtiers have defended Hanumanji and saved him from capital punishment, then this destruction seemed even more unjustified. To solve this question, Hanumanji, to check the intention of Lanka citizens, observed their participation in his tail-punishment. He intentionally staged up an act of looking frightened and in pain.

The demons like a novice gambler without assessing the repercussions, participated full fledged and arranged the cloth and oil. When Hanumanji was roamed around the city as a prisoner, they made fun of him, hurled abuses and even physically assaulted him. It was a clear indication that these foolish citizens like their king Ravan, have become hopeless and need to be taught a strict lesson, which even their future generations won't forget.

The Asuras of Lanka are an amalgamation of cruelty and cowardice. They were enjoying inflicting pain to a chained and alone Being. Torturing a helpless and strength less one is the instinct of cruelty which a sadistic mind-ego enjoys. Just a few minutes back, the same Lanka courtiers felt that Hanumanji who had single handedly destroyed the grand orchard, killed hundreds of soldiers and injured thousands, who didn't spare Akshay Kumar's life and thundered fearlessly in Ravan's court is not someone ordinary. That time, these cowards feared for their life. And by supporting Vibhishan's call, they wanted to show themselves as merciful, whereas in reality, they wanted to get rid of Hanumanji as soon as possible. This instinct of cowardliness in Asura is also an aspect of mind-ego that is to show off sympathy when dealing with a threatening opponent.

Hanumanji by burning every structure of Lanka devastated the pride and ego of the Asur species. All their houses, buildings and grandeur burnt in the fire of 'Dharma'. The whole of Lanka was shivering in fear and the soldiers were just standing and seeing Hanumanji in action like mute spectators. Hanumanji didn't torch Vibhishan's house because he was not a participant in the cruel and cowardly acts of Asura. The Leela of Hanumanji, the avatar of God Shiva was a grand success. Saint Tulsidas says that the destruction of Lanka in a few moments is not something unusual or special for God Shiva, who can destroy the whole cosmos in a split fraction of second through his third eye. God Shiva as Hanumanji wants to express His devotion for Lord Ram and says to the mortal Beings that no power in this universe can match the glory and the mightiness of a Devotee or 'Bhakt', who has surrendered in the lotus feet of Lord Siya-Ram.

Chapter 5.16

Hanumanji attains the 'Chudamani' of Mother Sita.

Sea was crossed and the search had ended,
Lanka got destroyed and Asura got punished,
Now Hanumanji, without a delay must return,
Lord Ram is waiting with impatience and concern.

'Mahaveer' Hanumanji had torched and devastated Lanka in a very short period of time. Now, when the task of Lord Ram or 'Ram-Kaj' was successfully accomplished by Haumanji, he finally accepted the Sea-God's invitation to refresh and energize himself. After bathing in the sea, his tiredness vanished. Goswami Tulsidas had depicted this 'Sea' as the symbol of Body-Identification or 'Deh-abhiman', that is the 'My Body' and 'I am the Body' aspect of mind-ego. We have already discussed that human-being is a consciousness of God. But, because of attachment with materialism, Being believes 'Self-consciousness' as mind and body.

For clarity on this, one must question that if human-being is the body, then which exact part of the body can be identified as consciousness? Does the consciousness reside in body limbs, brain, blood, heart or lungs? Modern medical science has advanced and we know that today it is possible to replace the body parts. So think logically and ask yourself that if you are this body, then does amputation, removal or replacement of a body part make any difference in your Beingness? People donate organs to other people who need those organs. Does the organ from another body change the identity of the receiver? If human-being is the brain, then even when the brain stops functioning (state of coma), still there is breathing function and body function doesn't stop. By logically contemplating, one will realize that no part of the body can be deemed as 'Self'.

Coming out of 'Deh-Abhiman' or body-identification is the toughest and the last test in the spiritual journey. Hanumanji had passed this test and had risen above body-identification. For him, the body is just a tool to be used in the service of Lord Ram. For him, the physical or body connections with friends, family and foe had evaporated. There is just consciousness and Oneness with God Ram, the Supreme-consciousness. He had realized that the purpose of the human body and intelligence is for 'Ram-Kaj' or for Lord Ram's service. A devotee uses his mind-body as an instrument only for the purpose of his deity or 'Ishta'.

So far, Hanumanji had successfully and quickly accomplished all the work but the last part of this assignment was very terribly painful for him that is bidding 'Bye' to Mother Sita. Leaving Mother Sita in this dangerous situation of Lanka, made him feel immensely guilty. But the work had to be finished. He had to return and inform Lord Ram about Lady Sita and participate in the great Lanka war. He could have taken Mother Sita with himself at that time also but that wouldn't have solved the purpose. The purpose of the Lanka war was not just about the abduction of Princess Sita or killing of Ravan, rather it was for ending evil and establishing Dharma and order in the whole world. And this can only be done through the hands of Lord Ram. Before departing, Hanumanji asked Mother Sita to give him some object as Her signage, like Lord Ram had sent the gold-ring or 'Mudrika' as His signage.

In this hour of separation, Mother Sita's heart ached. The joy She experienced with the advent of Hanumanji was fading and the visions of darkness and evilness of Lanka again flashed in Her eyes. Hanumanji felt that it was better to die than to see his Mother in tears and sadness. He comforted Her to be patient and just wait for a few more days. Soon Lord Ram with His army will defeat Ravan and free Her. Soon Lord Siya-Ram will be One again. She had no doubt about it and blessed Hanumanji.

She gave Hanumanji, Her most precious 'Chudamani' or 'Crystal-head-ornament' as signage. Till the seeker light's an oil-lamp, it remains his responsibility to ensure availability of oil in the lamp for continuity of the illumination. But when the seeker is bestowed with the crystal-ornament then this responsibility ends because crystal or 'Mani' illuminates by itself and doesn't need an external source. This means that once the seeker attains Mother Sita, the Goddess of Bhakti, he then becomes Her responsibility. Now, he doesn't need to light the lamp, his life will always be filled with divine illumination of Mother Sita. This is the highest form of Bhakti which Hanumanji had attained.

Through the 'Mudrika' and 'Chudamani' Lord Siya-Ram had exchanged their feelings. And it was Hanumanji, their true son, seeker and devotee who had become their medium. These two signage-pieces are the witness of the journey of Prince Ram and Princess Sita from Ayodhya. These two pieces are the witness of the greatest divine love. The love of Lord Siya-Ram is eternal. If there is a Ravan who can spoil this connection, then there is also a Hanuman who can re-establish the connection. If there is corruption which can spoil the Peace in our heart, then there is also virtue which can re-establish the Peace.

This love of Lord Siya-Ram cannot be seen from the lenses of logic. It is a matter of heart and only a loving heart can understand. This cosmos, these stars, this earth and its civilizations will come and go, nothing is permanent in this nature, but what is eternal and omnipresent is the essence of divine connection that is the Supreme Love of Lord Siya-Ram.

Hanumanji had destroyed Lanka and had taken leave from Mother Sita. Now, he must reach Lord Ram without any delay. There are no breaks, recesses or rests for the seeker, till the completion of 'Ram-Kaj'. I, along with my worldly responsibilities, am writing this commentary on Shri Ramcharitmanas. Years have gone by, but no day has passed where I have skipped working or thinking or planning on this work. I cannot stop and I must not stop. Like Hanumanji, a seeker must not stop till he attains his target that is pure 'Bhakti' or devotion in the lotus feet of Lord Siya-Ram.

'Ram-Kaj kinhe binu, mohe kaha vishram'

Chapter 5.17

Vanar group returns: Celebration at Kishkindha

Work is accomplished, orchard is welcoming, let there be celebration,
Freedom from apprehensions, doubts and fear, that is the fruit of devotion.

The impatient, worried and eager Angad with the Vanar group was waiting for Hanumanji on the 'Bharat' side of the sea. First, they heard a gleeful sound from far off and then, very soon they saw the gigantic flying form of Hanumanji appearing from behind the clouds. All of them started cheering and jumping in excitement. Seeing Hanumanji smiling, they knew that he had successfully completed the task of meeting Mother Sita. As Hanumanji arrived near them, they rushed to welcome him and were applauding him again and again. Some Vanar devotees even started worshiping the feet of Lord Hanuman. The one who had left them was the seeker but now he has returned as the Seer, Sage, Saint and God.

Hanumanji informed them about the wellbeing of Mother Sita. All of them sighed in relief and spoke in one voice, "It is but natural that everything becomes favorable for the one, who is blessed by Lord Siya-Ram". Now, all of them quickly packed and hurriedly began their return journey to Kishkindha. They got to reach Lord Ram and King Sugriv at the earliest. Throughout the journey, Hanumanji kept telling them about his Lanka experiences and in no time all of them reached the border of Kishkindha. There they saw Sugriv's dearest and most prized orchard with exotic fruits, lush green lawns, crystal clear water and cool environment. All the Vanars looked at the orchard with hungry, tempted and mischievous eyes. Their captain Angad understood and permitted them to go ahead and enjoy themselves. But, the guards of the orchards didn't like this and tried to stop them. But, the excited Vanars punched and pushed away the guards. The guards then ran and reached

Sugriv to complain about the trespassing and misbehavior of Angad's group. The guards expected Sugriv to take a strict action against this indiscipline but to their utter dismay, he too got overjoyed. He understood that the brave Angad and his group were definitely successful in their task.

So far, Kishkindha people believed that everything was not yet totally fine between Sugriv and Angad because of the Bali episode. They had witness the slaying of Bali by Lord Ram because of Sugriv and Angad being Bali's son, possibly was vengeful towards Sugriv. But with this incident, they realized that Sugriv is now a completely changed man. All the apprehensions were gone. Angad, the son of Great Bali had all the wonderful qualities. After Hanumanji, he was the most capable warrior. But earlier he was not able to free himself from apprehension and skepticism towards Sugriv. He had a fear that Sugriv would harm him to get rid of him. He had doubted Sugriv's intentions. But this 'Ram-Kaj' or the task and the Lanka experiences of Hanumanji totally changed his belief-system. All his apprehensions, skepticism and fears vanished. He felt that if Hanumanji deserves to have fruits of Ravan's orchard after meeting God-Mother Sita, then he and the Vanar group also deserves to enjoy fruits of Sugriv's orchard after meeting the great devotee-son of Mother Sita, that is, the same Hanumanji. Because, meeting God or meeting the devotee is one and the same thing. Angad's transformation happened because of the Satsang or company of a true devotee, the epitome of faith and loyalty, the great Hanumanji.

On the other hand, by not getting agitated with Angad's act of enjoying and disrupting his most precious and treasured orchard, everybody witnessed a pure and liberal hearted Sugriv. If he had been narrow-minded and egoistical like his brother Bali, then he would have definitely ordered to punish Angad for this indiscipline. He had a valid excuse to get rid of Angad and nobody would have objected that. But he had no ill feelings for Angad and now loved him like his own son. In fact, he got so excited hoping for good news that he didn't even realize that anything wrong was done by the Vanar group. This transformation is not unexpected for the one who has surrendered in the lotus feet of Lord Ram and had spent time in the company of the great Saint Laxman.

Today, both Angad and Sugriv got free from the last thorn, that is, the last trap of mind-ego. The days of confusions, hatreds, apprehensions have passed by. Now is the time for another 'Ram-Kaj'. Now is the time for the great Vanars to devote themselves in the service of Lord Ram that is by attacking

Lanka, defeating Ravan and freeing Mother Sita. The life of the seeker gets sorted and he becomes absolutely free from the clutches of mind-ego. This is the glory of Lord Siya-Ram and their devotee-son Lord Hanuman. This is the glory of Shri Ramcharitmanas.

Chapter 5.18

Hanumanji informs Lord Ram about Lady Sita: State of Devotee

When the 'Chitt' and 'Jibhya' are fixed on Ram,
There is no channel to escape, for the 'Pran'.

All this while, Lord Ram and Laxman were waiting with eager eyes for the return of the Vanar group that had gone in the South direction in search of Lady Sita. That day, they were sitting outside their cave when they saw Vanars coming towards them with Sugriv in front. The happy demeanor of the Vanars was the signal that they had succeeded in their endeavor. The Vanars arrived and bowed down in the lotus feet of Lord Ram. The Lord blessed and hugged each one of them. That day, He was not the eternal and omnipresent God but the music of a concerning and loving heart.

His eyes were set on every Vanar face, which was glowing with immense joy and satisfaction. They had successfully accomplished 'Ram-Kaj' or Lord Ram's task. Only Hanumanji's expression was filled with hesitation and anxiety. His thoughts were filled and his mind was fixed on the image of troubled Mother Sita in Ashok Vatika of Lanka. On one hand, there was joy of reuniting with Lord Ram while on the other hand, there was intense remorse for Lady Sita.

Lord Ram was first eager to know the wellbeing of Vanar group. To which Jambvanji replied that whosoever attains Lord's grace cannot be harmed, he becomes the epitome of victory, humility and flawlessness and his fame spreads in all directions. There is an art of conversation, that is, a very thirsty person drinks water sip by sip. Jambvanji knew the Lord's state, and so after a little foreword, he came to the point. He pointed towards Hanumanji and said, "Lord, what Hanuman has achieved cannot be explained even with a thousand mouths". After that, he narrated the whole story of 'Lanka-Dahan' or destruction of Lanka, to Lord Ram. Streams of appreciation, gratefulness and love flowed in the Lord's heart. He again embraced Hanumanji with immense adoration.

At the elemental level, Lord Siya-Ram is inseparable, but for the sake of Leela, they were playing the roles of separated lovers and Hanumanji was the bridge between them. Lord then spoke with a heavy heart, "My dear, tell me, how Princess Sita is protecting Her life in Lanka?" When leaving Ayodhya, He didn't want Princess Sita to come along with him in the forest exile but Her insistence and declaration that She will not survive without Him, forced Him to bring Her along. Now, ten months have passed since their separation and it was very rude for the unhappy Prince Ram to ask how Princess Sita is able to survive now. If on separation, an individual has objection to his or her partner's life, then is it truly love? True love is to see your partner being happy and flourishing even if she is not with you and even when you know that in this life she is not going to be with you ever. Is Prince Ram unaware of the meaning of love? Does He not truly love Princess Sita? There is always a deep and subtle meaning hidden in the words of great ones. The doings of Lord Ram is sometimes like an ordinary Prince and sometimes like Supreme God. Nobody can understand this play and that is why it is called 'Leela'.

Lord Ram was very well aware of what the extreme suffering that Lady Sita is going through. He knows that if She is alive today, then the only reason is that She doesn't want to die in such circumstances which will bring ill-fame to Her husband's name. If She loses Her life in Lanka, then people forever will blame Prince Ram and criticize Him for not being able to protect the life of His beloved wife. *If Ram cannot save Sita, then who will trust Ram, to become his savior?* What can be more humiliating and disgraceful for Raghukul Empire and 'Maryada-Purushottam' Ram? When Lord asked Haumanji that how is Princess Sita protecting Herself, He meant that He realizes that She is in a very sensitive and vulnerable state and to not to lose Her life, She needs to be very strong and cautious.

Hanumanji replied, "Life is desperate to leave the body but the passage has been obstructed in such a way that life is not able to escape. Her life is guarded day and night by continuous chanting of 'Ram-Naam'. In the absence of a guard, 'life' would have gotten away easily. But this guard is 'Lord's name' which is Supremely Powerful, which cannot be fooled or defeated. Also, this guard is worried that if in its presence 'life' is able to escape, then 'Ram-Naam' would be spoiled and the whole world will mock it that 'if Ram-Naam cannot save its dearest devotee, then what good is it for? How will it protect the seekers who have dedicated themselves in chanting Ram-Naam'. That is why, Ram-Naam is itself watching like a guard to not lose its honor." Here Hanumanji is expressing the influence and power of Ram-Naam which protects the devotee in the worst circumstances and to which even 'Kaal' or death fears to face.

Secondly, the mind is constantly thinking and visualizing the form of Lord Ram. Devotee Sita is not satisfied just with the name of Her lover. Her thirst cannot be quenched just with it and so She wants to see Her lover's and Lord's image every moment. If the mind is not submerged in the glory of the Lord's image, then it becomes the escape route for life. Lady Sita's mind is not giving this outlet to life and is blocking it with the constant 'Chintan' or Meditation of Lord Ram. This is a very high stage of Bhakti wherein the devotee without missing even for a second is constantly fixed on the image of the Lord. Meditation is the Gate. The 'Meditator' and the Object of Meditation are the two parts of this Gate. If they are not together, then they are of no value. But when they are aligned together, then they become powerful with divine force.

Ordinary seekers like us have to pull away our mind from worldly thoughts and fix it on God. Consistent Meditation is difficult for us. But for highly evolved devotees, it's effortless. Meditation, God's image, God's name and experience of Grace each and everything comes naturally to them. Here, Hanumanji through the example of Mother Sita is explaining the 'Bhava' or emotions of great devotees.

Finally, a devotee's eyes are either shut or fixed on an object that constantly reminds of her beloved God. Mother Sita keeps Her eyes closed and when opened then those eyes are focused only on Her feet. The formation of Lord Siya-Ram's feet is exactly the same. A devotee is only interested in fixing Her eyes at the feet of Her beloved Lord. She doesn't care for anything else. Any material or worldly object is of least interest for Her. So when Lady Sita closes Her eyes, She is mesmerized in the Lord Ram's image and when She opens Her eyes, She is again mesmerized in Lord Ram's feet. Along with that, Her speech and heart is continuously chanting Ram-Naam.

Hanumanji concludes by saying that when all the gates of the body that is eyes, heart, mind and speech are engrossed in Lord Ram, then neither life can escape nor death can enter. Goswami Tulsidas says that when Beings are trapped in a situation where they feel totally helpless and hopeless and there seems to be no option left, then like a turtle who rolls back his limbs inside the protective body shell, Being must also withdraw eyes, ears, speech, touch, mind and heart from outer world and fix them in the lotus feet of Lord Siya-Ram. Lord Ram has again and again promised that whosoever relies just on Him and not on worldly variables becomes His responsibility and then He ensures the wellness of His devotee. Mother Sita through Her Leela is inspiring the seekers that nothing is more fruitful other than surrendering in the lotus feet of Lord Ram.

Chapter 5.19

Hanumanji and Lord Ram: Who is the 'Doer' or 'Karta'?

This is the greatest conversation between God and Devotee,
Whoever understands it, attains the blessings of the Almighty.

This conversation between Lord Ram and Hanumanji, that is between 'Bhagwan' and 'Bhakt' is the greatest learning ever of 'Bhakti' or devotion. Goswami Tulsidas says that whosoever reads and absorbs this conversation will definitely be blessed with the love of Lord Ram. But what is so special about this conversation because of which it has made this conversation such an epic?

The conversation started with Hanumanji talking about how Mother Sita is protecting Herself in 'Ashok Vatika'? In the unfavorable environment of Lanka, She is constantly chanting 'Ram-Naam'. The dependence on God's name is the greatest spiritual practice. In whichever way, whenever and wherever 'Ram-Naam' is chanted by a seeker of any class, background and race, it will most definitely result in a wonderful, positive and unexpected outcome. If along with this chanting, seekers can focus on the image, form or story of Lord Siya-Ram, then it's an added bonus. Basic meditation is chanting the Lord names' using tongue but with it if also the mind can be fixed on the Lord's image, then it becomes extraordinary meditation. Also with tongue and mind, if the eyes can be focused on an object like a picture or idol or anything that brings a connection with the Lord, then the seeker herself becomes a divine entity and is in union with the Supreme Consciousness, that is, she is now no less than God.

In the second part of the conversation, Lord Ram praises Hanumanji for his great feats, and in return, Hanumanji desperately starts asking for help. It appears to be a weird response. The Lord is happy and favorable with His Devotee and this is a great achievement. But, Tulsidasji says that when God is kind to the seeker, that is, when the seeker attains glory, wealth, name and power with the blessings of God, then it is very common that pride, arrogance and ego increases quite a lot within the seeker. And if not checked, then this ego in due course of time becomes the cause of seeker's failure. It happened in Ramayan times and it is happening even today. And therefore, the seeker must be very cautious about his actions and very alert observant of his thoughts and of course must surrender in an even more devout manner in the lotus feet of the Lord. That is what Hanumanji did by asking for protection and help against ego from the same Lord who is also the giver of this ego.

In the third part of the conversation, Lord Ram sits with Hanumanji on His side and asks him how was he single handedly, able to destroy such a strong and gigantic fort of Lanka? Actually, this question is the most difficult test for a seeker. If the seeker sees a success or victory as his own doing that is 'Doer-ship', then the seeker also has to accept failures and defeats as his own doing. But the one who sees the Lord's Grace in every action-reaction & cause-effect and himself as just a medium that is 'Non-Doership', then he frees himself from the ownership of all actions. Hanumanji replied that not only in the destruction of Lanka but also at every step of life, he experiences the divine Lord's Grace and that he has surrendered gains, losses and everything about his life in the lotus feet of Lord Siya-Ram.

Hanumanji further says, "When I heard Trijita's dream, I was sure that the Lord had already decided to destroy Lanka. Whatever I have achieved in this journey is not possible for a Vanar. Can a dimwit Vanar who knows only to jump from one branch to another, can leap across the huge ocean? Can a Vanar who got defeated from Meghnad single handedly destroy the grand fort of Lanka? Can a Vanar who is a food for demons, can slay thousands of them? The orchard of Ravan where even my father Pawan-Devta (Wind-God) fears to enter, can it be destroyed by me, his son? All this happened because of Lord Ram's Grace. And nothing else."

Hanumanji opened about his 'Bhava' or feelings and passed the difficult test. Glory of Sundarkand is not about Hanumanji's attack on Lanka, but his teachings and quality of truly surrendering in the feet of Lord Ram. He had conquered the most difficult test of 'Maya' and 'Ahankar'. He has solved the most complicated ego. Lord Ram got even more pleased with him and blessed him with His pure 'Bhakti'. Goswami Tulsidas says that whosoever can truly understand this conversation between the Lord and his Devotee, will attain 'Bhakti' effortlessly. Whosoever can bring even one percent Surrender or

'Samarparn Bhav' of Hanumanji in his life, that is understands that he is not the doer but just a medium of Supreme Consciousness then he becomes one with it, he becomes God.

Fraction of God is also God.

Chapter 5.20

Sweetness of Sycophants: Narcissistic Ravan

Your Majesty has conquered the Devta and Asura, effortlessly,
Of what account, then, can these Manushya and Vanars be.

Lord Ram, after knowing about Lady Sita, called for Sugriv, "Make preparations for the march, we cannot waste a single moment. Issue orders to the Vanar army." Mother Earth smiled and the Devta who were witnessing this dialogue showered flowers in the lotus feet of Lord Ram. Time had come. God will now terminate evil. This is the beginning of the Ravan's end. And the world will be free from Adharma. Sugriv, at once ordered the commanders and the army marched forward towards Lanka. Millions of mighty, brave and great monkey, ape and bear warriors were joyfully marching. They had no weapons or instruments but just their limbs, claws and teeth. They were carrying rocks, trees and hills to fight the demons. They were full of enthusiasm because they have Lord Ram as their leader. They roared like a lion and the celestial bodies shook in salutation. This was 'Ram-Sena', the army of pure hearted devotees.

Ever since Hanuman left after burning down Lanka, the demons there had lived continuously in extreme fear . In their heart, they thought, "There is no hope for the demon race now. If his messenger was mighty beyond words, then what good would result when his master, Lord Ram, himself enters the city?" When Mandodari heard from her female spies what the citizens were speaking, she felt much perturbed. Meeting her lord in seclusion, she fell at his feet and with joined palms requested Ravan to return Lady Sita and save the family and Lanka from destruction. Lord Ram is invincible and will slay the evil-doers. But, the foolish Ravan ignored her words of wisdom and went to the court. There, he asked the courtiers to advise the next course of action against the threat of Lord Ram.

They however, laughed and replied, "What are you saying, my Lord? Your Majesty experienced no difficulty when he conquered the Devta and Asura. Of what account, then, can men and monkeys be?" Goswami Tulsidas says that when a minister, a physician and a preceptor, these three use pleasing words out of fear or expectation of reward, the result is that person, kingdom, health and righteousness, all the three are destroyed. The egoistic and foolish Ravan got elated on hearing his praises from this bunch of wicked sycophants.

Like Ravan, our mind-ego likes hearing sweet talks about self, but praiseworthy is the one who applies intelligence and welcomes the bitter truth. Most human beings speak and talk sweetly, just to be in the good books of others. There are very few who speak truth no matter how bitter it is and that is for the well being of others and society. Ravan was an adorer of flattery. But he didn't hesitate in speaking offensively and foully for others. Like common human beings, Ravan had set different parameters for self and others; sweetness for self and bitterness for others. And therefore, he had closed the doors for the truth to enter and reach him. He is disinterested towards the concern of Mandodari and blind towards the fear of his own citizens. Ravan teaches Mandodari the lessons for a wife and about loyalty, but never realizes a husband's morality. He wants his wife to be faithful and obedient, whereas he had himself abducted another woman and desired to indulge illegitimately with her.

Out of all Beings, only an owl can see in the darkness of night and can claim that he has the sharpest vision. But the owl is far from reality because in the bright day-light of truth, he turns blind. Ravan has the same traits of an owl and that is why he is unable to see the truth in the light of the divine Sun-Ram. Ravan was aware that the humongous army led by Prince Ram has reached the other side of the shore. It was a matter of grave concern for Lanka security. And initially, Ravan was indeed concerned but the flattery of sycophants made him ignore the reality. But, Ravan was a show off category person. He wanted only yes-man around him. Anybody who would give him sound advice would be pushed away.

If a doctor, teacher and colleague will not speak the truth, then it is definitely going to result in failure of the individual. The same happened with Ravan too. He had created his own aura in such a way that none dared to speak the truth but only his ego gratifying talks. Because of this ego and self-obsession, he destroyed his own life, kingdom and people. On the other hand, there is Lord Ram who had always accepted criticism all His life, be it killing of Bali like a hunter or Agni-Pariksha of Lady Sita or second forest exile for a pregnant Queen Sita. These incidences could have been hidden or not spoken or not written but Lord Ram never objected on opinions and criticism. Even today many people still criticize Lord Ram for these incidences. Everybody was free to speak his mind in Ram-Rajya. There was no fear of the authorities. For the Lord, the most important thing was truth and nothing else.

Ego denies truth and wants to show itself in a perfect and positive picture. Ego enjoys flattery. The one who is trapped in ego is limiting his growth. Acceptance for truth is imperative and is must for evolution. Following and learning the life of Lord Ram gives the strength and inspiration to embrace truth. And only a life of truth can evolve and attain higher level of consciousness that is 'Sat-Chit-Anand'.

Chapter 5.21

Vibhishan discards Lanka: Truth vs Tyranny

O Ravan, your insanity is going to destroy the Asur species,
hear my verdict,
I am discarding Lanka and surrendering to Lord Ram, the
Supreme Ascetic.

Readers of Ramayan have mixed opinions for Vibhishan. Some label him as a traitor who had ditched his brother and his nation and joined with Ravan's enemy. But without any doubts in the perspective of Ramcharitmanas, he is a great being, a Mahatma and a pure devotee of Lord Ram. Never ever did he, out of fear or greed, misguide his brother, Ravan. He always thought and said for the welfare of Lanka. Vibhishan advised Ravan, "Lust, anger, vanity and covetousness are all paths leading to hell. Abjuring all these, adore the Hero of Raghukul, whom saints worship. He is the Lord of the Universe and the Death of Death himself. He is the Brahma (Absolute) who is free from the malady of Maya, He is the unborn God, all-pervading, invincible, without the beginning or the end. An ocean of compassion, He has assumed the form of a human being for the good of the Beings. Listen brother, He delights His devotees and breaks the ranks of the impious and is the champion of the Vedas and true religion. Giving up enmity with Him, bow your head to Him; for the Lord of the Raghu relieves the distress of those who seek refuge in Him. My brother! You ought to restore King Janaka's daughter Lady Sita to the Lord Ram, and adore Him. On being approached, He forgives the one who has incurred sin by wishing ill to the whole world. Bear this in mind, Ravan, the same Lord whose Name destroys the threefold agony has manifested Himself in human form. Again and again, I fall at your feet and pray to you Ravan, abandoning pride, infatuation and arrogance, surrender in the lotus feet of the Lord of Kosala, Shri Ram."

Vibhishan had given the most beneficial advice for the well being of his brother. But the egoist and foolish Ravan, who has totally failed in recognizing friend and foe, humiliated and insulted Vibhishan. Not just this, he kicked Vibhishan on his chest and asked him to leave the kingdom of Lanka. Even though Vibhishan was hurt yet he had neither hatred nor vengeance nor did he try to conspire against Ravan. He, in front of the full assembly, challenges Ravan's decision and openly declares that he is discarding Lanka and is surrendering in the lotus feet of Lord Ram. If the meaning of patriotism for a nation and loyalty towards a brother is supporting immoral and unwarranted actions, then such loyalty and patriotism holds no value in Ramcharitmanas.

Earlier, Vibhishan had advised Ravan against hurting Hanumanji, the messenger of Lord Ram. Not paying heed to his advice, Ravan had faced major loss. Ravan was also hostile with Vibhishan because he couldn't understand that when the whole Lanka got burnt, how come Vibhishan's house remained undamaged. In this whole incident, Ravan felt that Vibhishan had conspired against him. He thought that if his initial decision of executing the Vanar messenger had been accepted, then Lanka would have been saved from being burnt and destroyed. It was Vibhishan who had advised against this executory order but Ravan had forgotten that putting fire on the tail of Hanumanji was not Vibhishan's idea but only his own.

Destruction of Lanka was Ravan's fault but the mind-ego of this evil Asura was not ready to accept his mistake and he baselessly blamed the virtuous Vibhishan. The mind-ego sees disrespect in the sound advice and conspiracy in an undamaged house. Ego's non-acceptance of own faults and putting the blame on others, has trapped human beings always. This Ravan-element in the Beings is the one single cause of disharmony and disturbance in their lives. Be it in business or in relationships or in any sphere of life, today humankind is wasting their energy in proving themselves as right and others' as wrong.

Vibhishan, in clear terms, condemns the obsession of Ravan towards 'Paristri' or another man's wife. He says that even if 'Paristri' is more beautiful and attractive in comparison to one's own wife, then too it doesn't give rights to forcefully abduct her. This action brings only disgrace and dishonor to the family and lineage. Comparison of Lady Sita with Mandodari is in no way justifiable. Vibhishan further says that when a man tries to forcefully capture someone else's wife, then that wife's man will not remain quiet and he will fight back, which is natural. Society and the world will be on that man's side and will be against the evil abductor. And in such a situation, destruction is inevitable. If a leader starts acting like a criminal, then how can his people ever respect him?

The culprit is the carnal desire and the greed, planted deep in Ravan as well as in the mind-ego of mortal human beings. An alcoholic forgets reality and lives in his own world, similarly in the ego of power and greed, one goes far away from reality. The choice between right and wrong was not difficult for Ravan. Lord Ram was the greatest and righteous personality ever and everybody knew it. He had slayed Khar, Dushan and Tardka who were equally strong as Ravan. Realizing His power Ravan could have easily mended his mistake and not bothered Lord Ram. But in his blindness, he failed to differentiate between black and white. Choices between right and wrong or black and white, are not so easy for mortal beings. Beings live in the gray zone. It is difficult for a mediocre mind to be totally righteous like Lord Ram or totally evil like Ravan. And so, this makes the choice difficult.

Vibhishan then praised and sang the glory of his 'Ishta' Lord Ram. Another wise courtier, Malyavan (Ravan's uncle) was in support of Vibhishan's thoughts. He also praised Vibhishan for his diplomatic intelligence. This further irate Ravan. He had always considered himself as the genius of political diplomacy. In front of him, his enemy Prince Ram was being praised and the one who was praising was appreciated in front of the whole assembly. This was intolerable for Ravan. He couldn't hold himself any longer and thundered, "Somebody throw both of them out of this court."

It was clear, how frustrated Ravan was? All the courtiers knew that both Vibhishan and Malyavan were saying right but out of Ravan's fear, could not gather the strength to open their mouth and thereby stood speechless. In this scene, we see three types of people. First type are one who didn't dare to speak the truth. All the courtiers were in this category. Second like Malyavan who had the guts to speak the truth but not the capability to bring it in action. And the third admirable ones are like Vibhishan who have the guts to both speak and execute the truth. And that is why, after being thrashed by Ravan, Vibhishan didn't return to his home and sit back, rather clearly divulged his thoughts to Ravan and the assembly. The sense of Right_Wrong or 'Sadbudhi_ Durbudhi' is equally present in every Being. But Ravan had set aside 'Sadbudhi' or righteousness and had only 'Durbudhi' or unrighteousness in his heart.

Vibhishan openly scolds Ravan, "Lady Sita is the worst nightmare for the Asur clan but you are hopelessly obsessed with Her. Even a challenged person wakes up from deep sleep when his house is on fire. But even after the roar of

Hanuman and torching of Lanka, your 'Sadbudhi' is still asleep."

Ravan wanted to insult both Vibhishan and Lord Ram and so he physically assaulted him. All the doors were closed for Vibhishan in Lanka. He had only one option left with him that was refuge in the lotus feet of Lord Ram. He decided to quit Lanka and walk towards his ultimate destiny. He was now clear that the end of Ravan had begun and nobody could save him and his Rakshas from death. He tried his best to make Ravan understand. He patiently tolerated the hurt and insult. He didn't try to harm or conspire against Ravan. And he openly declared about to leave Lanka and to join Lord Ram. These are the qualities of a noble, loyal and great soul Vibhishan had openly announced his intentions to the Lanka assembly and Ravan and this is not what a traitor does.Vibhishan was never against Asur clan. He wanted to save his clan from the sheer foolishness of Ravan with the help of Lord Ram.

It is not easy to discard your lifelong attachments like home, people, place and everything for Bhakti. The pain given by the people whom the seeker is attached with most, actually takes him closer towards the Lord. When Ravan hits him, Vibhishan felt as if the Supreme Lord had himself orchestrated this act to make him see the reality. Isn't this the Grace of Lord that Ravan didn't think of killing Vibhishan, instead ousted him from Lanka especially, when a lethal grand war is knocking the doors? Ravan lets Vibhishan go free when there is a high chance of him revealing the Lanka strategic secrets to the antagonist. But Ravan's pride and ego was at its peak. He wanted to show off that he is hardly bothered with Prince Ram's threat and that even after knowing the secrets, the enemies cannot harm Lanka.

This surprisingly foolish approach of Ravan proves that the Lord was Himself eager to take Vibhishan in His refuge. The act of Vibhishan is the ultimate Karma of every Being. The sooner one realizes the better it is. Vibhishan is a Mahatma and he did what every devotee does, that is to surrender in the lotus feet of Lord Siya-Ram.

Chapter 5.22

Vibhishan knocks at Lord's door: Apprehension of Sugriv

O Lord! Brother of Ravan has arrived and seeks Your refuge,
O Sugriv! Even if He has come to harm Me, I will not refuse.

Vibhishan left Lanka and reached the camp of Lord Ram but he was stopped by the Vanar guards. Sugriv is called and after hearing from Vibhishan, he goes to Lord Ram and informs Him about his arrival. Sugriv was very skeptical about Vibhishan and requested Lord to not trust him at all. Sugriv was the Prime Minister of Lord Ram and he was always focused on his duty, keeping in mind Lord's objective. He doesn't hesitate in putting forward his opinion to the Lord, even though he now was well aware of Lord's Supremacy and Divinity. Also valuing Sugriv's opinions is a proof of Lord's Grace for him.

Sugriv was very surprised that how come Vibhishan who knows every secret of Lanka that can be used to defeat Ravan , was allowed to leave and join the enemy's camp by Ravan, himself. Sugriv, while informing Lord, used the words 'Ravan's brother' instead of just telling his name, 'Vibhishan'. The hidden message was that the Lord must not forget that Vibhishan is the enemy's brother and should not be trusted at all. But Lord Ram very innocently replies, "Friend, what is there to ask about? Please let him come in." Lord hinted that it is not appropriate to stop Vibhishan from coming in His refuge.

In reality, Being is the part of Supreme God who has forgotten this connection. Vibhishan, the symbol of human being coming to Lord Ram, is returning back to his source. No matter how high and far the stone is thrown, it falls back on the Earth. The rivers are forever eager to reach the ocean. This is the nature of every element and every Being to return to its source. Being identifies himself with his ten senses, symbolized as Ravan. Like Vibhishan, Being considers Ravan as his brother. But when the Being applies

'Vivek' or intelligence and dis-identifies from the ten-headed Ravan, then he becomes one with the Lord. Lanka is a flourishing state with riches, wellness and luxuries. Vibhishan had not only discarded Ravan but also Lanka and moreover his near and dear ones. Lord Ram loves and appreciates this great sacrifice of Vibhishan and wants Sugriv to welcome him with respect.

"Nobody can escape the repercussions of his karma and for the evil doing of Ravan, his brother cannot be punished. Rather Vibhishan should be honored because even while staying in an immensely unfavorable situation in Lanka, he practiced his 'Swadharma' or self-duty and ultimately stood against Ravan and joined Me," said Lord Ram. But Sugriv was not convinced and didn't find Lord's statement reasonable. For him, it was a matter which ought to be seen in a political perspective and not spiritual. Sugriv believed that after arresting and torturing, the 'untrustworthy' Vibhishan, they could find out his real intention of coming to Lord Ram. Lord first appreciated Sugriv's concern and political acumen and then spoke.

O Sugriv, you are a wise diplomat and have given a very good advice,
But, I'll protect even the cruelest one who comes to Me, without thinking twice.

In a worldly perspective, there is a contradiction between political diplomacy and the Lord's verdict. Rule of diplomacy is not to trust who is untrustworthy but also if even one is a closest friend then too he must not be trusted in totality. One must always be cautious and alert against even the closest ally because in politics, it doesn't take long for friends to become enemies. Those who trust others easily are very often cheated by the same trusted ones. The urge for power, glory and pleasures is naturally embedded in the DNA of mankind. The idea behind alliances and friendships are based on an agreement and conditionality of give and take. It is impossible for two friends to be at par. Often a friend gets jealous seeing the other getting more respect and honor. And then, there arises a desperation in his heart like, 'How can I attain this superior status?'. And then, this desperation becomes a threat for the other friend. Therefore in politics, one needs to be very cautious towards both allies and enemies.

But Lord Ram's perspective was totally opposite to this rule of political diplomacy. He was just concerned for Being's welfare and happiness. Any relationship based on doubts, insecurity and caution was not agreeable to

Him. He wanted to remove the element of Fear from the core of society and from the heart of each individual. Fear is a good instrument to make others' work towards a righteous objective but then it can also be used for immoral objectives. And therefore, fear is neither the answer nor the solution of a any situation. The solution of fear is fearlessness and nothing else. Lord's message and effort was to eradicate fear from the hearts of His people. When He announced about His human incarnation, His first words were, 'Fear Not' and 'Be Fearless'.

An ordinary human being is already trapped in the web of fears. If he indulges in pleasures, then there is fear of diseases. If he tries to rise in life, there is fear of downfall. If he attains wealth, there is fear of being robbed. Lord didn't want to give one more fear to Beings. Lord knows that the Being is very troubled in his own mind-egoic complications. He is not able to get free from his past, he doesn't know what lies ahead in future and he is not able to get hold of his present. All this gives nothing else but pain and trouble to him.

Lord Ram promises freedom from all three fear zones of past, present and future. The one who surrenders to in the lotus feet of Lord Siya-Ram will not be punished for his past misdeeds and living in the shelter of Lord one cannot commit a bad deed in the present. And Lord's verdict is that He will ensure bliss and divinity to His devotee forever. This unconditional promise of love brought Vibhishan to Lord, and therefore, Tulsidasji says that the purpose of life and the 'Swadharma' of every Being, is in surrendering in the lotus feet of Lord Siya-Ram.

Chapter 5.23

Declaration of Vibhishan: Sufferings in Devotee's life

As per instructions, the Vanar-soldiers respectfully escorted Vibhishan to where Lord Ram was. He prostrated from a distance and got overwhelmed seeing Lord Ram-Laxman. His eyes stopped blinking and he stood stock-still with his gaze intently fixed on the Lord. The sight brought tears to his eyes and a deep thrill ran through his body.

Lord Ram immediately rejoiced at heart on seeing Vibhishan. He embraced him and sat next to Him and spoke, "You live day and night in the midst of evil-minded people of Lanka, I wonder! How you are able to maintain your piety, My friend!" To that Vibhishan replied, "Attachment to the world is like a dark night, delightful to the owls of attraction. It abides in the heart of a creature only so long as the Sun of the Lord's glory does not shine there. Having seen Your lotus feet, I am now quite well and my grave fears have been set at rest. The threefold torments of mundane existence cease to have any effect on the one who enjoys Your favor, my gracious Lord."

Vibhishan says that a devotee of Lord Ram doesn't get bothered with unfavorable situations of life. But many have wondered that if a devotee is dealing with bad times, then does it mean that either Lord Ram is not in his favor or he is not actually a devotee? But in the history of Sanatan Dharma, there is not one devotee, who hasn't faced tough periods in his life. In fact, sages have said that a devotee has to go through far more challenging situations than a regular worldly person. So if this is true, then how, as per Vibhishan, a devotee doesn't get affected with troublesome twists and turns of life?

It is better to say that in the life of a devotee, the threefold torments which are Adhyatmik or Spiritual, Adhidevik or Nature and Adhibhautik or Worldly, do come but they are unable to affect him. A devotee, with the Grace of Lord Ram, attains divine strength and immeasurable faith, as much so that even the most terrible events fail to concern him. There is an old saying, one reaps what he sows. Most of us believe in this Karma principle, that the cause of our today's situation is the outcome of our past action. This is not incorrect but for a devotee, his deity is superior and beyond the Karma principle.

Lord Ram has Himself given much importance to this cause and effect principle of Karma. And, has also declared that though he has designed this system yet he doesn't intervene in it. And yet there are many instances in the life of devotees where they witness that in a bad period, the Lord has been especially kind and has molded the Karma principle for His devotees. The principle of Bhakti is superior to the principle of Karma. The Supreme God is always available to the beck and call of His seeker. But a true devotee never asks for Lord's intervention while dealing with his painful Karma. He accepts good and bad times alike with only one request that with every passing moment his love and devotion for Lord Ram grows more and more.

Just like a regular materialistic worldly person, adversities are seen in the life of a devotee also. But unlike a worldly person, adversities and the pain doesn't affect the life, body and mind of a devotee. This doesn't mean that if a devotee is attacked physically, he will not get hurt or would not feel the pain. He would definitely feel the pain but his Vivek or intelligence, which is surrendered in the lotus feet of Lord Ram, will ensure solace and immense ability to tolerate it. He will feel the pain but would not suffer. You fear a criminal with a knife standing in front of you but you don't think in the same way when seeing a surgeon with a knife in front of you. A medical surgery on our body is definitely painful but there is a wishful hope attached with it that soon after the treatment, the patient will be fine and good to go. A seeker and a devotee see the adversities in the same perspective. He sees the unfavorable situations as the surgery of eternal doctor, Lord Ram, whose only purpose is to correct the past karma of His devotee, rectify the flaws and help the devotee in achieving perfection. After facing the challenges, the devotee surely feels healthier and stronger. He finds new strength to deal with situations which are intolerable for a worldly person.

The classic example is Vibhishan himself, who just a little while away was kicked and insulted by Ravan in front of a full assembly, of which he was a respected minister. If such a thing had not happened for him, he would not have discarded Lanka and sought the refuge of Lord Ram. From that incident onwards, his life changed. Lord Ram killed Ravan and crowned Vibhishan as the new King of Lanka. From an ousted nobody, Vibhishan became the supreme entity of Lanka. This is the Grace of Lord Ram. Also note that at the time of war, Ravan in his rage threw a weapon to kill Vibhishan but Lord Ram came in between and took the attack on his chest. Lord not just gave power but always protected his dear devotee, Vibhishan.

For a seeker of Lord Ram, this means that he must always be assured that the Lord is there for him. At times, Lord Ram will take the attack on Himself while at other times, Lord will let the devotee deal with the threat. Lord's only purpose for all this is well being and perfection for His devotee. Those seekers who believe that after indulging in Bhakti, there would be no problems in life are unripe. However, they are on the right track and eventually will become tough and indifferent towards the problems. A true devotee believes that the ups and downs of life are because Lord's Grace is taking him towards the Lord. He has firm faith and determination that one day he will attain his objective. Path of Bhakti is for brave-hearts, only the one who is ready to face adversity is eligible for the love of Lord Siya-Ram.

Chapter 5.24

Transformation of the evil Heart: Lord Laxman pardons Ravan's Spies

Lord Ram asked Vibhishan and Sugriv to come up with a solution about how to cross the deep ocean full of alligators, snakes and all kinds of dangerous aquatic animals. Vibhishan replied that Lord's arrow itself can dry up innumerable oceans, yet the right way would be that the Lord should approach the God of Ocean and request the passage. In this way, the whole army of Vanars will thus be able to cross the ocean without any problem. Lord appreciated the idea but Lord Laxman didn't like it all. He spoke, "O Lord! No reliance can be placed on the freaks of fortune. Fill your mind with indignation and dry up the ocean. Fate is a crutch for the mind of cowards alone; it is the indolent who proclaim their faith in fate." Lord smiled and pacified His invincible brother. He then sat at the shore for the 'Yagya' to please the God of Ocean for the passage.

In Lanka, just after ousting Vibhishan, Ravan had dispatched two of his best spies after him. They guised themselves as Vanars and got mixed with the Vanar army. They had witnessed the greatness of Lord Ram in accepting Vibhishan with open arms. Their hearts transformed and in the state of ecstasy they forgetting their disguise, openly and loudly commenced applauding the Lord. The Vanar Soldiers recognized them immediately and brought them to Sugriv who asked the soldiers to mutilate their bodies and send them back. The spies cried in fear and pleaded mercy. They gave the Vanars the pledge of Lord Ram, not to harm them. Hearing this, Lord Laxman laughed and pardoned the spies. He then asked them to inform Ravan that if he wants to live, then he must return Princess Sita and surrender in the lotus feet of Lord Ram. Bowing their heads, the spies immediately departed, singing the praises of Lord Ram.

Spies are used to find the secrets, strategy and the weak and strong points of the enemies. Commander Sugriv couldn't recognize the real spies but wrongfully labeled Vibhishan as a spy. If Lord Ram had accepted Sugriv's advice and captured Vibhishan then Ravan would have been a very happy person. If Ravan had any idea that Lord would embrace and honor Vibhishan, then he would have never let Vibhishan leave Lanka. Like every selfish and wicked ruler, Ravan believed Lord Ram will act like he, himself does. But this war, politics and diplomacy was totally unexpected and different.

Lord Ram's principles of rulership were not based on the past set norms of politics. Instead of doubting, trusting others is the core belief of Ram-Rajya. Lord's message is that those who are themselves untrustworthy, keep on doubting others. Secondly, a ruler and a leader needs to be confident of his own people and power and doesn't bother much about enemies knowing his secrets. But Ravan was playing like he had always played. So far throughout his life, his plans and strategies have given him victories. And on the old same lines, he had sent his spies. But seeing the compassionate and affectionate behavior of Lord Ram, the spies got bewildered. In this state of surprise, they must have lost their alertness and objective. In their minds, they must have been constantly comparing the acts of their King Ravan with Lord Ram. They knew how skeptical and doubtful Ravan is, who doesn't trust his own people. And here is Lord Ram, who had put all his trust in the enemy's brother in the first meeting.

The spies had also witnessed how Lord Ram managed two different opinions, one of which is Vibhishan's and second of his own brother Lord Laxman's, on crossing the ocean. Vibhishan's path was of request and worship where patience is imperative whereas Lord Laxman's path was of action and fighter-ship where courage is imperative. Lord knew that both the paths are correct but the question was which is to be chosen first? And here, he first gave priority to Vibhishan's solution. On seeing how the ever compassionate Lord values the one who surrenders to him, the spies got overwhelmed. Through this experience, they had accessed the infinite bliss of Supreme Consciousness which is in every Being, be it demons. They lost their control of alertness, behind the veil of evilness they found the goodness in them and forgot that they were Ravan's demon-spies. They in loud and clear terms started applauding and saluting Lord Ram.

Because of this, they got captured. Now, the Lord was busy in the Yagya and in His absence, Sugriv passed his judgment to mutilate the spies. Sugriv had his own reasons. Firstly, he believed that a soldier must stay away from any sort of kindness or sensitiveness towards the enemy. Secondly, he knew the Lord's nature and thought that just like Vibhishan, Lord might not only pardon them but also award them another kingdom. Thirdly, he remembered Ravan's act against Hanumanji, when he had gone to Lanka as the Lord's messenger. Sugriv by brutally punishing these spies wanted to give an apt reply to his enemy Ravan.

Hearing Sugriv's judgment, the asur-spies cried in fear and begged for pardon. The Vanar soldiers had already started thrashing the spies. Finally, the spies finding no way to escape used their last option and gave a pledge to the Vanar army that the one who harms them doesn't respect Lord Ram. In the perspective of war, politics and diplomacy, such a pledge is inconsequential. But in the perspective of Bhakti, this pledge holds immense value. For Lord Ram, a punishment was not for hurting the culprit but His purpose was transformation of the misguided heart. Today also, only such transformation can ensure peace in the society and not harsh punishments. The spies had already transformed, witnessing Lord's greatness. So, actually a punishment was not needed. Till the time, they were working as real spies in disguise then not one Vanar soldier was able to recognize them. And when they had found the truth and Bhakti of Lord Ram, they themselves discarded their disguise and revealed their real form.

Sugriv may ignore this fact but the great Lord Laxman could not. Laxmanji appears to be strict and angry but inside he is very compassionate and sensitive, just like his brother Ram. His purpose of life was the establishment of Ram-Rajya, built on the ideology of Lord Ram. Lord Laxman smiled and called the spies near him and immediately released them. Maybe he smiled hearing the clever pledge of spies or maybe because of Sugriv's judgment. Once when Sugriv knew, he was the culprit and Lord Laxman had gone to punish him, then he had begged for mercy on the grounds of kindness. And today, when Sugriv had become the commander, he had forgotten his past and was eager for harsh punishment for the spies.

Lord Laxman did what Lord Ram would have done. Point is that just in case someone thinks that probably the Lord is busy with something, then who is there to look after. So there is an assurance that if Lord is busy, then His brother Sheshnaag Laxman is there to take care of His Creation. Goswami Tulsidas says that the devotee is never alone and is always taken care of even in the worst circumstances. He inspires all human beings to discard their mind-ego just like the spies had discarded their false identity, and surrender in the lotus feet of Lord Siya-Ram.

Chapter 5.25

End of Sunderkand: The divine Bridge of Grace

Ravan's spies singing the glory of Lord Ram reached back to Lanka and bowed to Ravan. Ravan laughed and inquired about Vibhishan's whereabouts, who according to him is a foolish coward and will not be able to survive outside Lanka. The leader of the spies 'Shuk' then politely replied to Ravan, "Subsidizing your anger, hear me, O King! As soon as Vibhishan reached Vanar camp, Lord Ram immediately accepted him and titled him as the new King of Lanka. We were caught and were thrashed by Vanars, but on giving them the pledge of Lord Ram, they let us free." Shuk wants to convey that the Lord is very compassionate and He loves the one who surrenders to Him. Message is that if Ravan too surrenders, he will also be accepted by the Lord. Shuk then spoke, "The one who burnt our city, Hanuman, is actually the last in strength in comparison to other Vanar soldiers. The Vanars are in millions, very brave, huge and powerful. They have the blessings of Lord Ram and any one of them is capable to defeating you in battle."

Hearing this Ravan laughed again and spoke, "Acceptance of Vibhishan as his associate proves that Ram is not clever at all. He can neither be victorious nor will attain glory in this world." Goswami Tulsidas says that the criticizer of Lord Ram must be made quiet with the sword there and then. Shuk used Laxman's letter as the sword for Ravan to shut him up. In the letter, Lord Laxman wrote to Ravan not to destroy his name, fame and family on his own. Not even the Supreme Trinity that is Brahma-Vishnu-Mahesh can protect him. The only option is to surrender at the feet of Lord Ram. Hearing the command of the Great Laxman, Ravan got frightened inside but to hide his fear again started laughing loudly. Shuk again warned him and asked him to return Princess Sita, to save his life. Now hearing the name of 'Sita', Ravan lost his temper and hit Shuk just like he had kicked Vibhishan. Shuk too saluted Ravan and discarded Lanka like Vibhishan. He returned to Lord Ram and was liberated from this Asur life. Shuk the chief spy of Ravan was actually a hermit in his previous life, who was cursed by Sage Agastya and so he incarnated as an Asur in Lanka.

Here, three days had passed but the Sea-God did not respond to Lord Ram's Yagya - a request from the Sea-God to give passage for Lanka to the Vanar army. This irked Lord Ram and he furiously announced that He will teach this stupid and arrogant Sea-God a lesson and that his Fire-Arrow will evaporate this whole sea. It was strange that He didn't respond to the request of Lord Ram, the master of Hanumanji though he had offered Mount 'Mainak' to Hanumanji when he was crossing the sea to reach Lanka. Actually, He had seen the strength of Hanumanji and was impressed; so he came forward to help. But he had not yet witnessed the strength and power of Lord Ram and therefore, didn't bother to respond. Goswami Tulsidas says that this is a typical characteristic of a fool with lesser intellect.

Lord placed the arrow on the bow and took the hitting position. The oceans of the world started boiling in fear. Also all the aquatic life panicked in fear. Realizing the Supremacy of Lord Ram, the Sea-God appeared with a plate full of precious gems. Goswami Tulsidas says that no matter how much you water a banana tree, it grows only when its branches are chopped. Similarly, no politeness and humility is understood by a fool. The foolish Sea-God surrendered when shown the fear of destruction. He apologized to the Lord and spoke probably the most controversial lines of Shri Ramcharitmanas.

Dhol Gawar Sudra Pashu Nari,
Sakal Tadan ke Adhikari ||

Since centuries, people have criticized Tulsidasji for these lines as it ill-speaks about female kind. But before drawing a conclusion, one must carefully understand the context. When Ravan says that he will abduct Princess Sita and will forcefully marry Her, does that mean that Tulsidasji is saying so? Similarly, we must not forget that these lines are spoken by the Sea-God who has been already labeled as a fool by Tulsidasji. And a fool doesn't really think before he speaks. Secondly, the word 'Tardna' is misread by the people as 'Beating' but instead must be read as 'Disciplining'. Discipline is important in becoming a better human being. The words 'Gawar' and 'Sudra' are for masculine gender. So this discipline is for both male and female and there is no gender bias in it. Even, great ones have been disciplined whenever required by their well wishers. Also, we must understand that those who deserve discipline must be disciplined. We must not generalize. There have been highly respected ones, enlightened souls, sages, kings and leaders from 'Nari' or Female kind, or from the 'Sudra' or the Fourth Varna (Society Division). Our Supreme Goddesses including Mother Sita all are female gender, so can Tulsidasji or anybody can dare to discipline Supreme Goddess 'Devi' or feminine gender.

In this context, Mahatma Gandhi has said that in other religions there is no liberty to point out flaws in their scriptures although there are many. It is only in Sanatan Dharma does anybody have the liberty and authority to scrutinize the Holy Scriptures like Ramcharitmanas. Since times immemorial, it has been acknowledged that Ramayan is the greatest epic scripture which brings peace, prosperity and joy in our lives. It is because of divine Ramcharitmanas, we have faith, love and trust in the lotus feet of Lord Ram. Haters will say that there are many statements in it which speak against the female kind. But they must also remember that through this scripture, we are acquainted with the purest entity of the cosmos, Mother Sita.

Without 'Sita', there is no 'Ram'. Without Sita, there can be no Ram. Both "Sita" and "Ram" are One. Male and Female divisions are seen in ignorance or 'Avidya'. For pure consciousness, there cannot be any division but only Oneness. Glory of Lord Ram is based on Goddess Sita but the Glory of Goddess Sita is independent and doesn't need a base. And then, there are other great women of Ramayan like Kaushalya, Sumitra, Shabri, Ansuya, Tara, Ahalya, Urmila, Swayamprabha, Trijita and even Mandodari, who are till today and will always be worshiped by us.

Half knowledge is very destructive. Before criticizing something, one must study well and understand. Whatever Lord Ram did have a reason which is beyond the comprehension of ordinary human intellect. Believing that the Lord can never be wrong is the true faith. But justifying one's own wrongful acts based on the Leela acts of the Lord, is sheer stupidity. The word 'Pashu' or animal here means uncivilized. Here, it means that only those Gawar, Sudra and Nari who act in an uncivilized manner must be disciplined and not all of them.

The Sea-God is the devotee of Ram-Rajya. He used the word Tardna for education, discipline and evolution of himself and others like him. He has learnt that the society where there is no discipline becomes the Lanka of Ravan, leading to hatred and destruction. And therefore, he uses this phrase as the learning for the readers, highlighting the significance of order and discipline.

Lord Ram forgave the Sea-God and asked him the way across. He replied that the great Vanar architects 'Nal' and 'Neel' must build a Bridge of stones across the sea. And he and all the creatures of the sea will help in the construction work. Through this bridge 'Ram-Setu', the Vanars will easily cross the ocean. Saying this, the Sea-God prostrated at the feet of Lord Ram and returned. With this episode comes the end of the great Sunderkand. Goswami Tulsidas says that whosoever will recite and listen to this greatest canton of Ramayan will definitely attain the Grace of Hanumanji and will be blessed by Lord Ram.

LANKAKAND

Chapter 6.1

Establishment of Shiva-Linga: Faith and Knowledge

Lord Ram assembled the Vanars and ordered them to immediately start the bridge work. Under the leadership of Hanumanji and Sugriv, Nal-Neel and the Vanars began the construction of the legendary bridge 'Ram-Setu' that would connect the land of Bharat with Lanka. On seeing the constructed bridge, Lord Ram got pleased and announced that here at this point He will establish Shiva-Linga. And after completing the ritual He announced,

The one who worships Shiva and hates Me,
Or the one who worships Me but hates Shiva,
Will perish and cannot be saved even by the almighty.

Question is that why there was a need for Lord Ram to say this? What was Lord Ram's reason behind this announcement? Or does Goswami Tulsidasji wants to say something through the Lord?

Faith has given peace and prosperity to us but this also cannot be denied that in the name of faith, there have been countless instances of violence, intolerance and torture. Since ages, thousands of wars have been fought in the name of faith. In their blind propaganda of faith, missionaries have actually become ruthless and heartless manipulators. Faith and Religion have essentially two roles to play in human life. The first one is that how one individual must conduct his life and interact with other individuals. In Shri Ramcharitmanas, we learn about these values through the qualities and life story of Lord Ram and other characters.

The second role of religion is to show the light to the seekers who are inquisitive to know the unknown that is attainment of Supreme. Every religion has a different set of guidelines of seeking. And, this difference in guidelines and not the objective is the genesis of inter-religion struggle. Had the prophets of every religion had the same experiences and revelation, then possibly there wouldn't have been any dispute. But the ideology and practice of every religion is so different from each other that it is impossible to bring them on the same tangent.

The practioners of a religion, institutionalize it and work towards a resolution. Others, who identify with the resolution, join that religious institution. Ideally, there needs no resolution and the purpose of every religion is to free us from all resolutions but if there is no resolution, then there can be no institution. Irony is that the symbolic heads of every religious institution, are actually the most ambitious people whereas the founders of the same religion were the most dispassionate and stoic divine entities.

This one world is a small space for even one human-being's desires; then how can this world accommodate the ambitions of so many religious-institutions with billions of members? Every institution seeks supremacy, so that all other institutions are destroyed and only it survives and flourishes. This struggle of religious-ego has been the one main cause of loss of innumerable human lives and sadly even today there seems to be no solution. But fortunately from time to time, there have been incarnations of divine entities, the prophets and the sages who have successfully unified thousands of people of different institutions and brought peace in their lives. And one of the greatest one among them, is Goswami Tulsidas.

There was a time when Sanatan Dharma was divided between the followers of God Shiva and the followers of God Vishnu. However in North India, thanks to Tulsidasji, this difference and hatred ended. I have heard that in South India, even today this difference exists.

Tulsidasji writes that at Rameshwaram, Lord Ram, the incarnation of God Vishnu, worships God Shiva and seeks His blessing for the successful construction of Ram-Setu. Also, He established a Shiva-Linga and announced that nobody is dear to Him more than God Shiva and that the one who worships Lord Shiva and hates Lord Ram or worships Lord Ram and hates Lord Shiva will perish in hell. Both Lord Shiva and Lord Ram are always One. This episode of Ramcharitmanas written by Tulsidasji clarifies the doubts of the haters and brings together the previously divided followers of Lord Shiva and Lord Ram.

'God Shiva' is the symbol of 'Faith' and 'God Ram' is the symbol of 'Knowledge'. Faith and Knowledge always walk together with hand in hand. Faith without Knowledge is just an obligation and a compulsion. Let's say a blind person needs to reach somewhere and so he asks for help. A person comes forward and offers to walk him to the destination. The blind one agrees but in his mind there is always an apprehension that the one who is guiding him can be a crook and misuse his blindness. If by chance, the blind person stumbles while walking, he immediately loses faith in his guide and doubts his intention, even if it's not that guide's fault.

Same is the case with a seeker who wants to walk the path of spirituality. There do come rough patches where the seeker stumbles and the one who lacks faith in his guide and leaves in-between spoils his spiritual progress. And therefore, absolute Faith in your Spiritual Guide is must. Lord Shiva is the symbol of this Faith.

Now, if the seeker only has faith and no knowledge, then too there will be problems. One needs understanding that comes from knowledge to decide on whom to put his Faith on. For centuries and even today, people have been misused by Godsmen, Politicians and Leaders, because of this lack of knowledge in people. People without assessing and understanding trust the wicked and spoil their life because of this Blind-Faith. The blind man must have at least this much experience as to whom he should trust, for guiding him to his destination. It's better to not venture than to put blind-faith in the other. The knowledge that brings light in our life and cures our blindness is Lord Ram.

Point is, if one wants to progress, then he needs to have both Knowledge and Faith. Neither just knowledge nor just faith can help one reach his destination. The establishment of Shiva-Linga by Lord Ram at Shri Rameshwaram is a symbol of Lord Ram and Lord Shiva Oneness that is union of Knowledge and Faith. This was Lord Ram's message for His Vanar friends that if they want to defeat the Ego, that is Ravan and attain Peace, that is Mother Sita, then they need both the Knowledge, that is Lord Ram and the Faith, which is Lord Shiva. To progress on the path of Bhakti or Devotion, that is if one wants to attain Mother Sita, then one need to surrender in the lotus feet of both Lord Shiva and Lord Ram.

Chapter 6.2

The Three Ram-Setu: Vanars crosses the Ocean

With the Grace of Lord Ram, not one but three 'Ram-Setu' were created,
Vanars were free to choose the one, with which they felt most connected.

With the Grace of Lord Ram, the stones that were used for building Ram-Setu had attained a magical property. These 'Ram' stones didn't sink but effortlessly floated on the surface of the ocean water. Secondly, these floating stones could bear huge loads without any chance of sinking even a bit in the water. Everybody witnessed this miracle. This is, however, neither ascribed to any miraculous power of the ocean, nor to a virtue of the stones themselves and nor again to any skill of the monkeys. It was by the glory of Lord Ram that stones floated on the ocean. And the medium for this miracle were the highly skilled Vanar architects Nal and Neel who had been blessed since their childhood that whatever they touch will remain afloat and not sink in the water.

In spiritual perspective, Nal and Neel are the symbols 'Egoic Doer-ship' and 'Egoic-Expectations'. The meditation, penance or spiritual practices of even the greatest sages get spoiled because of these two factors that are Doer-ship and Expectations. Because of these two factors, all the hard work gets spoiled. Till the time the seeker will believe that he is the doer of all actions and achiever of all successes and also till the time he will have expectations of positive returns from the spiritual practices, his progress will get disturbed. If one works, be it worldly or spiritual and expects only good results, then initially he will be highly motivated but when there is obstruction in his expected outcomes, then his enthusiasm will sink.

The greatest spiritual practice and renunciation is freeing yourself from these two egoic factors, that is Doer-ship and Expectations. By Lord's Grace,

Nal and Neel had achieved this freedom by the practice of 'acceptance' and therefore, they were blessed that whatever they touch will not sink. The message here is that when one is freed from the egoic factors of Doer-ship and Expectations, and works just to serve Lord Ram, he will definitely progress without the menace of spoilage. It is not an easy achievement, but then also not impossible. It takes persistent practice, firm determination, patience and most importantly unshakable Faith in God.

Lord was glad at heart to see the hardwork of His beloved Vanars, the great 'Ram-Setu' bridge which had connected Lanka with Bharat. As the army marched, it was a sight beyond all verbalizing. The Vanar warriors were roaring as they were moving. Standing tall near the bridge, the Lord looked at the vast expanse of the ocean. Another miracle occurred, that is, all the aquatic creatures inhabiting the ocean appeared on the surface in order to have a look or 'Darshan' of the Lord. There were many kinds of alligators, crocodiles, fishes and snakes with humongous bodies. All gazed upon the Lord and would not stir even when diverted. They were all glad at heart and felt very happy. They had completely covered the water surface with their colossal bodies from one to the other end.

If the whole Vanar army had used the stone-bridge (one of the three bridges), then it would have taken long and days would have been wasted. And so many Vanars used the sea-creatures-bridge, which was the second among the three bridges, to cross the ocean. And again with the Grace of Lord Ram, that which was earlier doable for Hanumanji only, today was achieved by others also, who flew in the sky and crossed the ocean. This was the third bridge in the sky. The ten yojan broad 'Ram-Setu' being overcrowded, so some of the Vanars now flew across like Hanumanji did, while others crossed hopping over on the backs of aquatic creatures.

That day not one but three 'Ram-Setus' were built. The stone bridge symbolizes the Path of Action or 'Karma-Yog' that is the Path of Action or 'Purushartha'. For most of the human beings, this path is desirable and yet there are many who are unable to practice it. And therefore, another bridge of sea-creatures was needed where hardwork is not the only requisite and that is the Path of Devotion or 'Bhakti-Yog'. The sea-creatures symbolizes the turbulent state of mind which when focuses in the lotus feet of Lord Ram, becomes still and stable, ensuring the Being to easily cross the difficult ocean of egoic-identifications. And yet, there are some others who need a third sky-route, that is, the Path of Knowledge or 'Jnana-Yog'. The knowledgeable seekers want to walk, aloof and away from the crowd. They don't seek support and don't like waiting. They too with the Grace of Lord Ram and with their sincere practice of Knowledge, easily cross the ocean of mind-ego identification.

In this way, the Vanar army or the big cluster of seekers crossed the ocean of 'Ego' and reached Lanka, singing the glory of Lord Ram. Life becomes a celebration and no obstruction can stop the one who has devoted the 'Self' in the lotus feet of Lord Siya-Ram.

Chapter 6.3

Ravan got the Shock of his Life

Has He really bridged the waves, the billows, the sea, the ocean and the brine?
Has He actually crossed the lord of rivers, the blue, the deep, the tide and the hyaline?

The kingdom of Lanka was surrounded by a vast deep ocean from all four sides. It was believed that for an enemy with an army, it was impossible to cross this ocean. Ravan strongly believed in the same and never ever, even in his dreams, had he thought that a human being with an army of millions of Vanars can cross this ocean and invade Lanka. Ravan had always been an aggressive and offensive warrior. He was used to play on first mover advantage and he always got much success with his art of war. In very less time, he had defeated every King and had captured every part of the world. But in this last war of his life, he had lost his confidence. He had become defensive in his war approach. He had understood that this exiled Prince of Ayodhaya is not an ordinary human being but a divine entity.

Ravan had thought that after abducting Princess Sita, either Prince Ram would have committed suicide in desperation or would have brought his Ayodhaya army to combat him. Ravan played very unwisely this time as he should have realized this long back the power of Prince Ram when He had single-handedly killed Ravan's brother Khar, Dushan and Trishira at the Panchvati episode. It was ten months since Hanumanji had arrived and burnt Lanka and so again Ravan believed that the problem was over by that time itself. He had also got known through his spies that Ram is worshipping the Sea-God to give Him the path to Lanka. Ravan laughed saying that such a weak person who believes in praying and requesting can never fight wars.

Actually, Ravan had not been able to understand the unconventional ways of Lord Ram. Ravan had tried to assess the situation on the basis of his limited intellect, and therefore, it was beyond his imagination that a bridge that is Ram-Setu could be built across the ocean. He was surprised, frightened, perplexed and astounded after getting the news of Vanar army's arrival at Lanka through a bridge. In this 'Chaupai', Goswamiji has given ten different names of the ocean which Ravan, out of shock, spoke with each of his ten mouths.

In spiritual perspective, Ravan is the symbol of 'Moha' or attachment and the Ocean is the symbol of identification of the 'Self' with its Body or 'Deh-abhiman' attribute of mind-ego. 'Moha' or Ravan blindly trusts the invincibility of 'Deh-abhiman' or the Ocean. Moha believes that every Being that walks, swims or flies towards him, is trapped in the Deh-abhiman. Moha believes that it is impossible to overcome this Deh-abhiman which has entrapped every life form within it. Lord Ram had already sent Hanumanji, the symbol of 'Vairagya' or dispassion, to Lanka to let the Moha know that Deh-abhiman is indeed surmountable. Ravan, the Moha, had seen the impact of Hanumanji, the Vairagya, who had not only crossed the Ocean that is Deh-abhiman but also destroyed Lanka, which is the symbol of 'Bhog-Vilas' or obsession with pleasures and materialism.

The ten heads of Ravan signifies the Ten Senses (Five Jnana and Five Karma Indriya) which are eyes, ears, nose, tongue, skin, voice, hands, feet, anus and genitals. Moha believes that continuous enjoyment of the pleasure-objects for these Ten senses is the purpose of human life. A materialistic human being works obsessively to only see beauty with eyes, hear pleasing talks with ears, smell sweet fragrance with nose, taste delicious food with tongue and touch and feel the attractive things through the skin. Similarly, he wants to use his voice, hands, feet, anus and genitals to fulfill his desires, lust and greed. And this obsession with pleasures is the cause of suffering in human life.

The Devta who were earlier also trapped in the pleasures of Ten Senses had incarnated as the Vanars of 'Kishkinda'. They by serving and worshipping Lord Ram had been able to come out of the trap of Deh-abhiman that is identification with their bodies. And also soon by defeating Ravan, they would be able to be totally free from 'Moha' or attachment which is the main cause of mankind's pain or 'Dukha'. Ravan was dumbfounded to see the Grace of Lord Ram. This was a lesson for Ravan and for every selfish and materialistic Being, that real happiness and satisfaction is not in mundane objects but can be attained only by crossing the Ocean of Deh-abhiman and destroying Ravan of Moha and this can simply be done by surrendering oneself in the lotus feet of Lord Siya-Ram.

Chapter 6.4

Lord and the Four Elements: The Divine Scenery

Thus rested Lord Ram, the embodiment of benignity and beauty,
Blessed are those who remain ever immersed in Supreme Deity.

Ravan was terrified hearing about the construction of Ram-Setu. The way, one of his sons, Prahast condemned him and his ministers, dispirited Ravan. Then, the counseling given by his wife, Mandodari who adviced Ravan to return Lady Sita and to surrender himself to Lord Ram also irate him. To take a break from this, so as to speak, to be ignorant of the real challenging situation, he ordered to organize a music and dance program for his entertainment at the highest chamber of the fort. He wanted the whole of Lanka citizens to see that even though the enemy is at the gates yet Ravan is assured of his victory and is least concerned. That chamber was also visible to the Vanar camps. Ravan intended that the enemies too see him celebrating and get the message that the mighty Ravan is not bothered. Through this gimmick, he wanted to give confidence to his people and put down the morale of the Vanar army. He believed that by playing this one trick, he will influence both the Asura and Vanar, but the real truth was that he was trying to hide his own insecurity.

While the program was going on, on the other side, Lord Ram with His dear associates was seated on a hilltop. It was a special hill as it had an even and leveled surface on the top like a plateau. This hill had a deep significance. In the worldly life, the ones who are not successful appear to be polite and humble, whereas the ones, who have attained success, lose the even-mindedness. But to attain completeness in life, one need to be both great and humble, that is leveled like the mountain top. And this quality clearly sparkles in the persona of the Lord. For a balanced life, one not only needs to be disciplined but also soft and this was evident in the Lord.

Lord was lying on the couch prepared by Lord Laxman with leaves, flowers and deer skin. He rested His head on Sugriv's lap. On one side,

Vibhishan was kneeling down and whispering war strategy in the Lord's ear. Both the Lord's lotus feet were placed in the laps of Hanumanji and Angad. They with devotion and joy were massaging and giving comfort to Him. Laxmanji was standing right behind, watching all of them in an alert warrior posture. Lord had an arrow in His hands. He was casually sharpening the arrow's tip. Tulsdiasji says that the fortunate are the one who can do 'Chintan' or visualization of this divine scene.

Hanumanji, Sugriv, Vibhishan and Angad symbolizes the four elements of 'Antahkarana' or inner body of the Being, that is Mind or 'Mann', Intellect or 'Buddhi', Memory or 'Chit' and Ego or 'Ahankar'. Only when the Antahkarana of the human being is focused on God, the four elements come together else they wander in different directions chasing mundane desires, thereby giving only trouble to the Being. These four also signify the four types of Devotees or 'Bhakta' that is 'Aart' - one who wants to get rid of suffering, 'Artharth' - one who seeks fulfillment of desires, 'Jigyasu' - one who is inquisitive about spirituality and 'Gyani' – the Self-Realized.

Lord is conveying the message that He accepts both Asura (Vibhishan) that is ignorance of mind and the Vanars (Sugriv, Hanumanji and Angad) that is restlessness of mind. The seekers are always troubled with the unfriendly state of mind which doesn't allow them to practice spirituality or 'Sadhan-Bhajan', properly. Lord assures the seeker that it doesn't matter if the mind is not cooperating; what is expected is purity of heart and sincerity in quest.

These four also signify the four elements of politics. Hanumanji is the symbol of 'Sam' that is evenness, balance and agreement. He tries to convince Ravan to let go of his evilness and join the Lord. Angad is the symbol of 'Dand' that is punishment and discipline. Angad tells Ravan openly that if he doesn't return Mother Sita and surrender to Lord Ram, then he will lose his life. Sugriv is the symbol of 'Damm' or incentive. Lord removes Bali from the throne and crowns Sugriv as the king of Kishkinda. In return, Sugriv pledges to be a friend and serves Lord Ram forever. Vibhishan is the symbol of 'Bhed' or divide and rule policy. He, although a brother of Ravan, discards him and comes in the shelter of Lord Ram and divulges the secrets of Lanka, ultimately leading towards the defeat and end of Ravan.

In this way, if the Being wants to succeed in life, then he needs to bring all the four elements under the flagship of the Lord. And this is possible only when the human beings realize first that the only purpose of life is to surrender in the lotus feet of Lord Siya-Ram.

Chapter 6.5

Warning to Ravan: Oblivious Punishment

The imperceivable arrow cautioned the whole assembly,
Turn over a new leaf, or the next one will be very deathly.

Ravan seated high on his throne of entertainment theatre, with a proud smile on his face but with a concern in his heart, was observing the whole scene. He was least interested in the music and the dance but was only eager to scrutinize how much his demonstration of his boldness is influencing the other courtiers in the theatre. But then suddenly, the whole assembly got startled and stood up in awe. The magnificent royal shade under which Ravan was sitting fell on the floor and in the next moment the ten crowns on his head also flew in the air as if somebody had thrown them. Not only had that, but the diamond earrings of Mandodari also abruptly dropped on the ground. These occurrences shocked the courtiers. They were surprised as there was no earthquake, no storm, no person nearby and no weapon; then how come all this happened. They took it as an evil omen but as usual out of Ravan's fear remained mum.

Back at the hilltop, Lord Ram with His associates was relaxing and gazing at the moon in the Eastern night sky. He shifted His gaze towards the South and asked Vibhishan ignorantly, "Look there, how the dark clouds have enveloped the sky, there is a bright lightning and the thunder sounds so melodiously. Seems like there is going to be a hail storm". Vibhishan replied to Lord, "O King of Universe! It is not what it appears to be. This is the dark royal shade of the entertainment theater on the top of Lanka's castle that appears like a cloud. The diamonds on Mandodari's earring are sparkling like sky lightning and the melodious sound is of the musical instruments."

Actually, Lord Ram was indirectly conveying to Vibhishan that 'look your brother Ravan is sitting in the lap of death and still is engrossed in pleasures'; but poor Vibhishan couldn't understand the Lord's words. This is the state of every ignorant human-being trapped in the Maya of material pleasures.

The cloud thunders just like an egoist and arrogant person thunders to frighten others. The Being trapped in mind-ego is like a dark ugly cloud which in the reflection of its own lighting sees itself as very beautiful but fails to see its flaws. The sparkling of diamonds gives a proud feeling to the one who is mesmerized by worldly opulence but lacks the insight or 'Vivek', to understand the impermanence nature of the worldly objects. A thundering cloud is welcomed by the people as it is a sign of rain and water, bringing prosperity but nobody likes the cloud that brings a hail storm that destroys the farms and crops. And this is the character of Ravan who only brings destruction and no prosperity and who uses his might only to give pain and suffering to others.

After hearing Vibhishan, Lord smiled. He lifted an arrow and set the target. The next moment that one arrow throws off the royal shade, royal crowns and the royal diamonds from its royal places, which were for Lanka, symbols of power, prosperity and invincibility. After doing its work, the arrow returned and settled back in Lord's quiver. 'Kaal' or Death is the punishment of God, which is hidden and manifests itself as destruction. Nobody at the theatre could see who or what did but could see the dance of death in the falling of the symbols of Lanka's pride. This was a warning for Ravan and to the Beings, who can never know what is in wait for them the next moment and for those who forgets that their power and prosperity, the basis of their ego can be in dust the very next moment. And they can do nothing about it.

The message for the human beings is to mend your ways in time, the one that is 'Kaal' which is imperceivable, which has snapped the shade, crowns and the earrings can disbalance your life and won't even take a split second in destroying your head, the storehouse of your pride, arrogance and ego. If Ravan had understood the message of the Lord's arrow that is 'Kaal', then he would have corrected himself and surrendered in the lotus feet of Lord Ram. And like Hanumanji told him earlier, Ravan would have continued ruling Lanka and enjoying life. But even after this warning from Lord Ram, the polluted, ignorant and arrogant Ravan could not realize his mistake, and therefore, himself becomes the cause of destruction of his own self and of his kingdom.

Chapter 6.6

Mandodari counsels: Ravan, the Brainless Intellectual

Mandadori realized that Kaal had targeted her Husband-King,
One who has lost his judiciousness, impossible is his well-being.

The purpose with which Ravan had organized the grand concert at a place visible to every Lanka citizen, had failed miserably. His intention was to boost the morale of his people but with the fall of the royal symbols, the Asuras got extremely terrorized. The Lanka citizens started whispering that this is a sign of some change going to take place. The present monarch will fall and the new order will rise. Ravan's plan had backfired but the foolish tyrant didn't stop his attempts. Back in his private chamber, the bothered Queen Mandodari explains to Ravan to accept that Lord Ram is not an ordinary mortal and in the interest of Lanka, Ravan should return Lady Sita and surrender to Him. But the thoughtless Ravan didn't accept her wise words and gave illogical replies.

He said that once all his heads fell in the Bhakti of Lord Shiva and he got blessed with immortality, so how come falling of crowns is a bad omen? He was reasoning that for others falling off the head means death but he is special and that falling means prosperity and immortality. Therefore, falling of the shade and his crowns are signifying good luck and victory. But, Ravan had forgotten the difference between offering and falling. Offering depends on the will and endeavor of the devotee, whereas falling signifies the incapability and weakness of the Bieng. At that time, Ravan heads didn't fall but were consciously offered by him. If the royal shade and crowns had been offered consciously, then Ravan's reply would have been right. But now, they were not offered and they fell and Ravan couldn't do anything about it.

A person may demonstrate the loss or defeat as immaterial for him but this doesn't actually help. Damage has been done and Ravan knows it, and hence, he had immediately dispersed the assembly after this incident at the theatre. He didn't want to give the courtiers a chance to discuss this incident. He knew that it would spread terror in his people even more. He asked them to simply ignore this episode and go off to sleep. He believed that by doing so, his people would turn a blind eye towards the truth and live peacefully. But forget the courtiers, even his own family, Mandodari felt the fear. She couldn't sleep the whole night. Ravan may not have understood the call of death but his wife Mandodari had recognized it. The arrow of Lord was not visible but its impact was loud and clear. The invisible words spoke everything. There was also a message for Mandodari from the Lord, 'Ravan in his ego had turned blind but you are wise and aware and that you need to make him understand the reality and save Lanka'. Mandodari sincerely obeyed Lord's command and tried her best to show Ravan the Vishwa-Roop of Lord Ram and inspired him to devote himself in Lord's feet.

Death dances at the indication of His eyebrows,
Sun shines in His eyes,
Clouds are His dark hair,
Day and Night are the blinking of His eyes,
Ten directions are His ears,
Air is His breadth,
Vedanta is His voice,
Yamraj is His teeth,
Maya is His laughter,
Fire is His mouth,
Creation-Preservation and Destruction are His endeavors,
Shiv is His ego,
Brahma is His intellect,
Moon is His mind,
And Vishnu is His intelligence,
The Supreme Master of the Universe has incarnated as a human being.

Mandodari in many ways tried to explain Ravan saying that by not accepting the Supremacy of Lord Ram, he was sealing his own death warrant. But all her efforts went in vain. Ravan with his illogical reasoning and shallow humor instead replies that it's her attachment for him that is making her weak. In his foolish ego, he mistook the words of Mandodari and felt that she was actually praising him by referring to Prince Ram. Strange are the ways of intellectual idiots. Ravan's enemy was his own intellect which though very sharp and deep, but was totally polluted, that is trapped in the clutches of mind-ego.

When intellect is the enemy and supports the unreasonable activities of mind, then that human being is definitely doomed. Ravan considered himself as the most knowledgeable one, and therefore, to every statement of Mandodari applied reasoning which suits and gratifies his own ego. He totally failed to see the concern and truth in Mandodari's words. She remained silent to his idiotic comments and now understood that now well-being of her husband is not possible.

When 'Kaal' or death decides to destroy, then it doesn't attack using an object or weapon rather it destroys the intelligence and the thinking ability of its target. That day Kaal had annihilated Ravan's intelligence and so he had turned thoughtless and unreasonable. Therefore, Ravan's end was sealed.

Chapter 6.7

Angad: The Peace-Messenger

Lord wanted to give Ravan one more chance,
He wanted peace and not the death-dance.

Before waging the war, Lord Ram wanted to give one more chance to Ravan to realize his mistake. Although many had already tried to counsel Ravan to return Lady Sita and to avoid this war, but all had failed. So now who could be the best one to execute this Lord's work? Who has the capability to deal with difficult Ravan? The wise Jambvan suggested the youth prince Angad's name for this mission. In all perspectives, he felt that Angad had all the requisite qualities that could get the job done.

Jambvan had remembered the journey of Lady Sita's search. During that time, he had clearly noticed the guilt and despondency in Angad. Though Angad was the captain of that south-direction team, he was actually lonely and helpless. All the members of the team were Sugriv's loyalist who had taken Sugriv's side during Bali-Sugriv conflict. With the intervention of Lord Ram, the situation changed. The supporters of Sugriv and Bali got united after Bali's end and Sugriv's crowning. They were standing as one entity in the Lanka war, yet Angad was not able to come out of his apprehensions towards Sugriv.

When Hanumanji returned after successfully finding Mother Sita, all the Vanars got overjoyed and even Angad felt happy, but somewhere he was still not totally at peace. To accept the killer of his father, Sugriv as the new king and to work under him was difficult for him. Jambvan was eager to ease Angad and help him to come out of this dilemma and guilt. Jambvan wanted Angad to get his due. He wanted that by contributing in Lord Ram's work, Angad must gain importance in others' eyes and he should attain the confidence to accept Sugriv. Lord Ram too knew the power and talent of Angad and wanted His son-devotee to become eternal in the pages of Sanatan Dharma.

To talk to Ravan and that too for peace was not an easy job. The messenger needed to have the acumen to deal with difficult Ravan. If Hanumanji had been again sent for this mission, then Ravan would have assumed that other than him there is no good warrior in the Vanar army. There was another reason also. Earlier though in the fight, Bali had defeated Ravan but later both became friends. It would be easier for Angad, son of Ravan's friend Bali, to gain his trustworthiness. Also, Angad was an impressive and bright young man. Through him, the vigor of the Lord would spread in all directions of Lanka.

If Ravan had agreed to surrender to Lord Ram, he would be doubtful about whether the Lord would accept him after sheltering and crowning Vibhishan. In this case, through Angad, he would get to know that even after sheltering Sugriv, the Lord pardoned Bali and assured him a long life. Though Bali refused life and chose death, he did acknowledge the Lord's grace. The Lord also ensured cordial equation between Sugriv and Angad by crowning Sugriv as the king and Angad as the prince. He ordered Sugriv to run the affairs of Kishkinda along with Angad. In this way, the Lord ended the long going conflict in the royal family of Kishkinda and established 'Ram-Rajya'.

Knowing about Lord Ram's peaceful settlement of Kishkinda through Angad, Ravan would have gained the confidence that the Lord will be fair with him and will bring a peaceful settlement in Lanka also and would ensure cordial relationship between Ravan and Vibhishan. Lord Ram is the treasure of Dharma or righteousness. He is the pinnacle of order and justice. All the qualities and virtues reside in Him. And so all species be it Manushya, Vanar, Asur, Devta, Pashu and Pakshi can reside together under His shelter. Lord Ram agreed with Jambvan and decided to send him as a peace messenger to Ravan. Angad the great son of Kishkindha was now going to face the toughest challenge of his life. But he has nothing to worry about because he is a devotee who has surrendered in the lotus feet of Lord Siya-Ram.

Chapter 6.8

War of Words: Angad Vs Ravan

In the history of politics, other than Lord Ram no other leader had used the 'Trust' factor so liberally. For many, Lord Ram trusting Angad for the peace talks with Ravan, was not a very sound decision, considering that Lord Ram Himself is the slayer of Angad's father, Bali. So others were not very confident about Angad's loyalty towards the Lord and they had an apprehension that Angad might backstab by revealing the secrets of Vanar army to Ravan, making it vulnerable.

But like always, Lord Ram's decision was right. It turned out that no other one except Angad would have been able to execute this job with such magnificence and excellence. Angad was the greatest diplomacy challenge Ravan had ever faced. The great Angad emerged as a superb leader and loyalist of Lord Ram who brought Ravan on his knees, thrashing his honor in front of his own people. The devotion and faith of Angad towards Lord Siya-Ram shook the foundations of Lanka. Nomination of Angad for this assignment proves that the leadership of Lord Ram is beyond the understanding of mediocre minds.

The ruler-ship of Lord Ram was not based on showoff of power or grandeur but was based only on the well-being of His people. He had appointed Angad not just on merits but also for his welfare. The one who went and the one who returned was not the same person anymore. Angad reached Ravan and conveyed him the peace message. He proposed that even now, if Ravan returns Lady Sita and surrenders, then Lord Ram with the Vanar army would return from Lanka peacefully and Ravan can continue ruling. But as expected, Ravan replied offensively and in an uncompromising manner. Both Ravan and Angad exchanged witty and satirical words ending with no settlement. But through this episode, everyone came to know about the greatness of Angad who made Ravan bow down on his knees. This Angad-Ravan verbal confrontation is one of the most popular episodes of Ramcharitmanas.

Not able to persuade Angad to come to his side was Ravan's biggest political defeat. This scene opened with Angad introducing himself as the son of Bali who was a friend of Ravan and that Angad's purpose to come there is just for Ravan's welfare. Hearing the name Bali, Ravan didn't give any reaction, neither he appeared to be pleased nor welcoming. Actually, his friendship with Bali was more of a compromise which Ravan did after being badly beaten by Bali. The name Bali only recalled Ravan his defeat and not friendship. He didn't want his courtiers to see and believe that Bali was some important personality. Sharp Angad, immediately understood this and teased Ravan by asking him again that had he ever met Bali? To this, Ravan expressionlessly replied that he knows Bali is a Vanar.

Ravan then tried to provoke Angad against Lord Ram, reminding him that the One who he is supporting is the One who had slayed his father that too from ambush. Ravan very much wanted to make Angad leave Lord Ram and join him but he didn't want this intention to be revealed. He was constantly trying to prove that he doesn't care for anybody. Not just to Angad but also to his own people he wanted to flaunt that he can fight and win this war on his own. In his act of hiding his defeat from Bali, Ravan had forgotten basic courtesy. Being a friend of Angad's father and a king, a cordial and welcoming behavior was expected from him. The appropriate behavior would have been to ask Angad his well being, to express condolence on his father's demise, maybe talk about the injustice and sympathize with him. But instead of displaying basic courtesy, Ravan unabashedly tried to irk Angad.

Comparatively Angad's mannerism, wit and communication skills were far better than Ravan. He defeated Ravan in every aspect of this war of words. Angad very well knew that Ravan was aware of Bali's death and by asking Angad about Bali's well-being, Ravan was intentionally trying to poke him. Ravan was actually happy knowing about Bali's demise as this meant the ending of an enemy's threat. His pact of friendship with Bali was just another gimmick. And yet he was unhappy that Prince Ram had got the credit and fame for ending the rule of Bali. Through the speech and actions of Ravan, it was clear that he was a major victim of inner conflicts or 'Antardwand'. But Angad, being a wise person and also a devotee was totally free from any sorts of inner or outer conflicts, he could intelligently reply to every attacking questions of Ravan. The one who has freed himself from the trap of mind-ego becomes invincible. So when Ravan asked how Bali is, Angad with a smile replied that he himself will come to know after ten days when he will put by near his friend in the afterlife. Angad meant that since he had sparked off enmity with Lord Ram, Ravan would not be able to survive for more than ten days.

We may appreciate the greatness of Angad, but still a question arises in the minds of readers that can a self-respecting person take the side of the slayer of his own father? An ordinary person will always hate the one who has orphaned him and made his mother a widow. But Angad was different, not because that he was not self-respecting, but he had attained a higher level of consciousness which is not comprehensible for a mediocre intellect.

Every object, thing and relationship in this world is forever changing and volatile. So the duty-actions taken on the basis of these are always changing variables which cannot be stable and rightful. The only one basis of duty or Dharma for Beings can be that which is never-changing, that is, God only and nothing else. The relationship between two human beings is ever changing but the relationship between Being and Ram, Jiva and Ishvara, is constant and cannot be changed. Every human being must forever be grateful and devoted to his mother and father but the Being must also always remember the Creator of Self-Soul who is the true Mother and Father of the Being. When Angad had to choose between the father of his Body and the creator of his Self-Soul, he chose God Ram.

In the worldly spectrum, the family legacy of every Being can be different but at the true level of consciousness the family of every Being is one and same. Consciousness is the core and the world is one, in it's infinite manifestation. Enlightened is the one who understands this truth and Angad is one of them. He, unlike ignorant Beings doesn't choose the family legacy of this mundane world but only accepts the legacy of Ram-Consciousness. But, Ravan had taunted that Angad is a shame on his Vanar legacy and that Ravan is the guardian of his Asur legacy. Angad on the basis of Ram-consciousness-legacy replies back that being the scholar of Vedas, Ravan should be known the true meaning of legacy but even after having ten minds and twenty eyes and ears, he is far from it.

God Ram is the 'Adi-Purush', the First-Man. The one who goes against Him is the traitor of legacy, which is Ravan. To revere Him is the real commitment towards the legacy, Vibhishan discards Ravan and joined Lord Ram. In worldly perspective, he appeared to be a traitor of his family, but actually he was the genuine well-wisher of the Asur family. Foolish Ravan by earning enmity of Lord Ram had already signed not just on his own but also on every family member's death warrant. It was Vibhishan who protected Asur species and

Lanka from Ravan's destruction. If Lord Ram had crowned Sugriv with the King's throne, then He has also crowned Angad with the Prince's throne. Angad was the successor of Kishkinda though he was not Sugriv's own offspring.

In this war of words, Ravan's intention was to create a rift between Angad and Lord Ram. And Angad purpose was to explain him that if he had been able to understand the truth of Omnipresent Ram, able to put his faith in the principles of Vedas and able to realize the divinity, then instead of creating this rift, he would have himself surrendered into the lotus feet of Lord Siya-Ram. Angad wanted to make him understand that if his father the Great Bali, who was much stronger than Ravan, got destroyed by Lord Ram, then, what is the stature of Ravan. He should not repeat the same mistake and not waste his life foolishly. The purpose of life is only one and that is to realize the futility of this unreal world of ego and discover the Bhakti of Lord Siya-Ram.

Chapter 6.9

War of Words: Angad outwits Ravan

Angad speaks in amazement, "Is it true that that one Vanar torched and destroyed your kingdom? Probably out of fear of punishment for disobeying the Lord, he hasn't returned back to us." The diplomatic dialogue between Ravan and Angad was filled with high voltage drama, sarcasm, humor and taunts. They both were eager to defeat the other. Ravan had always labeled Vanar as an uncivilized and undeveloped race and had considered Asura and particularly himself as far more superior. He criticizes Lord Ram by accusing Him of slaying Bali from ambush. And then by quoting Bali as pitiful, he tries to show off his sympathy towards Angad.

Bali was not at all pitiful but Ravan by stating so, he just wanted to condemn Prince Ram, although everybody else and he himself was very well aware that the glory of Lord Ram had only increased manifold by bringing an end to Bali's cruel regime. What Ravan meant was that Bali could be physically very strong, but was still a brainless brute. Because of no sense of strategy and weapons, he had become a target of Prince Ram's hunting adventure. Naturally, Angad got very furious but he remained composed. Now, he decided that he will not only defeat Ravan in muscular strength but also in intellectual combat and ultimately get very successful. He made Ravan a laughing stock in front of his own Lanka.

Ravan tried to downplay the achievements of Lord Ram and Laxman. Without any basis and just out of his wicked imagination, he said that Prince Ram without His wife is hopeless. And his brother Laxman out of brotherly attachment is needlessly suffering. He indirectly taunted Sugriv and Angad, saying that they may have become the new rulers but because of their association with Prince Ram, their foundation has become vulnerable and in this war their end is guaranteed. He didn't spare his own brother Vibhishan also and criticized him by saying that he is an escapist who hid behind the sheath of spiritual life. What is the reliability of the one who in difficult times can leave his brother at a crucial hour, will stand with Prince Ram till the end? Then he picked on Jambvan that he may be an invincible warrior at one time but now he is old and fragile.

Ravan criticized everybody but surprisingly appreciated Hanumanji, but there was two reasons behind that. Firstly, before Angad would bring in the episode of 'Lanka-Dahan' or torching of Lanka by Hanumanji, he himself spoke about it, so that now, Angad would have nothing to boast about. Secondly, he wanted to demonstrate that he is an impartial person, that his criticism or appreciation is not based on enmity but on the merit of the individual. Ravan then tried to use this card of impartiality to bring Angad on his side. But, the smartest Angad turned the tables in the most unexpected manner. He cut Ravan in and with a fake-surprise and sarcastic expression spoke, "I can't believe it. Please be honest, King Ravan. A little monkey torched and destroyed the land of Ravan, who will believe this? But why would you lie and that means it must be true. We sent him just because he was aware of Asura's tricks. The one about whom you are speaking so highly is one of the many stewards of Sugriv. He was not ordered to attack and still he did it. Probably, this is the reason why he didn't return back."

Angad was not telling the truth but by portraying Hanumanji as an ordinary Vanar, he outsmarted Ravan with his clever and diplomatic tactics. Through these words, he made Ravan to realize that his world renowned Lanka is actually very vulnerable and easily penetrable, thereby mocking him. Ravan wanted to prove that only Hanumanji is a good warrior on his side but by stating the same Hanumanji ordinary, Angad outsmarted Ravan's diplomatic attack. Angad meant to say that when such an ordinary soldier can destroy your city, then what would happen when all Lord Ram's skilled warriors will attack? By saying that Hanumanji didn't have the orders of torching Lanka, Angad also wanted to prove that Vanars are very disciplined and each one of them is capable to defeat Ravan but they are quiet and waiting as per Lord Ram's instructions. By saying that Hanumanji didn't return out of fear and hid somewhere, Angad wanted to say that when somebody achieves a grand feat, he proudly returns but burning of Lanka was such an ordinary act for Hanumanji that out of hesitation he didn't return.

In this way, brave and brilliant Angad proved to Ravan that the one you are praising considers himself, that is Hanumanji, an ordinary servant of Lord Ram. By criticizing Lord and applauding the Servant, Ravan has achieved nothing but has made a laughing stock of himself. One needs patience and intelligence to deal with difficult people. Even a small loosening of grip gives mind-ego the window to spoil the peace of mind. It is more difficult to deal with your own Mind than with a difficult person. This ability to manage the most complicated situations is possible when one attains immense Faith. And the Power of Faith is easily and innately attained by the one who has surrendered himself unto the lotus feet of Lord Siya-Ram.

Chapter 6.10

Angad Challenges Asuras of Lanka: Roar of Faith

O Fool! Hear my challenge, if you can move my foot even by an inch,
Then I will accept my defeat and Lord Ram will return without Lady Sita.

The wise Angad had understood that Ravan's mindset cannot be changed just by verbal talks. Though Lord Ram had instructed him to remember two things while negotiating with Ravan, one is 'Success for us' and second is 'Welfare of Ravan'. But Angad's effort for Ravan's welfare failed. A doctor can just treat and ensure the health of the patient, only when the patient cooperates. Cure and welfare cannot be forced on anybody. And when the patient is in the wrong state of mind, then he doesn't realize that he is ill and needs to be treated. Ravan's both mind and intelligence was corrupted and so Angad had compared him with the patient of 'Sannipat' or Delirium.

Sannipat or this mental fever is the most difficult to be cured because the patient is hopelessly unable to trust his own healer. A patient more than his own needs to trust the intelligence of the doctor. If the patient is egotistically rigid and trusts only himself and not others, then he cannot be treated. In the perspective of Antaha-Karna, Ravan had corrupted his mind (mann), intelligence (buddhi), ego (ahankar) and mental conditioning (chitt). He had become so hopeless that he was not realizing who is with him and who is against. How his own son Prahastha had mocked him that he is despising the words of wisdom, just like a patient on his deathbed, detests cure.

Angad had already chucked the hope of Ravan's welfare. But, he had a duty and that was to ensure the success of 'Ram-Kaj' or Lord Ram's orders. And for it, he had to destroy the courage and morale of the Asuras. Along with it, he wanted to demolish the confidence and influence of Ravan over his people. The all-powerful Angad first punched the ground so hard that it trembled and because of its impact, the Emperor's throne shook and Ravan fell down on his face. Nobody in his wildest dream had imagined that the mighty Ravan would fall like this. But that day, the whole royal assembly witnessed it. All the ten crowns from his ten heads too toppled on the floor and Ravan, like a greedy animal, had hastened to grab them. But four of the crowns were picked and thrown by Angad, towards Lord Ram's throne. Ravan picked the rest of the six crowns and wore them again. It was a funny sight that crowns on his six heads and four empty heads.

Next, the lion-hearted Angad, with Lord Ram in his mind, fixed his foot on the ground and announced loudly - "Oh foolish and evil man! if you can move by foot, even by an inch, then I pledge that Lord Ram will leave Lady Sita in Lanka and return back." Many people when they read this part of Ramayan are not really appreciative of Angad's challenge. They get terrorized thinking, 'what would have happened, if Angad's foot had moved by Ravan as per the challenge'? Such apprehensions arise only in a weak mind which lacks faith. The pledge of Angad is a reflection of his unshakable faith in the Bhakti of Lord Ram. Lord by appointing Angad as His ambassador had expressed His immense trust in Angad. Angad had proved himself worthy of that trust.

Angad very well had realized the truth and that is why while taking leave from Lord Ram for Lanka he requested, "Lord, Yourself is the Consciousness itself. Yourself don't need anyone else for the success of your endeavors. Only to give me honor, you have given this task to me." Angad also had acknowledged Hanumanji as his teacher as he had got the inspiration for unwavering faith from him. Hanumanji had said to Ravan to decorate the lotus feet of Lord Ram in his heart and rule the kingdom of Lanka without any disturbance. Angad felt, if the lotus feet of the Lord are so divine, then the ones who serve Those, even their devotion and faith becomes divine. The challenge of Angad was based on his immense faith in Saint Hanuman and God Ram. This faith is very important for seekers, because if the teaching of Saints and influence of God are not effective, then the purpose of Bhakti or Devotion will be defeated.

Goswami Tulsidas says that to whom should I give credit for Angad's success at Ravan's court, the Glory of the Lord or the Faith of the devotee? Actually, the credit must go to both Glory and Faith. If there is no Lord's Glory, then Faith will be baseless and if there is no Faith in the Being, then Lord's Glory will be of no benefit for the Being. Human-Being's unshakable Faith in Lord and His Glory is the real victory of Bhakti.

Chapter 6.11

Ravan's Four Crowns: Righteous Politics

Seeing the corruption in Ravan they have come to the Lord,
One day everyone realizes the truth and surrenders to the Lord.

Before Angad would return, the symbols of victory had already reached Lord Ram and those were the four crowns of Ravan thrown from the court of Lanka. Seeing the approaching divine dazzle of the crowns, the Vanars got terrified. Some thought that it was a meteor shower and some thought that it was a missile-attack by Ravan to devastate the Vanar army. Seeing the Vanars frightened, Lord Ram in His signature style chuckled. Instead of Lord, if it had been someone else, then he would have got really concerned thinking about his own soldiers, 'how would such a petrified and cowardly army face an opponent like Ravan'. But Lord Ram's perspective is totally different.

Mind-ego is like a warehouse of contradictory elements. Logically, we may think that bravery and cowardice are contradictory to each other and cannot exist jointly in the same mind. But actually this is not true. Since the origin of mankind, the mind has been the center of contradictory emotions and fear is the first emotion of the Creation of Life. The God of Creation, Brahma Himself first experienced fear and later started His endeavor of creation (As per Srimad-Bhagwad, seeing Himself alone in the ocean, He got frightened and called the Supreme Lord Narayan for help). It is surprising to see Creator Brahma frightened but this fear has very deep value. This fear inspired Him to surrender in the refuge of the Supreme Lord. The significance of this story is to realize that when the Being feels lonely and scared, then he must devote his mind and surrender his energies in the lotus feet of Lord Ram. But the Creator knows that such is the mind-ego that not many Beings would be able to accept this truth. And therefore, at the lower level of nature or Apara-Prakriti, the emotion of courage was endowed to the Being to deal with their fears. And this is the reason for contradictory emotions that are fear and courage, existing together in the human mind.

Even the lion-hearts cannot claim to be totally free from fear. In ordinary Beings, fear is a permanent and constant factor. But the discerning one or 'Viveki' with his power of wisdom or 'Vivek' can conquer this emotion of fear. Most of us are ordinary Beings and the maximum part of our mind is always filled with fear driven thoughts. And these thoughts are mostly imaginative and do not have a solid ground. The fear of Vanars was also imaginary. The object that terrified them later became the cause of their merriment. Before the arrival of Angad, the four crowns symbolizing the success of Angad made the Vanars happy. If Angad had tried to keep the crown with himself instead of throwing, then surely Ravan and his Asura would have desperately tried to snatch back them. This is one perspective.

The other perspective is Angad's perspective. Out of the ten crowns which fell on the floor, Ravan was able to snatch six of them and the rest four were picked by Angad. Angad saw the four crowns as true loyalists of Lord Ram who wanted to discard Ravan and surrender to the Lord. To hold these four renunciants crowns, even for one moment was injustice towards them and therefore they should be immediately sent to the Lord. Lord Ram had recognized this intent of Angad and also the inclination of those four crowns and so had accepted them in His refuge. Later Lord asked Angad, how he was able to rescue these four crowns from Ravan, to which he replied that these four crowns are the four attributes of politics: 'Sam' or agreement, 'Daam' or lurement, 'Dand' or punishment and 'Bhed' or divide & rule. These four have clearly understood that if they now continue to remain with a person like Ravan, then their end is inevitable. So far, Ravan has been a very successful emperor who has used politics intelligently for his success. But later, his mind had corrupted and therefore the four pillars of politics (Sam, Daam, Dand and Bhed), the best weapons of Ravan had escaped his intellect and that means now, his end is not far.

Lord Ram had passed the judgment for Surpanakha as guilty which she was, but Ravan for his selfish interest, in attaining Lady Sita, accepted Surpanakha's act and didn't find her guilty. He was in agreement with wrong and disagreement with righteousness and so had misused the first attribute of politics that is 'Sam'.

The second attribute of politics - 'Daam' or lurement was used by Lord Ram for the benefit of all in larger interest but Ravan used his wealth as an instrument to attract others for his own interest. Ravan foolishly demonstrated his splendor to lure Lady Sita.

The third attribute - 'Dand' or punishment was executed by Lord Ram only to discipline the criminal and evil Beings who spoiled the peace and order of society. Whereas, Ravan tried to punish the noble ones who had shown him the righteous way of life like Marich, Vibhishan, Hanuman and Malyavan.

The fourth and final attribute of politics, that is, 'Bhed' or divide & rule, was used by Ravan on great devotees like Angad, who see nothing but righteousness in Lord Ram's verdicts. Ravan tries to divide them to separate them from the Lord and bring them on his side. Whereas, the Lord had used the weapon of 'Bhed' for those noble Beings who out of some compulsion had to support evil minded Ravan. Like Vibhishan, who although had never agreed with Ravan's actions yet because of circumstances had to continue living in Lanka. Through Hanumanji, the Lord was able to divide and separate Vibhishan from Ravan and through Vibhishan, ultimately established peace and order in Lanka.

Through this episode, Angad wants to give us the message that the four attributes of politics have understood that their right place and right utility is in the shelter of Dharma and Lord Ram. Ravan by misusing these political attributes had himself dug his own grave. Angad message is that sooner or later every animate Being or an inanimate particle realizes that the only purpose of their creation is to surrender in the lotus feet of Lord Siya-Ram and nowhere else.

Chapter 6.12

The Four Gates of Lanka Fort: Challenge for the Seeker

The Gates of Lanka Fort are very strongly made,
Need to find the way to break them and invade.

After embarrassing Ravan and his courtiers, the great Angad returned to Lord Ram and narrated the whole episode. It was clear now that truce is not possible with Ravan. He was not ready to change himself. And therefore, there was no other option but the war with Ravan. Lord Ram called the meeting with His ministers to discuss the strategy of the war. The objective was to chalk out the plan to invade the Lanka Fort. Vibhishan had already informed that the fort has four main entrance Gates. They had to decide whether the attack be focused on one main Gate only or it should be an equally divided attack on all four Gates.

In the history of Lanka kingdom, the first attack on Fort was done by Ravan. At that time, Lanka was ruled by the Yakshas or Kuber's men. That was the era of Ravan's progress and the young Ravan was full of enthusiasm. He did not have to try very hard and terrified with him, Kuber and the Yakshas soon surrendered to him. After winning Lanka, Ravan, like an aggressive warrior, invaded all parts of the world. But like it happens, with easy success, alertness reduces and the same happened with Ravan. Later, he had become complacent. Surpanakha in front of the assembly had scolded him, "Day and night, you are intoxicated and sleeping like an alcoholic, you are not realizing that your enemies are at your doors. You have forgotten the important political principle that enemy, fire and sins should never be underestimated or underrated."

Many years before, this war with Vanars, Ravan had come to know the rise of a new superpower, which was Prince of Ayodhya, Prince Ram. The elimination of Tardka and Subahu by young Prince Ram under the mentorship of Sage Vishvamitra was a warning for Ravan. A little later, at the bow-ceremony of Janakpur, Ravan eloped from the challenge but the Lord broke the bow and married Princess Sita. This was a clear indication of Ravan's beginning of the end of his supremacy. But it appears that Ravan mesmerized by pleasures and intoxicants was intentionally ignoring these indications. Possibly, he had felt relieved knowing about the forest exile of Lord Ram. He felt that when the Prince of Ayodhya had been ousted by his own father, then what threat now he could be for Lanka. In this way, repeatedly he became a victim of his own mind-ego's complacency.

Even after Surpanakha's news of the Khar and Dushan's episode, Ravan could not dare to lead his army and attack Lord Ram at Panchavati. Instead he did a cowardly and dastardly act by abducting a lady, finding her alone and escaped from the scene like a rodent. He had become defensive and insecure, and so confined himself within the boundaries of Lanka, believing that exiled Prince Ram can never reach this most protected island. For this war, Lord Ram could have called an army from Ayodhya but instead he built the Vanar army and was now standing at the doors of Lanka. This was none less than a miracle and a shock for Ravan and now the whole of Asur clan got defensive, waiting for the enemy's move.

Lord Ram's courtiers decided to attack all the four entrances of the fort, simultaneously. The Vanar army was divided into four parts. And with this planning, began the destruction of Ravan. This war of Lanka is very significant not only in historic perspective but also in spiritual perspective. It is a reflection of the constant struggle which every seeker has to deal with. It is the war between the polluted egoic conditioning versus re-establishment of Dharma or righteousness, in the 'Antahkarana' or intellect of the seeker.

The materialistic worldly life also has four Gates like Lanka Fort:

Bhoga Dvar or the Gate of Pleasure

Sangraha Dvar or the Gate of Accumulation

Sanrakshan Dvar or the Gate of Security

Samman Dvar or the Gate of Importance

The main Gate or the main hurdle in directing the worldly life towards the Lord is Bhoga Dvar or addiction for worldly pleasures. The more the aspirations for pleasures the more intensified is the materialistic mind-set. Where there is high importance for Bhoga, there is concern for Sanrakshan Dvar or security of the pleasures. To ensure continuity of pleasures in the future, accumulation or Sangraha Dvar becomes the priority. The more one has the resources of material, the more the urge to see Samman Dvar or self-importance in others' eyes.

A spiritual seeker must break these four Gates of materialism and win over the fort of mind-ego. He cannot be ignorant or indifferent, he must fight the war. Seeker cannot win this war on his own. But as soon as he attains the support and strength of the Lord, he initiates this grand struggle of his life and with relentless efforts, ultimately, he conquers the mind-ego, and that is how the Lanka Fort is conquered. The rule of Ravan or Ignorance collapses and is replaced by the rule of Self that is Supreme Ram. This is not an easy test but it has to be passed.

The chains, the conceptions, the notions, the perceptions, and the karma of thousands of lives are broken, giving immense pain in the heart of the seeker. He cries in pain, fear and anger. His mind confuses him, pulls him back, asks him to return and that this struggle is not worth it. It seems that he is all alone in this war, there is nobody with him. There is no physical entity perceivable by senses with him. It is only his faith in the invisible subtle grace that keeps him going. And when his efforts are sincere, he gets the attention of the Supreme. It is when the war ends, then he realizes that he was never alone and that he was always protected and guarded. And then, he with absolute conviction tells the world that the purpose of human existence is nothing but to move in accordance with divine will and surrender in the lotus feet of Lord Siya-Ram.

Chapter 6.13

The Roar of Vanar: The War Begins

Although the Vanars just had trees, rocks, stones and claws for the war.
Yet the highly skilled Asur warriors got nervous, hearing their roar.

The planning was done, the conch shell was blown and the ever compassionate Father of a zillion Universes, Supreme Lord Ram blessed this part of His Creation, by commanding the Vanar army to attack the Fort of Lanka, the symbol of Adharma, tyranny and hatred. The most enthusiastic Vanars with zeal and eagerness ran and roared. Their 'Singhnaad' or Lion's Roar or war-cry, terrorized every soul of Asur clan. The Vanar who were earlier considered small monkeys, just capable for jumping on trees and fighting for food and who would hide in fear even from a cat-cry, were now fearlessly standing to confront the mightiest Asur warriors of all times. Goswami Tulsidasji through Vanar's Singhnaad indicates the grand transformation of Vanar's 'Antahkarana' or self-conscience.

The confidence of Vanars was seen from their Singhnaad. The commander of the Lanka army was Prince Indrajit, the brave son of Ravan. Even his roar was already heard and well-known in every part of the world and his more popular name, Meghnaad, symbolized this same lethal thunder like roar. On one side was Meghnad or thunder-roar and on the other side was Singhnaad or the lion-roar. The reason for Vanar's confidence was not their newly found strength but their ultimate surrender to Lord Ram's Grace and Glory. They were sure from the core of their hearts that when Lord Ram is with them, nothing in this eternity can harm them.

The Asur army was also no ordinary but specialist of war-crafts. They had highly sophisticated weapons and vast experience of wars. They had fought and won many battles before, whereas, Vanars in comparison were novice in war. Vanars had no special weapons but had their claws, tree barks and rocks as their arms. The war scene appeared to be unusual as one side was an organized Asur army with sophisticated artillery, whereas on the other side was the Vanar army, which was without proper formation, strategy, skills and weaponry. But the ideology and philosophy of Shri Ram Charitmanas is very clear in this context, which is, 'Wars are not just fought with numbers, weaponries and strategies but with the most important factor that is 'Morale'. Here the Question is what is it that wins the war, with which every Being can overcome life challenges, is it Muscle or Material or the Morale?

If we see the History of India and believe that our Indian rulers lost in the battles against the invaders just because of lower weapon technology, then this argument doesn't look appropriate. The invaders who have the courage to attack a great country like India, proves that their firm determination was way superior to the Indian rulers. To march an army from a far off region to invade India, cannot be an endeavor of soft hearts. In the Lanka war, this strong determination was with the Vanar army and also they had the Power of Dharma with them. The Asur army was already vulnerable as their stand was against Ravan, the Dharma. Secondly, if Ravan and Meghnad had sophisticated weapons, then Lord Ram and Lord Laxman were no way lesser. In fact, there was no warrior in eternity who could face the might of the insurmountable Princes of Ayodhaya. So when the leader is like Lord Ram and captains like Lord Laxman, Hanumanji, Sugriv and Angad, then the morale of that army is bound to be high. The leader and the captains who are skilled as well as high in Dharma do attain superpowers.

For Worship or Devotion of the Lord, no special or unique object is needed, whatever is easily available must be utilized; this is the principle of Bhakti or Devotion. Feelings are the centre point of Spirituality, not the objects like wealth, beauty or muscle. If it had not been so, then spirituality would also have become like business, whoever invests more money and resources gets higher returns. Had virtue, like vice, for its success needed resources, then there would be no difference between spirituality and materialism. The Vanars are the symbols of virtue, that are the good qualities in Beings and for the victory of good over evil, just an intention is required and no support of Material or Muscle. The bad side of human nature albeit equipped with advanced resources, shrewdness and deception still cannot defeat the good. The good loses where the intention is weak and this weakness is because of an impure mind-ego resulting in greed, insecurity and cowardice. The mightiest

Ravan was actually the most insecure Being in this war.

The Ram-Setu or the bridge across the ocean was not built on the basis of advanced technology rather was made with whatever simple things that are available there like stones and trees. Even the great Hanumanji also fought with no special weapon and yet thrashed thousands. The happiness in a materialistic individual is dependent on worldly objects, whereas the basis of joy and enthusiasm of a spiritual seeker is just his own 'Antahkarana' or the self-conscience. The challenges, the pain and problems of life are dealt by a seeker by the power of high morale, intent, and virtue which sprouts inside. Like Vanars, he is not dependent on external objects or resources and like Vanars he marches ahead with whatever he has.

The lion-roar of Vanars inside the heart of the seeker is subtle. He may appear vulnerable, uninterested or dispassionate to the world but the power to rule the cosmos resides in his heart, for his heart has become the seat of Lord Siya-Ram. A spiritual seeker and a devotee of Lord Ram never loses, cannot lose, for he has surrendered his vices, his evilness and his impure mind-ego and himself in absoluteness, in the lotus feet of Lord Siya-Ram.

Chapter 6.14

Purpose of War: Divine Duty vs Immoral Duty

More than success or failure, it is the purpose that matters,
In front of one divine cause the army of million devils scatters.

Goswami Tulsidasji has compared the Lanka war of good vs evil, of Vanar vs Demons and of Ram vs Ravan, as a game of gamble where warrior is the gambler, weapons are the stakes and strategy is the dice. Without playing the game, nobody can know who is going to win and who is going to lose. Birth and Death are the opposite sides of the same coin, called life. We cannot ignore either side. But Being wants to welcome only one side and avoid the second side. Being celebrates the birth, the arrival of a child with much enthusiasm but is compelled to accept death with much agony and pain. This episode of Ramchaitmanas that is Lanka-War inspires the seekers to accept Death gracefully and with enthusiasm just like he celebrates birth. In this context, Vedanta declares - 'Only two types of great ones can break and escape this Maya of birth and death and can attain 'Samatva' or even-mindedness in pleasure or pain, one is a Yogi or mystic and other is the Yodha or warrior'.

Appearance wise there is hardly any similarity between a Yogi and a Yodha, but inwardly, the perspectives of both are very similar. They both are well aware that a regular worldly person has tremendous attachment and dependency on his 'Pran' or life and 'Deh' or body. The expansion of material and this world and things beyond this planet earth is because of a Being's mind-ego which craves for expansion of identities and for the same, it achieves great grand things. And therefore, the attachment with life and body, which are the medium for execution of mind-ego's desires, is not unnatural. But both the Yogi and the Yodha, to be successful in their endeavors, have to go beyond this attachment. Both of them realize that there is 'something' which is imperceptible to the senses, which is priceless and is way more important than a life and a body. They believe that for the same 'something' life and body can be sacrificed.

Both the Yogi and the Yodha yearn for 'Samatva' or evenness, Yogi needs it to attain the 'Samadhi' or super-conscious state and a Yodha needs it to successfully fight a war, else his material attachments won't let him risk his life in a war, making him weak. The one who fights after assessing confirmed victory can never become a warrior because war is not a business of profit or loss. But it is a situation of absolute surrender of life, where one puts his everything at stake with just one objective in mind, which is fulfillment of his duty without knowing and without even bothering about the consequences. And in this state, he rises above the sphere of ordinary Beings because now his duty, his role and his responsibility has become more important than his life. A real warrior is always prepared to embrace death with pride and honor. Ravan and the Asur clan had these qualities of 'Yodha', they were forever prepared to offer their lives for the war. Not many villains were as brave as Asura in the history of Sanatan Dharma. But the problem with them was their 'Purpose' of war, which was immoral and unjustifiable.

War between Vanar, the noble and Asur, the evil warriors was a grand one, never witnessed before. In the beginning, the Asurs were not able to face the lethal attack of Vanars. In the heart of Vanars, there was always an intense fire to fight and achieve a divine purpose. They knew that they were fighting for justice and Dharma or righteousness. The enthusiasm for a divine purpose must not be underrated. When the purpose is pure and clear, there is no right or wrong and moral or immoral factors which can stop the fighter. And this purpose pushes him to march ahead unstoppably. Lord Ram in the very beginning had entrusted Vanars for the search of Mother Sita and gave them this feeling and a responsibility that the liberation of Mother is their endeavor. Lord had already given them a divine purpose and showed His confidence in them, and this multiplied their own self-confidence. And therefore, nothing could stop or slow the mighty roaring Vanars.

Vanars knew that they had the backing of God Ram with them and also the swift victories of their captains Hanumanji and Angad increased their enthusiasm a hundred fold. And therefore, the Asur army was not able to face the lethal attack of the Vanars. The weaponry, strategy and skills of Ravan's soldiers went into vain in front of brave Vanars' enthusiasm. Just like strong winds disperse the thick black clouds in the sky, similarly the storm of Vanars scattered the Asura army on the battle-ground. Asurs were neither weak nor coward but they didn't have that righteous and strong purpose and enthusiasm like that of Vanars. Because, inside they were well aware that their king Ravan, by wrongfully abducting Lady Sita, had done an immoral act and they were, knowingly by fighting for their King Ravan, were actually confirming and contributing in the same immorality.

Asur Beings knew that their King didn't honorably challenge Lord Ram and Lord Laxman in Panchavati. Then, Vibhishan's insult and oustment by Ravan had further reconfirmed Ravan's immorality. The proposal of peaceful settlement from Angad also cleared that Lord Ram is not eager for war, violence and blood like Ravan. They didn't know whether their stand was right or wrong and whether they should fight or not. All this had put them in a dilemma and the result was their defeat in the first round of the war. But their King Ravan, who could read their minds and who was a shrewd diplomat, was not ready to accept defeat.

Ravan knew that he could never justify his act of kidnapping Lady Sita, and therefore, he didn't speak about it at all. But he reminded his army about their duty. He had always taken good care of his Asur clan and warriors with the best of facilities, security and pleasures. He had let them plunder innocent Beings, fulfill their carnal desires and ensured illegitimate pleasures for their families. So far, the Asur people, with the support of their King had enjoyed their life thoroughly through immoral means and now today when in return, their King wanted their support, they were retreating. He furiously warned them that if even one of them backs off, then he will not be spared from a harsh punishment. Very often, people forget or do not care about their associations. Whoever fulfills their desires and satisfies their ego, without thinking judiciously, they attach themselves with that entity. And then, they are obliged to stand with that entity even though they know that what they are doing is totally wrong.

Ravan's warning shook Asur soldiers and they returned back to fight with a purpose, that is duty to stand for their King. This was just the beginning of a long, great and grand Lanka war. On one side were Lord Ram's devotees, that is Vanars and on the other side were loyalists of Ravan that is Asur. And just like the roulette wheel, the wheel of victory and defeat, and survival and death was continuously rotating. But like Vanars, the one who has surrendered in the lotus feet of Lord Siya-Ram doesn't worry for he knows that such, infinite number of wheels are just petty slave of Maya, who is just a small pawn, in the court of Lord Ram. Victory-Defeat and Birth-Death are all puppets who dance at one small indication of Supreme Lord Ram. And God has Himself declared that He dances to the tune of His pure devotee or 'Bhakta'. Can there be anything like Lord Ram who is all-powerful and yet so loving and compassionate?

Chapter 6.15

The Retreat of Vanars: Power of 'Dharya'

Vanars were surprised with Asurs' aggression and fell back,
But in the end, they are sure to win and thrash every attack.

Fear, as well as, sense of duty for their King Ravan, stopped the Asur army of Lanka from retreating. They then, like true Yodha, jumped back in the battle and confronted the Vanar army with a fierce attack. Vanars were shocked with this sudden change in the situation and got nervous, and now, they started scattering. Both Asur and Vanar were equal warriors who had kept aside the fear of death for this war and for their Kings. And therefore, their retreat from the battle seems strange. But, there is a difference. Death and Pain are not one but two different things in a war's perspective.

In comparison to death, the pain of physical injury is much more frightening. The soldier believes that the pain experienced before death is of few moments or for few minutes whereas nobody knows when will the pain experienced in an injury end, or how will one live with permanent damage of a body part, the rest of life. This is for the same reason that many times patients who are suffering from long terminal illness at one point of time are not able to bear the suffering any longer and so commit suicide. Clearly, the pain and fear of unending illness overshadows their fear of death. Also, those who intends to end their lives selects that method of suicide which gives minimal pain. An ordinary Being as well as a great warrior both fear the injury or illness of the body more than loss of the body. The pain experience can jolt even the greatest of the warriors.

The great Gidhraj Jatayu is the symbol of bravery and valor. He with his old and decayed body tried to stop and attack Ravan, when he was escaping away after abducting Lady Sita. Ravan sliced Jatayu's wings and he, in immense pain, fell on the ground. But it was not that his physical pain didn't trouble him. The injury was tormenting for him and he wished to end his body to free himself from the pain. Everyone, even Ravan saluted him for his grand courage but Jatayu himself felt that like a sinner and whose body strength is cowardly because even after promising for Princess Sita's protection, he had failed. Ravan fled away with Her in front of his eyes and he could not do anything to stop him. But more than this, Jatayu was in immense agony for he didn't want to die without informing Lord Ram about the abduction of Lady Sita by Ravan. He got free from this dilemma when Lord Ram and Lord Laxman found him and he could divulge to Them the mishap.

It can be concluded that to overcome fear of death, valiantness is needed. But the capacity to deal with physical and body pain is not related to bravery but with an individual's 'Dharya' or tolerance and patience. Even the greatest of the warriors in absence of Dharya will cry in physical pain, wriggle in sickness and run away in the battle field. To be composed in extreme physical pain is a divine quality which is attained by a real hero who has 'Dharya'. Jatayu had overcome both the fear of death and also had immense 'Dharya'. He tolerated the intense pain but didn't succumb to his injuries before informing the incident to Lord Ram. He is the true Yodha and a true Yogi. Such a great 'Dharya' is seen in just one in millions. And that is why Lord embraced Jatayu like His own father who did everything to protect his daughter Princess Sita. Vanars too had the 'Dharya' but not as much as Jatayu. Not every Vanar can be like Hanumanji or Angad. So to label Vanar as cowards is not correct as by getting nervous against Asur attack and scattering they just reacted to the situation just like how any soldier would have.

If the Vanars had been really cowardly ones, then they could have escaped from the battle field and could have fled to Kishkinda in the security of their home kingdom; but their fall back was just for a distance from the battle ground. They were injured and tired and so they were just desperate to secure their lives and weapons. Unlike Asur, they never did think of leaving their King in the battlefield. And therefore, while God Shiv narrating this incident to Mother Parvati says that this action of Vanar might appear strange but is momentary and that one should not be judgmental towards them.

In the perspective of spirituality, when a seeker really tries sincerely to go deeper in awareness of truth then the mind-ego in the form of intense fear and negativity fights back. The seeker has to deal with many such inner confrontations mixed with external challenges and shouldn't expect that since he is chanting Ram-Naam, he will always be victorious against the traps of mind-ego. Many times or actually mostly, he loses. While many of the seekers in such situations give up, but the one who is like the Vanar army, learns his lessons and doesn't give up and is sure to win in the end. This is the guarantee given to the seeker by Lord Himself.

In every endeavor of worldly life, obstructions and problems are bound to come, where one is expected to deal with them, with his self-'Purusharth' or efforts. He might also get support from others. In the path of spirituality and 'Bhakti' or devotion, to deal with the challenges, the seeker can only depend on the Grace of enlightened Sages and Lord Ram. The temporary defeats in the Bhakti path actually are very helpful as they prepare the seeker for more difficult challenges which lie ahead. A victory gives pride, enthusiasm and joy but then it also increases the chances of giving strength to vanity and ego. A seeker who believes himself as the doer, an achiever and the victorious one, will most definitely, eventually lose and will fall. The defeats remind the seeker that he cannot win over the traps of mind-ego by his own efforts or 'Purusharth' and that on every step and in every moment he needs Grace of enlightened Sages and Supreme Lord Ram. And in this way, he is able to deal with his mind-ego because he has shifted from doership to non-doership. The same happened with Vanars. In this moment of defeat, they depended on the greatest enlightened Sage that is Hanumanji.

In the battle of Vanars against Asurs or seekers against the negativity of mind-ego, one may win or may lose and so one should neither lose hope nor be overjoyed. Ultimate winner will be 'Satya' or the Truth. Truth, that the master and operator of this whole universe is none other than Supreme Ram. A seeker might become pessimist reading or listening about this incident of retreat from the battle of great ancient warriors Vanars. He might think that when the great Vanars are not able to deal with Asuras or the negativity of the mind-ego, then how can he, an ordinary mortal Being, be able to? And therefore, God Shiva ensures that this defeat is momentary and later victory will be of Vanar, that means of the seeker. And till that 'later' comes great 'Dharya' needs to be practiced by the seeker. The best way to attain 'Dharya' is by 'Prarthna' or Praying from our own Lord Ram. For whosoever even for once, even in his dream, surrenders in the lotus feet of Lord Siya-Ram and asks for Their shelter, will without any doubt win this Lanka war, that is the battle against mind-ego and will attain his ultimate objective.

Chapter 6.16

Liberation of Angad: Thrashing of the Asur

Seeing Hanumanji on top of the Lanka Fort in full action,
Angad too joined him to thrash the foolish Asur aggression.

The Lanka war was on. Sometimes, it was Asur dominating and Vanar retreating while most of the times it was Vanars thrashing Asur brutally. The mala fide ways of the Asur army irked Hanumanji too much so that he broke the Gate that was defended by Meghnad. He then beat Meghnad, barged in the fort of Lanka and climbed up on the highest point of Ravan's palace. On seeing this single-handed lethal invasion of Hanumanji, the mighty son of Bali, Angad too thrashed many Asur warriors like a child's play and climbed up the palace to give company to Hanumanji. They then together brutally started assassinating hundreds of Asur soldiers. The people of Lanka saw this dreadful sight and cried in f ear, "Earlier one Vanar came and burnt half of the kingdom, now they are two, God knows what will happen to us. Our foolish King will get us all killed."

This incident was another feather in Angad's cap. Everybody can see his evolution in courage, skills and determination. Like how Lord Ram and Lord Laxman did many adventures together, similarly Hanumanji and Angad also executed many adventures together. Angad had a deep respect for Hanumanji. He saw him as the true and greatest devotee of Lord Ram. He had seen how Hanumanji had achieved great feats and had done unbelievable tasks with the power of Lord's Bhakti or devotion. The previous time, when they had come in search of Mother Sita, Angad was not very confident in jumping the ocean and reaching Lanka. But this time, he had no reservations and he could, without any apprehensions walk hand in hand with Hanumanji to face the most dangerous challenges. Angad, in the mentorship of Hanumanji, had now attained higher level of surrender in the lotus feet of Lord Ram.

In other perspective, Angad could have harbored ill feelings against the Lord because his father was killed by Him, but Angad was a man of righteousness and 'Bhakti'. He knows what is right and what is wrong and no attachment of any sort could change or confuse his ideals. Also, just before dying, Bali had offered Angad in the shelter of the Lord Ram and so it was Angad's duty to follow his father's judgment. Angad worshiped Lord Ram but it was the company of the great Sage, Hanumanji that he learnt the true meaning of devotion and surrender. Although for him, Lord's orders were the final verdict, yet initially, he didn't like his uncle Sugriv's crowning as the King of Kishkindha. In fact, his aversion towards Sugriv was not hidden to the Lord and the Vanars.

For Angad, Sugriv was an undeserving and unqualified person for Lord's love and throne of Kishkindha. He saw him as a very pleasure seeking materialistic one who after getting his brother Bali killed for the throne, forgot his commitment towards Lord Ram and involved himself in satisfying his carnal desires. He didn't even bother to look after the affairs of his kingdom. Also, Angad doubted that whenever Sugriv would get a chance, he would eliminate him. But Angad's doubts were baseless. Anybody can clearly see the transformation in Sugriv and also when Lord Ram and Hanumanji had accepted him as the King, then nobody should question their choice. But that is how the mind-ego functions, making it difficult for the Being to get rid of his 'Sanskara' or old habits, doubts and apprehensions. But Angad is a true devotee who has the mentorship of the greatest Sage that is Hanumanji and so Lord knew that soon he was going to come out of the trap of 'Sanskara' and the same happened.

While slaying the Asur soldiers, both the divine warriors Hanumanji and Angad, were not only demonstrating their valor but were also spreading 'Bhakti' of Lord Ram. While hitting, they were loudly declaring to the Lanka people that their sad state is because of their lack of worshiping or 'Bhajan' in the lotus feet of Supreme Lord Ram. They would also pluck off the heads of the slayed Asur soldiers and throw them towards Ravan, which would break like 'Dahi-Handi' or Earthen pot of curd right in front of him. Being attains the human body after much deliberation and good deeds of past lives. If the Being doesn't use this body for Devotion and Worshiping of the God, instead uses it for egoistic desires, then that simply means he has wasted this Body and this Life. The heads were thrown to Ravan to warn him that even now there is a chance for him to mend his ways and surrender to Lord Ram.

Also, they were throwing some of the slayed Asur warriors to where

Lord Ram was. Vibhishan would then tell the Lord about those warriors and then Lord would give them salvation. In the first case, they wanted people to see the consequences of not worshiping or Bhajan, and in the second case, they wanted people to realize the loving and caring nature of Lord Ram. The ever compassionate Lord was liberating the most evil Asura who have just harmed others, throughout their lives. Hence, in this way, Hanumanji and Angad highlighted the loving as well as punishing attribute of Godly forces.

In spiritual perspective, Hanumanji is 'Siddhi' or spiritual accomplishment and Angad is 'Sadhna' or spiritual practices. From day one, Hanumanji is free from all mind-ego's traps, even the 'Satvik' trap, that is, seeing self as religious and righteous. His devotion and surrender to the Lord was absolute but Angad's complete surrender or 'Samarpan Bhav' came later. Hanumanji in the first instance didn't hesitate in jumping the ocean to reach Lanka in the search of Mother Sita. Then, Angad had doubts about his capabilities. In reality, he was no less capable but he was not 'surrendered' in totality, like Hanumanji, and therefore, had apprehensions. But after the successful return of Hanumanji from Lanka, Angad learnt the lesson and was able to match the devotion-levels of Hanumanji. In the war, it was Hanumanji who could break the Lanka Fort gate guarded by mighty Meghnad. But then, Angad was no less and he too participated in the struggle with complete enthusiasm.

In spiritual perspective, Meghnad symbolizes 'Kaam' or lustful and greedy tendencies of the human mind. To break the gate of Kaam is the most difficult task for the seeker. Hanumanji is an enlightened saint and the teacher of all seekers and so first he showed the way to freedom from 'Kaam'. Angad the seeker, then followed the footsteps of the enlightened teacher and was too able to get past the 'Kaam'. In this way, the seeker through his 'Sadhna' attains 'Siddhi'. Hanumanji chanted Lord's name, the great 'Ram-Naam' and by seeing him, Angad then too learnt the same. Our spiritual teachers or Gurudev are avatars of Hanumanji who wants to teach every Being and their beloved student-seekers that to get free of sufferings and challenges symbolized by the 'Asur', the only way is to surrender in the lotus feet of Lord Siya-Ram.

Chapter 6.17

Light Vs Darkness: Illicit Asuri Act

Seeing the Sun setting, the foolish Asurs attacked unethically,
But with Lord's Grace, Vanars again thrashed them brutally.

Very often success or failure of an endeavor is put on one individual but one individual is not capable of doing everything. The most important factor that decides success or failure is 'Kaal' or time. This creation is made up of the three 'Gunas' that are Satogun, Rajogun and Tamogun. All these three modes or Gunas of nature are consistently and equally active at all times. However, the equation of these Gunas changes in different time phases, as proclaimed by the Rishis of Sanatan Dharma. For instance, in the morning time, Satogun or the mode of purity is dominant, while in the day time, it is Rajogun or the mode of action. In the dusk, the Tamogun or the mode of ignorance starts rising and by the night time it overpowers the other two Gunas. In this perspective, it can be concluded that the 'Satogun' predominant daytime is for Godly or Devayi powers and the 'Tamogun' predominant night time is for the Devilish or Asuri powers. Satogun with Rajogun is Devayi and Tamogun with Rajogun is Asuri.

The courageous Vanar army of Lord Ram in the daytime under the captainship of Hanumanji and Angad defeated Asur army of Ravan, in many rounds of attacks on that first day of the Lanka war. On seeing the Sun setting, it was but natural that Demons of Lanka found a new enthusiasm within themselves as now it was their time, the 'Tamogun' time, which depletes the power of 'Satogun' or Vanars. After all, this war was between the Light and the Darkness, Divine Vs Nocturnal. The Asur army found a new strength in the sundown light of the dusk and then they, hailing the name of Ravan, again attacked the Vanar army.

Nature had created the principle of day and night. Both complement each other and are equally important. One needs to know how to manage the self in both the phases and by effectively doing so, both day and night become equally beneficial. This is possible only when the day time is used for action and night time is used for rest. But when the Tamogun darkness of night is used for action, then it brings imbalance and becomes devastating for the Beings. The Asur or the demons of Ravan by not ending the war in the sunset, against the war protocol and by continuing the attack proved that their only agenda is selfish benefit at the cost of principles of nature and war. The nocturnal Asur had learnt to use the Tamogun powers in their interest, and therefore, their strength increased manifold in the Sun setting. Whereas, the highly ethical Vanars were instructed not to attack after the Sunset, and also to retire from the war.

The darkness of night signifies the time of retirement and rest. This rest is much needed for energizing the body for the next day's activities. This is the principle for the whole creation which is supposed to be accepted and practiced by every Being. But the arbitrary Asur are not ready to accept the laws of nature. They use the system of nature as per their own interest and not how it should be utilized. Under the influence of their ignorant mind and intense ego, they don't care for any rules and order, they rather feel proud, in spoiling the system. Their desperation was to use or misuse others to fulfill their desires which gave them pleasures in the beginning but ultimately became the cause of their destruction.

This Asur practice can be connected with the criminal mind. It is the night time when crime, violence and brawls happens the most. In the day time, most of the same ignorant minds are in their senses. There is a specialty in Asur lifestyle. It brings a lot of success because unethical actions do bring quick results but ultimately it destroys the doer. This can be seen in this Lanka war sequence. The Asur got some success by attacking in the falling light of the Sunset and the Vanar got really troubled. But on seeing His dear Vanar devotees in distress, Lord Ram asks Hanumanji and Angad to go back on the battlefield and take care of the situation. Not only this but also the Lord shot 'Pavak-astra' or divine arrow towards the sky which lit the sky and earth with bright light. In that light of truth, Asur lost the advantage of darkness. The Light of Satogun overshadowed the force of Tamogun. They could no longer deal with the counterattack of Vanars and ran away.

Lord's 'Pavakastra', destroys the darkness just like 'Gyan' or knowledge destroys the 'Sanshaya' or doubts. Night is the symbol of 'Agyan' or ignorance and Day signifies 'Gyan' or Knowledge. In the light of Gyan, the Satogun Vanar army was strong whereas in the dimming light of the dusk, the Tamogun Asur army became strong. This constant shuffling of day and night or 'Gyan' and 'Agyan' gives rise to 'Sanshaya' or doubt in the mind of the seeker. This inner dilemma makes the seeker weak, making him disoriented. In the state of 'Gyan', a seeker is fully motivated for spiritual practices while in the phases of 'Agyan', no matter how hard he tries but he loses the enthusiasm in seeking the Truth. This constant fluctuation between 'Guna' confuses the seeker, making him lose confidence and doubting the path of Bhakti or Devotion, sometimes to the extent that he questions even the existence of the Supreme Lord.

This is a very natural state for a seeker and in such a time he needs help. The ever compassionate Lord then sends the Pavakastra, symbol of Gyan and Hanumanji and Angad who symbolizes 'Vishwas' or Faith and 'Vichar' or contemplation. To overcome the situation of 'Sanshaya' and 'Agyan', one must work hard with 'Vishwas' and 'Vichar'. Though not once but thousand times the Asur of ignorance will vanquish the Vanar of devotion but the seeker must not lose hope and keep trying. After all, every seeker has to fight this Lanka war to attain the Grace of Lord Ram. For it is the law that whosoever tries, does attain the special help and 'Kripa' or Grace of Lord Ram.

While on the way of seeking, many a times, the seeker doubts whether he is going in the correct direction and questions the very purpose of spirituality but once he crosses this ocean of dilemma and wins this inner war or the 'Lanka war', like Vanar he too realizes that the only purpose of life is to surrender in the lotus feet of Lord Siya-Ram.

Chapter 6.18

Unsurmountable Meghnad: Power of 'Kaam'

Meghnad's attack was baffling and gruesome,
The dejected Vanars were about to succumb.

The grand success of the Vanar army in the first phase of the Lanka war shook the core of even the finest warrior Ravan. But even in that situation, one individual from Asur clan, whose self-confidence was unshaken was mighty Meghnad, the son of Ravan. In thought, speech and action, Meghnad was an ardent follower and supporter of Ravan. He was a devotee of his father. Never ever did he find inappropriateness in any action of Ravan. When all wise men were suggesting to Ravan to not indulge in this war and surrender to Lord Ram, it was Meghnad who gave courage to Ravan to not give up. He was the greatest warrior or 'Yodha' of Lanka. In the very next phase of the war, Meghnad displayed his valor and openly challenged the Vanar army. But the one who was the center of his fury was none other than his uncle, Vibhishan.

There were particularly two reasons for Meghnad's hatred towards Vibhishan. He felt that Prince Ram-Laxman and all Vanar clan were although his enemy but by waging this war were righteously fulfilling their duty or 'Kshatriya-Swadharma'. But he believed that Vibhishan's act was totally immoral as he discarded his own clan as well as his own family and joined the enemy. Meghnad and Vibhishan had a heated argument over right and wrong. The angry Meghnad blamingly says to Vibhishan that he was born and brought up in Lanka, secondly he is the real brother of his father Ravan and was also like a father-figure to him also and yet Vibhishan had turned against his own family and people.

Meghnad went on criticizing, "You don't care for your family and the honor of your Asur clan. Also you don't have a sense of right and wrong, brotherly love and Dharma. You neglected your own people and accepted slavery of the enemy." The righteous Vibhishan aptly replied to these allegations, "Although

I am born in the family of evil Asur, yet my nature is not Asur like. I hate cruelty and immorality. It was my own brother and your father Ravan, who first ousted me from Lanka. Ravan has lost all values and has decided to act sinfully. The one who loots others' wealth and abducts others' women has no right to live. And so, I have to discard this venomous snake Ravan and take refuge in the Supreme Lord Ram."

Meghnad's life's philosophy was just 'I' and 'You'. In every situation, be it right or wrong he just wants to defend those who are 'His'. Like every selfish pleasure and power seeking individual his focus of 'I' and 'You' is on material pleasures of the physical body. He wanted victory for the Asur army and Ravan, so that his own name, fame and power would spread even further. But like every selfish person, he also had immense fear of losing his position. He feared that since Vibhishan knew the secrets of Lanka and his own magical powers, he could reveal them to Lord Ram and spoil everything, which the Asur had built. Therefore, he first wanted to kill Vibhishan in order to protect Lanka.

On that day of war, Meghnad wanted to end Vibhishan and so attacked him with his power-arrow, but Lord Laxman came in between and took it on himself, thereby saving Vibhishan. For Lord Laxman, not just Vibhishan but every devotee who has taken refuge in Lord Ram is very important. He could do anything even give away his life in protecting that Devotee.

The war skills of Meghnad were unmatched. He was the only unfazed Asur, fighting that war. His lethal attacks astounded the Vanar army. Reading about Meghnad, one would realize that there were two unique specialties in his attack. One, he had such a chariot which could invisible itself, making it impenetrable and invincible from the attacks of the enemy. Secondly, there was simultaneous usage of elements of 'Fire' and 'Water' in his attacks. If it was fire raining from the sky, then there was water springing out from the earth. To face such a difficult and unfamiliar attack was out of bounds for the Vanars.

In spiritual perspective, Meghnad symbolizes 'Kaam' or Lust for pleasures. 'Kaam' is the most influencing force of mind-ego in a Being's life. 'Kaam' encompasses everything related to desire, insecurity, passion, greed and lust. In comparison to the other disorders of mind-ego, Kaam is the most difficult and the strongest. In Bhagavad Gita, Lord Krishna orders Arjun not only to overcome Kaam but also to admit that it is not easy to deal with. But the Lord also says that 'to win over a thing which is difficult to overcome is the real success'. Kaam without having any physicality, distresses the human body. When Kaam rises there sprouts not one but two contradicting 'Vritti' or thought-ideas and they are 'Raag' and 'Dvesh' or Like and Dislike. If Raag is Water, then Dvesh is Fire.

In 'Kaam' what one Being desires, the same object others also desire. And when many Beings aspire for the same object, conflict arises. And in this conflict, every participant in the desperation of victory develops 'Dvesh' or Dislike for the other. So on one hand, Being in the 'Raag' of his desires enjoys the water, while on the other hand, burns in the fire of 'Dvesh'. The force of 'Kaam' that is Meghnad played with the psyche of the Vanar army by using both Water and Fire elements. Water was springing from the land while the Fire was raining from the sky. To save themselves, the Vanars were trying to escape from the raining Fire and embracing the water springs. But neither the springing water nor the raining fire were real and fixed. It was an illusion, like a mirage. As soon as the Vanar would come close to the water, it would vanish and no matter in which direction they ran, everywhere there was fire. In this intense manipulation of Kaam with confusing Raag and burning Dvesh, the human being loses his identity and his sensibilities. The same was happening with the Vanars, and they were lost.

Beings cannot protect themselves from this play of water and fire. No umbrella can resist the raining fire and no shoes can save from the marshy land where water is springing. In spiritual perspective, umbrellas and shoes can be symbolized as 'Vichar' and 'Vivek' or thoughtfulness and intellect. The seeker who has good command on his Vichar and Vivek, most definitely saves himself from ill effects of mind-ego. But when Kaam attacks with his full force, then even 'Vichar and Vivek' fails. The same was happening with the Vanars. They were trying their level best but were not able to protect themselves from the lethal attack of 'Kaam', the Meghnad. Their senses, mind and intelligence were all confused and they were losing.

On seeing the play of Meghnad and Vanars in deep anguish, Prince Laxman started showering arrows on him and destroyed his resources. If Meghnad is 'Kaam', Lord Laxman is 'Kaal' or the God of Death. Meghnad got scared for his life. He felt that Laxman would not spare him now. The Vanar army regained their confidence and returned back in the battle with full enthusiasm chanting 'Ram-Naam'. The War of Lanka was not between two entities, Ram or Ravan or two armies or two clans but it was the clash between two ideologies, that is the 'Right' and the 'Wrong'.

Goswami Tulsidasji says that whoever, whenever and wherever surrenders to Lord Ram and is well-taken care of by the mightiest force of this Universe that is Lord Laxman. The path that leads to the Lord is not easy and is full of challenges but then there is Divine Energy symbolized by Sheshnaag Laxman which supports and helps the seeker to walk ahead and attain his objective that is Lord Ram.

Chapter 6.19

Leela of Lord Laxman: Illimitable 'Adhar'

Struggling with the 'Adhar or foundation of the Creation' Lord Laxman, Meghnad with every passing moment was losing his strength He had weakened and felt defeated. Meghnad got scared on seeing the power and mightiness of Lord Laxman and felt that now at any moment he would get killed. Lord Laxman had already destroyed his chariot, and had injured every part of his body. To save his life, Meghnad finally used his ultimate special power 'Veerghatini' against Lord Laxman. The power hit Lord Laxman and he felt unconscious. Meghnad was overjoyed. Excitedly, he rushed to carry Lord Laxman back and present him to his father Ravan to brag about his grand victory. He then with all his strength tried to lift the unconscious 'Illimitable Laxman' but even after trying very hard he couldn't even move him by an inch. He was astonished and dejected. Then many of his Asur warriors joined him and together tried to lift Lord Laxman but again to their astonishment, all of them failed miserably.

Meghnad was bewildered and couldn't understand this miracle. 'How come so many of us are not able to lift one unconscious person?' he thought to himself. By making Lord Laxman unconscious, what Meghnad felt was his victory was not actually a success but just another 'Leela' or humanly-sport of Lord Laxman. He is the Master-Teacher or 'Paramacharya' of the Beings and through his various Leela, he teaches us the ways to contemplate on the Truth. This entire Meghnad's incident of getting unconscious was just one of His divine Leela. Lord Laxman is the Avatar of 'Shesh', who is the 'Adhar' or base and the support of the entire creation. And to try to defeat the Adhar is a laughable thing which an Asur or an ignorant person is never able to understand. How can one cut the same branch of the tree, which is holding him? A wise person would never do that but a foolish one to demonstrate his strength often does that.

Asuri or an ignorant one always neglects the importance of Adhar or the base, on which the entire life-form, including his 'self' is existing. Heonly values himself and takes others for granted. He never understands that to understand the Adhar of the Creation, he needs to deeply contemplate with gratitude on his inner-self. While walking on rough terrain one must be watchful of his steps so that he may not tumble down by hitting the stones and obstructions that lie on his path. An arrogant one who is overconfident doesn't look downwards but only forward with a high-head, believing himself beyond the reach of the obstructions. It is the trap of mind-ego which makes one feels superior and neglect the divine Supreme energy which is running the whole system.

When one is able to free himself from mind-ego trap, when there is humility and no vanity, then only he lowers his eyes in surrender-ship and is able to recognize the real terrain which is supporting the whole Creation. This Leela of unconsciousness was done by Lord Laxman to divert the ignorant mind of Meghnad from ego to truth. It was an opportunity for Meghnad to apply sense and understand the truth. It was indeed Lord Laxman's Grace for Meghnad which he failed to realize. If Meghnad had been wise and matured, then he would have realized the reality of Lord Laxman and also, that his battle against him was nothing but a suicide attempt. Adhar 'Shesh' is Infinite, Immortal, Omnipresent and Almighty.

Lord Hanuman arrived on the scene and on seeing him, all the Asur soldiers eloped. Then, on seeing Lord Hanuman easily lifting Lord Laxman in his arms, Meghnad got utterly confused. What thousands of them were not able to do was so easily done by one Vanar, Lord Hanuman. The secret behind this Leela was that in actuality Lord Laxman was never unconscious. 'Consciousness was just appearing to be Dead'. Lord Hanuman lifting the Infinite was not about his strength but was about his love, reverence and devotion towards Lord Laxman. Lord Laxman, pleased with the Bhakti of Lord Hanuman, allowed him to carry himself on his lap. No dead or living Being, not even Ravan could have moved Lord Laxman by an inch. Out of pure love for Lord Hanuman, Adhar Laxman lightened his weight.

At gross level, Beings can only see the ground on which they dwell. To attain the subtle perspective one must question, if his base is the ground, ground-base is the Earth, then what is the base of this Earth? What is this infinite Adhar, the base on which this Earth, Solar System, Galaxy, Universe dwells and is functioning? Can the Creation exist without this Adhar? Maharishis have given a form and a face to this subtle and Supreme Base or

Adhar as 'Shesh-Naag', the eternal servant of God Narayan. When Narayan took avatar as Lord Ram, Shesh-Naag to serve Him took avatar as Lord Laxman.

Lifting Lord Laxman for Meghnad was like lifting the entire Infinity which is impossible. Even if one has the power of a thousand Hercules, he cannot lift himself. The Adhar of this Adhar Shesh Laxman is Supreme Lord Ram. And only a devotee like Hanumanji with the blessing of Lord Ram can lift the Infinite Lord Laxman. This episode has a philosophical perspective, inspiring the reader to contemplate, what is that which is supporting the whole system and because of which there is Life and Existence? Can there be Creation without an Adhar or Base? The seeker realizes that this is something which cannot be comprehended with logic but is 'That' to which he must surrender with love and gratitude. And also to devote himself to the One, to whom the Infinite Adhar Laxman surrenders to, who is the Ultimate Adhar and that is Lord Siya-Ram.

Chapter 6.20

Cure for Lord Laxman: Mission Impossible

The medicine was to be brought before the sunrise,
Only he could do it whose speed can split the skies.

The war was called off that day. On seeing His brother Laxman unconscious, Lord Ram worriedly rushed to the scene. Vibhishan advised that now, only Sushern, the royal doctor of Lanka can cure Prince Laxman. Although it was next to impossible to convince Ravan's doctor to treat his enemy, yet Lord Hanuman, like always, took the initiative and immediately went to the Lanka city and brought the doctor. The medicine 'Sanjeevani Booti' prescribed by Sushern was not available in Lanka and it was to be searched and brought from faraway 'Dronachal' Mountain in the Himalayas. On top of that, it had to be brought before Sunrise and only then Lord Laxman can be cured else he would not survive. These were the instructions of Sushern.

Sushern was on the payroll of the Lanka kingdom. Sushern knew that Ravan would not spare him knowing that in these times of war, where the existence of Lanka is at stake, a royal doctor of Lanka has helped and cured the greatest warrior of the enemy camp that is Prince Laxman. Lord Hanuman already understood this point and so he carried the complete house of Sushern with Sushern inside, while he was asleep and brought him to Vanar side. Lord Hanuman knew that if Sushern is accused for helping the enemy, he can now give the excuse that he didn't go intentionally but was unknowingly abducted and forced to do the treatment. But Sushern knew that Ravan was very cunning and might not buy this logic but he was sure that after knowing about the cure that he gave for Lord Laxman, Ravan would definitely accept his excuse and pardon him. Because, the solution was very difficult rather impossible. It was already midnight and someone had to bring the medicine from Himalaya which was sixty thousand yojan away from Lanka and that too before Sunrise. And the same happened, later on when Lord Laxman got cured, Ravan didn't punish Sushern. Also, if Sushern had refused to cure Lord Laxman, then there was this fear that Vanar would not spare him. So he played in such a clever way that he remains safe from both Asur and Vanar side. Lord Hanumanji could read behind the lines but for him cure for Lord Laxman was on top priority.

This incident also reflects the philosophic equation between birth, death, disease, medicine and cure. Is medicine more powerful than disease? Can divine medicines defeat the Kaal or death? Can one elude his 'Kaal'? Some believe that birth and death of the Being are already fixed based on his 'Bhagya' or destiny and they cannot be changed. We see that even after taking the best of the medicines, some patients are not able to survive. And at times, even without the availability of basic medicines, some patients get cured. So in the context of death, medicine or efforts don't actually play much of a role. But this theory doesn't appear to be right in totality. If everything is fixed and Being has no other option, no liberty and no right to fight for his survival, then actually God is very unkind. But that's not true, God is most kind and ever compassionate, and therefore, he bestows the gift of 'freedom to decide' for every Being. And so everything in this 'Prakriti' or nature is based on duality, if there is night then there is a day and if there is disease then there is medicine. However, if Being could achieve everything he wants to and there are no failures in his life, then his arrogance and pride would not let him accept the existence of God. Commonly those who have seen more successes than failures often get trapped in the ego of vanity. If there are no failures, then Being would have considered himself as God. And so these failures and limitations in our life make us realize the supremacy of God.

One needs to be a good swimmer to cross a river. But the irony is that even the best of the swimmers sometimes drown in the same river in which they have learnt swimming. And therefore, along with the swimming skills there are some other uncontrollable variables which ensure the survival of the swimmer and help him cross the river. Strong flow of the river, underwater currents, whirlpools and strong winds can spoil the effort of the swimmer and so he needs the support of both water and air. In this perspective, Tulsidasji emphasizes on these three factors-

1. 'Purusharth' or self-effort
2. 'Prarabdha' or destiny
3. 'Ram-Kripa' or Grace of Lord Ram

River is Prarabdha, the swimming activity is Purushartha and the flow of water and the wind is 'Ram-Kripa'. Only when these three factors are in harmony, the Being can overcome the challenges and achieve his target.

The same factors can be seen in this incident of Lord Laxman's treatment. The 'Sanjeevani Booti' cure was Prarabdha, Hanumanji was Purushartha and the overall enviorment to get the cure in timely manner was Ram-Kripa. If the resources are available but not applied in the right time, then there is no use of these resources. And the responsibility to bring balance in these three that is doctor, medicine and timing was put on the shoulders of the greatest hero and the epitome of 'Karma-Yog', Shri Hanumanji. Ravan was shocked and unhappy knowing that the cure has been given by his doctor but the time limit of Sunrise, brought immense hope in him. He believed that it was impossible for Lord Hanuman to bring the medicine from the Himalayas within such a short span of time. But he didn't want to take chances, and therefore, sent his demon 'Kaalnemi' to spoil this Purushartha or effort of Lord Hanuman.

Kaalnemi had a gift. He could travel very fast, even faster than Lord Hanuman. Ravan was hoping that his fast and shrewd Kaalnemi could not only spoil but might also kill Lord Hanuman. In Kaalnemi, Ravan saw Death and Time as his slave. But the intelligent Kaalnemi knew his limitations. He knew that every successful one believes that Time is running as per his accordance. But the truth is that both Time and Death are slaves of one and only Lord Ram. And so after hearing Ravan's orders, he was filled with remorse. He regretted joining Ravan and showing off his magical skills to him. Like Mareech, Kaalnemi too tried to convince Ravan, that Lord Ram is God Himself and that he should discard his stubbornness, surrender in the feet of the Lord and forever worship him, and in this way benefit himself and the Asur clan. But Ravan wouldn't pay heed to the sound advice and insisted Kaalnemi to go and do the job.

Kaalnemi, again like Mareech, thought that rather than being killed by Ravan, it is far far better that he dies in the hands of Lord Ram's messenger that is Lord Hanuman. Lord Hanuman is the avatar of God Shiv who wears Time and Death as ornaments. Lord is the creator of Kaal and his devotee uses Kaal as his ornament. Neither the Kaalnemi of Ramayan nor the Ravan of today is capable of defeating the devotee, because more than 'Purusharth' or self-efforts, the devotee relies on 'Ram-Kripa' or Grace of God Ram. Kaalnemi knew the truth which Goswamiji always says that the only purpose of this life is to surrender yourself in the Bhakti or devotion of Lord Siya-Ram.

Chapter 6.21

Guardian of Ayodhaya: Hanumanji meets Prince Bharat

Laxman, Hanumanji and Vanars are all great devotee,
But there is no other one like Bharat, the Ayodhya's trustee.

Asur Kaalnemi traveled faster than Hanumanji and in his way created an illusionary but pleasant Hermitage. Lord Hanuman while flying towards the Himalayas saw the hermitage and decided to take some rest there and then carry on with His journey. Kaalnemi, disguised as a sage, welcomed Him and offered to drink water from the nearby pond. But as soon Lord Hanuman took a dip in the pond he was attacked by a female-crocodile. Sensing the danger, He immediately killed her and then that female-crocodile divulged her real self. She was a cursed maiden or 'Apsara' who got now liberated because of Lord Hanuman. While leaving, she told Lord Hanuman the truth of the disguised sage and Ravan and Kaalnemi's conspiracy. He decided to teach a lesson to this Asur. Returning back to hermitage He killed the sage guised Kaalnemi but before dying he too came back in his real Asur form and chanted 'Ram-Naam' while taking his last breath. Lord Hanuman felt elated seeing that like Marich, even Kaalnemi was a devotee-Asur of Lord Ram. Without wasting any time, Lord Hanuman took off and now reached the Great Himalayas.

There He found many herbs on the Drona mountain but couldn't figure out the 'Sanjeevani-Bootti', the medicine that was prescribed by Sushern. He couldn't find a solution for this dilemma and so He uprooted the whole mountain 'Drona' and carried it on his hand, to Lanka. On the way back while he was flying over Ayodhaya kingdom, Prince Bharat saw Him and mistook Him as an enemy entity and shot an arrow. The arrow hit Lord Hanuman and He fell on the ground chanting 'Ram-Naam'. Prince Bharat was startled realizing that He had hurt a Lord Ram's Devotee. He prayed for His recovery, and Lord Hanuman got up immediately. They then greeted each other and

Lord Hanuman narrated Bharatji the whole story. Bharatji blessed Him and Lord Hanuman again flew towards Lanka where Lord Ram was eagerly waiting for His arrival.

This episode not only shows the courage, skills and focus of Lord Hanuman but also shows the enlightened intelligence of Prince Bharat. It was midnight when Lord Hanuman was flying over Ayodhaya. Naturally, every Ayodhaya citizen was in deep sleep. But at that moment, there was one great entity who was alertly watching and protecting the people of Lord Ram. Bharatji had accepted the throne of Ayodhaya but always considered Ayodhaya as the property of Lord Ram and himself as His servant. While protecting Lord's property, he had wrongly mistaken a devotee as an Asur yet he made sure that the arrow used must only stop and not harm him. This reflects the alertness of Bharatji. He made sure that the suspect must be least harmed, what if, if he is innocent. In this way, this reflects the great sense of duty and capability of Bharatji, the guardian of Ayodhaya.

That night Lord Hanuman too, while performing the great task for Lord Ram which humanity was always going to remember, witnessed a greater servant-devotee than himself. Lord Hanuman and Lord Laxman had sacrificed everything to serve their Lord Ram and were fighting the greatest army of Asur to free Lady Sita, the beloved of Lord Ram. Their contribution, service and duty are always praised by us but here Lord Hanuman realized, what Bharatji was doing was even greater than their service. Millions of Vanar warriors were devotees of Lord Ram and were ready to go to any limit to serve their Lord but here in Ayodhaya there was just one guardian-devotee who had taken the responsibility to protect millions of lives of Ayodhaya kingdom. And that night, though Lord Hanuman got hit with Prince Bharat's arrow and fell unconscious yet understood in His heart that Bharatji is the one greatest example of devotion who had from the core of his heart and soul had devoted his life and surrendered in the lotus feet of Lord Siya-Ram. There is no other one like Great Bharat who had in true sense attained the purpose of life, in the service of Lord Siya-Ram.

Chapter 6.22

Kumbhakarna: Desires vs Dharma

He scolded Ravan for taking enmity of the Lord, whom He admired.
But soon forgot righteousness and began gulping what he desired.

Here in Lanka at the Vanar Cantonment, Lord Ram was anxiously waiting for the return of Lord Hanuman. He was very sorrowful and upset seeing the condition of his beloved brother Laxman. The whole Vanar army that day saw tears in the eyes of their God Ram. Goswamiji says that Ram is indestructible and omnipresent but was doing this human-leela to display the emotions of mankind. The ever compassionate Lord knows the intense suffering and pain that human beings have to deal with. Everybody then saw a strange sight that Lord Hanuman was descending from the sky with a huge mountain in his hand. Lord Hanuman narrated the whole story, and the doctor, Sushern, using the 'Sanjeevani-Booti' cured Lord Laxman, who at once got up. Everyone was overjoyed, filled with new found enthusiasm they were now again ready to fight the Asur. On the same night, Lord Hanuman dropped Sushern back to his house in Lanka city and returned.

Here Ravan as soon as got the news of Laxman's cure got very disconcerted and went to wake up his brother, the mighty and invincible Kumbhakaran. As soon as he got up, Ravan narrated the whole story and asked him to fight Lord Ram and the Vanar army, on his behalf. Kumbhakaran instead got upset with Ravan for abducting Goddess Sita and taking the enmity of Lord Ram. He scolded Ravan for his foolish act and asked him to return Mother Sita and surrender in the lotus feet of Lord Siya-Ram. Kumbhakaran contemplating on the qualities of Lord Ram got overwhelmed in Bhakti or devotion. But Ravan wouldn't listen to any counsel and immediately asked to bring uncountable pots of wine and buffalos to feast, the gluttonous Kumbhakaran.

In the beginning along with Ravan and Vibhishan, Kumbhakaran had also performed tough penance. Satisfied with their dedication, God Shiva and Brahma manifested to give boons to all three of them. Seeing Ravan and Vibhishan, Brahma didn't feel any different but on seeing Kumbhakaran, he got really perturbed. His humongous body was proof of his gigantic appetite. Brahma the Creator felt what would happen to his lovely creation that is Earth, if Kumbhakaran would continue consuming its resources every day. Devta with the help of Mother Saraswati manipulated Kumbhakaran and the boon he got was that he would be awake and conscious for just one day after every six months. This way he would consume resources just two days in a year. This way Earth's survival was ensured by Brahma.

Kumbhakaran, on one hand wanted to satisfy himself by consuming more and more of the resources and food but didn't want to work as hard as was required to consume this quantum of resources. He wanted to fulfill the expectations of Rajogun or materialistic appetite through the medium of Tamogun or idle way. In simple words, he symbolizes those who want many things in life but don't want to work hard for it. If the mind-ego compels the Being to attain more of everything, then the same mind-ego also encourages the Being to work harder for it. But there are some Beings like Kumbhakaran whose mind-ego is such that they want things but do not want to bear the struggle to achieve them. And so, it was Ravan who took care of his brother's needs and let him live the way he wanted. It was but natural that Kumbhakaran felt obliged and grateful to Ravan for looking after his lethargic lifestyle.

Ravan had accepted the 'Kumbhakaran-Burden' with pleasure. But a mind like Ravan wouldn't do anything if it doesn't suit his selfish interests. His taking care was not just about brotherly affection. He knew that an active Kumbhakaran could one day become his own opponent and spoil his ambitions. Kumbhakaran was a devotee of God Narayan and physically the strongest one and so had the capacity to create problems for Ravan. By making him dependent and obliged, Ravan wanted to keep Kumbhakaran under his control and use him in difficult situations, whenever needed, like in this time of war.

Kumbhakaran had many flaws but he was indeed a devotee of Lord Siya-Ram and had deep respect for Saints and Sages. He had blessed Vibhishan in the war for quitting Ravan and joining Lord Ram. But his 'Rajogun vritti' or animalistic desire for wine, food and resources had overshadowed the little 'Satogun' or purity he had. And so, at the battlefield, he hastily asks Vibhishan to move aside as he is failing to understand right and wrong, and thereafter, he right away attacks the army of Lord Ram, whom he was praising a little while ago.

Ravan knew the nature and flaws of his brother very well. He knew that all sermons of Kumbhakaran could be stopped by providing him wine and food. On one hand, Kumbhakaran had closed his eyes and was engrossed in the 'Darshan' or vision of his Lord Ram but as soon he opened his eyes, he started gulping the wine and flesh. Just after worshiping the qualities of Lord Ram, he starts worshiping Ravan for providing him what he was always desperate for. Goswami Tulsidasji here shows the impulsive and contradictory nature of Kumbhakaran. A flickering minded, wine and flesh obsessed individual can have some reverence for the Lord but this is not good enough for Dharma and Bhakti. Worshiping God when it's convenient and forgetting righteousness and indulgence in pleasures the rest of the time is not spirituality. Even today we see many of us with the same attitude, visiting temples in the morning and cheating, lying and amusing ourselves, the rest of the day. A little practice of 'Satogun' cannot justify an irresponsible lifestyle. A true devotee is the one who at least tries sincerely to be stable in Satogun and without any fluctuations, surrenders in the lotus feet of Lord Siya-Ram.

Chapter 6.23

Yagya of Meghnad: Good vs Evil Intentions

He was a great scientist but used energies for evil intentions,
Even today such ones are the actual cause of world's tensions.

Kumbhakaran had launched a lethal attack on the Vanar army. The Vanars scattered and ran here and there in fear. Even the great warriors Hanumanji, Sugriv, Nal and Neel were also not able to stop this unstoppable giant. They all felt helpless and went to Lord Ram. Lord then asked Sugriv and Vibhishan to look after their soldiers while he would take care of the Asur force. Lord then shot hundreds of arrows which further multiplied in lakhs and showered on Asur army like a heavy rain. So thick was the cloud of arrows that it ambushed the Sun and brought darkness though in broad daylight. Kumbhakaran then ran towards the Lord in anger. He knew his end was near and he was now going to be liberated from his animalistic life. The Lord's arrows destroyed Kumbhakaran by chopping his body parts one by one; first arms, then head, and then legs. He dropped dead on the ground and his consciousness got united with Lord Ram. His sliced head was flown by the Lord's arrow back in the palace of Lanka and in the lap of Ravan. Ravan and the whole Asur clan seeing the devastation cried at this great loss.

On seeing his family in deep sorrow and in such a pathetic state, Meghnad then swore to destroy Lord Ram and Lord Laxman. He reached the war field in his flying chariot and used magical tricks which were against the rules of war. All the Vanars got trapped in his illusion and lost their alertness. His 'Nag-Pash' arrows then tied Lord Ram-Laxman and made them unconscious. Here, Tulsidasji says that what can tether that Lord who has tied the whole cosmos in His one finger. Lord Ram was playing the Human-Leela by becoming a victim of Meghnad's attack. On seeing this situation, Lord 'Garuda' the King of Birds and the mount of God Vishnu arrived and untied the 'Nag-Pash' arrows, bowed to the Lord and flew back.

In the meanwhile Jambavan had attacked Meghnad who fainted and with his chariot fell back in Lanka palace. Meghnad got very embarrassed, on seeing himself defeated in front of his Asur clan, especially Ravan and pledged to do the 'Yagya' or prayer for immortality. Vibhishan got this news and he requested Lord Ram that this 'Yagya' of Meghnad must be stopped at any cost. Vibhishan's apprehension was that if Meghnad succeeds, then it will be impossible to defeat him.

Meghnad with firm determination was totally committed to the victory of his father Ravan. His spirit and confidence was exceptional. It was clear that he was not going to give up at any cost. But he could clearly see that the Vanar army had an upper hand in the war. Death of Kumbhakaran was a big blow for the Asur army. Meghnad could not have imagined that the mightiest warrior of the world would be defeated and slayed in the war in just one day. And his own war skills had failed in front of Ayodhaya Princes Lord Ram-Laxman. So now Meghnad had decided to obtain and use supernormal powers in the war and so for it had begun 'Yagya' or oblation for the Goddess of Darkness. Meghnad was a one, stubborn and corrupted mind-ego which was not ready to give up or accept its defeat.

Human Being is a combination of virtues and flaws. Even a very virtuous one cannot claim absolute perfection. At times even the greatest and noblest ones speak or commit something wrong and are then criticized. But then the wise ones immediately realize their mistake and out of remorse try hard to correct their mistake. Here, Goswamiji says that it's not right to put all the blame on any individual but to remember that mistakes are governed by 'Kaal' or time, 'Karma' or actions and 'Guna' or qualities. The same was said by Lord Ram for Mother Kaikeyi at Chitrakoot. She repented for her mistake and was revered by the Lord and this proves that she was indeed a wise and noble soul.

But there are some people who have a sadistic nature, who enjoy committing crime and who like to spoil others' lives. To commit a crime is neither their impulsive nor their conscious decision, but their way of life. They may at times do some good deeds but that is because of the company of virtuous people. Or there is hidden some selfish motive. But such ones are unable to change their negative nature. Meghnad was of this kind. He had never felt guilty or remorseful or repented for the crimes he had committed. And so to spoil the Yagya of such a person, one must not hold back. Yagya is a holy ceremony but if the intention is evil then it cannot be justified. Vibhishan conveyed to Lord Ram that Meghnad without an iota of righteousness is one person who is using his right or wrong resources just to win this war at any cost. There are rules also for an event like war which both the sides adhere to but Meghnad never cared for it. And therefore, the Lord must not hesitate in spoiling his Yagya and to punish him, without any delay.

In today's times, most of us fail to understand the significance or the relevance of Yagya. In the beginning, we see that Vishvamitra comes to Dasaratha to talk about Asuras spoiling his Yagya and now we see Meghnad initiating a Yagya which might be lethal for the Vanar army. So the question arises what exactly is a Yagya? Yagya can be understood as a combination of 'Mantra' or set of specific words and 'Vidhi' or set of systematic actions. The Vedic Teachers believe that Mantras when recited properly, unleashes tremendous creative and supernormal powers. No matter what is the intention of the doer, with systematic Yagya, he does attain Siddhi or divine powers.

The Yagya process can be compared with the General Science of today. Science is about knowing the potential in an object and then finding a way to use that potentiality. Once the scientific principle is established, then anybody using the same principle can create the same energy and use it for other purposes. Once when the understanding of Nuclear energy was established and technology to use it was designed, then not just the founder authority but many other organizations have used the same technology and understanding and started using this energy. This Nuclear energy was used by mankind as a weapon to destroy their enemies but also used it to generate other useful energies like electricity for the benefit of the people. So energy is always there, it depends on the Being whether to use it judiciously or immorally.

In every object and in every particle on this planet, there is a hidden potential power. However, in the perspective of Spirituality the subtle body holds more power than the gross object. And Mantra is considered as the superior most subtle energy. The Science of Mantra gives maximum importance to the 'Word/s'. Through the process of Jaab or chanting words, the power of Mantra is initiated. Ravan was a great scholar of this Science of Mantra and so was Meghnad. Both of them through this science had obtained supernatural powers and energies. But they had mostly misused these powers for their own selfish interests. Sage Vishwamitra too had such powers but he didn't even use them to protect his own people because he felt it was unlawful. A Sage never uses these special powers for their own purposes and this is the fundamental difference between a Sage and an Asur.

Both Ravan and Meghnad had understood that they cannot win this war against Lord Ram within the boundaries of rules and so found it necessary to initiate the supernatural powers through Yagya. There is a difference between Yagya of evil Beings like Asur and 'Yagya' of Sage-Devotees like Vishvamitra. The purpose of Asur is not faith and surrender or 'Samarparn' towards the Deity instead it's about attaining powers and to use them in whatever way he wanted. Meghnad wanted to use the Yagya powers for his Egoic selfish interest. It's far from the Yagya of a true Devotee where from the beginning to the end, the only purpose and intention is faith and surrender to God, realizing own flaws and asking the Lord for forgiveness.

For Asur faith, surrender, acceptance of mistakes or asking forgiveness does not hold any significance. The same applies to any selfish Being of today's times. But they forget that the one who is doing a Scientific Yagya to create a Nuclear Bomb is not immune to the destructive impact of the same bomb when it explodes. Destruction of Meghnad by Prince Laxman while performing the Yagya is a proof of this principle. Goswami Tulsidasji says that Asur-like Beings do attain early success but then they are doomed for a tragic ending. The same happened with Ravan and Meghnad. Goswami says that no Yagya is complete unless it's done with faith and surrender in the lotus feet of Lord Siya-Ram.

Chapter 6.24

Liberation of Ravan: Destruction of Source

Like Ravan's heads and hands, 'attachment' rises again and again,
One needs Grace of God Ram, to overcome this last round of pain.

Recalling the might of Lord Ram, Prince Laxman defiantly fitted an arrow to his bow and shot it at Meghnad. On being hit, he abandoned his magical disguises at the moment of death. While taking his last breath, the changed Meghnad recited the name of Lord Ram and Lord Laxman. On seeing him dying as a devotee, Angad and Hanumanji smiled and said, "Blessed indeed is your mother!". Lord Laxman had successfully destroyed both the Dark Yagya and Prince Meghnad and then all of them returned back to the lotus feet of Lord Ram.

The moment Ravan heard the news of his son's death, he dropped unconscious to the ground. Mandodari too was shocked and was crying relentlessly. The citizens were all smitten with grief and everyone blamed Ravan for Meghnad's tragic end. Ravan in anger got ready his chariot and his best warriors, and rushed forth like a storm. Many ill-omens occurred at that time but the arrogant Ravan didn't value them. He ordered his army to march forward. When the Vanars received this news, they too rushed forth chanting the name of Lord Ram. The gigantic and brave apes and bears of Vanar clan stood tall with claws and teeth, rocks and huge trees as their weapons. They were all very powerful and fearless.

Vibhishan was disconcerted when he saw Ravan mounted on his chariot and King Ram on His foot. He bowing to Lord's feet spoke, "Lord, You have no chariot to carry You nor an armor for Your body or shoe for Your feet. How, then, can You expect to defeat this devil Ravan?" Lord smiled and replied, "The chariot which leads one to victory is something else. Valor and fortitude are the wheels of that chariot, while truthfulness and good conduct is its banner and standard. Strength, discretion, self-control and benevolence are its four horses that have been joined to the chariot with the cords of forgiveness, compassion and evenness of mind. 'Bhakti' or devotion is the charioteer, 'Vairagya' or dispassion is the shield and 'Santosh' or contentment is the sword. There is no other equipment for victory as efficacious as this chariot. And the one who owns such a chariot shall have no enemy to defeat anywhere."

On that side, Ravan threw his challenge, while on this side Angad and Hanumanji invited him to a contest. The war of life and death began that day. When the Devta saw that the Lord was on foot, their King Indra sent his own chariot, on which Lord Ram gladly mounted. The enraged Ravan challenged the Lord of Universe, "My name is Ravan, whose glory is known all over the world, and whose prison holds the Devtas and Beings of all worlds." Lord replied, "There are three types of men in this world, first one gives flowers alone, the second one gives both flowers and fruits and the third one yields fruits alone. Eventually, the first one talks, the second one talks as well as does, while the third one simply does but never brags about it. Stop using empty words and show some action."

Saying this Lord shot many arrows towards Ravan. Those arrows shot down Ravan's heads and arms to the ground. But miraculously, they grew afresh as soon as they were cut. Time after time, the Lord smote off his arms and heads; but they were renewed as soon as they were blown off. Again and again the Lord tore off his arms and heads. Ravan, on seeing the failure of his opponent's attack he laughed wickedly in his great pride and rushed forward. On seeing Vibhishan, in intense anger, he threw a weapon on his brother but Lord Ram put Vibhishan behind Him and took the weapon on Himself. Lord fainted for a while.

When Vibhishan saw that the Lord had been hurt, he seized his club and in anger rushed and struck his brother Ravan right on the chest. Tulsidasji says that Vibhishan was always so meek and submissive that he could have never dared to even look Ravan in the face. But that day with the Grace of Lord Ram, he fought like 'Kaal' or Death itself. He had discovered his hidden potential and had overcome his fears. This was just another Leela of Lord Ram for the benefit of His devotee.

Here at Ashok Vatika, Trijita narrated the whole story of that day's battle to Lady Sita. When She came to know about magical re-growth of Ravan's heads and arms, She felt much dismayed at heart and Her mind was filled with anxiety. Guilt and pain filled Heart as She blamed Herself for the cause of this struggle. Trijita consoled Her and said, "My dear daughter, Ravan will surely die if an arrow pierces his heart but the Lord is careful not to strike him there, for He knows that You abide there. Ravan will perish in less than a moment whenever the Lord intends so." These soothing words consoled Her for a while.

Here on the battlefield, Ravan's heads grew up as soon as they were chopped. Vibhishan then divulged the secret to the Lord, "Nectar abides in the depth of his navel, by virtue of it Ravan doesn't die."

One after the other, all the main and mighty warriors of Lanka had fallen but Ravan like a true immortal hero stood tall in the battlefield. So far, it has become almost impossible to defeat this last standing warrior. No matter how great Kumbhakaran and Meghnad were but after their heads were chopped, they perished but Ravan was like a difficult mystery of death. And to solve this mystery, the Lord had to take assistance from Vibhishan. 'Is Ravan immortal?' Everyone, be it Asur or Vanar, was thinking about it. Even the arrows of God were not able to stop him. The Devtas from the sky who were watching this spectacle were horrified. Even Lord Ram appeared to be tired. Drops of sweat were shining on His face.

Well the truth was different. God was not showing His Almighty and All-Powerful attributes, purposefully. In His Godly perspective, merely a thought could have ended Ravan. If God had not wanted, then Ravan would not have been even born, let alone his boons of immortality. Clearly, God doesn't interfere in the ways of the world. He is the mute observer of the movements of nature. Indifference is His innate attribute. God only interferes in this Maya created world when the Being through true love and prayer calls Him for help. And when God incarnates as a human-being in this world, then His Avatar, who is although beyond the domain of Maya's created universe, yet accepts and practices the same laws that are applicable for every Being. Therefore, any of God's human-avatar, whether as Ram or Krishna, doesn't show a Leela openly which may appear to be humanly impossible.

Even those acts of God which we believe as divine are actually not so. Perspective of Beings is very limited. What seemed to be magical, supernatural or divine are actually those movements which fall in the domain of nature's laws and are actually possible for a Being to achieve. But since we don't see them happening, commonly we consider them as divine.

Birds flying in the sky are an ordinary sight but a story of Yogi flying awe struck us. A yogi can transform himself through his practice of yogic sciences.

We may not know what is the science behind a yogi flying but still it is a science and so doable. To accept Lord Ram as God because of His divine and supernatural powers is not right. Even Ravan possessed such divine powers. And his immortality is the part of the same powers that he had. Re-growth of heads and arms on Ravan appears to be an impossible occurrence but there are so many plants we know about which after being chopped regrow themselves. It is a very common occurrence in the field of Botany. But this attribute of re-growth in a human-being is considered unbelievable by us because we haven't witnessed such things ever in our lives. And therefore, we start believing such epic stories like Ramayan as fictitious mythology.

In today's time, medical science has advanced a lot and organ transplant through surgery has become a doable feat. But some years back in the past, it appeared to be impossible. Today we are talking about cloning, artificial intelligence and what not and if not soon but later in the future these things will too become unsurprising. Is it really difficult to accept 'Pushpak-Viman' as a marvelous product of AI? Science is about understanding a nature's phenomenon in one field and applying it to other fields. Why is it so difficult to accept that Ravan was a science genius who had learnt some skills which were a way to advance for others in those times? Through hard and dedicated penance, he had tried to learn to overcome death and he was, though not in totality, but was very successful. His mistake was to consider these scientific achievements as something which was beyond the realm of nature and something divine, impossible for any other one to achieve. He foolishly started believing himself as immortal and this success made him proud and arrogant.

To kill Ravan, it was not necessary for Lord Ram to use His Godly powers. For it, what was needed was the right solution and that was to focus the target right in the center of Ravan's energy source. And this solution was given by Vibhishan who had seen Ravan works and methodologies. Vibhishan therefore knew exactly where to hit him. The energy source that was re-growing limbs, heads and organs countlessly was centered in the navel of Ravan's body. It was required to destroy that 'Amrit-Nabhi-Kund' or Life-Giving source. Lord Ram then targeted the arrow towards it and destroyed it.

In spiritual perspective Ravan is the symbol of 'Moha' or Attachment of a man with his body and owned things like house, family, car etc. This is the illusion of 'I' and 'Mine', which is the fundamental cause of human suffering. On the path of spirituality not once but hundreds of times, the seeker feels that he has escaped the trap of 'Moha' but very soon like Ravan heads and hands, 'Moha' again rises in the mind-ego of the seeker. Moha cannot be destroyed just by chopping off its heads and hands. Just by intellect and good deeds too, Moha cannot be destroyed. To successfully destroy it, one needs to target the center-source or 'Amrit-Kund' and this center lies in 'Chitt-Sanskar' or conditioning of uncountable past lives imprinted on the hard-drive of memory inside the mind. This conditioning cannot be washed off just by the seeker's own intellect and logic. For it, the help of the Teacher and Grace of Lord Ram is needed.

The thirty arrows that were shot by Lord Ram which chopped off Ravan's heads and hands symbolizes the multiple efforts of the seeker, who believes to have chopped off the Moha every time and yet is not able to destroy it. The thirty-first arrow of the Lord which had targeted the energy-source that killed Ravan, symbolizes the Grace of God on the seeker who under the guidance of the Teacher, here symbolized by Vibhishan, is then able to finally erase both the good and bad conditioning from the hard-drive of memory and liberates the himself from his most difficult challenge that is Ravan, the Moha.

Liberation from Moha means the ultimate and permanent state of divine peace and the final evolutionary stage of human-consciousness, which is the purpose of every Being's life. And so, Tulsidasji says that for every Being, the only concern should be to find his way that leads to surrender in the lotus feet of Lord Siya-Ram.

Chapter 6.25

End of Ravan: Lord liberates the Devil

That day was the end of world's most dreaded dream,
Ravan's consciousness got united with the Supreme.

Lord's arrow hit the pot of immortality in Ravan's belly and the great Asur King fell. Leaving the 'Tamsik' Asur body, his consciousness or the pure spirit got united with Lord Ram. The onlookers were surprised, how can Lord bless such a violent and evil Being like Ravan. 'What about the Law of Karma?', was the question everybody was asking. Karma principle is that one has to reap what he sows. Ravan ought to be punished for many lifetimes for the unrighteous deeds and crimes he had committed all his life, was the call of justice. By abducting Mother Sita, he had done such a hideous act which cannot be compared with even the worst of the sins. But like Kumbhakaran, his consciousness or Beingness attained Oneness with the Supreme.

The liberation of Kumbhakaran and Ravan seems to be against the Karmic law but we must also not forget that nothing happens without a reason and without the will of Lord Ram. God's incarnation is not based on Karmic principle but happens because of the love of His devotees. God's purpose is to fulfill the desires of His people. In Leela or play of God Avatar, His punishments though appear like an effect of the cause but behind the punishment, it is actually His Grace. And the liberation of Ravan and Kumbhakaran is the greatest example of Lord's Grace and love. A devotee, even when he takes up enmity with God, expects welfare from God. Tulsidasji says to Lord Ram that, "O Lord, if there cannot be love between us two, then let there be intense hatred between us." He believes that instead of having affinity with others, it's better to have enmity with Lord because any relation with Him is it of hatred or enmity, ultimately brings welfare of the Being.

Waves, be it subtle or rough, though appear different but are part of the same ocean water. Similarly, 'Jiva' or individual consciousness in the human body appears to be separate but is actually part of the One Supreme consciousness or 'Ishwar'. The Jiva, because of its attachment with the body and material based on 'I' and 'Mine', then starts working for the happiness and against the suffering of the body, in whatever ways it feels as righteous. It is because of forgetfulness of truth and ignorance that the Being believes itself to be the body and experiences unhappiness. But an inquisitive one in the light of knowledge realizes the illusion of this body-attachment and is able to free himself. The 'Jiva' which was standing in the form of Ravan was at the level of Beingness actually a part of God's consciousness. But because of intense body-attachment or 'Moha', Ravan's ignorance level was also high and so he acted unrighteous and became a demon.

Even after being counseled and educated numerous times by so many knowledgeable ones like Hunamanji, Ravan was unable to come out of this ignorance. Even after realizing to some extent that Lord Ram whom he was earlier taking as an ordinary prince of Ayodhaya was actually God Himself. Ravan was unable to come out of his foolishness. On the stage of the Lanka war, the body of Ravan was torn into pieces by the arrows of Lord Ram. That body in which feet once the world used to bow had now become the feast for jackals and vultures. But in that impure body dwells a holy soul which like all other souls had to someday attain self-actualisation.

No wonder how unpalatable it seems so yet this is the truth. Even the biggest criminal of the world is eligible for the love of Lord Ram. This must not be seen as unjust but be accepted as the will of God. And what God does cannot be questioned because He is the knower of everything and all pervading. Almost everything that Ravan did was wrong but one wrongness became a blessing for him and that was taking enmity with God. A man like Ravan cannot ever be a figure of inspiration but it is also true that there cannot be another Ravan in this world ever.

Lord Ram loves every Being and is the symbol of Grace and Care and so Goswami Tulsidasji says that the purpose of every soul and of every Jiva is to be united in the Supreme Consciousness that is Lord Siya-Ram. We may like it or dislike it but that day Ravan too had attained the purpose of his existence.

Chapter 6.26

Lord Ram embarks the Pushpak Viman

Vibhishan was crowned as the new Lanka King,
Lord Siya-Ram got reunited in the Vanar's ring,
And yet Lord was only concerned for Bharat's, waiting,
Off they flew back without taking any Lanka's, thing.

The story of Ravan came to an end. God Brahma and God Shiva came to see the spectacle. The Devta clan rained down flowers. The Vanar army bowed in the lotus feet of Lord Ram and celebrated in excitement. The whole universe resounded with the Glory of the Lord. Queen Mandodari and the whole of Asur clan, on seeing the state of Ravan, felt miserable and cried in pain but Mandodari like a true devotee had no bitterness and she too with others sang the glory of Lord Ram. Everybody was now in relief. Lord then asked Vibhishan to perform the funeral rites of Ravan with royal honor. For the crowning ceremony of Vibhishan, Lord then sent all the Vanars with Laxman in the Lanka city but Himself stayed back. Lord then sent Hanumanji to Lady Sita to tell Her about the victory and to prepare Herself for reunion.

As per the arrangements of Vibhishan, Mother Sita seated in a beautiful palanquin, with Asur maids and soldiers, reached the Vanar camp. Lord Ram and Mother Sita then played the Leela of 'Agni-Pariksha' or fire-test, where to prove Her purity She crossed the blazing flames of fire, unharmed. The most criticized Agni-Pariksha was actually a Leela of Lord Siya-Ram which they had played in Aranya Kand where the real Sita went with the Agni-Devta and her place was taken by Her reflection. Ravan had kidnapped Sita's reflection and had never come in contact with the real Sita. Now was the time to end this leela and so the trick of Agni-Pariksha was played so that the Agni-Devta could then bring back the real Sita and dissolve the reflection of Sita. No one, not even Laxman would know this secret Leela of Lord Siya-Ram.

Standing on the left side of Lord Ram, Goddess Sita shone resplendent in

Her exquisite beauty like the bud of a gold lily beside a fresh blue lotus. The beauty of Lord Siya-Ram was beyond all measures. Everyone rejoiced at the sight and shouted, "Glory to the Masters of the Universe!".

King Dasratha too manifested from heaven to bless his sons Prince Ram and Laxman. Lord bowed to His father and requested him to forgive Mother Kaikeyi which he did gladly. Lord Ram then asked Devta Indra to restore the lives of martyred Vanars. Devtas and God Shiva sang the glories of the Lord. When they all had left Lord Ram requested Vibhishan to do something so that He gets to meet His Brother Bharat without any delay. Vibhishan arranged the 'Pushpak-Viman' or the flying machine which can carry any number of travelers and can fly at the speed of thought. This was the same machine which was snatched by Ravan from his half-brother Kuber and used in the abduction of Lady Sita. Lord Siya-Ram with Lord Laxman, Hanumanji, Vibhishan and other Vanar leaders embarked it and flew towards Ayodhaya.

Lord Ram had established full control over the Lanka of gold but the question is, what was the purpose of this war? Is it a war of revenge? Is it the defeat of Ravan or Asur clan or Lanka? If it had been so, then this war would also be recorded as just another war in the history of India. But this war was not against any individual, country or clan. Nor was this war waged in anger, hatred, revenge or for ambitions.

This war was against those flaws which had along with the whole world had also engulfed Lanka. When one part of the body gets infected or injured, then more than the other parts of the body it hurts itself the most. A qualified surgeon doesn't hesitate in removing that failed organ from the body. And in doing so, the surgeon doesn't hold any attachment or grudges against that organ. His only objective is to save and heal the body.

In the perspective of Lord Ram, this whole world is one entity and Ravan a very meager part of that entity; Ravan was that part, which had got infected. Lord Ram first tried to cure through sweet and bitter medicines of Hanumanji and Angad but it didn't work out. And now, the infection had become so grave that cure of this infection was not possible. So in this circumstance, there was no other option left but to amputee that infected part from the world. By slaying Ravan, Lord Ram followed the same procedure. He had removed the infection and the flaws and ended the pain of the humanity-body. The end of Ravan was the celebration of victory over all the flaws of mind-ego. And in this war, nobody lost anything but only gained. Even Ravan and Asur clan didn't lose anything. They had lost the throne of Lanka but had attained the Heavenly abode of Lord Ram, the ultimate destination of every Being. Queen Mandodari while grieving on the dead body of Ravan said, "You had committed only sins and crimes throughout your whole life and yet ignoring your 'Paap' or Sins, the One who had liberated you is Lord Ram. I surrender and prostrate in the lotus feet of the Lord."

The Asur clan, its soldiers and each one of them who had supported Ravan was also guilty and a prisoner of war. Hanumanji had witnessed the Asur maids troubling Mother Sita in Ashok Vatika. But as soon as Ravan was slayed all their sins were forgiven. In the perspective of Lord Ram, 'Past' is not such a prison from which one cannot free himself. Lord believes that if the Being attains purity and wisdom in the 'Present' then his misdeeds of the 'Past' must be taken as a bad dream and should be forgiven.

Had Lord Ram wanted, He would have taken over the throne of Lanka. If Lord had wanted, then He would have entered the city of Lanka on the pretext of Vibhishan's crowning ceremony. But away from victory-defeat and ceremonies-celebrations, He remained seated equanimously or 'Samatva-Bhav' on His divine 'Asana' or seat. To be indifferent in this victory was only possible for Lord Ram. Even though He was so close to the most prosperous land on Earth yet He was only thinking about the Great Mahatma Bharat, His brother who like Him was staying away from the luxuries and prosperity of Ayodhaya and was living an ascetic life in Nandigram waiting for His return. The feelings of Bharat were the only thing which were filling the eye ocean of Lord Ram and flowing down like streams of tears. Goswami Tulsidasji says that who can be so caring and compassionate like Lord Ram, who has no interest in celebrating Lanka victory but is only concerned for His beloved brother-devotee Bharat. And therefore, Goswamiji says that whoever for once understands the nature of the Lord finds nothing worthwhile in this world but to surrender in the lotus feet of Lord Siya-Ram.

UTTRAKAND

Chapter 7.1

Hanumanji meets Bharat: Glory of Ram-Katha

Hanumanji informed Bharat about Lord Ram's location,
But he was more interested in the 'Ram-Katha' recitation.

Lord Siya-Ram with their whole clan flew off in Pushpak-Viman to Ayodhaya. For the first time, in fourteen years, Lord seemed enthusiastic, for now He will be seeing His beloved Ayodhaya and His people after a long period. But equally, He was anxious for the well-being of His beloved brother-devotee Bharat and so He was very eager to reach on time. While flying, He was showing spots to Princess Sita like where Ravan and Kumbhakaran were killed, the Ram-Setu and Rameshwaram, then the points where they had traveled in Her search in Kishkindha and so on. Princess Sita was overwhelmed on seeing the love of Her Ram, the love of God who didn't sit at peace till He had rescued His beloved Sita . On the way, they visited the hermitages of the Saints in Dandakaranya and Chitrakoot. They then stopped at the banks of Ganga to meet the King of Hearts, Nishadraj couldn't believe his eyes, for him the Raghukul King had arrived and kept His promise. Lord then first sent Hanumanji to Bharat to inform him beforehand about their victory over Ravan and their arrival in Ayodhaya.

Here, at Ayodhaya the people, the family and the mothers all were both excited and anxious simultaneously. They were excited because tomorrow was the last day of fourteen years of exile and that means the arrival of Lord Ram and anxious because so far they had no news of Him. A little away from Ayodhaya, at Nandigram, sage Bharat was getting restless every moment. He had decided that if the Lord didn't arrive at tomorrow sunrise, he would end his life. He was in deep sorrow and remorse thinking of the past events of their lives. Then suddenly, he had some good omens and he saw a 'Bhramachari' or celibate seeker coming towards him. The Brahmachari broke the news of the arrival of Lord Ram and came back in his original form. He was Lord Hanuman.

Bharatji was overjoyed and felt relieved. It took a while for him to absorb such exhilarating news after such a long time. He requested Hanumanji to sit with him for a while and sing the 'Ram-Charit' that is the qualities and the legend of Lord Ram.

Bharat had expected that Lord would come via the territory of Nishadraj by foot or by chariot and then he would get the news of His arrival beforehand. He couldn't imagine that Lord would be taking the aerial route through Pushpak-Viman. Since Bharat was not getting the expected news his heart was sinking day by day. He was depressed thinking that the Lord must have discarded him because of his flaws. Along with that He was praising the commitment and qualities of Lord Laxman. In these moments of despair, the arrival of Hanumanji was like a life-saving boat for a drowning soul in the sea-storm of life. Bharat's joy knew no bounds. He hugged Hanumanji and asked him to sing again and again the Lord's story for him. This appeared to be strange because Hanumanji had already told him before and again now. Instead of sitting and listening to Ram-Katha repeatedly, it was expected that Bharat would rush to Ayodhaya, inform everybody else about the good news and organize the grand welcome. But Bharat didn't do so because there was one thing which he loved more than Lord Ram and that was 'Ram-Katha'.

After Hanumanji had finished, Bharat asked him, "Did Lord Ram throughout this time, ever think or say anything about me?" Bharat, wanted in some manner, to get connected with 'Ram-Katha'. He himself didn't see any goodness within him. However, once Lord Ram had said to him, "O Bharat, there was, there is and there can be no noble soul like you in the three worlds." The epitome of humility, Bharat had replied, "If a monkey dances nicely or a parrot sings beautifully, then is it the talent of the monkey or parrot? No, actually it is the quality of their trainer who gave the training where the inborn skills got exposed. Whatever goodness in me that You are seeing is because of You." That day with the same humility he asked Hanumanji about the Lord's remembering him. To this question, the great Hanumanji bowed in Bharat's feet and said that he was more dear than life to the Lord.

Bharat was still eager to listen more about Lord Ram. This is the heart of a true devotee which is never satisfied listening to the glories and attributes of his beloved Lord. But time was short and so Hanumanji took his permission and left. More than Lord, Bharat loves the qualities of Lord, that is, Shri Ramcharitmanas. It appears like through Bharat, Goswami Tulsidasji has spoken his heart in this story. A devotee's thirst is never quenched, the more he listens the more thirsty he gets it. A devotee seeks nothing else from his life and from this world. He is least bothered about anything, even his own life. Because, he doesn't want to lose the bliss of 'Ram-Katha'. Such a pure devotee then becomes the duty of the Lord. More than devotees, it is the Lord who is impatient to reach them. He ensures their well being. And so Goswamiji says that, today, tomorrow or after a hundred lifetimes, every Being would realize one day that the only purpose of his Beingness and of his existence is to surrender in the lotus feet of Lord Siya-Ram. And then nothing more is left for the devotee to accomplish or do and he becomes One with the Lord, forever singing just one thing, which is 'Ram-Katha'.

Chapter 7.2

Shri Ayodhaya Dham: The Land of Lord Ram

If you find difficult to practise Ram Bhakti and Devotion,
Simply visit Ayodhaya once and your work will be done.

The people of Ayodhaya were impatiently waiting for the arrival of their King Ram. All the eyes were set towards the sky. By now through Prince Bharat, everybody had come to know that Lord is coming through 'Pushpak-Viman', a flying machine.

Here, flying in the Pushpak-Viman, Lord was none less impatient to meet and greet his beloved people of Ayodhaya. Tears fell from the eyes of God. His companions were startled to see this. This face which had never shown a sign of pain, trouble or fear even in the great war of Lanka was now displaying deep heartfelt emotions of love and anguish. The Land of Awadh appeared on the horizon, Lord held himself and spoke to His companions, "See Sugriv, Vibhishan and all of you, this is my holy land which is very beautiful. Though everybody sings the praises of Baikunth the Heavenly abode of Vishnu, but it's not as dear to Me as Ayodhaya. Not many but just one in thousands knows this secret."

Fourteen years back, Lord had got separated from this mysterious and holy land. It was the call of Dharma or duty and Maryada or protocol. At that time, with the ease, He had left it, created an impression in others' minds that He had no special adoration for Ayodhaya. Like a traveler who doesn't mind leaving a comfortable motel to carry on with his difficult journey, Lord had departed from this land. The question is, was the Lord actually disinterested and indifferent? Didn't He have a bit of attachment with His homeland? No, that is not the case. Even in the pleasant days of Chitrakoot many times, He would get emotional and remember Ayodhaya. He had always loved His country but He didn't want Laxman or Lady Sita to see tears in His eyes. And hence, when departing from Ayodhaya, He kept a straight and stern face.

Even in the days of exile whenever He would see His tears upsetting them , He would immediately hold Himself, as He never wants others to get bothered because of Him.

Had He got emotional and cried while leaving Ayodhaya, then people would have got agitated to the extent of harming Queen Kaikeyi. If Mother Kaushalya had seen tears in the eyes of her beloved son Ram, then she would have got shattered in pain. Prince Ram was very much attached with Ayodhaya but He never was attached with the throne or glory. Lord's love and emotions proves that in God resides a tender heart which is the lifeline for devotees. Devotees don't want an indifferent and dispassionate God. Such 'Antaryami' God already exists in the heart of every Being, who doesn't react or respond to the call of the Being. And that is why seekers are not very attracted towards such 'Antaryami' God.

God is everywhere and omnipresent, but does this knowledge help any of us? Can we see or feel Him? Can we hear His voice? Can in any way we experience His love for us? Truth is that God is always expressing Himself but because we are not that spiritually evolved we are unable to realize Him. But if we are spiritually not that evolved, does that mean we must lead a dry and cold life. A seeker and a devotee has the right to rejoice and find joy on his spiritual journey and so he needs a God who, on seeing him in pain, comes to him, looks after him, consoles him, gives hope to him and ensures care to him. And so a devotee doesn't get attracted towards a formless or 'Nirakar' God but a 'Sagurn-Sakar' or Avatar God with form, who looks, talks, feels and expresses just like humans, who has a life-story of successes-failures and joys-sorrows like that of mortal Being. And such God is Ram.

Lord Ram feels that Baikunth Dham, the Heavenly abode is no doubt divine but because it's inaccessible for the Beings, therefore it has earned a special importance. On the other hand, Ayodhaya is easily accessible for all. This Holy land makes the formless God to manifest and becomes approachable for the Beings. Lord Himself has rejoiced the beauty of human life which He could have never experienced in Baikunth. Sleeping in the lap of Mother Kaushalya, playing with friends and working physically like a human for the well-being of all His devotees was that He had yearned for. Lord announces to His companions, "Friends, have a look at this land of Awadh. Even though the whole world is eager to attain the dust of My feet, I am only eager to touch the dust of this land. Today my wish is going to be fulfilled. After a wait of fourteen years, I am returning to My abode. And I want all of you to be part of this most beautiful moment of My life."

This was true then and this holds true now and will forever – whoever has attached Himself with Shri Ayodhaya Dham, will one day attain the dust of Lord's feet and His love. Once the Being attains his Creator, there is nothing left for him to do or to think. His journey has ended. And therefore, here Goswami Tulsidasji says that one should surrender in the lotus feet of Lord Siya-Ram and also find the affinity in self for Ayodhaya.

Chapter 7.3

Advent Of Ram-Rajya

Ram Rajya is not a place but is a divine Consciousness,
Attained by the one who lives life with devotion and awareness.

Lord Ram saw hordes of people rushing towards Him and so He asked to land the Pushpak-Viman outside the city. After disembarking the flying machine, He asked Pushpak-Viman to go back to its real master which was Kuber. Lord Siya-Ram and Lord Laxman then rushed towards their kins and first prostrated in the feet of Teacher-Sage Vashishtha. Then they met each one of their family member that is Prince Bharat and Shatrughan and mother-queens Kaushalya, Kaikeyi and Sumitra. This union was very emotional. The family had reunited after fourteen long years. To satisfy thousands of people, Lord Ram did a miracle. He manifested Himself in countless forms and met each one of them individually and personally. In an instant, the agony and pain of the people ended as soon as the Lord casted His benign look on them.

Hanumanji, Sugriv, Vibhishan, Angad and all other Vanars and Asuras who had accompanied Lord took guise themselves in charming human forms. Lord introduced them to His family and people. They all greeted each other with immense love and affection. The sky was covered with beautiful flowers showered from the Heavens. All of them then marched towards the palace. Every inch of the city was decorated and was filled with utmost joy and merry. Even the Gods from different cosmos came to see the celebration of Ayodhaya. Lord Ram, knowing the remorse of Queen Kaikeyi, again went to her and relieved her from her guilt. Vashishtaji then initiated the crowning ceremony of Lord Ram. It was a grand spectacle. Lord Ram was sitting on the throne and on His left side shone Princess Sita, the mother of universe. Brahma, Shiva and all Devtas came to see this unforgettable view. Lord Laxman, Bharat, Shatrughan with Hanumanji, Vibhishan, Sugriv and all comrades stood behind the throne.

The wait was over. Evil was destroyed and finally Ram-Rajya was established. In that divine kingdom, all the males and females were always engrossed in the Bhakti of Lord Ram. In Ram-Rajya, nobody died in a young age and nobody felt any pain or suffering. Everyone was healthy and beautiful. The sufferings that arise out of death, life, time, karma, nature and attributes were nowhere to be seen. Neither Ego nor Maya were able to trap the Beings. Every Being had got rid from the clutches of ignorance and were eligible for ultimate bliss.

From the beginning till today and forever, mankind has lived with one purpose that is attainment of happiness and elimination of suffering. In the perspective of Rishis, this was achieved in Ram-Rajya. The people of Sanatan-Dharma from ages believe that there is no other place like Ram-Rajya. But can it be actually real? Can there be a place where there is no pain or suffering of any kind? Can a mortal Being attain that position where no problem can disturb his life? We all have experienced that, unhappiness is always attacking us from all four sides. When we cannot deal with one side, then how is it possible for us to survive in attacks from all sides?

Even when all the parts of the body are working fine but one-part malfunctions, then the person considers himself unhealthy and cannot sit in peace till he gets the part treated and makes it function normally. In the same manner, if even one person in the society is unhappy and dissatisfied, then that society cannot be considered happy and healthy. Lord Ram is not one individual or Being, He is 'Virat-Purush' or the Alpha-Man and this whole universe is His own body. He cannot sit in peace till every part of His body doesn't function perfectly. This is the vision of God. When Ravan was a part of Lord Ram, how can He take enmity with Ravan? The problem starts when that part becomes so infected that it's beyond cure and starts destroying other parts of the body.

The journey of Lord Ram from Ayodhaya to Lanka was a small link of the God's vision of healing His body that is this world. And so, we see that in this journey not just humans but animals, birds, monkeys, demons all came closer to Lord Ram. Hanumanji's visit to Lanka and counsel Ravan to return Mother Sita and surrender was part of Lord's treatment. But when the infected part stops responding to the treatment, then it needs to be surgically removed from the body to ensure that it doesn't spoil other parts. Slaying of Ravan was the same surgical procedure to ensure the well-being of the society. After the end of Ravan, the last obstruction in the advent of Ram-Rajya was eliminated.

When a person starts believing that in others' well-being there is trouble in his own life, then he starts spreading the same ideology in others also. This results in corruption, violence and failure of the society.

Knowing that there can be no situation which doesn't change, no matter how dear to us, yet we, all our lives just try to do one thing, that is to maintain the same comforting situation. No matter what, there are some things, be it self-beauty or wealth or fame or children which traps a person's mind and he doesn't want to leave these things at any cost. But things do come to end, beauty fades away, fame goes to another one, wealth is never enough and sometimes children discard their parents. And then, this ends his ride of joy, and brings immense pain and unhappiness in his life. The nature of each and every thing is ever-changing, it cannot be one, same and unchanging. This understanding of impermanence brings stability and peace in our mind. The way how we accept day and night & light and darkness likewise we have to accept happiness and unhappiness, good and bad, and birth and death. There is no option. There is no escape.

In Bhagavad Gita, Lord Krishna tells Arjun that the one who is born will have to die and after death the soul takes rebirth in a new body. This cycle keeps on going. And therefore, to cry for the deceased is not a wise thing to do. This is the universal truth of our existence. But not just for common people like us but even for very spiritually evolved and experienced ones, the truth of death is very difficult to accept. But when Goswami Tulsidasji says that in Ram-Rajya there was no 'Death', then what does he actually mean? Were the people of Ayodhaya had become immortal? Well, he meant to say that death in itself is not the problem rather untimely death is the biggest pain. Tulsidasji meant that in Ram-Rajya, there was birth and so there was death but there was no untimely death and so no sorrow. But just a long life is not good enough. Life is enjoyable when it's free from illnesses, pain and deformities. In Ram-Rajya, there was long life and with it was good health, pain free and beautiful human beings. In this way, Ram-Rajya had overcome the agony that arises out of death and fear of death.

The other reason for sorrow in our lives is Karma. Even when born in the same family at the same time, two persons experience different gravities of joys and sorrows in their lives. The only reason for this is understood to be their actions or Karma of their past lives. Simply putting, the law of Karma states that what you sow you will reap. All of us can see the play of Karma in our lives too. But in Ram-Rajya, there was a change in the Karma Law. Lord

Ram had declared that the punishment for the sin of servant-devotee will be given to the master. Sometimes, when the eyes couldn't see an obstruction, the whole body tumbles down and brings pain to the Being. At that time, can we blame just the eyes for not seeing properly? Being is also the part of 'Virat-Purush' that is God Ram. And therefore, the punishment is not just for the Being or the eyes but for God or the whole body also. And therefore, the ever loving Lord Himself became the bearer of the Karma of Ayodhaya's people. And in this way, He freed His people-devotees from the sorrow that is brought by Karma.

The third reason for pain in our lives is our own individual and personal nature or 'Swabhav'. Some people are pessimists, full of fears, anxiety and negativity. Their focus is so much centered on flaws and troubles that they fail to admire the beauty and joys of life. The one who lives in the guilt of Past and worries of Future, can never have a joyful Present. Some people are just not able to come out of the bad experiences of their past. Their memories become the cause of their suffering. But then, God has gifted every Being the power to Forget and therefore, in a new lifetime, Being forgets everything about his innumerable past lives. God wants the Beings to forget their past. To discard or to keep on holding is a choice in our hands but most of us don't make this choice wisely. Those who cling to their past, even when it's not desirable by God, are like the ones who want to sit in a polluted chamber even when the Creator of the chamber had got it sealed knowing about the lethal pollution inside. The one who enters such a chamber will die, this is but natural.

Similarly, God has also programmed the future with secrecy, mystery and uncertainty. He doesn't want the Beings to know what lies in the future. Because He wants the Beings to make use of the Present with best efficiency and learn to live with satisfaction that the Present moment brings. In actuality, only those who worry about the Past and the Future are the ones who don't know the way to properly utilize their Present. In Ram-Rajya, the people were experiencing a divine bliss which is attained by spiritually enlightened ones. And when Being attains the ultimate state of Bliss, he wouldn't want to leave it for the Past and the Future. The only reason for the bliss of Ayodhaya's people was their unwavering and one-pointed focus on the Bhakti or Devotion of Lord Ram. And in this, they had overcome the suffering that is brought by human being's nature or 'Swabhav'.

Most likely a person acts as per his nature. It is not impossible but still difficult to transform an individual's nature. But in Ram-Rajya, actions were not based on individual's 'Swabhav' but inspired by God. Not just there was the formless God or 'Antaryami' inside the hearts of people but there was the human avatar of God in the form of Lord Ram outside also. And the experience of God both inside and outside made them free from all confusions that are created by Maya. Generally, a common person acts according to his or her individual nature but in Ram-Rajya actions happened not on the basis of 'Swabhav' or nature but as per inspiration of God. In the inner-self as well as the outer-self of the people of Ram-Rajya, there was only direction and inspiration from Lord Ram.

'Prakriti' or universal nature is based on 'Gunna' or the three modes which are Satva Gunna, Rajas Gunna and Tamas Gunna. In the creation, preservation and destruction of 'Prakriti' all these three Gunna are must. And these three Gunna also govern the Beings. The most difficult challenge in our lives is to bring balance between these three Gunna. Satva brings purity and sacredness but too much of Satva makes the person idealistic and non-performer and so brings Tamas. But we all know that with good thoughts, action is also a must, otherwise it's not of any use. Action happens only in Rajas but then where Rajas inspire us to act and perform in our lives, it also brings attachment to the result of the action and so gives rise to pride and vanity for our achievements. Again, this results in overconfidence and complacency in the person and he falls in Tamas.

But Tamas is not all wrong. If Tamas makes the person lazy and idle, then because of the same it brings rest and sleep. Sleep appears to be against the attribute of Action but sleep is important. It provides rest, healing and peace in a person's life and makes one fit and healthy to face the next day's challenges. Noble ideas, right actions and rest all three are required to lead a balanced life. Ideally, the individual must govern these three Gunna but mostly it is the Gunna that governs him. And when they govern, then there is no proper balance and discipline in a person's life. It just brings disturbance, chaos and desperation. The only way to free from the attacks of Gunna is to surrender to God who is beyond these three modes of nature or Gunna of Prakriti. He is the Creator of the Prakriti and Gunna but is Himself untouched by them.

The people of Ayodhaya who were the citizens of Ram-Rajya could now always feel the presence of God that is Lord Ram in their lives. They were blessed because for them God Ram had physically manifested and so they could see, touch and hear Him. For a spiritual seeker, this state is attained after much progress. Mostly a seeker experiences God in his 'Bhava' that is thoughts and emotions. In Ram-Rajya, there was no ego, pride and vanity. Their King Ram, who had defeated the mightiest empire of Lanka in those times, gave credit to Sage-Mentor Vashishta for this success. This was an inspiration for the people that had opened the door to freedom from the ego of doership or 'Kartatvabhiman'.

In this way, Ayodhaya people freed from the clutches of Kaal or death, Karma or destiny, Swabhav or nature and Gunna or modes of nature, had attained the ultimate state of peace and bliss, that is Satchitananda. Even God Shiva, the speaker of Ramcharitmanas could not explain the joy of Ram-Rajya. But God Shiva through Goswami Tulsidasji ends the epic by saying that every human-being today and tomorrow can attain the state of Ram-Rajya simply by singing the glories of Lord Ram and surrendering in the lotus feet of Lord Siya-Ram.

Chapter 7.4

Exile Of Mother Sita: The Sin Of Ayodhaya

It is a well known fact that the story of Mother Sita's exile was written in the 'Uttara-Kand' canto of the Ramayan of Maharishi Valmiki. But in the case of Ramcharitmanas of Tulsidasji which was written much later, there is no reference of it. Tulsidasji's Ramayan ended with Lord Ram returning to Ayodhaya and the advent of Ram-Rajya. In just one chaupai or verse, Tulsidasji mentions that later Lord Siya-Ram had two beautiful sons whose glories are written in the scriptures and their names are Luv and Kush. They were brave, strong, courteous and charismatic and were just like their father, King Ram. The other three brothers Laxman, Bharat and Shatrughan too had two sons each. After giving this information Tulsidasji moved ahead with other aspects of the story, so there is no reference of Lady Sita's exile in his work.

So why did Tulsidasji skip this bitter part of the story? Why didn't he speak about Her exile? Maybe because this part of Ramayan had pained him so much that he didn't find it worth talking about it. This is one part of Lord Ram's story which has for infinite years hurt the hearts of devotees, and even now it continues to do so. In today's times, this question has become even more relevant and important and is the most talked about episode of Ramayan. In my own experience, no talk on Ramayan is ever complete without somebody raising this question, "Why did Lord Ram discard Lady Sita?" I have observed that people are less hurt because of the false accusation of Ayodhaya people on Queen Sita, but are more hurt because it was their very own God-Father who had exiled their Mother Sita. The fact that Lord Ram discarded His beloved wife Lady Sita is shocking and unacceptable for the devotees. We cannot blame those who criticize Lord Ram and Ramayan for this. The most pained are the true devotees who get very upset thinking about the troubles that Mother Sita had to go through in the exile.

About a hundred years back, one of the greatest devotees of Lord Siya-Ram, named 'Bhakt Kokil Sayi' spent the maximum part of his life in

Vrindavan and never liked going to Ayodhaya. This was not something usual. A devotee, that too of the stature of Kokil Sayi, cannot live peacefully till he lives or at least regularly visits the abode of his God or 'Ishta-Dham'. The devotees of Lord Krishna visit Vrindavan, Lord Shiva devotees visit Kashi and so devotees of Lord Ram go to Shri Ayodhaya. But Kokil Sayi's perspective was different. The citizens of Ayodhaya had criticized Mother Sita and accused Her of infidelity. And this was not tolerable to him. For twelve years, he was engrossed in the 'Bhav' or visions of separated Lord Siya-Ram. There was no question of justice, injustice, right or wrong for him. The circumstances which had orchestrated the separation of Lord Siya-Ram made him weep.

Even the feelings of Tulsidasji on Their separation were similar. While describing the citizens of Ayodhaya, he didn't mention any qualities of them. Maybe because for him, they had criticized Mother Sita, so they were not worthy of any praise. But the love of Lord Ram towards them had saved them from this historic-sin and also made them attain the heavenly abode of the Lord that is 'Saket-Dham'. Clearly, Tulsidasji also didn't like them and spoke sarcastically - 'O people of Ayodhaya! Your goodness lies in the fact that Lord Ram loves and cares for you.'

The true devotees may see Queen Sita's exile as the shortcoming of the Ayodhaya people but they don't see this as an injustice of Lord Ram towards Her. Many times, we have heard that the cause of Her Exile is a 'Dhobi' or washerman of clothes. He had accused his wife of infidelity by giving reference to Queen Sita's abduction in Lanka. But could this be the only reason for Lord Ram exiling His beloved Sita?

We need to understand that the vision of Ram-Rajya was even superior to the system of Democracy. In Democracy, the opinion of the majority matters whereas in Ram-Rajya, the opinion of each and every individual matters. So, when one individual accused the Queen of infidelity, King Ram passed His judgment of Her exile. The culprit is not this one Dhobi, rather the culprit was the whole of Ayodhaya. Why? Because none of them objected or rejected the accusation of the Dhobi, none of them stood for injustice and none of them showed their support for their beloved Queen Sita.

There are people who cannot but blame Lord Ram for Mother's exile. Similarly, there are people who accuse Lord Ram for asking Mother Sita for 'Agni-Pariksha' to prove Her purity. I accept that on the level of intellect, it is very hard to not blame Lord Ram. But then, we must also contemplate that didn't Maharishi Valmiki and for that matter, historians of Sanatan-Dharma, know that later and forever, these two objections, blames and allegations will always be labeled on God Ram? Was the creator of Ramayan, an ignorant? Surely, he was well aware that these questions will rise in every generation, Kalp and Yug. Till there is Ramayan, there will be these allegations. And yet, even after knowing that this can make people speak against Lord Ram, he didn't try to change or hide anything.

History has been written to glorify the great and the victorious. History has been written by those who are loyalist followers. Lord Ram is the greatest emperor of the world. Who can be a greater devotee of Lord Ram than Maharishi Valmiki. And yet, he wrote these episodes knowing the repercussions. Sages never speak a lie, this is true. But there could be one more reason, and that was that Valmiki wanted the seekers to find their own answers for these episodes. He knew that those who will not like this episode, who will disapprove, they will see flaws in God, and will stay away from the Bhakti of Lord Ram. This is one way to keep the unprepared, undeserving and ineligible ones away from Bhakti. Bhakti is precious and not everyone is qualified for it.

The people of Ayodhaya didn't say anything or protest even after knowing about Laxmanji secretly taking Queen Sita to the forest and leaving Her there to bear the fourteen years of exile. When because of Queen Kaikeyi, Lord Ram had to leave for exile, then not only they in the harshest words criticized her but also in thousands followed Lord Ram to the forest. But in Mother's exile, no such reaction happened, although this was a much much more painful, difficult and terrifying episode as compared to Lord Ram's exile. A lady bearing two babies in her womb was left alone in the wild forest. Queen Kaikeyi was condemned for her conspiracy but here it was the judgment of Lord Ram. Ayodhaya people had so much devotion and so much faith in their Lord Ram that even in their dreams they could not have gone against Him.

A person can accept a fact on the basis of intellect and logic but that doesn't necessarily mean the emotional-mind too accept it. And this is a tough challenge which every Being has to go through. Let's say a man's son commits a crime and it is clearly proven that he is guilty. The man too accepts that yes, his son has committed the crime and deserves the punishment. But will the emotional-mind of the man accept it? He will not sit at peace thinking about the harsh punishment that his son has to go through now. This conflict between intelligence and emotions is the main reason for mankind's pain and suffering. The people of Ayodhaya knew that their Queen Sita is no less than a

Goddess whose purity and character cannot be questioned and yet they know how wicked and carnalist Ravan was. They had heard many stories of Ravan abducting women and misusing them.

The people and their collective mind could not forget that Lady Sita had spent ten months in Ravan's territory. They must have also heard that Lord Ram had Himself asked Lady Sita for 'Agni-Pariksha'. The great Goddess Sita passed the test unharmed and proved Her purity but the emotional-minds of Ayodhaya took it as an act of divine miracle instead of accepting it as the greatness of Lady Sita. People see what they want to see and what they want to see is often designed by fictitious narratives based on conditioning of the society.

A Dhobi or washerman eyes are always set on spots and dirt on the clothes. With the same set of fault-finding eyes, he was seeing society and his Queen. Can we expect the washerman to apply intelligence before passing a statement? He might keep on banging and crushing the clothes till the dirt is removed even though that spoils the cloth. Can we expect the washerman to take a balanced approach in doing his job? Similarly, in today's times there are people who have become the flag-bearers of justice and purity but are only involved in finding faults in the society.

That washerman sees himself so greatly that he starts seeing faults in the character of Lord Siya-Ram. Before pointing the finger on others that too on Lord Siya-Ram, a sensible one will always contemplate on his own self. Lord Ram had given the freedom of speech in Ram-Rajya which was misused by that washerman. So what should have Lord Ram done with the washerman? The common opinion is that the washerman should have been punished for speaking loosely for Queen Sita. But Lord Ram had also wanted that the need of punishment should not be there in Ram-Rajya.

Firstly, just because of one person misused the freedom of Ram-Rajya, must the principles and the vision of Ram-Rajya be altered? Secondly, Lord Ram must also have thought that the punishment cannot be the only way to end rumors, suspicions and doubts. Suspicion is one such thing which when tried to be suppressed by force sprouts in multiple different forms and spreads with many-fold velocity. The Ram-Rajya way of ending suspicions and doubts was to create such a situation where the one who had started the rumor himself realizes the baselessness of his allegations and burns in the fire of guilt realizing his mistake. After all, the exile given by Mother Kaikeyi to Lord Ram was also based on suspicions and doubts with no solid proof.

That time too, the Lord didn't protest or punish her or talked about justice and injustice. Instead he, by going to exile, created such a situation that very soon she had realized her mistake and for a very long time burnt in the fires of guilt. The same policy was adopted by Lord Siya-Ram, in this case too. In this exile, Lord Ram had never left or discarded His beloved Sita from His heart. His pain was no less that of Her. This was another difficult test in the life of both Lord Ram-Sita. This was the most difficult test ever which only the true lover of Lord Ram that is Lady Sita could have accepted.

Lord Ram had never discarded Lady Sita. She was always in His heart and thoughts. This fact came to light when in Ashwamedh-Yagya, He got a gold statue made of Queen Sita and seated it beside Him in the ceremony. This seat is for the wife of the King and this act of Lord Ram made the people of Ayodhaya rethink about their stand for their Queen Sita. Goswami Tulsidasji describes Luv and Kush as the victorious sons of Lady Sita. Although they were children yet they had the courage to stop the horse of Ashwamedh-Yagya and not just fight but defeat every great warrior of Ayodhaya who were individually capable of destroying huge empires and armies. How was it possible? This was because those Ayodhaya warriors had doubted the incredible 'Maha-Shakti' Sita. Their doubts resulted in loss of their Dharma and righteousness and so they could not face the mighty sons of 'Maha-Shakti' Sita.

Those who question justice, injustice and punishment in this episode of Lady Sita's exile are seeing the relevance of Ram-Rajya in present life or world circumstances. Whereas, Ram-Rajya is less about justice and injustice but more about contemplation, tolerance and acceptance. Ram-Rajya is the kingdom of God which is inside every Being. Goswami Tulsidasji just gave a hint about it but didn't go into details of this episode of Lady Sita's Exile, which was not at all in his liking. Whatever happened justified or unjustified was unbearable for the sensitive heart of devotee like Tulsidasji and so for every devotee of Lord Siya-Ram. Mother Sita has set the highest level of tolerance for the generations to learn and incorporate in their lives. Instead of aspiring to become like the great and large-hearted Sita, the questioning and criticizing of the people against Ramayan had given them no beneficial fruits but only disagreement and argument.

Accept this or not but God's Grace sometimes comes dressed as sorrow. Lord Ram felt that though he had acquired immense fame and loyalty, people had not realized the greatness of Lady Sita. So, He made a scheme to send Her, a pregnant royal lady, into the forest, without informing anyone. Because of this, the position of Lord Ram became secondary in Ramayan and the nobility of Goddess Sita was given the highest position. No personality of Ramayan shines as brightly as Her. Tulsidasji's Ramayan ends with Lord Ram and Lady Sita living together with the Raghukul family in Ayodhaya and that is what I too want to know and believe in. The exile part of Mother Sita is not acceptable to us and must not be thought about. Ramcharitmanas is a celebration of Bhakti and joy. It is one complete book that covers every aspect of Love, Bhakti and Dharma that every Being needs to know. And most importantly it is a tribute to the eternal story of Lord Siya-Ram that echoes the corners of creation from time immemorial to the end of time and beyond. And so Goswami Tulsidas says that the only meaning of our life is to live fruitfully by surrendering in the lotus feet of Lord Siya-Ram.

Hari anant Hari katha ananta,
kahahi sunahi bahu vidhi sab santa.

Lord Ram is infinite and infinite are His Leela.
His stories have been narrated by many saints in many ways.

Nana bhati Ram avatara,
Ramayan sat koti apara.

In numerous ways Ram incarnates.
And so numerous are Ramayans.

■■